THE FOOLISHNESS OF GOD

JOHN AUSTIN BAKER

'*The foolishness of God is wiser than men*'
ST PAUL: FIRST LETTER TO THE CORINTHIANS

DARTON, LONGMAN & TODD
London

231
B

First published in Great Britain 1970
by Darton, Longman & Todd Limited
85 Gloucester Road, London SW7 4SU
Second impression 1971
Third impression 1972
© 1970 John Austin Baker
Printed in Great Britain by Cox & Wyman Ltd,
London, Fakenham and Reading
ISBN 0.232.51075.X

TO THE MEMORY
OF MY BELOVED FATHER

ANIMA NATURALITER THEOLOGICA

CONTENTS

Foreword   9

PART ONE – THE ULTIMATE QUESTION

1 God and the Gods   13
2 The Logic of Creation   40
3 The World's Sorrow   54
4 Moral Good and Evil   70
5 Freedom, Guilt, Forgiveness   103
6 Love and the Nature of God   128

PART TWO – JESUS OF NAZARETH

7 The Loss of the Christ   137
8 The Recovery of Jesus: (I) The Method   160
9 The Recovery of Jesus: (II) The Portrait   182
10 The Lord's Doing   244
11 The World's Joy   275

PART THREE – WHAT THEN MUST WE DO?

12 The Church and the World   317
13 The Word and the Words   359
14 Man in the Presence of God   373

Postscript: The Simple Truth   400

FOREWORD

ANY WORK which like the present one tries to set out a reasonably unified vision of the whole Christian faith and life is bound to be indebted to a host of people – family, friends, colleagues, teachers, pupils – impossible to list not merely because there are too many of them but also because some, alas, the writer has himself forgotten. What they gave to him has become too much a part of himself. To all, however, known or unknown, I wish here to return formal and quite inadequate expression of my gratitude.

In the sphere of the written word the same holds good – indeed, memory is here further bedevilled by the fact that works which one consciously admires often have had less influence than others ungratefully overlooked. The perceptive reader will identify the true sources of whatever good there may be in these pages far more accurately than I myself could hope to do.

Specific acknowledgements connected with the actual writing of a book can, however, be made. Here it gives me great pleasure to declare my debt of gratitude to Trinity College, Hartford, Connecticut, who in 1967 did me the honour of appointing me a Dorrance Visiting Professor in the Department of Religion. It was my six months at Trinity which gave me the opportunity to work out the ideas of the present work as a coherent whole, and to test them in the liveliest of arenas. To my friends in the Faculty and to my vigorous and keenly intelligent classes during Summer School and the Fall semester I send my warmest thanks.

Nearer home, I wish to express my gratitude to those friends who have constantly urged me to write on the present subject (may they not regret it!), to the Rev. Leslie Houlden, Fellow of Trinity College, Oxford, for valued help with the reading of the proofs, and in particular to Tim Darton for kindness and confidence far beyond the line of a publisher's duty.

Finally, a debt which I can only indicate but never hope to describe: my debt to my parents – my mother, whose support and encouragement have been unfailing, and my father, to whose memory this work is dedicated, and to whom more than to anyone else I owe it that I found my way into the indescribably exciting, rewarding, and privileged vocation of theology. He would have been very glad that I had tried to write this particular book. I can only hope that it is not altogether unworthy of him.

Corpus Christi College,
Oxford.

JOHN AUSTIN BAKER

PART ONE

The Ultimate Question

I

God and the Gods

THE ROOTS of religion strike far below the layers of historic human culture into the unrecorded experience of primitive Man. The myths and legends, the rituals and customs, the philosophical theories of all religions, even the doubts and questions which they evoke, all derive from a vast complex of sources, some of them of incalculable antiquity. Any attempt to state and explain the heart of the Christian faith must therefore begin by tracing, at least in broad and diagrammatic outline, the story of the quest for ultimate truth which led up to it. This means in effect the story of the religions of the ancient Near and Middle East and Mediterranean worlds, but not that of Hinduism or Buddhism, though these will demand our attention at certain points later.

Whether we like it or not, we cannot start from scratch in talking about God; but it would in fact be extremely silly to grumble about this. The record of human experience enables us, if we will, to take up old truths and learn from old mistakes, and to discern our own faces in the portrait gallery of the past. In an age when we are beginning to discover how much we have in common with other animals it is somewhat ludicrous to talk as though we were a different breed from our human forefathers. Man's circumstances and his store of information change far more drastically than his basic nature and needs, though the wide variety of forms in which the latter find expression often disguises this fact. In talking about God, as in so many other fields, we need to ask where we have come from, if we would rightly understand where we are going and why.

At one time it used commonly to be argued by defenders of religion that the fact that all human societies at some stage in their history believed in a god or gods pointed to the truth of that belief. To us, however, such universality at once suggests an origin in some aspect or aspects of human nature; and when we take into account certain features of Man's psychological make-up and the character of the world in which he lives it is far from surprising that an idea of this kind should have emerged.

The first significant feature is Man's built-in tendency to project his own characteristics on to his environment. The most familiar example of this is our habit of attributing faults or feelings or even good qualities in ourselves to other people with whom we are closely associated. But projection is not limited to particular aspects of the personality. At a very early stage we project on to our surroundings the fact of person-ality itself. This is probably connected with the way in which the infant learns of the existence of any environment at all, namely first by becom-ing aware of himself as distinct from the mother, and then of the mother as one among other persons. He has to pass through many finely graded stages before he is able to distinguish accurately between the personal and impersonal objects around him.

We have only to watch a tiny child at play to realize how naturally he personalizes his whole environment. The phase of talking only to doll or animal toys is a relatively advanced one. Before that he has talked freely and naturally to anything he comes across, and is not in any way put out by the lack of response – which as likely as not he will supply himself. This habit can have its practical uses. A toddler explor-ing unfamiliar territory, a strange garden for example, will bolster his courage, make himself feel welcome, by talking to the things he finds and so convincing himself that they are on his side. This practice may often continue as a silent internal colloquy for quite a long time after the child has grown up enough to learn that others will think it silly of him to speak out loud. Similarly, the small child is perfectly convinced that inanimate objects feel pain – a piece of paper on the fire, let us say, or something run over by a car.

The classification of the world into 'Thou' and 'It' is something which has to be learned. It does not come naturally. The 'natural' or, more correctly, primary stage is to treat all beings as personal. And this attitude, as we shall admit if we are honest, is never completely eradi-cated. The fact that a man knows perfectly well that his motor-mower is a machine does not in the least inhibit him, when it refuses to start, from the irrational feeling that it is being 'difficult'. Of course it is childish to mutter to something one has lost, 'Damn you! where have you got to?' – but lots of people do it. And in more serious contexts, when men are fighting for survival at sea, in deserts, or on mountains, the forces of Nature quickly take on the character of personal enemies to be overcome. Indeed this personalization is of considerable help by stimulating energy and endurance in the same way that physical combat has done throughout the history of the animal kingdom. In cold logic the sea is not cruel, but we need a phrase like 'the cruel sea' to express the truth of one aspect of our dealings with 'her'. Men who occupy their business in small ships on great waters commonly develop a love-hate relationship with the sea of an intensely personal kind.

The ability to distinguish between 'Thou' and 'It', therefore, is something acquired. But men acquire it by virtue of another fact about themselves, namely the way they think. The change which came with the scientific age was not, whatever some anthropologists may say, the introduction of a new way of thinking, but the rigorous and exclusive use of an old one. That this has meant enormous alterations in our attitudes and in our mythology no one would deny; but in the broad sense the 'scientific method' has always existed. To collect evidence by observation, to generalize from your information, and then to test your general pattern by prediction and further observation, is not a procedure invented by Western Man since the Renaissance; it is the activity which made all human civilization possible. And there is good reason to suppose that this activity also played its part in the emergence of the idea of God.

It is easy to forget that effective scientific reasoning depends first of all on access to evidence, and that without a number of basic technical aids the vastly greater part of our relevant evidence would still be hidden from us. Without the telescope and the microscope modern science would never have got started. Ancient Man was, by our standards, unimaginably limited in his access to the facts. How, for example, was the primitive inhabitant of Egypt to discover the reason for the annual flooding of the Nile on which his life depended? The rain which caused the river to flood fell far beyond his ken in the mountains of Central Africa, and there was not enough rainfall in Egypt from which to argue by analogy. Hence any attempt on his part to work back along the real chain of cause and effect was immediately baulked; and the only solution left to him was that the changes in the river were self-caused. Now, the only beings which are self-moving, which have 'get-up-and-go', are living things – humans, animals, plants, and so on. In the circumstances the conclusion that a river which possessed this capacity was a living being was the result not of unscientific thinking but of inadequate information.

Similar difficulties must have beset primitive Man's interpretation of many natural phenomena. The rising and setting of the sun and its daytime journey across the sky naturally suggested the idea of a return underground during the night hours to account for its reappearance in the east at dawn. But what made the sun behave in this way? Or there was the mystery of the rain. To us there is no mystery. Every schoolchild is taught about the cycle by which water is taken up out of the sea and deposited over the land. But how could ancient Man have discovered this cycle? He knew that clouds were a sign of rain; but he did not understand what a cloud was, nor is it apparent how he could have found out. In the circumstances the hypothesis, adopted by some ancient peoples, of a solid sky with reservoirs of water above and sluices through which this water was released was far from unintelligent. Again, the growth of vegetation was inexplicable, given his means of access to knowledge. What is interesting and significant is the relatively large number of instances in which he did in fact invent a naturalistic explanation. When this proved beyond him, however, he had no rational alternative but to regard the phenomena in question as, like himself, living and self-moving beings.

Thus the spontaneous psychic tendency to project personality on to the environment co-operated with the deliberate exercise of reason to produce the same effect. The opportunity to unlearn the child's first spontaneous interpretation of the world as a 'Thou' was restricted by the practical obstacles in the way of his discovering the true nature of things.

What has been said so far, however, is a conjectural reconstruction of a stage before the dawn of history. For any time of which we have written records, that is to say, for all the civilizations of the ancient world, the position is far more sophisticated. Here men have made a step forward of immense significance, one indeed of which the effects are still with us today. They have come to regard the actual objects around them no longer as in themselves living beings but rather as the media of the activity of spirits. Intertwined with the world of sense is another, omnipresent world, the realm of the supernatural.

Once more it is possible to make a reasonable guess at the way in which Man arrived at the concept of the supernatural. In part it would seem to be prompted by the fact that the same characteristics are found in all members of a class of objects, and are not affected by the ending or death of any particular example of the class. In ancient Mesopotamia salt was regarded as the medium of a salt-spirit. The active properties of salt when used for curing and preserving, the sharp pain which it causes when it touches bare flesh, its emetic effects, any or all of these may originally have given rise to the idea of salt as a living thing. But salt may be eaten, dissolved in water, or burned, without making any difference to the properties of other quantities of salt. No one piece of salt, therefore, can be absolutely identified with the living being that produces these effects. His condition is unaltered by the fate of the material through which he works. By the same token no one ever actually sees this living being. Along such a line of thought it is not far to the conception of a spirit of salt, an invisible power present and active wherever material salt is to be found. Similarly, the acres of reeds along the marshy margins of the rivers impressed people as being alive; and anyone who has listened to them and watched them moving in the wind can well understand why. But however many reeds were cut down for thatch or matting or a thousand other uses, an endless supply remained with the same properties; and so the conclusion that there was a deity of reeds (in this case a goddess) seemed highly probable. The ancient Phoenicians clearly had a similar conception, when they sacrificed to the spirits of the great cedars of Lebanon before felling the annual quota on which their internal building works and external trade balance so largely depended. In many such instances we can see how the conflict between the tendency to see objects as personal and the evidence or demands of practical experience forced men to the ingenious solution of a world of invisible beings interlocked with their own. In this way they were enabled at one and the same time to explain the otherwise inexplicable, to treat things as things to be used and manipulated, and yet to preserve that feeling of reverence for and one-ness with their environment which was and is of such deep emotional importance to Man.

Given a belief in such beings, omnipresent, indestructible, with a mind and will of their own, it is understandable that men should have tried to enlist their aid by direct appeal. Prayer and magic are closely linked. The texts of many prayer rituals making magical use of material objects or substances have come down to us from the ancient world. In these, belief in the spirit associated with the object or substance has gone beyond the point at which he is thought of as able to do whatever the material itself can do. He possesses power in a quite general sense. Hence he is entreated (or even commanded, if the power of a greater spirit or god can be enlisted) to bring about all kinds of results – causing an enemy to fall sick, winning a return for unrequited love, curing some disability. Such rituals can, of course, be paralleled from many parts of the world to this day.

Some supernatural beings, however, are deaf to entreaty or cajolery. Their activities are malign and can be overcome only by the use of superior force. These are the demons, especially of sickness. They are understandably associated with lonely and sinister places, with animals which are untameable and with which it is seemingly impossible to communicate, which inspire revulsion, or which keep far from human habitation. Snakes, jackals, lions, certain birds of prey, for example, are commonly regarded as the media of demons.

The supernatural world is not made up simply of a multitude of minor beings, good or evil. The great dominating features of the cosmos also have their spirits. The Egyptian felt that the inescapable sun with its tyrannous fire must be the vehicle of a supremely powerful being. In other lands it is the sky which seems to have been personalized at the primitive stage as the All-seeing One. When the attempt to provide a naturalistic explanation for phenomena like that of rain led to theories such as the one mentioned earlier of a solid dome of heaven, there was no problem. The device of the supernatural simply modified the primitive ascription of personality to the overwhelming fact of the sky into belief in a great universal being above and behind the sky. It used to be held that men's religious beliefs developed from a phase of belief in spirits inhabiting individual objects to an eventual notion of a single, universal Great Spirit. It is now clear, however, that belief in such a High God or universal divine Father (not always equated with the Creator) is quite as old as the belief in spirits. The two conceptions run side by side; and in view of the mechanisms involved it would indeed be surprising if they had not.

By contrast to the High God the being behind that other great cosmic fact, the sea, was thought of as cruel, dangerous, and hostile, a monster ramping and roaring at the apparently arbitrary barrier of the shore, striving to engulf the safe and stable dry land where alone men could live. Since it was impossible to detect any physical reason why this destructive power was thus held back, the conclusion suggested itself that this was the merciful work of the other great gods who in this and other ways showed themselves guardians of the cosmos and of the security of its inhabitants. From this kind of reflection it was not a great leap to regarding them as also the patrons and protectors of those virtues and qualities and institutions without which human life itself so quickly dissolves into chaos, and on which men's hold is so precarious and intermittent – truth, justice, wisdom, mercy; the family, the tribe, the city, the state.

This picture is enormously over-simplified, and takes no account of the mass of variation in detail between different cultures, or of the chronological relation between them. Its purpose, however, is not to be a condensed history of the rise of religion in the ancient Near East, but only to give samples, based on evidence from that area, of the kind of processes by which Man, with his particular characteristics, might quite easily and naturally have arrived at his belief in gods. Any encounter with occult or parapsychological phenomena must, of course, have strengthened this belief.

To achieve the imaginative elaboration characteristic of religion in historic times, however, a further element of a different kind was needed. This was Man's passion for story-making and story-telling. Once men had acquired all these mysterious *dramatis personae* with their superhuman powers, it was too much to expect that they would refrain from weaving whole epics about them. In the resultant stories of the gods and of their dealings with men we find an immense wealth of motives and interests. Sometimes, it is clear, the poets and their audience are identifying with these immortals, with their power and passions and freedom from human restraints, and thus satisfying the deep inner longings of creatures who can always imagine so much more than they are able or allowed to accomplish. Sometimes the stories are the vehicle for profound and tragic reflection on life and death, and on Man's own subjection to the whims of the unseen. Sometimes again they are epics to be recited in worship, describing in vivid and dramatic form the outcome which prayer and ritual are intended to win from the gods, such as the return of the rains and the revival of life and fertility. Yet again they can even be opportunities for asserting Man's independence by making fun of the powers which control his destiny. (Some at least, and arguably all, of these motives find expression still in the very different stories of our own culture; and no doubt this process will go on until the race comes to an end.)

Having suggested what may in principle have been the story of the emergence of religious belief in those societies directly ancestral to our own, it is time to consider the implications of these beliefs, and to trace the way in which they led to questions about God and about the meaning of life as we know them in our own society.

It is usual nowadays to think of the concept of the supernatural as a barrier to rational thought, as a source of tyranny over the mind and behaviour of Man. That it has been so in history at various times no one need bother to deny. But it ought also to be remembered that its initial effect was not one of tyranny and suppression of thought but of liberation to think objectively. While gods were identified with the visible world, there could be no hope of studying that world intelligently. By shifting the arbitrary into the realm of the supernatural men tacitly assumed that the natural would prove to be reliable and predictable. If the behaviour of something in their environment failed to fit their expectations based on experience, then admittedly the lazy solution of assuming supernatural intervention was too ready to hand; but the possibility of an increasingly objective or scientific understanding was also open in a way that it had not been for primitive Man. Thus, for example, we find quite staggering achievements of accurate astronomical observation co-existing with belief in astrology and astral deities.

The idea of the supernatural, therefore, gave the human mind a certain amount of room to manœuvre. But by the same token it produced a dramatic new development as irreversible as it was unavoidable. The conception of an invisible world made it inevitable that sooner or later the existence of that other world would be questioned. Where the thing and the god are one, it is silly to ask, 'Does the god exist?' – there he is. You can touch, hear, see him. But of a god supposed to 'lie behind' some physical phenomenon it is not at all silly to ask, does he really exist? No man has seen the god at any time. The standard taunts against idol-worship used, for example, by Judaism from the sixth century B.C. onwards – 'They have mouths and speak not; eyes have they, but they see not; they have ears and yet they hear not, neither is there any breath in their mouths' – are not as irrelevant as some would-be fair-minded modern commentators make out. The carved shape of wood or gold is but a thing. How are we to tell whether the god which it is supposed to represent, and in some sense to mediate, exists or not? There is no evidence that he or she exists at all, once the image itself is no longer thought of as imbued with power. The concept of the supernatural world ensured that from that day forward God could never be 'proved'. Men would always have either to argue to him as a probability or to believe in him by an act of personal commitment.

One by-product of this situation is the supernatural 'event' or 'manifestation'. The existence of the invisible world is attested by some happening supposedly impossible to produce by natural means. Oracles, visions, miraculous cures, the thousand and one physical phenomena of mysticism (as well as outright jiggery-pokery staged by cultic officials) have in all ages characterized supernaturalist religion. The hope that the invisible world may somehow be verified is, of course, a vain one. If an event happens, then however wonderful it is – and some very wonderful things have happened from time to time – by the very fact of happening it is a natural phenomenon. If its causes are natural, they may be discovered; but unquestionably if they are supernatural they cannot be. There can be no such thing as an event which demonstrably comes from the invisible order. The idea is self-contradictory. That strange and wonderful events have happened in many different ages and places is beyond reasonable doubt; but they can never serve the purpose men wish them to serve. The supernatural is beyond either proof or disproof.

Such events must anyway be peripheral to a living belief in a god. If the religious believer thought his god responsible only for the odd exceptional occurrence, his belief would hardly be of much importance even to himself, let alone anyone else. In fact it may be stated as a law that all higher religions of the theistic type strive to maximize the number of events for which the god is responsible. The god is manifested not just through the image or the sanctuary, in the cult or in miraculous actions, but in the world and all that happens there. This is yet another development made possible by the concept of the supernatural. If a god is too closely identified with particular physical phenomena, then first it is difficult to ascribe to him events quite unconnected with these phenomena, and secondly his character tends to be dictated by them. The idea of the supernatural realm detaches the god from the events a little more, and makes room for the religious imagination to develop the picture of him as a more fully rounded person. Natural phenomena then become simply the impersonal tools with which he carries out his purposes.

Furthermore, since the god is capable of commanding and manipulating the visible world, there is no reason why these tools should be limited to such things as fire, earthquake, storm, disease, and famine. They can now include human agents. The god thus grows from being purely a 'god of Nature' into what is commonly called a 'god of history' as well, the fundamental implication of the latter phrase being his ability to direct human as well as non-human affairs. Where such a god is worshipped as the patron of a particular social group, a city-state or nation, for example, then his control of history will be focused naturally enough on the disposal of their destinies. Even if he is venerated as the supreme god of the universe, and thus the ultimate arbiter of all history, the peoples of the world will not all be of equal significance or insignificance to him. He vindicates his own position by his special concern for the community in which his worship finds its home and centre.

The gods of the ancient Near East (and to a lesser extent those of Greece) exhibit this general theory very clearly. It is, however, a striking fact that though all over this area religious development follows a very similar course it does so only up to a certain point. From that point onwards one culture only, that of Judaism, carries the argument further.

The god of Israel was a god of Nature and of history; he was also a universal god with a special concern for one particular people. In these respects he was not essentially different from, let us say, Marduk of Babylon or Ishtar of Arbela. But the fact remains that while the Jews developed this common religious material until they arrived at a pure ethical monotheism, thus creating the classic pattern for all theistic religion thereafter, the surrounding nations never did so. And the reason for this is, to say the least, disconcerting.

We might put it like this: the other nations were too objective and realistic. The details of the life of Nature and of history are complex and confusing. To discern in them a coherent rational and moral pattern without ignoring or distorting some of the evidence has in all ages proved beyond the wit of Man. If this chaos of happenings was in truth the work of the supernatural order, if the character of that order was indeed to be read off from the facts of life, then that character too must be to some extent morally and rationally incoherent. God, or the gods, could not be perfectly good and perfectly wise all the time. There must be limitations which prevented their achieving such an ideal. Taking a panoramic view, it may be said that the ancient world invoked three major limitations to reconcile belief in the divine with the facts of life.

The first was limitation of goodness. No more than men were gods impeccable. It is important to remember that this was not apparently felt at first to provide grounds for resentment or contempt such as we find in Greek thinkers of the fourth century. Mesopotamian society, for example, was one of intense social divisions. The privileged position of the aristocracy and free citizens under the law strikes us today as morally offensive; but it was plainly taken for granted as an inevitable fact of life. The ruling classes had a right to escape virtually unscathed in some societies from the commission of crimes for which the proletariat suffered mutilation or death. Ordinary folk were lucky if the king or the lords chose to behave with decency and generosity above the required minimum. And what was true of the earthly social order was all the more true of the cosmic. The whole nation was but slave labour for the gods, labour organized by the king as the gods' bailiff. If a god behaved 'badly', that was after all his privilege. On the whole one could only be glad that deities behaved as well as they did – better, indeed, sometimes than the earthly rulers. Even so there were days when the wise man remained inactive at home to avoid the irritated anger of the gods. Such was the Babylonian 'sabbath', the day for pacifying the incensed heart of the god by abject submission, or the *dies nefastus*, the day of ill-omen in Rome. The erratic moral standards of the Greek divinities, too well known to call for comment, also probably owe something to this concept of quasi-aristocratic privilege. Nevertheless, whether this explanation of the religious attitude is correct or not, the fact is incontestable. Moral perfection was not attributed to the gods.

The second limitation was that of power. Here the idea of Destiny as the ultimate ruler comes into play. Neither are the gods exempt from Fate themselves, nor are they able to deliver their protégés. This conception forms a major motif in a number of Homeric stories. Another concept of the same kind is that of a balanced duality of light and darkness, good and evil powers, such as we find in developed Zoroastrianism, if not in the teaching of Zarathustra himself. The dominion of good can never be absolute or complete.

The third limitation was that of responsibility. Even the sophisticated concept of the supernatural did not give these societies sufficient scope to rid themselves of the gods many and lords many inherited from the primitive past. In a world where men were still overwhelmingly ignorant of Nature and at her mercy there was naturally deep emotional pressure not to abandon the polytheistic world-view. Furthermore, once deities had become persons in their own right, it was natural to think of them living in community. (Absolute mono-theism, that is, belief in a God who was personal yet completely alone, would be a very strange conception, which may explain why, theo-logical theories notwithstanding, it has never in practice formed part of the imaginative piety of any living religion.) Hence there was no incentive from that angle to demolish polytheism – it did in fact make the gods more believable and imaginable. Again, the attachment of particular communities to their own gods meant that in the age of the great empires, uniting so many diverse cultures and languages under one administrative machine, monotheism would have had to be im-posed by decree, backed by force, and it would have been politically most unwise to try. Ikhnaton's attempt to impose the worship of one god, the sun-disk, on Egypt at the end of the fifteenth century B.C. proved a disastrous failure. The efforts of Nabunaid, the last king of Babylon, to displace Marduk with his own favourite, the moon god Sin, merely caused the priests of Marduk to support the Persian in-vader. By contrast, Cyrus, to all intents and purposes a true mono-theist in the manner of early Zoroastrianism, tactfully recognized and subvented the religions of all his subject peoples. In such a world polytheism for anyone but a philosopher or a prophet was the natural way of thinking.

Perhaps the greatest asset of polytheism, however, was this limitation of responsibility. No deity was in a position to control all events. He or she had a sphere of influence, and beyond it could do no more than appeal to or argue a case with the relevant authority. Especially striking in this respect is the adamant dividing-line in all the polytheistic religions between the gods of life and the gods of death or the 'under-world'. In Hades the writ even of the creator of heaven and earth does not run. Another interesting divide is that between the gods of earth and sea. The sea, as mentioned earlier, was for the ancient Near East a realm of fearful and dangerous powers. Even in the late and somewhat sophisticated and effete Greek mythology Poseidon, the sea god, sig-nificantly still operates very much apart from the other gods, in a world and on terms of his own. He is 'the Earth-shaker', the threat of chaos-come-again, and even great Zeus cannot overrule Poseidon within the latter's jurisdiction. In addition to these major divisions, however, it is common for the myths to imply a whole complex of interlocking rights and prerogatives, expressed often in terms of the rank and family relationships of the gods and goddesses within the pantheon. Some of these rights and privileges derive ultimately from the ancient personalization of natural forces. It is a motif common to many mythologies, for example, that the goddess of fertility should complain to the High God that procreation by man, beast, and vegetation has ceased because of the death of the male deity at the hands of the underworld god. On occasion this male deity may be represented in the cultic drama by the earthly king, and then the plea in heaven becomes simultaneously a prayer for the resurrection of the life of Nature and for the preservation or deliverance of the human king from sickness or danger. Such a theme comes close to the Homeric scenes where various gods and goddesses protest to or plead with Zeus on behalf of their human hero-protégés who have incurred the enmity of some other divinity. In all these ways it came about that the fate alike of individuals and of communities was conceived as the resultant of conflicting forces in the divine realm. Man might secure the most favourable possible terms if he offered prayer and sacrifice to the god with the greatest appropriate power (taking care to do so through the intermediary divinity with the strongest personal influence); but clearly one could not expect always to be successful. In short, the polytheistic view of the supernatural made it understandable that all was not for the best for everyone in the best of all possible worlds.

In these ways, therefore, the ancient world gave its account of the fact that life was far from ideal. But by this realistic approach they also ensured that in the end their religion would fail to satisfy them. The gods, who, as we saw, came to be credited with, among other things, presiding over desirable moral qualities and attitudes, such as justice, truth, compassion, and so on, were manifestly either incapable of or prevented from ensuring that these qualities controlled the character of life on earth. It was true, of course, that men too either could not or would not live by these things. But the whole point of moral or ethical rules is that whether or not they are kept they ought to be. That is what men are saying when they express something in the form of a rule or law. And to have a god who invests the rules of your community with his own personal authority, and then does not — or so it would seem — act himself in accordance with the principles underlying these rules, is a very unsatisfactory position. But how could one look honestly at the facts of life, and come to any other conclusion?

It is interesting to see how this problem continually confounds even the finest religious endeavours of ancient Man. In the seventh century B.C. the Persian prophet Zarathustra tried to replace the polytheism of his society with a simplified faith of high moral quality. Scholars differ over the exact theology of primitive Zoroastrianism; but one plausible reconstruction is as follows. Zarathustra himself taught that there was one supreme god only: Ahura Mazda, the Wise Lord. Under his sovereignty, however, life was the arena of a permanent struggle, which might be described as between Asha and Druj, 'truth' and 'the lie', or between Angrya Mainyu, the 'evil spirit', and Spenta Mainyu, the 'holy spirit'. Zarathustra was here, we may think, inspired to do skilful justice to two ways of seeing life in religious terms, those which we call the metaphysical and the existential. Metaphysically, at the level of what may be termed 'eternal reality', that is, the realm of Ahura Mazda, goodness is supreme and unchallenged; at the existential level, that of daily life and experience, good and evil are locked in an unending combat which sways now one way now the other, and which demands that each person should commit himself to one or the other side. The reconciliation of these two visions or orders of reality comes at 'the end of Time', when good is finally victorious at both levels. It may be in the very nature of such an end that it is perpetually receding, or rather, let us say, like de Chardin's 'Point Omega', a quasi-mathematical infinite. But, for a religious conception like that of Zarathustra, faith in the ultimate arrival of such an end is essential, because anything but the eventual triumph of good is intolerable to those who have taken the existential decision to fight here and now on its behalf. Given this, however, it might be thought that Zoroastrianism could provide a perfectly adequate account of the mixture of good and evil in the world, and certainly one vastly superior to the prevailing polytheism. Nevertheless, it failed to endure. At the existential level its austere simplicity suited the self-conscious rectitude of the all-conquering Persian military caste, but perhaps appealed less to the ordinary man. At the metaphysical level the idea of an ultimate but infinitely distant resolution of the problem of evil failed to satisfy. It seemed simpler and more convincing to believe in an eternal dualism, where Ahura Mazda (Ormuzd) and Angrya Mainyu (Ahriman) remained in unending if dynamic equilibrium.

In another area, that of hellenistic culture, men were also seeking to dispense with the conventional gods. One line of thought, starting from scientific speculation on the nature of the physical universe, tended towards philosophical atheism; but where this drastic conclusion was unacceptable, the Greeks still found it necessary to differentiate in their own way between the divine in itself and any sort of power behind the world. God, to be worthy of the name, must be perfect; but perfection could not be responsible for, or active in, the world as it is. Moreover, the Greek mind saw perfection as essentially unchanging or static, for the very straightforward reason that if you are perfect obviously any change must be for the worse. Anything impassive and immobile, however, was clearly very unlike what we call a person. Thus it is, therefore, that we find Plato distinguishing on the one hand the 'divine', the absolute Good, which is an object of intellectual contemplation, not an active personal God, and on the other a cosmic Craftsman, the Demiurge, a personal figure who had organized the universe out of pre-existent matter, guided to the best of his ability by the vision of the Good but restricted both by the nature of matter and by his own limitations. In Aristotle again, there is an entity of absolute static eternal perfection, which does in fact cause the world to move and evolve, but only because of the attraction which it exerts. The imperfect is always striving to attain perfection; and though it never succeeds, yet the fact of striving is the very essence of its life. The ideas underlying these Greek approaches to the problem are enjoying a revived popularity today in the 'process theology' of Hartshorne and others. Widely different though the Greek solution was in almost every detail from that of Zarathustra, at bottom both have this in common: they accept that any god worthy to be called God cannot possibly be the sole ultimate reality behind the universe. Some other being or factor must be introduced to account for things as they are.

Only one society in the ancient world rejected the necessity of this. Judaism alone clung defiantly to the conviction that life could be understood as purely and simply the 'kingdom of God'. This is, in the last resort, the reason why the Jewish Scriptures (the Christian Old Testament) are of unique importance for all mankind. They and they alone have the courage to present without qualification the challenge of belief in God. This gives ancient Israel an importance quite independent of either Judaism or Christianity. The latter may be described from one standpoint as different answers to the same Old Testament question, as indeed are Islam and many later forms of philosophical theism. It was ancient Israel who worked out the only meaning of the word 'God' for which it is worth bothering either to accept or to reject belief in him – though to say this does not mean, as we shall see, that she had also worked out correctly the implications of this belief either for human life or for the nature of God.

How was it that Israel succeeded where all her contemporaries failed? A slightly flippant answer might be that throughout her history there were always some Israelites for whom the sensible, realistic, and pragmatic religious schemes of the rest of the ancient world were abhorrent. It has been said that Israel's picture of her own national story was written 'in defiance of the facts', and from one point of view this is true. What is meant by saying this may be illustrated from the Old Testament reactions to the most important single event which befell Israel during the first millennium B.C., namely the capture and destruction of Jerusalem by the armies of Nebuchadnezzar in 586 B.C.

This disaster put an end at one stroke to the political independence of the nation, the rule of the dynasty descended from David, and the worship in Solomon's Temple, which was razed to the ground. The land was put under the administration of an official directly responsible to Babylon. Many leaders of the community were deported to Meso-potamia. In short, the nation as a nation was extinguished. This event could not but have enormous religious importance for the Jews for a very particular reason, namely that the fate of the community formed a central and indispensable part of their faith in God. They believed not just in a deity, but in one who had promised to preserve and bless the nation for ever, who had chosen Jerusalem as his dwelling-place on earth, who had laid down the details of Israel's peculiar way of life, and who was, so to speak, personally and emotionally committed to her continuance. Thus the end of the nation shattered her creed in a way no other event could possibly have done.

The Old Testament shows us how various groups within Israel reacted to this apparently devastating blow. Some drew the straight-forward conclusion that their god was less powerful than the foreign gods; others decided that he was unjust. In both cases the result was that the nerve of their religion was cut, and that they lapsed into either paganism or despair. Others, however, looking back on the moral failures of the nation's past life, saw in the disaster a just retribution which, if anything, enhanced the righteousness and majesty of their God, because it seemed to prove both that his righteousness was not to be bent by any considerations of his own reputation and that his power and self-sufficiency were independent of any human fellowship or worship. The catastrophe was no more than the community had deserved. This, however, still failed to satisfy some, who pointed out that the consequences had fallen indiscriminately on good and evil members of the nation. One rejoinder, at a rather superficial level, was to deny that this had been so; all who suffered had been guilty. There was, however, an unknown poet who went deeper than this, and declared that though the sufferings of the good and the evil were outwardly the same their inward value was different. The miseries of the wicked were punishment for their sins; the agonies of the righteous were a sacrificial offering to God which in fact served to atone for the sins of their brethren. Nevertheless one final question remained: however just the punishment, did not the fact that God had been compelled to execute it and thus to nullify his own promises to the nation mean that he had been defeated by the nation's sin? To this came the triumphant affirmation even in the darkest hours of exile that the divine purpose would in the end somehow be fulfilled in a restored nation by means of a seemingly impossible miracle, in corporate terms nothing less than a virtual 'resurrection from the dead'.

During the earlier centuries of her existence Israel had been moving towards practical if not theoretical monotheism by way of increasingly exclusive claims for her own particular god. There had always been powerful voices within her to urge that the God of Israel was the only god worth worshipping, that he had done so much for her that to pay homage to any other was ingratitude and infidelity. As more and more areas of life were ascribed to his exclusive control – the growth of crops, oil, and wine, the rain and the seasons, the creation of heaven and earth, the fortunes of war, and the fluctuations of international politics – he became so big that there was in effect no room for any other gods in the universe. 586 B.C. posed the question: had all this been simply illusion? Could there be an event so terrible that it could not be fitted into this framework? – rather as the Lisbon earthquake shattered the optimistic rationalist theology of eighteenth-century Europe. The positive answers outlined above were Israel's attempt to cope with this challenge, and they were successful in the sense that they enabled the community to survive until in a new and unique form the miracle prophesied did in fact happen. Jerusalem did arise from the ashes, and a state with control over at least its internal affairs sprang from the shattered stump of the old. This restored society maintained a belief in one God, all powerful, all holy, who was responsible for everything that existed or happened in heaven and in earth, and who was righteous, nay merciful, in all his dealings even down to the micro-cosmic level of the individual life-history. The creation was good, very good. There was no need to postulate a hierarchy of gods in conflict, or a second, imperfect deity, or an equal and hostile power of evil, to explain the evidence.

The principles on which, so it was argued, God's actions could be understood were, first and foremost, that of reward and retribution, and then by way of secondary qualification, those of vicarious expiatory sacrifice, and of testing and education – suffering on the latter view being sometimes to lead Man to an increasingly refined loyalty to the good. In short, the universe exhibited a moral order. This faith did not, however, stand the test. It was already being challenged in Old Testa-ment times, as the books of Job and Ecclesiastes show. It became neces-sary to modify it by projecting the reward of the righteous into an unverifiable life after death, where, for example, martyrs whose faith-fulness availed to expiate the sins of their fellow-countrymen could receive their due glory – the moral glory of their sacrifice not being its own reward.

It is easy enough to point to the failures and shortcomings of the theory by which Israel sought to justify the ways of God to men. But these defects belong quite unquestionably to Israel's response to her own challenge rather than to that challenge itself. Experience had con-fronted her with a choice: on the one hand, make the obvious common-sense evaluation of your predicament, and change your view of God to correspond; on the other, hold fast to your belief about God, and change your evaluation of experience in the light of that. She chose the second; and that is the sense in which it can be said that she interpreted her history 'in defiance of the facts'. But her story contains fundamental implications of principle and method for the whole of later belief in God; and it will be as well to conclude this historical survey with an analysis of these and with a summary of certain other lessons which it will be necessary to bear in mind in the exploration on which we are embarked.

Before the great crisis which, as we have seen, determined Israel's fate in the sixth century B.C. her religious traditions already contained all the elements which she was to use in her solution. She already had the idea of her god as a universal god; she had long thought of him as intervening in human affairs to reward the innocent and punish the guilty; and she had a real sense of individual and corporate sin in a moral and not merely in a tabuistic sense, even though it might fluctuate greatly in intensity. What was new in her sixth-century synthesis was that these traditional ideas were now rigorously and universally applied. Her moral failures (which like those of all nations in all ages were real enough) were now seen as deserving rejection and death. Thus, by acknowledging her corporate and individual guilt and the justice of her sentence she was enabled to put God in the right, and in the very magnitude of the disaster to find proof of his holiness and omnipotence. The result was that her dogma of God itself acquired a new and absolute degree of definition and clarity. If this extreme test-case could be successfully accommodated, then the hypothesis could be generalized. In future it could be taken as an axiomatic starting-point that God was all-powerful, all-righteous, and all-merciful, executing justice in all the earth. There would never be any need now to treat this picture of God as a tentative conjecture, liable to proof or disproof by new turns of fortune. It was the unshakeable truth in the light of which all else was to be understood.

Such an attitude, however, was in the end impossible to maintain. The law of retribution on which it relied, and which had seemed so convincing a key to the riddle of life in the midst of one particular historical crisis, proved increasingly inadequate in other situations. But those who were alive to this fact, and who tried to think through the problems which it raised, found that questions were no longer permitted. The theory had become a dogma, and any criticism of it was blasphemy against God. Moreover, criticism was an attack on the very foundations of the life of those who held the dogma. In obedience to it they had staked all on the possibility of achieving perfection. Naturally, therefore, any questionings which suggested that this was a futile exercise provoked their bitter anger and hatred. What the dogmatists failed to realize (as indeed they always do) was that the view enshrined in the dogma had commanded men's assent, and given them new life and creative power, only because it had very strikingly fitted the facts of life as they had known them. It had been a good hypothesis on the available evidence; as more evidence became available, so it became less adequate. And one of the elements which later appears in the teaching of Jesus is a brusque rejection of this theory of God on the basis of simple and obvious facts of life: 'Your Father who is in heaven . . . makes his sun rise on the evil and on the good, and sends rain on the just and on the unjust.'

Because the supernatural order can by definition never be accessible to direct observation, anything that can be said about it must be based on the evidence of the natural order considered as in some way the work or expression of the supernatural. God can be known only from what happens here. If there is a God, then he meets us in our earthly experience or not all. It might seem, therefore, that any theory of God which contradicted the facts of life could not possibly be true. But matters are not quite as simple as that.

The religions of the ancient world had made quite a good job of accommodating all the facts of life; and so long as they were polytheistic, and could therefore allot to each god a more or less coherent sector of the whole, their deities each possessed a character at least as consistent as that of the ordinary human being. But as soon as every aspect of reality has to be ascribed to one god, there is an imminent risk that the deity will become either superfluous or chaotic. If everything that happens is equally 'God's will,' then what even marginal insight do we gain by saying so? What meaning can be attached to the word 'God', if he is apparently at one and the same time moral, immoral, and amoral, rational, irrational, and non-rational? The point may be put another way by considering the statement that 'God is love'. If everything that happened in the world was indisputably a manifestation of love (always assuming that we could agree what that word implied), would the affirmation that God is love be of any interest? Is not a God of love an idea worth considering solely because the world is not a world of love? But if it is not, where is the evidence that God is a God of love?

There are only two moves that can be made if these traps are to be avoided. Either it must be said that God is not equally manifest in everything; or everything must be made to yield a satisfactory moral meaning. The dogmatists in Israel took the second course. The weak points in their theory are, as we have said, well known and well canvassed; the strong point is often overlooked, namely the insight that there was no future for belief in God at all, unless some such move was made.

The same result was arrived at along a slightly different route by those thinkers in Israel who developed the old idea of a decisive divine *dénouement* at the end of Time. Judaism, like the religions of other ancient Near Eastern peoples, asserted, as we have seen, a personal deity. In this idea, however, she detected an implication which her neighbours missed. If a god were truly personal, then the possibility must always be open that the universe was only one of his potential achievements, and that he might have some completely unprecedented project in mind for the future. Thus the very idea of God meant that even the whole cosmos could never be an exhaustive key to his nature. This created a further important consideration for faith. Even if all the evidence at present available could not be fitted into a morally and rationally satisfying whole, there was always the chance that God would do some new thing that supplied the key to the story, and made sense of the confusion. This future hope was more than just a consoling thought for the world-weary. It was a fundamental theological concept, which enabled men to give real and independent meaning to the idea of God while still maintaining his universal sovereignty.

The two moves just described correspond to the two main types of religious thought in Judaism at the time of Christ: the static view, which saw Man's vocation as that of maintaining the morally complete and satisfactory divine order as already instituted in the world; and the dynamic view, labelled in modern times the 'eschatological', which was found in many varieties sponsored by many different groups, and which looked for a final intervention of God to resolve the problem of life. It is the latter which is found as the predominant approach in the New Testament, and which has become a standard item in traditional Christian theology.

The time has come to sum up the legacy of the ancient world in this matter of God. Once the primitive stage, at which the environment itself was regarded as imbued with personal life, was left behind, and the supernatural, the invisible world interlocked with the visible realm of Man and Nature, had become the frame of reference within which men's thinking about God was done, 'God' could never again be a certainty. It was no longer possible to say, 'Behold the god!' The divine must henceforth be the object of faith, upheld or attacked by rational conjecture. It is a matter of historical fact that from the options thus opened to them men have chosen to doubt or deny the existence of God or the gods since at least the sixth century B.C.; and that the reasons for taking either option have not essentially changed in the intervening period. The emergence since the sixteenth century A.D. of a science-based culture has not for the most part added to or altered the basis of

c

any of the major arguments. It has simply increased the supply of relevant information, thereby closing a large number of loopholes, and making much traditional religious language very difficult to use.

It will be as well to ask at this point what light if any has been thrown on the vexed question of 'myth' and 'mythological language' which plays such a part in modern religious discussion. It will by now be apparent that some of this language is not religious in origin, but simply incorrect science. The 'three-decker' universe of heaven, earth, and the underworld certainly fitted the religious scheme of ancient Man, but it was not constructed simply to a theological specification. This very natural and obvious diagram of the cosmos did indeed have the added advantage of providing suitable homes for the inhabitants of the supernatural order, and the details of these homes were elaborated with happy speculation. But it is important to remember that it was speculation, and that when the evidence of the physical world seemed to call for modifications in the general picture, speculation had to adapt itself to the change. It is true that such modifications were of secondary importance – as, for example, the effect of astronomical observation on the supposed number of heavens – and that in ancient times nothing comparable to the Copernican revolution came to test men's theological flexibility. The fact, however, remains that it was religion which fitted into the notion of what the universe actually was like, and not the other way round. Heaven and hell were not symbolic terms seeking to express unimaginable realities; they were natural science which seemed to bear out religious teaching precisely because it was natural science. The world had room for the gods.

When we come to mythological stories, matters are not so straightforward. It is necessary to distinguish various elements. First, as in the cosmological picture, there is an element of explanation based on observed (or supposedly observed) facts. Why is the snake reborn every year (an incorrect interpretation of the sloughing of its skin)? Because it swallowed the flower of immortality which Gilgamesh dropped while bathing in the river. Why do the peoples of the world speak so many different languages? Because their titanic ambitions threatened the heavenly realm – are not the ziqqurats of Mesopotamia, modelled on their mighty tower, evidence of this? – and God defeated the enterprise by causing them to speak different languages so that they were unable any longer to co-operate. It will be obvious, however, that explanation is not all or even the greater part of the interest behind such stories. Their second ingredient is the dramatic formulation of truths about Man and his predicament. It is his pain and desolation at the death of his friend Enkidu which drives the hero Gilgamesh to over-come heartbreaking hardships and dangers in order to secure the flower of immortality. Then, when he is almost home, a moment's inadvertence and the treasure all men most desire is lost for ever, not only to him but to us. Here something very profound about Man is given poignant expression. He is capable of imagining immortality, and of desiring it for not ignoble reasons. Death is an ultimate contra-diction of all that is good and creative and happy. Why should this be so? Was it the jealousy or cruelty of the gods? Or was it some fault or carelessness in Man that threw away the one blessing without which all other blessings turn to dust in his mouth? Such questions are not really meant to be 'answered'. Both the asking of them, and the stories that purport to answer them, are in fact dramatic and poetic statements of the human condition, revealing it with greater subtlety and realism than can be achieved by any 'objective' description. Similarly the bibli-cal story of the Tower of Babel crystallizes some major themes of human life: Man's ambivalent feelings about his own capacities, the scope of which fills him with pride and ambition but also with guilt and anxiety, and also his puzzlement and dissatisfaction at the seemingly compulsive disunity of the human race. Sometimes the implications of these stories are almost impossible to analyse with certainty by any strictly intellectual approach. What these implications are becomes apparent only from the kind of attitudes which the archetypal power of the stories stimulates in those brought up on them. This would apply, for example, to the narrative of the making of woman out of man in the book of *Genesis*. Sometimes the psychological sources of the stories lie in primaeval levels, beyond our capacity to recover, as in the account of the making of Man from the blood of the dragon Kingu in the Mesopotamian Creation Epic. By contrast, the biblical picture of God moulding Man from the clay, much as the artists of ancient times made their figurines, voices unambiguously the awareness of human transience, and anticipates at the very moment of creation the decree: 'You are dust, and to dust you shall return.'

In practice, then, many of these stories – and in theory perhaps all of them – could be 'translated' into plain descriptions of Man as he is and of his situation. The element of explanation, however, even though on matters of fact it is usually false, is by no means irrelevant, since it expresses the insight that these situations are inherited. No generation starts with a blank sheet. There is an entail of evil stretching back to time immemorial; and the reason for it (since reason there presumably is) must be earlier still. The kind of reason which the writer suggests, and which his society accepts, in its turn throws further light on the way in which they regard the contemporary human situation. It is quite wrong, for example, to treat the story of the Fall of Man in the Old Testament as some do, namely as an account of human life as it is, *and nothing more*. The writer does not think that every human being starts where Adam and Eve started, with the same options open. He knows perfectly well that they do not; and to that extent the story is a real story, and the explanation is meant as a real explanation. But the kind of explanation which he constructs is still entirely typical of human beings and the human situation as we know it, and uses these elements from experience to pass judgement on what is ultimately at issue in human life: the refusal to be obedient to the given terms of Man's existence, and the determination to decide for oneself what is to be right and what wrong; the irrationality and fraud of evil.

Another type of mythological story presents far less complex problems. This is the category of Nature myths. The most celebrated examples are those which connect the annual cycle of the seasons with the slaughter of the male deity by the forces of death, his resurrection and conquest of death, and his triumphant intercourse with the goddess. In this form the story dates from at least the second millennium B.C. Different versions, in which the central theme is the search of the goddess of fertility for her murdered lover, are familiar from the Isis and Adonis-Tammuz cults. Such stories formed the scenario, so to speak, of the great annual festivals at which by quasi-magical rituals the worshippers attempted to ensure the right outcome of the supernatural drama, and thus the regularity of the seasons and the fertility of Nature for the coming year. (It is worth noting that in Israel these results were made to rest simply on a once for all promise by God.) In instances like these the explanatory element has virtually no relevance to human life or conduct. It throws no light on Man's situation; it enjoins no activity save a ritual one. What it 'explains' is simply certain phenomena in Nature. If then we have reason to believe that these gods and goddesses are fictions, and that the explanation is bogus, there is no further value left in the stories.

A fourth class of material is that of imaginative description of the supernatural. In this group come the accounts of the courts of heaven, the councils of the gods, their appearance and behaviour, the hosts of angels and other spiritual beings and their functions, the realms of the dead, visions of the future, especially of the final consummation of history and the judgement, the torments of the damned, and so on. Here again two purposes are served. The descriptive element, whatever the extent to which it is intended or taken literally, serves to arouse appropriate emotions and attitudes. Its importance indeed lies in this emotional truth, that is to say, it is assumed that, whether heaven or God corresponds to the imagery used or not, the feelings aroused by the imagery will still be the right ones for us to have when we discover what these realities are actually like. The second purpose may be roughly termed metaphysical. The pictures give concrete and dramatic expression to various general beliefs about God, such as his omniscience, omnipresent activity, holiness, or about the eternal destiny of human souls to bliss or woe. In either case the details are unimportant. They are, in fact, essentially unimportant, not just because they may be wrong or inadequate in any given instance, but because they must be fashioned out of the world men know and the kind of experience by which they are moved. Therefore whatever images in any given culture produce the 'right' response, or express the 'right' beliefs, are all equally valid.

It will be seen that the mythological writing of the ancient world is of more than one type, and that each type raises its own kinds of question, and calls for an appropriate response from us with our new and different knowledge and understanding. There is, in short, more than one way of 'demythologizing'. It is the basic error of much contemporary thinking on this subject to assume that there is not, that one composite method will do for everything. Because some mythological language is unbelievable as straight statement – the 'three-decker' universe, for example, or the existence of nature deities – it is taken for granted that all straight statements in myth are unbelievable. Because some myths can legitimately be understood as comments on the human predicament, or as implying certain values or obligations for human conduct, then all myths are to be 'translated' in this way. Because the imagery of some mythology is valid only in so far as it evokes particular feelings or value-judgements, it is assumed that this is the purpose of all mythological imagery. The question is then posed: To what do we attach the value which the myth attaches to life or

death, heaven or hell, or to God himself? The answer to this question
becomes the demythologized meaning of the myth.

We must ask: Is this not simply a crude and insensitive approach?
In particular, is it not completely blind to the real nature of the
Israelite, Old Testament material, from which, as we saw, the classic
form of the question of God derives. Here there are no Nature deities;
the primitive personalization of natural phenomena has vanished as an
effective element, and survives only in metaphors and literary flourishes.
What is said about the world and Man is intended first as factual
statement, at least akin to that which we call science and history,
whatever its other important implications. The making of the universe
in six days, the forming of Man from the clay, the descent of the human
race from a single primal pair – this is the way they thought it was.
We have good reason to conclude that as a factual account their version
is wrong. Does this rob it of all interest for us? The answer to that
question depends on what we think of their central affirmation.

This is the statement that there is a God. The word 'God' is not just
a symbol to describe the indescribable. It is a term to which a clear
meaning can be given; and the assertion that there is a God – and such
a God – is one that can be argued on the basis of what is agreed to be
relevant evidence. At the very centre of the whole system there is again
a statement of fact.

Of the possible moves to be made at this point one might be expressed
as follows: 'The greater part of this mythological material, considered
simply as statement of fact, is false. So far as the statement about God
is concerned, it is of course impossible to prove conclusively that it is
false, but we have a number of good reasons for thinking that it is;
and the probability that it is false is, if anything, increased by the fact
that the statement comes in the general mythological package. We
have, after all, seen that the whole scheme of supernaturalism, of which
mythological language is the characteristic expression, was in the first
place the product not of rational reflection but of an attempt to ration-
alize already existing irrational beliefs when forced to do so by the
facts of life. There is no very convincing reason to think that an idea
produced in this way is likely to be correct. It is much more likely to
be of purely emotional value, a childish defence against the terror of
cosmic loneliness, and defended for that reason. The sensible thing to
do is to demythologize it along with the rest.'

To this there is, of course, an obvious riposte: 'Most of what you say is simply imputing guilt by association. It makes no difference whatever how a statement comes into being. Once it exists it can be examined on its merits to see whether it is true. To argue "Because it would be nice if this belief were true, it is probably false", is a purely statistical argument and not a very decisive one at that. What is really at issue is whether the reasons for thinking that there is a God are valid, and bring down the balance of probability on that side. Until that issue has been settled, no decision about demythologizing the idea of God can legitimately be taken.'

Of these two positions the first is roughly that known today as 'radical', the second is traditionalist. Both in fact rest on a foundation of 'natural theology', the exercise of deciding about the existence and fundamental nature of God by rational argument from evidence. As such they are united in antagonism to various other approaches, ranging from the extreme fundamentalist to the sophisticated anti-rationalism of Karl Barth, all of which have this at least in common, that for them one of the distinctive marks of God is that he confounds human rationality.

In the present work it is proposed to adopt a rationalist approach, but to work it out in a way rather different from any of those mentioned. The chapters following, as far as the end of the first part of the book, explore the question: If we assume the existence of a God of the traditional type, what on the evidence available today would he be like, and what would be his relation to the cosmos and ourselves? The point of taking this stance is that, while giving full play to opposing arguments that the existence of such a God is incredible, it may have two new advantages. First, it may enable us to avoid as far as possible attributing to God our own ideas, moral and metaphysical, of what he ought to be; and secondly, it may show whether any new light can be shed on the old dilemma, analysed above, that God must be either a nullity or unsupported by the evidence. The second part of the book will then examine the relation between the picture of God thus constructed and the God of the Christian revelation. The third and final section will consider what paths the Christian Church and Christian theology ought to take in the light of the conclusions already suggested by the preceding chapters.

2

The Logic of Creation

MAN HAS been defined as 'the animal who can think about what is *not* there' – and that, in a nutshell, is the reason why he will always worry away at those problems which we call 'ultimate questions'. Ultimate questions are those which ask about the origin, essential nature, or meaning and purpose of all that exists, the universe considered as a single system. Two simple and basic forms of this kind of question may be phrased as follows: 'Why are things the way they are?' and 'Why does anything exist?' Because no answer to such questions can ever be scientifically proved, it has been suggested, for example by Wittgenstein, that there is no point in asking them. Whether such a standpoint is sound will have to be discussed later. First, it must be made quite clear that it is a waste of time to tell human beings not to ask ultimate questions, for the simple reason that, whatever the situation, they can always conceive that things might be different. And if you can imagine that things might be different, it will always seem perfectly reasonable to ask why they are as they are.

At the present day, however, there is a widespread feeling that to argue about such questions is not the best way to arrive at an understanding of ultimate reality. Man has constantly been haunted by a 'mystical' feeling that everything in his world, himself included, is transient, insubstantial. This is partly a natural product of the trait mentioned above. If we can imagine a different universe from the one we have, we can equally well imagine that it might not be there at all. Hence nothing can ever seem to us to be 'necessarily so'. It is hardly surprising, therefore, that we respond to the idea expressed in Prospero's famous speech about the 'cloud-capped towers'.

This general openness to the idea of transience and instability is, however, greatly intensified by what is called 'mystical experience'. In the past this kind of experience has, for the majority of people, had to be cultivated. To achieve it sophisticated techniques were long ago developed, techniques which for all but those psychologically most susceptible required long and patient practice. Today, however, it can be had more quickly and easily by chemical means. It is an interesting fact that, if we discount the differing ideologies, the accounts given by many mystics of all religions, philosophies, and periods concerning their sensations not only closely resemble each other (something which has long been noted) but also resemble the sensations made available by drugs such as LSD. The feelings of personal transience and nothingness in face of an ultimate reality, of insight into hitherto impenetrable mysteries, of dissolution, insolidity, and absorption into the infinite, and of remaking and rebirth to a new mode of existence, constantly recur in all these cases.

This similarity is only to be expected. 'Learning' plays a much larger part in Man's make-up than in that of the animals. When, therefore, surface thinking is suspended, and there is a 'descent' into the substrata of the living self, it is possible that there may be a loosening of the current organization of the personality. This gives the individual a sense of renewed contact with the raw material of existence, a chance, as it were, to be put together differently, to start again, as well as a frightening awareness how superficial and precarious a structure is the 'self' which is the be-all and end-all of normal daily life. Similar effects can be discerned in the experiences of the schizophrenic as revealed, for example, in their art-work.

This does not mean that mysticism, experiences with certain drugs, and psychosis can all be equated. It simply suggests that in all of them certain mechanisms are brought into play. The value to be put on each of them is quite another matter, and, so far as the first two are concerned, depends on the ideas and images imported into the experience or used to interpret it. These ideas and images are definitively formulated in the conscious rational life. Jewish, Christian, and Islamic mysticism, for instance, are differentiated by the religious ideas and images proper to each; and these, whatever their roots in the archetypal human unconscious, are products of conscious creative thinking. The understanding of the mystical experience is controlled by the theology of the religion.

It is possible, however, to adopt exactly the opposite approach, and instead of interpreting mystical experience in the light of a conscious theology or philosophy to derive material for theology or philosophy from the mystical experience. This, broadly speaking, is the line taken by Hindu and Buddhist mysticism, and by some schools of thought in the contemporary West. But there is no good reason for supposing that in these experiences men are directly in touch with ultimate reality. At best they are picking up signals from the limits of their own identity. That human beings are capable of such experiences is an important and interesting fact about them, and as such can have its place in philosophy or theology. If, however, the experience itself is allowed to dictate the images and concepts in which we talk about the nature of ultimate reality, and answer the ultimate questions, then we run the risk of falling back into the primitive error, and of putting our faith in some aspect of ourselves which we have projected. Indeed, we may be in even worse case than the primitive, since the aspect we project is relatively chaotic and fragmentary, and not the integrated system of conscious and unconscious, mind, feeling, and will, which is the person in its full glory.

Let us return, then, to our ultimate questions. Of the two forms mentioned above – 'Why are things the way they are?' and 'Why does anything exist?' – it might be thought that the second had the better right to the title 'ultimate'. In fact, however, they each come to very much the same in the end, since it is impossible to ask the second in any meaningful way without implying the first as well. When we ask, 'Why does anything exist?', we are forced to refer to some specific entity, even if it is the whole cosmos, since the question could not be asked about something which did not exist. Even if the totality of things was changed every five minutes, the question would always have to refer to the universe of the moment. Someone may object nevertheless: 'But I am not asking why things have the character they do. I am merely asking why they exist.' It is true that one can distinguish between 'existing' and 'having a certain character', but that is not the point. The point is that everything has a character of its own, without which it does not exist. If nothing had the character we associate with a lettuce, there would be no lettuces. Hence to ask, 'Why does X exist?', is to ask why something with the characteristics of X exists. And when this question is asked about the universe as a whole, it inevitably involves (though it is not logically the same as) the question: 'Why are things as they are?'

One advantage of sorting out this particular confusion at the start is that it delivers us from the temptation to become immersed in the old argument about contingent and necessary being. So long as attention is focused on the fact that the cosmos does not have to exist, the tendency is always strong to insist that it must ultimately depend on something that does have to exist. But the idea of a necessary being is logically vacuous. It is really an image from a very sophisticated kind of poetry, voicing a deep feeling in response to the idea of God – as indeed is the whole Ontological Argument. Much more useful is to make a different distinction, namely that while the existence of everything else is derived, God's alone is underived.

In the religious history of most reasonably intelligent children the following dialogue is apt to occur:

'God made the world.'

'Who made God?'

'Nobody.'

'How do you know?'

The answer, of course, is that we don't. It is for a different reason that we affirm that God's being is underived; and it is essential to understand what that reason is.

It is all very well to be precise in formulating the ultimate question, but what if it cannot be answered? In scientific terms obviously it cannot be; and if we believe that only answers which can be scientifically verified are acceptable, then clearly the question is unanswerable. But equally clearly the question is, in a different sense of the word, answerable, in that throughout the centuries people have answered it and been satisfied with their answers.

Fundamentally there are only two of these. Either 'things are so because they are so', or 'they are so because of some determining factor other than themselves'. To believe in God is to opt for the second answer, and to understand this determining factor as of a particular kind, namely a free, personal being. If we pursue this option, then what is absolutely vital is that our idea of God should be adequate to answer the question from which we began. If we posit a God who does a particular job, then he must have the characteristics necessary to do that job, otherwise our hypothesis falls to the ground. This is the reason why we say that God is underived being. If he were not, then it would be necessary to assume another determining factor behind him, and so on *ad infinitum*. In the end, to provide an adequate answer you are forced to an underived God. We do not know that God is underived. We only know that if he were not, he would not answer our question.

It will be as well at this point to make some remarks on the possibility of talking about God at all; for this is often said today to be impossible. There are two foci of discussion here. First, can we make any positive statements about God, or can we say only what he is not, or what he is, approximately but not exactly, like? And if the latter, then are we really saying anything? Secondly, can theological statements be considered to have any meaning, in view of the fact that they are apparently non-falsifiable, that is, that there are no conceivable situations which would count decisively against their truth? The first area of argument is concerned with the nature of God in himself, and the second with the meaning of statements in which God is the subject. Thus, is there anything which would make a believer deny that God loves his creatures? and if not, if God's love is apparently compatible with anything that could conceivably happen, does it have any real meaning?

The contemporary attack on theological language depends on keeping these two areas sharply separated, and then dispatching the enemy piecemeal. For it must be pointed out that when critics are arguing in the second area, about, let us say, the problem of evil, they find no difficulty whatever in giving positive content to the word 'God'. He is 'the One responsible'.

The other area of theological statement, the description of God in himself, is worked out from this simple usage as its necessary logical foundation. It is not an area which will be explored in the present work, because the nerve of religious faith does not run through it. It may, however, be worth pointing out that for all its abstract terminology and labyrinthine arguments it is based on a perfectly straightforward principle, namely that if God is to be accorded even preliminary consideration as an adequate answer to the ultimate question he must have the characteristics needed for the job ascribed to him. The researches of metaphysicians into the divine nature, the language of analogy, the negative theology, all these are simply the product of attempts to work out the answer to this question: In what ways must God differ from us to be able to do his job? In itself this is no more bizarre an activity than asking, 'If there is organic life on Venus, what would have to be its characteristics?', and producing the answer, 'Flat, bladder-like, water-absorbing objects floating on the underside of clouds.'

Of course, if one succeeded in penetrating the Venusian atmosphere (or lack of it) it might be possible to check this particular hypothetical reconstruction. The God-hypothesis cannot be checked in that way. But this is far from saying that it cannot be checked at all. It is absurd to say that religious assertions are not falsifiable, because people falsify them to their own satisfaction every day. They look at the world and say, 'I just cannot accept that there is a God'. When they say this, it is not that God has been conclusively disproved, but that the balance of probability has tipped against his existence in their judgement. And since a being such as God is conceived to be is inevitably beyond logically valid proof or disproof, to go by the balance of probability is the only rational procedure.

What, therefore, we are asked to decide is whether such statements as 'God is good', or 'God loves us', can be used without depriving 'good' and 'love' of any sort of normal meaning. If we think they cannot, then we have no business to go on professing Christian belief. And with these falsifiable assertions stand or fall all those other types of theological utterance which, as it has been expressed by Crombie in an illuminating phrase, are simply there to show 'in what direction' our meaningful 'statements are to be referred'. All that the onslaught of linguistic analysis has done is to show how very wise Jesus was to focus the issue on the one word 'Father'. Either we can say this or we cannot. When the reader of the *Daily Express* says that he cannot, it is not because he thinks the implied assertion meaningless. He knows quite well what it means, and he thinks it is wrong.

The evidence on which such conclusions are reached is first and foremost not that of the story of Jesus, nor the contents of Scripture, but the experience of people's own lives and of the world as they see it. And the basic concept underlying the discussion is that referred to earlier of God as 'the One responsible'. This idea of God's responsibility is summed up in the concept of *creation*. In theology the title Creator can be applied properly only to God, and the verb 'create' used only with 'God' as subject. An analysis of the internal logic of this concept will serve two important purposes. It will illustrate the way in which we use language about God; and, more vital still, it will show more exactly and fully what kind of God would provide an adequate answer to our ultimate question.

In ordinary parlance to 'create' has affinities of meaning with a number of words, among which the chief are 'conceive', 'invent', 'design', and 'make'. On the common frontier with 'conceive' the emphasis is on the producing of something new. We speak, for example, of a completely new or original conception, when a designer has gone back to ask himself basic questions about function or beauty, and has tried to work out his design from scratch. In theology this idea of 'new' or 'original conception' is pushed to extremes by saying that the conception involved is that of the basic terms of cosmic existence – something which might be described as a 'homogeneous space-time continuum of mutually convertible mass and energy'. The Creator is the one from whom this conception derives as something new.

Turning to the affinity with 'invent', an inventor may observe certain properties or relations in the physical world, and by making use of them work out a device or method which serves a particular purpose. But his invention may have other potentials as well, of which he is unaware either because there are further properties in his material unobserved by him, or because his understanding of the nature of what he has observed is limited. Hence at a later stage new observations or better understanding may result in revolutionary new applications of the original invention or of developments from it. But when we analyse the logic of 'creating', that is, the production from scratch of a conception that really is completely new, then it does not make sense to suppose that any properties or potentials of this conception could be unknown to the Creator. A thing in its totality is the thing plus its whole potential – for anything without these potentials is not that thing but something else.

If we bring to bear on this extended idea of 'creation-invention' our present scientific understanding of the cosmos, we might say something like this. The nature and scale of the universe are such that from its basic properties, its fundamental particles and organization, it was statistically inevitable that at an indeterminate number of points within it organic life would emerge from the inorganic, and sentient, rational life from the organic and so on. In short that Man, and no doubt many other kinds of being superior to Man, with all their spiritual and moral values, were implicit in the basic terms of existence, the fundamental conception, and as such must have been present to the mind of the creator of that conception.

A third way into the notion of creating is from design. The aspect of creative activity stressed in ordinary use by the word 'design' is that of purpose or intention. We 'design for'. The degree to which this aspect is prominent varies. If a cabinet-maker reproduces an existing model, the design element is minimal; he merely recognizes an appropriateness to function that is already there, and which may not be very great. But when he asks basic questions about function, and works from scratch, 'design' is maximized. He intends or purposes to meet the requirements of some function known or envisaged; and this intention controls his reasoning and decisions. In the theological use of the word 'create' this element also is pushed as far as it will go. The Creator's conception is the result of an intention to bring about results which do in fact ensue.

The last facet of the ordinary use of 'create' is the one which in theology is given the most staggering extension, but not one essentially different from the others. In ordinary usage we recognize a difference between our cabinet-maker's 'thinking up' a desk and his actually making it from wood, metal, or plastic. This realization of the design is an essential element in artistic 'creation'. The sculptor has not 'created' the statue until he has surmounted the problems of producing his design in the stone or bronze. Theology sees a comparable difference between conceiving, inventing, designing the basic terms of existence, and actualizing them in the cosmos; and it makes the Creator responsible for both. Indeed logically, if the cosmos is a completely original conception, fully known to the Creator and expressing his purposes, then it must owe its concrete actuality to him; for if it already existed in its present form, then it could not be his conception.

It is important, however, to realize what is the crux of the matter here. To resort to pictures, as of God gazing at nothing like Rodin's 'Thinker', and then waving his hand and with a triumphant cry causing basic matter to appear, is unhelpful. What is asserted is that the character of the cosmos as it is derives from God alone. He was not limited or constrained by any other factors, such as the nature of already existing material if it did exist, or its absence if it did not. His conception, his purpose, was and is the sole determinant. This is what 'creation' means; this alone makes him the 'One responsible', and an adequate answer to the ultimate question.

It will by now be apparent what we are doing with language when we use it in this way. We are taking ordinary human situations, with all their complexity and compromise, and pushing them to an ideal extreme. In so doing we automatically make our words refer to something we cannot imagine or picture or even analyse. The last example,

that from 'create-make', illustrates this. The logical problems surrounding the idea of God's bringing this cosmic system into being are
immense. 'Before ever the earth and the world were made, thou art
from everlasting.' But what meaning can we give to Time, to words
like 'before' or 'everlasting' in a situation where a space-time continuum does not exist? If, like the learned mobs in fourth-century
Alexandria defending the full divinity of Christ, we march down the
town shouting, 'There was not a time when he was not,' what do we
mean? We mean that even if God has always had his creation in
existence it must still be his creation; his thought and purpose and
decision must still be logically prior to its becoming. And, more
important still, if he should wish to change the basic terms of existence,
he is at liberty to do so. Only so is he our adequate answer.

We use language about God to point to a condition which language
cannot directly describe. This may seem a very odd way to use it.
Perhaps it is, but it is not confined to theology, as a very simple example
will show. The first stage in mathematics beyond the purely elementary
levels is the calculus. In the differential calculus we soon encounter an
explanatory phrase which operates in a way very similar to that of the
creation-language which we have been considering. This is the phrase,
'instantaneous rate of change'. As a direct description it is meaningless.
But it is not a direct description. It points the mind, so to speak, in a
certain direction. It says, Continue this process until you cannot take
it any further, and what you have just beyond that is what I am referring
to. If we try to describe this, we come out with linguistic nonsense; but
thousands of school pupils every year pick up quite easily what it
means. So it is with statements about God as Creator.

When, however, we try to take this limiting-point indicated by the
language about creation, and use it as a starting-point for further
thinking, we come to grief, because we have never really been 'there'.
We can extend usage to point to that which cannot be directly described,
we can indicate in what direction our meaningful, ordinary-life statements are to be referred; we cannot then use the point indicated as the
zero for another exercise in extension and indication, or even for
descriptions of the scenery from there. If we could have described it,
we would not have needed to indicate it in this oblique way to begin
with.

It is this failure to recognize our limitations which gives rise to a
number of assertions about God which have no discernible basis in the

logic of the situation, and which certainly cause confusion. Such are the
insistence that God is 'outside' or 'beyond' the creation. It does not
help much to balance this by stating that, of course, he is also 'inside',
or 'in the depth of one's own being'. Here we have left behind the
method of 'indication-by-extension', and have resorted to bald incom-
patibilities. If such statements were absolutely indispensable in the light
of the principle that any answer to the ultimate question must first of
all be an adequate one, then no doubt one would have to do one's best
with them. In fact, however, they are far too crude philosophically to
be anything of the kind. Their original value lay in the pictures which
they conjured up, and in the feelings which these aroused. In the
relatively homely and compact cosmos of ancient Man these pictures
worked fairly satisfactorily, because they stressed God's supremacy
without making him utterly remote. Like the king of a small nation he
could weigh up the suppliants who came before him, scanning them
through half-closed lids; or his emissaries, like those of the great kings
of the world-empires, could run to and fro through the earth to keep
him apprised of all that was done, writing every significant incident in
a book of remembrance. But with the cosmos as we know it the effect
of the picture is utterly changed, and becomes alien and inimical to all
the most important affirmations which the believer in God wishes to
make.

If the ideas 'outside', 'beyond', 'transcendent', were exact and
necessary theological concepts, this would create a serious problem.
But they are, in fact, positively misleading. To talk of God as 'outside'
the cosmos carries a hidden assumption that God himself has a spatial
location, is 'in' an environment. Just as we are in the universe, so God
is here pictured as 'in' something outside the universe, something which
we may call 'heaven' (if we are simple) or 'eternity' (if we are sophisticated). From this it is but one easy step – and often taken – to thinking
of God as conditioned by his environment in the same way as we ourselves are conditioned by our world. He is described, for example, as
'static, unchanging', because that is what it is like 'in eternity' as opposed to the flux of becoming and change in Time. But this is quite
irreconcilable with the logic of the creation-concept. This, if taken
seriously, involves us in affirming that apart from the creation (whether
or not that is limited to the universe, which is all we know) there is
only God. There is not something else as well 'in' which God is. If we
are to 'go' anywhere that is not identical with the creation, then God

D

himself is the only 'place' to go. It makes much more sense to say that the universe is 'in God', than that God is 'outside' the universe; but even this phrase is still clinging to the inadequate spatial imagery, and is far inferior to the language of personality and activity which alone can carry the sort of statements needed to provide an adequate answer to the ultimate question.

What has been said of Space applies inescapably just as much to Time. Mention has already been made of the logical difficulty involved in thinking of a time 'before' Time, a difficulty which is unaffected whether we choose a 'big bang' or a 'steady state' view of the origin of the universe. Efforts to overcome this problem tend to result in talk about God existing in an 'eternal Now', where all those events which from within the time-process appear successive are simultaneously and perpetually present. All that this would seem to offer is a disastrously distorted view of reality. One of the absolutely fundamental attributes of beings within the universe is that they change continuously. If we could take every moment of a person's life, let us say, and see them all simultaneously, the total of which we were aware would not be a 'truer' picture than a synopsis of him at any given moment. It would in fact not be true at all. At this instant you are a person with a particular present condition and a particular past. Your present condition includes an awareness of that past (no doubt highly censored) and certain plans and vague previsions, hopes or fears about the future. In a few moments all of these elements will be different – almost imperceptibly, no doubt, but different none the less. Mysteriously indeed you retain your identity, a kind of recognizably continuous organization of these elements, but within that organic continuity nothing is precisely the same as it was. Any one of the possible millions of such instantaneous 'four-dimensional' portraits would be a true picture of you as an existent being. But to add them together makes not more sense but nonsense. That is what it means to live in and by Time. Unless, therefore, we wish to make nonsense of God's awareness of his creation, we had better be just as careful of our picture-language about his relation to Time as we discovered we had to be about his relation to Space. Cosmic time is in any case not adequately to be pictured by one straight line, a single scale applicable anywhere in the universe, since its rate of change is relative to one's movement in Space. It is to be regretted that in the past so few theologians and philosophers (with the noble exception of Farrer) have tried to understand and use modern concepts of Space and Time; but the scene is at last changing for the better in this respect.

The universe as we see it today is a dynamic and fluid system, its regularities the statistical regularities of behaviour in mass. If anything, then, we would expect a God characterized by dynamic and flexible activity, working in each of an infinite number of different situations in the way appropriate to each of them, and to the change and development continually going on within them. Moreover, we have to reckon with the fact that even if new marvels constantly emerge from the cosmos yet they do so from a level of potential which is ever sinking ineluctably towards total inertia. Time is running out in more senses than one; and, so far as anyone can foresee, there is a deadline not just for our own planet but for all the worlds. On the basis of the God-option this deadline too is part of the purposive, fully comprehended design. To see it as such, however, at once raises the question, 'After the deadline – what?' The only possibility, if a God is not to be left contemplating an infinite stillness, is that a new environment would have to be provided in which creatures with their own peculiar nature could function once more. What such an environment would be, and whether God would bother to provide it, are questions to which answers can be suggested only if we can reach some conclusions about his purposes and values on the present evidence. This means that any useful and relevant statements about this or any other fact of the creation will be made not by using totally inadequate metaphors from the physical world to describe what we know to be logically indescribable, but by the language of personal and moral relationship. For this and this alone has a cutting edge, this alone makes a difference to life about which it is possible to argue on evidence, and which can therefore be rationally believed or disbelieved. It is essential to recognize that in theology as, for example, in nuclear physics, there are conditions which it is beyond the resources of language to convey, and that therefore the only practicable and sensible course is to confine oneself to those affirmations which can be made or effectively indicated.

Three points may be made in conclusion. The first is a declaration of principle. We have said that an adequate answer to the ultimate question in terms of God must present the cosmos as a thought-out, purposive system. It is, of course, fallacious to argue from the fact that a system 'works' to a conclusion that it was consciously designed to work that way. But the argument in the opposite direction is not so vulnerable. If we can point to any prominent or general characteristics of the system, and say, 'These serve no good or useful purpose,' then this does count against the belief that it is the thought-out production of a good mind and will. If such characteristics predominated they would be sufficient reason for abandoning such a belief. It would be quite wrong to accept the thesis that 'nothing can be allowed to count decisively against belief in God', or the view that belief is a 'blik', an attitude not open to alteration by argument. The test mentioned is a real one; and if the system could not pass this test, the only honest course would be to abandon one's faith unless or until someone could convince one that it did pass it. The real difficulty, however, as will become apparent in the next chapter, lies in deciding whether certain pieces of evidence are to count for or against; and here it is doubtful whether any amount of argument can do much to help one's decision.

The second point concerns an objection to belief in God which is not infrequently voiced but which does not properly come under the main head of evil and suffering. This is the charge of waste, the apparent pointlessness and inefficiency of a vast and largely empty cosmos, or, within this planet, of the evolutionary and reproductive processes.

To this there are two replies at least. First, it was remarked earlier that given the scale of the universe as it is the emergence of life and of rational life was statistically inevitable. It might, therefore, be that a more restricted scale would not have provided sufficient chances for this to happen; or, to put it the other way round, to ensure that all the potentials of the basic terms of existence were realized, a certain space-time scale was required. This is not to say that the ultimate purpose of the cosmos was to produce Man, merely that the space-time scale may have been necessary to ensure the working out of all the potentials of the cosmos, of which Man is one, but including no doubt beings higher than Man, unknown to us in distant galaxies. Nor is it to say that this realization of potentials is the purpose of the cosmos or of its hypo-thetical Creator, but merely that the scale enables certain results to be achieved which might not be achieved if that scale were different; and this would not count against an ascription of purposiveness.

It is hard, however, not to feel that this argument is not really an argument at all, but rather a thinly disguised cry of Pascalian terror. On what grounds do you call millions of light-years of inter-galactic space a 'waste'? A waste of what? Of space? On this basis, in proportion, a hydrogen atom is a shocking example of waste, for that is mostly space

– as are you and I for that matter. There are variations on this theme, of course. It is often urged that because Man is but a dot on a speck, and a dying speck at that, in the vastness of the universe, he cannot be anything but an accident, and belief in a Creator a bad joke. But on what principles do we correlate significance with size or density of distribution? Or, to recall our suggestion of a moment ago, if the vastness were necessary to ensure the speck, one would not be demonstrably an idiot to assume the exact reverse. Anyway, what is wrong with vastness? Is not a sense of splendour and excitement as sound a response to it as this time-and-motion tutting? Or again, take the question of terrestrial waste – the profusion of unnecessary life-forms, the methods of reproduction, the ephemeral organisms. Quite apart from the role of these phenomena in the evolutionary process, by what right do we call them a waste? Is the dragon-fly a waste because it lives but twenty-four hours? Are the denizens of the Pacific floor a waste because they have no discernible relevance to any other living creatures, not even that of swimming around in a tank for their entertainment and edification? Why should not a creature just be? Why should there not be infinite diversity, whether there are hearts to leap at it or not? This small and anthropocentric criticism is not an argument. It is nothing more than the thin, complaining voice of mean, utilitarian, gutless, heartless, cerebral, twentieth-century, profit-margin Western Man.

The third point is just this. When we consider the simplicity of some basic unit of the universe such as the hydrogen atom, and the fact that its potential for change is apparently limited to the rise or fall of its energy level, to the greater or lesser excitation of its components, and reflect that with this were made the humming-bird and the whale, the mind of an Aristotle, an Einstein, a Kierkegaard, the music of Handel and the utterance of Shakespeare, the Wiltshire downs and the green mountains of Vermont, Michelangelo's David and the courage of good men, no miracle, no portent, can ever arouse more wonder than the fact of the natural order and the mystery of the human soul.

3

The World's Sorrow

ALL DISCUSSIONS of the world's sorrow are to some extent distortions. Sorrow is at most only one half of reality. In a thousand, often surprising ways our humanness is matched to its environment, and enabled to find it good; indeed, the ways in which mankind finds or makes its pleasures are far more varied than its pains.

There is the relish of food and drink; the satisfaction of hard, tiring work alternating with rest, leisure, sleep; the precious sense of physical health. There are the joys of love, of friendship, and of family life, the pride and excitement stirred by the achievements of one's children, fellow-workers, and neighbours, one's nation or race, be it in football or philosophy, outrigger racing or space exploration. Almost every culture takes pleasure in music and dance, in making things that are beautiful or useful, in solving problems. There are the delights of the senses. Visual beauty – not only present in the people and the works of art or Nature generally agreed to be beautiful, but liable to descend with a sudden nuance of the light, even if only for a short while, on the most unlikely objects; and the more acutely or whole-heartedly we look, the less bored or sated we are with what we see. Beauty of touch – the feel of polished wood, of water through the fingers or swilling all over you, of the solid earth under you, of the sheets of muscle in a horse's neck. Beauty of hearing – an old song worn to a perfect line by centuries, ripples against a running boat, a bird, a drum, a smooth powerful motor. Beauty of smell – wine, the first frost, green things after rain, the fur of a healthy animal. To catalogue every man's tastes and every man's happiness would be a fool's project. The pleasures already mentioned are of the kinds open to all societies, poor or rich, simple or sophisticated, in every continent. Once we start investigating those peculiar to each culture or sub-culture – pop music and pigeon-racing, bullfighting and beer, Stravinsky and stamp-collecting – there are more than enough entries for a large encyclopaedia. And that in itself tells us something of enormous importance about our experience of the world. Are we to count only the hate, never the love, only the ugliness, never the loveliness, only the misery, never the joy?

Such a plea does not, of course, exempt those whose faith in a good God creates the problem of evil from giving some viable account of the other half of experience. It is entered here simply as a necessary corrective in face of the tendency of thinkers and writers in our own old, tired, and decaying society to consider only the dark side of life, as a reminder that the problem we are now to consider is not the whole story. We are not starting from nothing, trying to scrape together a few good points out of a mass of misery and corruption. The world already has a score of something like fifty per cent to its credit. Nor is that good half all lavished on certain groups of Haves, while the bad is the only ingredient in the life of the Have-nots. That the balance is often criminally, gigantically unjust we may agree; but no man's life is a journal of unmitigated ills.

Nevertheless, everyone who reads these words, and who has normal human feelings, has at some time exclaimed, 'Why? Why did it have to happen? or to happen like that?' The question may not expect an answer. The questioner may be certain that there can be no answer. The word 'Why?' may merely be shorthand for a violent protest, a shout of anger into emptiness, a blow across the face of the dark. But it is a well-chosen word. It declares that there can be no good reason for these things, no way of justifying them.

Human suffering derives from three principal sources: the working of the natural order in accident, sickness, and disaster; the sense of futility and transience, commonly most acute in the contemplation of death; and the wickedness of allegedly free agents. In the present chapter we shall be concerned primarily with the first two. Most people make a rough and ready distinction between suffering caused by Man and those ravages of Nature for which God, if there is a God, is held to be more directly responsible, even though he is not exempted from blame for both. We shall, therefore, concentrate first on those evils for which no intermediate whipping-boy can be found.

As one would expect in a matter which has occupied Man's attention through most of his recorded history, a number of standard arguments and counter-arguments have been elaborated over the centuries. In most instances the defence of suffering is based on some form of the idea that it is a necessary evil, that is to say, that it serves essential purposes which justify the distress caused. It will be advisable to proceed in three stages: first, to give a brief account of these classic defences, together with the major criticisms which can be made of them; secondly, to question some of the assumptions underlying the whole discussion; and thirdly to see what happens when the whole matter is placed in the context of belief in God.

Before starting on this examination, however, it will be as well to dispose at once of two traditional approaches to the problem. The first is the conviction (it cannot be called an argument) that everything which happens is for the best, because if it had not happened, then something worse would undoubtedly have ensued. Islam has tales on this subject (e.g., in the Koran, chap. XVIII); and similar compositions, in which a devout believer protests at some cruel disaster, and is allowed to see in a vision the fate which would otherwise have befallen the persons concerned, occur in Judaeo-Christian piety. Something of the sort is often implied by the comment, 'God knows best'. It is hardly necessary to point out that such a view is quite unprovable; nor would it be particularly relevant to do so, since it is, as has been said, not an argument but an expression of piety, of complete faith in God. It is perhaps more to the point to ask where is the mercy in staving off one appalling end by another only a degree less horrible; and indeed, in view of the sufferings some people have to undergo, it requires considerable ingenuity to imagine what could be worse.

The second such approach is the theory, mentioned in an earlier chapter, that all suffering is retribution for sin. It is important to say a word about this view, not because there are very many people in our society today who believe it to be true – almost certainly there are not – but because there are far more who talk as though they wish it were. 'Why should this happen to me? I've always lived a good life.'

The dogma that all suffering is retribution, however long after the crime, is false, but we need to state the nature of its falsity with some precision. There is a sort of rough retributive justice in the world; and it is this which provides the basis for common-sense popular morality. Habitual idleness, folly, cruelty, cowardice, or dissipation, for instance, do tend to have disastrous results both for individuals and for communities; but these results are as likely as not to fall on those who had no part in the crimes and stupidities that produced them.

'The fathers have eaten sour grapes – and the children's teeth are set on edge.' In the age of 'one world' we know only too well that evildoing at one point in the world community will sooner or later bring evil fortune somewhere – but where? If there is a broad justice for the totality, there is very little for the individual, the local community, the province, or the nation. If we think in terms of the part and not the whole, good and evil fortune are morally random.

What those who gird against this fact do not seem to realize is that we ought to be thankful for it. If it were not so, if the theory were correct and it were demonstrably the case that in the long run honesty and all the other virtues were the best policy for each individual and group, then it would become impossible to do good for its own sake. We could never say, 'I am going to do this because it is right, and be damned to the consequences.' Enlightened self-interest would be the only way of life open to us. Furthermore, the theory only makes sense in the context of a particular view of right and wrong. There would seem to be two possibilities here. If justice is not only to be done, but to be seen to be done, then we have to assume criteria of good and evil which can be adequately applied by an outsider. I must be able to say with certainty that Jones was a wicked man, if his dying of a painful cancer is not to outrage me. The alternative is that justice should only be done, in which case either there is no sufficient evidence for the theory, or I am driven into the unspeakably nasty attitude of saying, 'Because Jones died of cancer he must have been a very wicked man.' Neither of these possibilities would be tolerable for a moment to a person with a grain of intelligence or human sympathy, any more than would the implied assertion that it is possible to regard, let us say, losing your children by drowning as an appropriate sentence for ruining several thousand small investors by shady financial practice. The whole conception is as nonsensical as it is depraved.

To turn then to theories more worthy of consideration, we may begin with the argument that physical pain acts as a warning system which helps us to survive. In some cases, as in the reflex withdrawal when we touch anything too hot, it saves us from serious or fatal injury; in others, such as head or stomach pains, it warns of threatening or actual illness. This explanation does not pretend to cover more than a small sector of human suffering anyway; but even within this sector it may be said in reply that the mechanism is of very uneven effectiveness. It is not uncommon, for example, to discover that a cancer has reached the inoperable stage before the patient has felt any significant discomfort. Moreover, why should it be necessary for pain, in fulfilling this function, to get so monstrously out of hand as it sometimes does? A flashing light is enough to give the controller of a power station notice that something is wrong. We do not give him an electric shock as well. One possible counter to the first objection might be to point out that in animals this system of warning by pain or discomfort seemingly works much better, and that therefore both its unreliable operation and the afflictions of which it fails to notify us may be the results of our 'unnatural' human existence. Alternatively, it may be that Man, whose great asset is that he arrives at conclusions by thinking instead of by instinctual programming, has to pay the penalty for this in the form of an insensitivity to signals from the physical organism which in an animal would be early enough, strong enough, and specific enough to evoke the response most beneficial for its health. On the subject of extreme pain any defence would probably have to resort to the argument from the regularity of the physical world, which we shall consider later.

Many have wondered whether, if there were no pain, we could experience pleasure. Montaigne, who for many years endured great distress from recurrent stone in the kidneys, commented: 'Just as the Stoics say that vices are introduced for our profit, to give value and assistance to virtue, we can say with better reason and less rashness, that nature has given us pain so that we may appreciate and be thankful for the absence of pain. When Socrates was relieved of his fetters he felt agreeably stimulated by the tingling which the weight of them had set up in his legs, and took pleasure in reflecting how closely pleasure and pain are allied, being linked together by a necessary bond, so that they follow and engender one another by turns.' The relationship may sometimes be closer even than this. The pang of hunger increases the pleasure of the food; the deprivations of the dark, interminable Northern winter make the return of the sun a silent ecstasy such as the Southerner can never know; the greater the anguish of separation or mutual anxiety, the more overwhelming are the joy and satisfaction of lovers. The pain here is not just the occasion of pleasure by contrast; it actually intensifies it. Such a view, however, says nothing about those pains which are never followed by any pleasure – unless the blessed relief of approaching death be so regarded.

A third justification urges that pain is necessary to the formation of character. In considering pain it must be borne in mind throughout that what we commonly call 'mental' or 'spiritual' agony is still experienced as physical pain. The difference lies not in the nature of the pain itself but in its being caused by the impact of ideas or events on the psyche rather than by direct injury to the body. Emotional distress occasioned, for example, by fear, anxiety, or bereavement, is accompanied by such clinically observable symptoms as pallor, faster pulse-rate higher blood-pressure, headache, abnormal sweating, sleeplessness or stomach pains. It is through the discomfort of such symptoms, or simply through those equally physical ones which result from the frustration of some desire, that 'moral temptation' exerts its pressure. The way out lies in the subject's own hands; he has only to break some rule or obligation and the distress will end. If he succumbs often enough, however, to set up a habitual pattern of behaviour, then it will not be necessary for him actually to feel the pain. The awareness at the back of his mind that resistance to the relevant impulse will bring it on is by now sufficient to make him give in without so much as considering the possibility of a fight. It is true that in many cases the onset of pain or illness of physical origin will displace these purely psychogenetic states. Even a cold in the head may put an end for the moment to the pangs of unrequited love. This does not mean that the pangs are not real or not physically experienced – merely that, for very good reasons connected with survival, external physical events make a more emphatic impression on the normal person than those of internal mental origin.

It has rightly been said that no virtues are of any use without courage; and courage is the strength of will not to be diverted by pain or the prospect of pain. It might be thought, therefore, that there was a good deal of truth in the view that pain was necessary to the formation of character. If we never had to endure anything daunting or unpleasant, would we not be totally lacking in backbone or determinatio ? This argument, however, ignores the special conditions that have to be observed if pain is to be educationally efficient. The situations in which courage is most needed and most difficult are those where, as we saw, the way out is in a person's own hands, but because of some overriding loyalty he does not take it. Hence hardship voluntarily undergone in pursuit of some goal held to be of great value (physical fitness, learning, a way of life) does build up moral stamina and stability. Even pain inflicted by another may do so – sometimes, indeed, to the disastrous point of total moral inflexibility – provided that the value in question is truly accepted by the victim, and the person administering the pain is not regarded as an enemy. There is a case on record of a violent, habitual criminal who was totally unmoved either by reasoning or by the severest sentences, because while he was a boy his father had conditioned him by constant beatings 'never to give in'. The boy admired his father, and accepted this as a worthwhile value. He therefore voluntarily co-operated, as it were, in the perverted purpose behind his beatings. The kind of pain with which we are concerned, however, is not voluntarily undergone, nor is it clear in any given case what good we are helping to bring about by enduring it. The result, as experience shows only too plainly, is that 'educationally' it is grossly inefficient. It is as likely to destroy morale as to build it. Moreover, this criticism is additional to more obvious rejoinders. Are babies who starve to death in some barbarous war capable of learning from their experiences? Does the agony of a husband and wife in some doomed airliner, visualizing during those last moments their children's orphaned future, help to build their characters?

In a variant form of the same defence it is argued that every single instance of suffering is productive of some secondary good of a moral or spiritual kind, and is thereby justified. But there would seem to be little evidence for this view. The most appalling tragedies fail so much as to ruffle the indifference of those who pass by them daily, or, where concern is aroused, they merely add to the total of fruitless pain, since there is nothing constructive that the sympathizer or anyone else can do. Even where some good is evoked, it will as likely as not be but a distant and general mitigation. The spastic child, the man or woman in the prime of life blighted by an intractable mental disease, the elderly sufferer whose heart is too strong to release him from the dehumanizing terminal agonies of cancer – all these may arouse concern, which may in turn lead to help or relief for future sufferers. Their misery may point us to radical errors in the way we live our lives, to faulty regimen both of body and mind. But no one with a grain of feeling would expect such considerations to reconcile the victim or his family and friends to their distress. One might, of course, modify the defence to say that all pain would produce good if people would only react to it in the right spirit – meaning, no doubt, with practical remedies, if possible, and with courage and serenity, if not. But is this not to beg the whole moral issue? The fact that we can find ways to make the best of a bad job does not make the job itself any less bad. Only if we think that such responses to pain are good in themselves, good absolutely, does this argument go any way at all to justifying the pain which is necessary to evoke them. If they are merely the most we can do to accommodate evil with dignity, then they may vindicate us – they certainly do not vindicate the pain.

Nevertheless, we are beginning to come close to the crux of the discussion. Some of the arguments so far considered have some limited validity. They nibble away at the mass of evil from various sides, and so do something to reduce it to manageable proportions. The warning-system argument applies in certain cases; the pain-pleasure argument in others; the formation-of-character theory in yet others. None of them, however, comes near providing a general rationale of pain. It is quite clear from all that has been written on the subject down the centuries that this can only be done with any hope of success by framing the argument differently. It is no good using the formula, 'All instances of pain produce the good result X,' because there is no one value of X for which this is true. We can, however, ask the question, 'What would necessarily be lost if the world were such that there could never be pain above an easily tolerable level?' By phrasing it this way we avoid the assumption that every instance of pain has the same good outcome – or even any good outcome at all.

The world we have is one where the regularities of the physical order make it possible for pain to take extreme forms. A world where gravitation keeps you on the ground is one where you will be dashed to pieces if you fall off a cliff on to the rocks below. A world where you can take advantage of the properties of steel to make a motor-car is one where the tie-rods in that car will break under certain conditions with the result maybe that someone is maimed or disfigured. A world where the nerve-endings in our fingers are sensitive enough to make delicate craftsmanship or surgery possible is one where crushing or burning will send appalling shock waves through the system. There are only two ways in which such situations might be avoided. We might have a world where pain was physically impossible, a world, let us say, of globular creatures in sterile, unbreakable plastic rolling about on an endless foam-rubber sea. Or we might have a world where, whenever something was about to go seriously wrong, an interventionist God by a special act saved the day. He would have to intervene thus on every such occasion, or obviously he would be unfair. One basic question, therefore, is, 'What would be lost in a world subject to this kind of intervention?' There would necessarily be a serious limitation on our ability to discover regularities in Nature; but the major loss would seem to be control of our own affairs and the responsibility that goes with this. To opt for an interventionist God would be to say that these things do not matter very much. (Christians who expect more than a marginal proportion of miraculous answers to prayer would do well to remember this.) To decide that they do matter leaves you with a choice between a regular but painless universe and one much like that in which we live at present.

'What would necessarily be lost in a regular but painless universe?' Intellectual life would be unaffected. The observation, collection, and comparison of evidence; the formation, testing, and application of theories; the general systematizing of knowledge – all these would still be possible, though some of the incentives that at present seem needed to stir men from mental lethargy would be lost. Social and individual relationships of an intellectual kind would remain. Hatred, fear, jealousy, envy, cruelty, loneliness would have gone. War, injury, death, disease, and starvation could all in theory continue – but no one, not even the victims, would care.

And that, of course, is the point. If someone's death causes me no pang, is it possible for me to care about them? If no word or act of mine, or of anyone else's, no accident of nature, no defect in themselves, can cause pain either to them or to me, can I have any concern for them? In short, to our list of losses do we have to add – love?

Surely too there would be an end to that constellation of qualities we call disinterestedness, loyalty, sacrifice? I could not choose to do what was right even though it was to my disadvantage, for nothing would ever be to my disadvantage. The idea of loyalty would lose its meaning, because there could never be any stress or pressure sufficient to justify one in speaking of it. I could never choose someone else's good at the cost of my own hurt or disappointment, for nothing would hurt me enough to count. I could not sacrifice all for an ideal or a precious thing or a defenceless fellow-creature that had put itself under my protection; I could not even practise self-denial. I could do my best for others, and for myself, in various ways, but I could never suffer for them.

Another forfeit which a painless world would exact is adventure in all its forms. The runner's pain barrier, the mountain-climber's North

Face, the yachtsman's solo voyage round the world, the potholer's exploration miles into the unknown hill, the racing driver's lap record, the crossing of Antarctic snows, all these would lose their essential meaning. It is true that when such activities are condemned because of the waste and danger involved – families bereaved, bodies shattered, rescuers imperilled, and all for what? – an obeisance is commonly made to outraged moral feeling by the thin pretence that what is done is in some way useful. But in all these largely 'pointless' pursuits it is not the technical achievement, it is the life-enhancing fear of danger, the overcoming of both the hostile environment and oneself, which contributes the large measure of deep and even ecstatic satisfaction. If love is the first great quality conceivable only in a world of pain, the second is undoubtedly courage.

We have now reached the farthest point to which the classic arguments can take us; for if we suppose that any of these replies, true and important observations though some of them may be, could possibly answer the original question, then we have failed to see how radical that question is. The issue is not whether this world is in all respects as bad as some maintain, or whether we might not make it more tolerable than it is, but whether any system which admits excessive pain can be regarded as the work of a good and intelligent being. The way things are is condemned not in detail but in principle, and on these grounds. We, if we had had the planning of it, would have made it otherwise. Our moral sense would have insisted.

The argument that without significantly costly pain there could be neither courage nor self-denying love takes for granted that these are desirable qualities absolutely and in themselves. But is this true? Certainly they may be desirable in the world as we have it; but it is precisely the fact that the world requires them which is under attack. On what rational grounds is it a good thing that I should suffer for the benefit of a fellow-creature? So long as I can see what is good for him, and pursue it to the utmost of my ability, what conceivable purpose is served by my getting hurt in the process? It may be true, as things are, that 'greater love hath no man than this, that a man lay down his life for his friends'. But if we assume that such love is the highest good in some absolute sense, then have we not been brainwashed by the universe? Have we not refused to face the fundamental problem at all, and swallowed without question the faith that this, the only world we have, must be the best of all possible worlds?

Between these two positions there can be no rational method of adjudicating. Our decision must be a naked act of choice, and for the following reason. When talking about this subject we tend to fall into the trap of treating experience as something that happens *to* one ('A funny thing happened to me on the way to the studio'). What I experience, however, is not just the external event, nor, as some have thought, simply my own inner sensations, but the complex reality of 'myself-experiencing-the-event'. I am aware that something real is happening outside me and impinging upon me, that I have become involved in an event that exists in its own right. But normally I am also aware at the same time of my own response to it, what it is like to live through it. (It is a matter for remark when our sensations lead us to comment: 'Somehow it didn't seem to be happening to me at all. It was as though I were watching someone else.') The way in which we react to events is just as much a part of our experience of them as the events themselves. When, therefore, we are asked to compare a system under which we have never lived with one that is our permanent environment – in this case a pain-free universe with one such as we now have – we do not have the basis on which to make the evaluation. Imagination soon becomes exhausted, our guesses about the effects of such a change highly tentative. We cannot 'know good and evil' except from the inside, inside the event and inside ourselves.

To adjudicate in this way between two systems, of which one is known from the inside, the other only from the outside, is, however, precisely what the classic debate about the problem of pain attempts to do; and it is this which gives it so marked an air of academic unreality. The question, 'Is this universe the work of a good and wise God?' can never be answered on the basis of the world's own evidence, for any answer depends on a prior judgement about what is good and wise, and this can be made only in terms of the actual environment in which we find ourselves. The real question that we have to answer, indeed the only question we have any hope of being able to answer, is this: 'Taking things all in all, am I glad that I was born?'

We already become aware of this limitation as soon as we try to assess the sufferings of other people. These sufferings are indeed a part of our own experience, but only in our capacity as spectators. 'Spectator' may seem a wholly inadequate word to use of those people whose deep and intuitive sympathy enables them to read the mind and heart of a sufferer, and even to share in part his actual physical pain.

Yet, however intense the sympathy, the one who feels it cannot truly cross the line that divides the spectator from the participant. In fact the greater our awareness of the agony, the more helplessly and miserably we are conscious of being just a looker-on. This limitation of being able to live only our own life is nowhere more apparent than in the moral judgements we make about pain. A famous philosopher once remarked to the present writer: 'If I thought there was a God, I would kick him in the teeth for what he did to my father.' Many of us have wanted to make a judgement like that, but has anyone the right to make it except the one who knows the exact quality of the experience in question, the person himself? He, if he chooses to do so, may have the right to resent it. Are we, who cannot live his life, in a position to resent it for him, or to say that he ought – or equally that he ought not – to resent it? 'Then Job's wife said to him, "Do you still hold fast your integrity? Curse God and die!" But he said to her, "You speak as one of the foolish women would speak. Shall we receive good at the hand of God, and shall we not receive evil?"'

This same impossibility of judging from the outside bedevils another way in which the problem of pain is sometimes approached. We might say: 'God is supposed to be perfect. Surely then the crucial question is not whether the universe is in any respect well and wisely ordered, but whether it is perfectly so? And obviously the answer must be "No".'

Human beings are prone to think in this way in terms of a 'perfect' solution. The idea of perfection is a natural one. It seems so obvious that if we can draw an imaginary line to represent the change from what is bad to what is good, then it must be possible to go on extending this line from 'good' through 'better' to 'perfect'. In coming to important decisions we take it for granted that one of the courses of action open to us must be the 'right' one and all the others 'wrong'. In fact, however, several of the possible courses may simply be good in different ways. If I take this new job or turn it down, if I marry this person or that or not at all, if we have another child or stay as we are, there will always be a profit and a loss side to the account, whether or not we are able to foresee it now or ever become aware of it later. In such situations the question, 'Am I doing the right thing?' is the wrong question, because it implies at the very least that if we knew all the factors one decision would stand out as correct. Of course, we may find ourselves in a situation where only one course of action seems to us even thinkable. Here our decision will undoubtedly be the 'right' one, but it may still be far from an ideal solution of the problem. If Sydney Carton could have saved his friend without himself going to the guillotine, would not that have been better still?

Experience thus suggests that while there may be 'better' or 'worse' or 'equally-good-in-different-ways' solutions, there are no 'perfect' ones. And the same would seem to apply to the possible 'worlds' which would of necessity dictate the nature of any experience we might have, as indeed they would dictate the kind of beings we were. The world in which we live has certain qualities, certain potentials, all of which spring from the basic terms of existence. Change those terms, and you change some at least of the qualities and potentials. Remove significant pain, and, as we saw, you remove certain moral possibilities; demand an interventionist God, and you are voting for the surrender of certain intellectual possibilities. 'The best of all possible worlds' remains a contradiction in terms. The assessment we are required to make is an existential one – do we or do we not say of the world we have: 'Behold, it is very good'?

When modern Man, however, has tried to make this existential assessment, to do justice in his thinking to the fact that he is indeed involved in the world, the result more often than not has been a deep melancholy, a sense of futility and nothingness. Nothingness, the nil, is the Devil of this generation. It is the mythical symbol for our defeat and desolation when confronted on the one hand with a cosmos so vast that our brief existence seems without significance of any kind, and on the other with our failure to manage even our own lives and the minute polity of this planet. But why this particular symbol? Why Nothing rather than Satan, Non-being rather than malevolent being?

Partly perhaps because we have become aware of the nothingness at the centre of our own selves. There is indeed a reality which may rightly be called by my name and my name only, there is an 'I' which has a continuous history despite the fact that its body is continually changing, an 'I' which is not just a freakish by-product of my brain and nervous system, but which exerts real influence upon them. Whereas, however, many of our forefathers thought of this 'I' as something actually 'there', like a ghost and equally indestructible, for us it is a phenomenon dependent upon the proper functioning of the physical organism. While all goes on more or less well, life retains this strange extra dimension. When physical functioning breaks down, the 'I' may become unrecognizable, or vanish altogether. The senile hulk lingering on in some old hospital, admission to which signals to everyone in the neighbourhood that hope is gone – is it the man or woman, gay, kind, intelligent, whom we knew? Where is the 'I' that used to say, 'I think,' 'I see,' 'I love'? What was it that it should crumble at so light a touch? At the heart of our personal system there is a void; it is not built round anything at all. We are a feat of organization.

Primitive Man projected his personhood on to the environment. We have not changed. We do the same, but the image which we project is naturally the hateful truth about ourselves which we normally repress out of consciousness – the hollow man, ephemeral impotence. The awareness of the nothingness within us looms over us as the infinite abyss of the impersonal void without; and our hold on some sort of individuality, so temporary, so easily prised away, becomes a gesture of defiance expressed either in an explosive nonconformism or a pragmatic, self-seeking acceptance. Both are understandable ways of trying to keep one's sanity in face of a conviction of ultimate nothingness.

Contemporary Man sets about solving the enigma of the universe in two ways. Sometimes he tries to argue to a solution by reason, but does so from a standpoint of detachment which it is logically impossible to occupy. Sometimes he reads off a solution from his emotional reaction to certain mental pictures which he takes to be 'objective' fact about the cosmos, but which are really unconsciously projected facts about himself. Sometimes he combines both methods (as in the case of the 'Death of God' theologians, Hamilton and Altizer), and is greatly impressed by the fact that each approach produces much the same answer. Two incompetent arguments, however, are no better than one. The conclusion still remains unproven. And both the lines of argument mentioned are incompetent, because they are untrue to our situation, which is one neither of detached rationality nor of affective intuition but of 'rationality-in-involvement'. We must reflect, but we must reflect on the actual position in which we find ourselves, individually and corporately, where certain thoughts can be thought and others cannot.

When we examine this position, as we have tried to do in this chapter, and come to sum up our findings, we are led to an interesting observation. We see that we are beings capable of great and varied happiness within the terms of our existence. We see too that we may have to endure great and varied suffering in the forms of pain, futility, wickedness, and death. And we also detect a strange relationship between them. Happiness cannot be sought for its own sake. It comes as a by-product of doing other things, making objects of beauty or use, making love, helping in a corporate achievement, seeking knowledge, being with friends, breaking records, celebrating. All such activities involve a concern for something or someone other than the self, by which the self in self-forgetting is fulfilled. But concern and self-forgetting are attitudes possible only in a world where pain also is possible. In short, if beings such as ourselves are to be happy, they need to be open to pain.

Of the good ends which the universe as it is makes available to its inhabitants some could be pursued under a different system. The search for truth and for understanding of the nature of things; freedom to plan and conduct one's own affairs, and to take responsibility for them; these need not be exclusive to such a world as ours. But we do need our kind of world if these good ends are to be combined with certain others: adventure, courage, disinterested goodness, loyalty, concern, sacrifice, and love. What is more, the latter are of primary importance for two reasons. First, without a world where they were possible, there could be no happiness, as we know it, of body, mind, or heart. Secondly, these are the only purposes that might be called good for which the specific qualities of our universe are required. If these are not goods, and the most important of all goods, then neither is the cosmos good, nor can we claim that a good and wise God is an adequate answer to the ultimate question Man is driven to ask about it.

It is quite impossible to over-emphasize the crucial significance of this point. Neglect of it has vitiated almost all traditional thinking about God. Unless we have faced the radical question which, as we saw, the fact of suffering puts to us, and have *already* made the naked choice to hold love, sacrifice, concern, and the rest, of greater value than exemption from pain, we cannot rationally believe in a God of goodness at all. To invoke a supposed divine revelation to make this value-judgement for us would be to beg the question; since if we decide against love God ceases to be even remotely plausible. The judgement has to be made simply and starkly in face of the facts, an existential commitment which can be arrived at by no road of rational argument. This is the necessary logical order of events: commitment to love first, faith in God second. It may indeed not be the historical order in any given individual's life; but at some time or other, if he wishes to retain any intellectual integrity and to give his religion a foundation in reason, he has to face this most searching of all challenges, not to his mind, but to his heart and will.

One happy consequence of recognizing this fact is that we can take up all the agonized and convoluted arguments by which religious thinkers down the ages have sought 'to justify the ways of God to men', and pitch them into the depths of the sea. The only person to whom it is necessary to justify God is someone who does not accord this supreme value to sacrificial love, that is to say, someone who cannot rationally believe in God anyway. To anyone who does believe with mind as well as heart there is no need of learned vindications.

A second implication, which leads us directly into the subject of the next three chapters, may be less immediately welcome. If what we have said is true, then the nature of moral good and evil is not an open question. The system has been 'rigged' so that we are not free to start from scratch in deciding what is right and wrong. In a rather strange and oblique way love has been required by law.

4

Moral Good and Evil

OUR CONCERN in the next two chapters must be to apply the general approach already developed to the question of moral good and evil. We shall examine Man's nature and situation, the given terms of his existence, to see what light these may shed on the problems of the good, of the methods and conditions necessary to realize it, and of Man's failure to do so. If, as we have argued, God can be God only in so far as he provides an adequate answer to the ultimate question, then there is no other way of proceeding. Any clue to possible values or purposes behind the way things are must be found in the way things are, not in some ideal construction of our own moral preferences.

In one respect, however, it is quite inaccurate to speak of the 'nature' of Man, because by definition he is never found in a 'natural' state. His life is always marked by some element of that detached and reflective organization which we call 'culture', for it is by the presence of this element, evidenced maybe in nothing more than a few rough but unmistakable artefacts, that we recognize his arrival. From the start some at least of his responses have lost the spontaneity of those of the other animals. He is tackling his problems differently, and will develop his own methods more and more, at the same time becoming more and more aware both of what he is doing and of himself doing it.

Nevertheless, the living self of which he becomes conscious does have a given character of its own, which mind and will have to accept and with which they are obliged to work. The appropriate diagram for the normal human being is not a circle with its single centre but an ellipse with two foci, the self and its 'world' – the latter term being used here in the technical sense of the total environment as the person himself apprehends it in a more or less unified vision. Man cannot be understood in terms of a static being with certain 'qualities' or 'attributes' but only as a dynamic process with a recognizable overall character. He is in continuous action and reaction with his world. It is the to-and-fro, the interplay between them which constitutes him a person. It is no use asking which comes first, the self or the world which the self perceives and with which it interacts, for the one is never found without the other.

In this interplay the self may adopt a predominantly assertive or subordinating role at any given time. Man's approach to Nature is a good example of this. Far more often than not, it is true, he is attempting to impose his own ideas on Nature; but he may also subordinate himself to it for its own sake, as in preservation projects. Nowhere perhaps do we see more clearly than in art how indissolubly linked are these two aspects of Man. The artist is in one way a highly self-assertive person. He is striving to create the perfect expression and communication, precise, complete, and convincing, of his own vision. Yet if he does not take trouble to discover and conform to the nature and capacities of his medium he will achieve nothing worth while. To every man in his own particular way of life fulfilment of body, mind, and heart comes only if he can respond appropriately in both these ways in the unceasing dialogue between his self and his world.

This dual character of Man's responses is of special importance in his relations with his fellows. A human being needs the group not just as a helpful adjunct to his own life but absolutely. A child deprived of the society of other persons never itself develops into a full person. The family, the pack, the clan, the tribe – these organic systems are in their way ultimates. Without them, or something like them, the individual as such could never exist. His relationship with them, however, is not purely one of self-subordination – yielding, taking his allotted place, endangering himself for the common good, even dying in an attempt to ensure the survival of his mate or young ones or the whole community. He also needs room for self-assertion through status, authority, leadership, expertise, anything which will command from others the recognition that he has his own unique value. In a vast, shapeless, and coercive urban society, where a man's work does nothing to distinguish him from thousands of his neighbours, this need will often be supplied by his leisure activities. He may satisfy it by nothing more glorious than being a saloon bar knowall. But for every human being both these aspects of his nature are necessary both to him and to the species; and a member of the species who is not characterized by both in something like reasonable proportions is a misfit and inadequate. He becomes either a psychopath, unworried by his own socially unacceptable aggressions, or a mere cipher who has almost ceased to be an individual and who contributes little to the group that a machine or a domesticated animal could not provide.

Pulpit moralists are apt to say that Man is by nature self-centred. Sometimes they attribute this to a Fall, sometimes they hold that there never was a time when Man was not like this. It makes absolutely no difference, since the statement is so gross an over-simplification that it is useless anyway; and it is this defect in the premiss which makes the moralizing built upon it so untrue to life. Here wickedness is defined as selfishness, and all self-assertion then becomes at least *prima facie* suspect as wicked. Goodness is correspondingly identified with unselfishness, and self-subordination, even in highly undesirable forms, is automatically presumed to be virtuous. All of which is so repugnant to common sense and common observation that not surprisingly it fails to carry conviction.

The fallacy is really a very simple and obvious one. 'Self-assertion' and 'self-subordination' (or whatever equivalent terms we prefer to use) refer to observable phenomena in human beings. They are in intention as purely descriptive as the language of anatomy or neurology. 'Selfishness' and 'unselfishness' are words expressing a value-judgement. It is quite inadmissible to assume any correlation at all between the two pairs. A human doormat may be extremely selfish precisely in his readiness to have feet wiped on him, and a decisive leader may be very unselfish in his willingness to take command and risk and responsibility. The true criteria of selfishness do not come within the scope of psychological investigation.

Two other features of Man, closely connected with that already described, are relevant at this point in our discussion. The first is his psychic fragility. In animals neurosis can be induced by confusion or frustration, when it repeatedly happens that learned behaviour does not meet with the expected response, or that instinctive behaviour fails to match the situation which has evoked it. Analogous breakdowns can be elicited in human beings by forcing them to endure inconsequential and irrational responses at unpredictable intervals.[1]

---

[1] This is the theoretical basis of psychological torture. It is interesting to note that the techniques of Zen Buddhism are designed, among other things, to increase a person's capacity to tolerate such treatment, which is seen as a parable of life

In addition, however, Man is liable to neurosis, and even to complete psychic dissociation from reality, as the result of internal conflict. In the animal's confusion- or frustration-neurosis its inner coherence is not destroyed; the system as a single whole breaks down because its running dialogue with its world is not proceeding properly. In a human conflict-neurosis the dialogue is again disturbed, but this time with the added complication that the self is divided.[1] Sometimes the individual may be able to solve his problem by living a double life, of which the second stream may be pursued in reality or in fantasy. If both these avenues of escape, however, are barred to him, either by circumstances or by early conditioning, then complete breakdown may ensue; and if at this point some safe and undemanding haven, to which the sufferer can for a time withdraw from the struggle with reality, is not available, then insanity and suicide, the final havens of dissociation or death, are the only options left.

The second relevant feature is Man's ability to stand at a distance from himself, to observe himself as though he were another person with a certain objectivity and detachment. This ability is part and parcel of the radical difference in structure which distinguishes Man from the other animals. Without it he could not have any of that particular kind of knowledge which, as we shall see, makes possible a margin of freedom. As usual, however, this immense advantage is paid for by an immense risk. The individual forgets that the observer is also the observed. He may then try to dissolve the unity of the person in a different way, allotting to the observed all those elements which he or his world finds distasteful, while crediting the observer with any good qualities. In extreme cases the latter may consist of nothing more than the capacity of the observer to condemn – 'If I know I am no good,

---

[1] The specific content of the conflict, and the factors which make this particular area the person's weak spot, are of course the familiar subject-matter of clinical psychology. The present discussion would be uselessly inflated by any attempt to include a survey of this vast field. We are concerned here rather with what may be called the basic terms of human existence, not with their detailed working out in the individual life-history. It will be sufficient for the reader to bear in mind the general relation just indicated between psychological analysis and our main theme.

---

itself. If we can train ourselves not to expect rationality, we shall not resent irrationality. Here, as in so many other ways, Buddhism shows itself a more radical alternative to Judaeo-Christian theism than any offered by Western humanism. This is no doubt part of the reason for its increasing appeal in the West.

then I cannot really be so'. Naturally this must not be explicitly claimed, for then the self-condemnation would not be severe enough to justify it; but as an unacknowledged assumption it enables the observer to carry on in the confidence that his dialogue with his world is conducted by his 'better self', and thus avoid ever facing the truth.[1] All the various abuses of this human capacity for detachment come down in the end to this: the flight from reality. An animal cannot escape from his own reality, but neither can he be aware of it. Man uses his privilege of being aware as a means of escape, sometimes even to the extreme point of creating a multiple personality. His universal readiness – and compulsion – to do so in some degree is further testimony to the fragility of his psychic structure and to the instability of its normal equilibrium.

These elementary facts about Man, taken in conjunction with other information, help us to compile a list of his most important needs. We can begin simply enough with the necessities of any sort of life: security from attack, a balanced diet, clothing, light and air, adequate shelter, sleep, freedom of movement, opportunity for mental and physical exertion, stable conditions for the upbringing of children. A more basic list it would be hard to imagine. Yet, as we know, there are millions of human beings, some of them in the most unexpected places, for whom even this cannot be guaranteed.

Once we move beyond some such list as this we are concerned not with mere survival but with a minimum tolerable quality of existence. In this connection outstandingly important, as we have seen already, is contact with other human beings – and not simply contact but effective communication. The most deleterious of all situations is permanent solitude; but to have as one's only society people with whom communication, except of the most rudimentary kind, is impossible is also destructive of mental and physical health. A shared language, culture, values, and intellectual presuppositions, serve not only to create a strong community but to maintain the stability of the individuals who make it up; for by virtue of these things they are given a framework within which true communication is possible. The tragic effects of a decay of communication may be illustrated from the plight of so many

---

[1] It cannot be too strongly emphasized that all the moralistic language about our 'better' or 'worse' self, our 'higher' and 'lower' nature, is the product of this illusion. It has now penetrated even into the English-language versions of the New Testament, in the *N.E.B.* version of Paul's Epistles, thus converting a serious moral challenge into a piece of harmless conventional religiosity.

old people. Because after a certain age they have less and less in common with those around them, all concerned (themselves included) find communication more and more demanding, and cease to make the necessary effort. The result is a swift and largely unnecessary deterioration of the faculties and personality.

Furthermore, most people need a structured community in which to live, where they have a recognized place and usefulness. Here again the old in our own society point the moral. A world of high mobility and rapid technical change places a premium on youth, which has fewer roots and is open to new ideas. By the same token age, which in the past commanded respect as the repository of wisdom and the medium of tradition, no longer does so. If we want to consult the past (always assuming we believe it has anything to tell us) we expect to do so more conveniently and accurately in books or on computer tape. Thus after retirement, which arrives at a progressively earlier age, it is all too easy to become and to feel 'useless'. Worse still, the family, within which the old might properly look to find status accorded by gratitude and respect for all that they have been and done, is fragmented. As a large federation linking the basic units of husband, wife, and children, it is less regarded than it was; nor have these basic units, living each in its own small, independent house or flat, either the physical or the emotional space to accommodate the oldest generation without strain. What is the outcome? Men and women who are no longer powerful or indispensable enough to command status are denied the satisfaction of a fundamental human need. They are shunted off to Homes for the Aged, the lumber-rooms where society keeps the accumulated rubbish which it is – as yet – too sentimental to destroy. While still alive and human they are treated as having no role save that of waiting for the formality of bodily death. The results are seen in symptoms of depression, withdrawal, and emotional retrogression.

In the light of what has just been said it may at first sight seem ridiculous to suggest that our society also provides too little opportunity for the adolescent to feel himself part of the organic whole. Yet consider the position of many a boy who leaves school at the minimum age. He has no domestic responsibilities, no part to play in politics or local government or trade unionism. His first job commonly makes even less demands on his effort and intelligence than his lack of training makes inevitable – and that at a time when he has more nervous energy than he knows how to use. If he has also developed no real interests for his leisure time, he finds himself wandering the streets every night with others similarly unoccupied, bored to distraction in a world where everyone else has something to do and to be. The result is the auto- nomous teenage sub-culture, which from time to time forays out to smash the property or persons of the larger world. The futile, irra- tional, and often self-destructive nature of these behaviour patterns suggests their morbidity. That a sense of exclusion from the total community has a part in causing them is confirmed by the fact that they are abandoned by most on entry into adult life and responsibilities, and generally speaking do not arise at all in those whose fuller life and leisure satisfy their need for status and occupation.

To interpret these phenomena as a crisis over 'authority' is to go only half-way in thinking the matter through. Authority is stable only where those in authority and those under it all see themselves as members of one genuine community with broad agreement about aims and ideals. Where this condition is not met, be it in a nation, a military force, a school, a church, a university, there rebellion, followed either by repression or by appeasement, is never far away. It is significant that among university students, for example, revolt and protest are notice- ably less common in those who already have a clear idea what they wish to do with their lives in adult society than among those who can find no career that attracts or inspires them. The former see the university and their training within it as having an obvious coherence with society as a whole. To dismiss this with the comment, 'Oh, those are just the conformists', throws no further light on the matter, since 'conformists' is simply another word for those who share the aims and ideals of society as it is. Moreover, though some of those who are dissatisfied have definite reforms in mind, a disquietingly high proportion seem to be antagonistic and nothing else. In discussion they prove to have no clear or concrete aims nor any concept of society as a stable framework for creative living, and try to conceal this vacuum from themselves and others by high-sounding talk of 'continuous revolution'. In this respect they are quite different from the classic revolutionaries of 1789, 1848, or 1917. The irrational violence of their reactions, as opposed to the readiness of those with a practical programme to use constitutional methods, points to the fact that this is in some ways a blind and emotional response to some sense of deprivation. A plausible explan- ation, to put it no higher, is that society seems to many no longer to have a place within its body for those who do not share its values nor to provide any natural mechanisms of change for them to use. Hence reform seems mere tinkering, and is replaced by revolution or rejection. In this respect we have become partly moribund, and have lost the openness and vigour of the mid-nineteenth century. This is at least not contradicted by the attitude of cynicism and apathy towards politics which characterizes many older people.

Another constellation of human needs is that which may be generally described as privacy and space. It is a corollary of the fact that human life is, as we have said, a dialogue or interplay between the self and its world that the two should be distinct. Among the most basic and essential ways of keeping the self distinct from its world is the right to be separate and alone both in space and in time. The human being needs physical space. Overcrowding has dangerous effects on his mental equilibrium. Just as hens crowded too closely in a battery become vicious and, given the chance, savage each other, so the self-control of the human animal is subjected to intense strain by lack of room. The same applies to lack of time to himself. (The fact that dread of being left alone is a neurotic condition confirms this from the opposite direction.) If there is never a chance to get away from other people, or at the very least to ignore their existence for a while, tensions build up, and easily reach breaking-point. It would be miraculous if there were not gang warfare between youths in crowded slum areas. The combination of two factors already considered – inadequate mental and physical outlets, and lack of any real function or status within society as a whole – with minimal privacy and space is so destructive of personhood that a violent reaction is statistically inevitable. Significantly this takes the form of a retrogression to animal methods of solving the same problems: the pack marking out its 'territory', and attacking all aliens who enter it, to a great extent indiscriminately. Here, in a dehumanized form, members of the group at last have organic community, status, usefulness, power, and room. Slum clearance, community centres, and suchlike, cure these ills not, as is fondly supposed, by the moralistic mechanism (concern and education evoking a change of heart) but by removing the pressures that produced the sub-human reactions. It is only when the pressures are off that any worthwhile observations can be made on the moral qualities of most of the people involved.

Other needs take us beyond survival or tolerable levels of health into the more debatable area of growth and fulfilment, including certain questions of freedom which will occupy us again shortly. Here may be mentioned the security of a loving and stable home in childhood, the security provided by the right to think for oneself and express one's conclusions (less accurately called freedom of speech and thought), the security of equality before the law, the enlarging of the options of life by educational and health amenities, a social order sufficiently developed and flexible to allow of choice of occupation, a physical environment that is beautiful and varied rather than drab, offensive, or monotonous.

It is tempting to suppose that an ethic might be constructed with the building-blocks of these needs and of numerous others of the same kind which the reader will be able to name from his own experience. After all, life will not be full or happy either for the individual or the group unless such needs are largely met. It is therefore a 'good' thing that they should be satisfied, and a 'bad' thing that they should not. Here at once we have solid practical content for a scheme of ethical guidance. The fact that any particular description of human needs may be inaccurate or incomplete does not affect the principle. All we have to do is to go back to the study of mankind and of his environment, to ask what are the real needs of men, and to discover more adequate answers.

Are matters, however, really as simple as that? By speaking as we have done of 'need', have we not presupposed a norm? Is it not implied that if these requirements are not met then men and women will differ from some concept of ideal Man? and if so, is not this ideal concept the basis of our ethic, and how is it to be justified?

This objection is to some extent a valid one. When, for example, we justify the need for privacy and space by saying that without these things there is a likelihood of violence, we are taking for granted that the sort of violence normally produced by these conditions is socially undesirable. But one can easily imagine a society where this was not so, where violence was deliberately induced as a means of selection in order to develop, let us say, a warrior caste capable of enriching the community by plundering its neighbours. Plato was prepared to deny the ruling class of his ideal state the satisfactions of family life, because he believed that the specialized task of governing called for special qualities to which this was inimical. The main strategic end in view will always influence decision on points of detail.

To this, however, it may be replied that to a certain extent we are talking about health, and that health is a descriptive term which can be empirically defined. Failure to supply many of these needs can create serious, clinically observable malfunction – psychosomatic illness, impotence, inability to work at the level normally associated with the individual's physique and intelligence, and so on. Moreover, if we include in our account of health such aspects of the human person as the ability to discern, communicate, and act in accordance with external reality, then even such of the items mentioned above as freedom of speech come into the picture, since to be compelled to keep one's view of reality to oneself, and not to tell it or act on it, would seem to be a misuse and stultification of the equipment with which Man is endowed. It may also induce a morbid split in the personality, a destruction of 'the bond of integrity between the private and the public self' (Raymond Chapman), or, in the terms we have been using in this chapter, a blockage and distortion of that interplay between the self and its world which in fact constitutes the person. Here the only question we are asked to beg is that it is better to be healthy than not.

This is, however, only a partial answer. First, if the concept of health is to be of any use in this context it must refer to something measurable and verifiable, some level of functioning which is demonstrably more efficient than another. ('We painted the canteen pale yellow, and offered interest-free loans for house purchase, and output went up by 17 per cent.') But can such a test be applied rigorously enough to give valid results for every type of need on our list? Secondly, the needs themselves are identified on a statistical basis. A sufficient number of cases have been investigated to show, let us say, that an unhappy childhood or the lack of stable circumstances in which to bring up children can lead to malfunction in the individual and trouble in the group. But equally there are many people who overcome these hazards successfully, even light-heartedly. 'A list of human needs' can never mean that each person who is unprovided for on any one of these counts will inevitably suffer. Human life is so rich and complex that individuals may manage surprisingly well on a very limited range of fulfilments. What such a list does do is to give an aid to diagnosis. If there is trouble, then somewhere on this check-list we are likely to find some factor at least partly responsible.

Should our aim then be by social engineering to attempt to supply as many of these needs as possible for everyone in the community?

Here again we run into insuperable difficulties. To ensure that no person lacks in regard to need A may very well entail denying them need B. This is the classic problem of the welfare state. Can you make certain that people have the food, the physical regimen, the housing, the education, the amenities that they 'need' without taking away their privacy, their freedom, their need to exert themselves to make sacrifices for those dependent upon them, and so forth? The answer is that you cannot. Or again, how can any system ensure that each individual has security and love in childhood or respect in old age? It cannot. These are things which cannot be organized. Human beings have to do them for each other out of their own inner resources. The most society can hope to do is to provide a framework in which the satisfaction of some needs is attainable for those who can make the effort and available for those who cannot – provided that they want it. Only so can the most fundamental need of all, the unique dialogue between each self and its world, be met.

An approach from the angle of typical human needs is thus unquestionably useful. It gives us the best chance of creating a setting within which as many men and women as possible can say, 'I am glad I was born'. But it involves us in so many imponderables and incompatibles that we have to proceed by trial and error and settle for temporary and compromise solutions. These nevertheless will be infinitely preferable to the marble immobility or the fiery emotion of simplistic *a priori* ethical systems. For Man himself is a complex and composite being; and his own nature rules out the possibility of any straightforward and unchallengeable good.

There is, however, one special complication which must be mentioned, and which causes a good deal of confusion in the discussion of moral questions. This is the difficult problem of the relation between needs and desires. In principle, there is a distinction to be drawn here which is important. When we talk about 'needs', we are trying to frame statements which apply to all human beings simply because they are human. The psychical and physical nature of the species is such that all its members, whatever their individual, social, racial, or cultural differentiae, have these basic requirements. 'Desires', however, are a phenomenon of the individual, and are as diverse as human beings themselves. The satisfaction of a need can be defined only in general terms, because it may be possible to fulfil it in a number of ways. A desire is always directed to a particular object.

There is no one standard relation between needs and desires. Sometimes, quite obviously, a desire exactly expresses a need. The hungry man both needs and desires food; and the mechanism of desire may even be sensitive to particular deficiencies in the metabolism, causing a person to crave certain kinds of food or drink which would supply a lack (of which he is quite unaware) of some element in the body. On the other hand, a sufferer from malnutrition, whose need for food is desperate, may have reached a stage where he has no desire for food, while someone else may passionately desire food for which they have no need whatever, since they are grossly overweight already. In the latter case the desire may indeed be ludicrously inappropriate, when, for example, the over-eating is simply appeasing some emotional need which cannot find its proper fulfilment.

The complex phenomenon of addiction is a widespread and tragic illustration of the difference between need and desire. The alcoholic needs alcohol 'like he needs poison', as the saying is. Strictly speaking, no one at all needs alcohol or tobacco or drugs in the sense in which we have been using the word 'need'. Yet the desire for these and other objects of addiction can, as we know, destroy. Are we right then to press our distinction so far? The junkie may be so drastically disabled a personality, whether as a result of his drug-taking or from earlier and more hidden causes, that he is no longer capable of accepting the fulfilment appropriate to his real need but only the crude and fatal substitute. This problem is bound to arise where the root cause is or was an inability to form satisfactory relationships. It may have been the denial of some basic need which led to this inadequacy in the first place. But matters have moved so far beyond this stage that any attempt to supply that original deficiency now does no good. The victim's personality now rejects love just as his body rejects ordinary wholesome food.

Not that desire as such is a symptom of a deprived person; quite the contrary. The happy and fulfilled person may have intense and varied desires which are the excellent and natural expression of a vitality and interest in life above the ordinary. It may be doubted, however, whether such desires are inordinate, compulsive, or destructive of personality. When desire takes on this tyrannous and insatiable quality, then is the time to ask what lies behind it. Is it a signal of some need unfulfilled? If so, is this a need which must be met if life or health are to be preserved, or is it just one of the many possible ways of contributing to our

F

well-being? When a man is dying of thirst, he does not need to go through such a pompous formal process of diagnosis; he knows what he must have. When a housewife is going to pieces from being alone in the house all day, it is also imperative that something be done, but a little more care and analysis is needed to make sure what it is really best to do. But there are needs, as we saw, which are not so importunate. All of us have to manage without fulfilments of one sort or another which would be very good for us, but which simply cannot be had. We make up for them, perhaps, in other ways, if we can; we may have special limitations because of them. But they do not incapacitate us as full and normal human beings. Before we can come to any truly mora decision what to do about a desire, we obviously have to come to some conclusions on these questions.[1] To classify a need or desire as essential when it is in fact non-essential puts an unnecessary and damaging limitation on the number of ways open to us of meeting the challenge both of our neighbour's situation and of our own, and throws away one of the richest assets of the species, namely that there are many different ways of being a fully human person.

So far we have been principally concerned with the question of the good ends which behaviour is planned to achieve; but this inevitably has brought in the subject of means. These two aspects of morality are so intimately linked that any discussion quickly becomes unreal unless they are studied more or less concurrently. It will be as well, therefore, to pay more attention than we have so far done to the

[1] It is obvious, for example, that the views both of conventional morality and of immorality on the subject of satisfying the sexual desire share the common assumption that a man or woman cannot be a proper human being unless this is done. This begs the question. Sexual desire may indicate a need, but there is good reason to think that it is not a need of this kind. The distortions of personality often observed in the celibate, in so far as they are related to this question and are not simply defects of a different origin, occur where such emotional attitudes as fear of the physical nature, self-hatred springing from an inhuman perfectionism, resentment and self-pity at an involuntary deprivation, are present. There is plenty of evidence in history that the man or woman who is as happy and proud of the physical as of any other aspect of human nature, but is content to live with the internal tensions and ride them out because of some prior claim which can be met only on these terms, and who adopts a mode of life intelligently designed to compensate, not only does not suffer from the lack of physical sexual fulfilment but in fact develops aspects of the human potential which otherwise tend to remain inert. The celibate misses certain elements of human experience, as we are always being reminded; but so does the non-celibate, and this is ignored.

inquiry: How can we give ourselves the best chance of achieving our ends? Here too we shall find that the terms of human existence, the exigencies of our situation, force us to conclusions of a certain general type.

A discussion of means may be said to be concerned with the formulation of practical moral policy; and at the start we find that it makes a considerable difference how you do your formulating. We shall examine several of the ways that have been proposed or used, beginning with the one which has enjoyed the greatest vogue in human history: the moral rule.

The term 'rule' itself covers a number of forms of directive or injunction which vary in their origin and method. At one end of the scale we have the absolute and unqualified command issued by authority, often divine, and not necessarily supported by any sort of justifying commentary from reason or experience. At the other we have the maxim of proverbial wisdom, characteristic of all societies – 'If you wish for peace, prepare for war'; 'spare the rod and spoil the child'. The present discussion will begin from this kind of rule, which may be defined as 'a generalization from experience indicating the means to a high probability of good'. The content of the good in any instance is determined empirically; but, as will appear, the logic and use of the rules themselves is also very much a matter of experience.

These generalized directives characterize Man's emergence from the animal level. The behaviour of animals is basically controlled by 'instinctual programming', which means that their responses to certain situations are pre-set. The response should not be thought of in too sophisticated terms. It can be shown, for example, that reaction is not by any means always reaction to the total situation – such as the approach of a predator – but to one element in it, perhaps a particular colour or movement. Normally this stimulus may occur, let us say, only in a situation of danger commonplace in the life-history of the animal concerned; hence the reaction is in most cases highly appropriate. If, however, the stimulus is imitated by some quite different set of circumstances (such as the hand of a harmless human observer) the reaction follows as usual, quite inappropriately. Such responses can be suppressed and overlaid by learned behaviour, as when we accustom wild birds or animals to take food from us, or when a police horse is trained not to yerk with its heels, bite, lash out with its fore-hoofs, or use any other of its natural fighting techniques when struck or frightened by a crowd. Under conditions of stress, however, or without constant practice, the animal may revert to its natural reactions. In the case of performing animals, pursuing highly artificial routines, these natural responses may be hopelessly or ludicrously inappropriate, but they take charge none the less. 'Learned behaviour always tends to drift toward instinctive behaviour' (K. Breland).

In Man total instinctual programming has disappeared. The functioning of bodily organs is indeed largely automatic, under the autonomous direction of the central nervous system, and this produces involuntary actions; but these are not what we mean by instinctive behaviour-patterns. Vestiges of these patterns have come down to us in our evolutionary inheritance, and may influence us both as individuals and in our social patterns of life more than we realise. These legacies, however, are relatively weak or intermittent in effect, and for the most part have long ceased to be usefully and reliably matched to the typical situations of human life. (The study of human aggression, for example, shows that in some contexts they are at present doing markedly more harm than good.) Man cannot, therefore, rely on his instincts. Instead he has to depend on that capacity for observation, memory, generalization, and prediction, which we call reason. This has given him pronounced advantages over the other animals, because despite its slowness and crudity it is flexible. If conditions change rapidly or radically, a species controlled by instinctual patterns which are stereotyped and which take many generations to modify, may easily perish. Reason, because it can be used to analyse any set of circumstances, gives its possessor that extra chance to survive. Moreover, when corporate experience can be called upon to supplement the individual memory, and if techniques can be developed to generalize and predict on this broader basis, then the marginal superiority of reason is greatly enhanced. The improvement of such techniques, from oral tradition through the use of books by individuals of high intelligence to the computer, exhibits a fascinating diversity of detail; but its purpose has never varied.

The proverbial maxims of conduct mentioned above exemplify this evolutionary change especially clearly, replacing instinctual control of behaviour by rational generalizations. But there is one important feature which they share with the animal programming. They are matched to typical situations. 'Many hands make light work,' and 'Too many cooks spoil the broth,' are, to quote a standard example, each true in the appropriate situation. We could easily combine them into an umbrella maxim ('Making is work for many but creating is for one'), but this would still have to be broken up into its components, to see which of them was relevant, before it could be used. Provided, however, that this general principle that rules are matched to situations is borne in mind, their value and necessity may be seen to be far greater than much current ethical thinking is prepared to admit.

The first and most obvious value of a rule is to guard against some universally disastrous event. There can be no exceptions to such rules, because the context in which they apply can never be bent sufficiently to make them irrelevant. A small everyday example is that of 'No smoking' at petrol pumps. A gigantic example which overshadows our times is the menace of modern war, nuclear, chemical, and biological. The minimum safeguard is that the whole race should agree never to use such weapons in their conflicts; but the pressures towards escalation of a conventional war make this a very poor precaution. The only sensible course would be the recognition by all that war had now become too potentially catastrophic to be tolerated as a means of settling disputes, and so must be outlawed altogether; and this in turn would have to include the use or show of force to achieve an end on the assumption that there would be no retaliation. There could be no exceptions to this rule. Its value would depend wholly on its being as unbreakable as the instinctual inhibitions for which it would be the human equivalent.

There is a second value of rules, which is an extension of this. One of the most delicate types of ethical decision-making is that which is colloquially referred to as 'knowing where to draw the line'. The general principle involved here will best be illustrated by taking a particular case and examining it in detail.

One of the less remembered atrocities of Nazi Germany during the Second World War was the liquidation of the insane or mentally deficient. Among those condemned were the six thousand inmates of the great hospital at Bethel. It proved impossible to carry out this particular decision, however, because Pastor Bodelschwingh, the head of the institution and a man revered throughout Germany for his devoted work among these people, made it clear that the authorities would have to kill him first. In terms of a crude form of utilitarianism it would not be hard to justify the official line. The survival of the nation was at stake; passengers who might be carried in easier times could not be afforded now. A more refined pragmatism might have argued that the psychological shock of such an atrocity, even in a country so hardened and wilfully blind as Germany then was, would not be worth the material benefit. It might suggest that matters really were desperate, if it was necessary to slaughter not just criminals or subversive elements but harmless lunatics and cretins. Pastor Bodelschwingh's stand, however, was not motivated by pragmatism of any sort but by a conviction that it was wrong to kill helpless and innocent human beings, no matter how much of an encumbrance they might be.

To which there is a counter-question: when does a human being cease to be human? Ancient social morality held that a man might forfeit all human rights, put himself outside the pale of the race by crime. He became an 'out-law', and anyone finding him might kill him without risk or remorse. In a number of societies today the position is rather different. No crime, however horrible, can forfeit the right to life – but perhaps an involuntary defect may do so? Already it is argued that if there is good reason to think that a child may be born with some serious defect then the pregnancy may properly be terminated. It would, of course, be safer for the mother and more just to the infant to wait and see what the degree of defect really is, and if after examination it proved intolerably high to kill the infant then, that is to say, immediately after birth in the case of physical deformity, later on in that of mental deficiencies. No doubt it will not be long before this proposal is seriously made as the more 'humane' and 'rational' course. At the other end of the life-span callous indifference is quite a normal attitude – 'He's lived too long; it would have been much better if he had died years ago' – and 'voluntary' euthanasia, with all the risks of pressure on the aged or the chronically sick to take advantage of it, is a concrete issue. Theoretical discussion has already moved on, in the Press and on television, to the prospect of 'compulsory' euthanasia at a certain age as the only way to protect the interests of the species in an era of population explosion. It calls for no special prophetic gifts to see that the sub-normal and incurable of all ages (why not physically incurable as well as mentally?) will soon be proposed for the list of 'expendables'.

The crucial difficulty for a pragmatic, 'situational' ethic in such questions is precisely that of drawing the line. Once it is admitted that there is any degree of defect or handicap which can justify the extinction of life, or which entitles one to say, 'This is not in any meaningful sense of the word a human being,' then the queries are bound to arise, 'Why not half a degree less?' and 'How do you decide?' For all such cases form a continuum, and it is no easy matter to place an individual even approximately within it. In assessing his chances of a tolerable life we have to look not only at him but at the context in which he will have to live, the specialized care which may or may not be available now or in some problematic future, the moral and emotional and material resources of his family. In the case of mentally defective children we have to predict the maximum level to which they will develop, a prediction which in many instances may well carry a big margin of error. There is the whole question of the values and attitudes of society at large, and the various ways in which these may shift. In short, the mass of imponderables is so immense that it is hard to see how anyone but the most insensitive and unimaginative of individuals, with the most grossly materialist values, would ever dare to make such a decision. Yet, when the 'right' to such a 'service' comes to be recognized in law, professional men and women are then required to make it as part of their regular duties.

Nor, if we are to look at matters with at all realistic an eye, must we ignore the hidden motivations which lurk behind our assessment of the defective human being's right to live. How far is it really their miseries that influence us? How far the strain and sacrifice they inevitably impose upon us? This question probes the conscience not only of those close to the afflicted, on whom the main burden must fall, but that of society as well. Life is so much simpler if we have to develop only those rudimentary spiritual capacities needed to deal with the able-bodied, well-adjusted, and intelligent, if the community can get by with just those conventions that suit the clubbable who have something to contribute. But what if there are buried glories in both the human individual and the group which cannot be unearthed save by the demands of the weak and the helpless, of those who can at first be discerned only by their outward form as human – and even then perhaps as no more than a pathetic approximation? And what if our intuition rightly warns us that the price of these glories comes high? The same meanness of spirit which refuses to pay that price ensures that the prospects of the afflicted will be that much the poorer, poor enough, no doubt, to justify easing them out of the harsh world altogether.

This is but one example, if an important and pressing one, of the problem raised by a continuum of cases, a scale with such infinitesimal gradations that there is no room between any of them where a line can honestly be drawn. And at the bottom of the particular continuum we have been considering, but even so no longer safely out of reach, are the perfectly normal. For we have mentioned so far only instances where perhaps, on pragmatic grounds, some case might be made for the taking of life. But what of those who do not hesitate to abort a foetus which there is no reason to suppose in any way abnormal, and which, given ordinary care, would become a human being capable of a full and happy life? and that on no better grounds than the convenience of the parents, married or unmarried, who have been 'unlucky' enough to bring it into being? This attitude, which is morally indistinguishable from that which exposed healthy but unwanted infants in the ancient world, is found not just in the worn-out and desperate wife with already too large a family but in the robust and affluent suburban mother of two who for her own 'well-being' demands the ending of her careless third pregnancy. But why not? If the gap between these two cases were empty, and we had to label one right and the other wrong, the matter might be different. But the gap is not empty. It is filled with a dense mass of cases, each differing from all the others in some particular, each slightly more justifiable than its neighbour in this respect, slightly less in that. How are you going to divide them? You cannot, not on any rational principle. Any decision to do so must either abide by purely arbitrary criteria or be made on the basis of 'feel', intuition, moral hunch. Once you have admitted the principle of weighing the individual's right to life on pragmatic grounds, you can never define where the line is to be drawn.

The Nazi authorities, therefore, were not behaving irrationally when they provoked Pastor Bodelschwingh's heroic defiance. They were merely following the logic of their cause. For if A can forfeit his right to life because his race makes him 'an enemy of the State', then B can forfeit his because some other fact about himself which he cannot help makes him a burden on the State. The continuum runs into zones unsuspected by those whose one ethical principle is the minimization of pain. The only safeguard is never to step on to that slope at all; to ban absolutely the taking of human life, defined as the life of any progeny of human parents. The same must apply to the abortion of a human foetus, except when clear indications that the life of the mother is threatened by the continuation of the pregnancy force a choice between lives – a situation which today is happily growing rarer wherever proper obstetric, contraceptive[1] and ante-natal facilities are available. And even here the choice should be a real choice. It is no accident that the ancient Hippocratic oath, which enshrines these principles, should be under constant propaganda attack today. That such a rule occasions 'hard cases' is undeniable; the prolongation of human life by modern medicine, for example, produces some of the most heartrending. But the abyss which opens up if the rule is abandoned is immeasurably worse. Wherever a continuum of cases exists, a rule will always be needed to keep Man from entering it, and to protect the helpless not merely against injustice and cruelty but against the impersonal humanitarianism of the public good.

A third great service which rules, and only rules, can perform is the creation of a good, free, and happy social climate. They may indeed equally create one that is joyless, anxiety-ridden, and repressive; and no doubt it has been revulsion from such a climate (and, more influential still, the revulsion from an exaggerated legend of its gloom and tyranny) which is partly responsible for contemporary abhorrence of rules as such. But this abhorrence does a great disservice by blinding people to the fact that rules are the one method by which we can make life safely open to some very valuable freedoms. Thus, the observance of a rule against theft in all its forms can do more to make life happy and secure than all the apparatus of State welfare. In a community where there is no need to lock, bolt and bar doors and windows every time you leave your home for more than a few minutes; where property that you lose or leave behind is returned to you or kept to be claimed; where buying and selling everything from a house to a loaf of bread is not a matter of constant vigilance and of knowing all the tricks if you are not to be swindled; where savings that you invest or accumulate against old age will not be embezzled or utterly devalued by negligence or lack of principle on the part of individuals, businesses, or governments; where communal amenities will not be smashed or looted time after time; such a society lives in an atmosphere of mutual confidence and lack of strain which is of incalculable benefit to all.

The observance of a rule to tell the truth at all times would equally certainly transform human life for the better. (There are the well-known classic exceptions to this rule, such as that of the duty to

---

[1] It ought not to need saying, but it obviously does, that the stronger the rule against ending life once begun, the greater the need to ensure that we do not irresponsibly create it.

misdirect a man bent on violence or murder; but even here the success of the manœuvre depends on the criminal's taking it for granted that the truth will be told. Any significant proportion of failures to do so would make the exception impracticable.) We may find this prospect less immediately appealing than that of a ban on theft, both because we have come to depend on the comforts of evasion, half-truth, flattery, and the double-talk of official statements, and because there is much in everyone's life which it is so painful to reveal that even the most hopeless falsehood seems worth trying. Once we had acclimatized ourselves, however, we might find the liberation even greater. Truth is an ardent and exhilarating virtue. Half the difficulties which men foresee in loyalty to truth-telling – the fear of giving offence or distress, or of bringing despair – arise because people are accustomed to lies and require them. The other half could largely be avoided by a greater liberty to keep silent. Nor should it be forgotten that those who will not be bothered to include the good in what they say are just as much liars as those who suppress the bad. A climate of truth would not necessarily be one of keen winds and cold seas only.

It will be seen that the essential purpose of rules in this aspect is not to restrict but to liberate, to create a setting in which human beings can realize more possibilities for their life than they could ever do without them. The rules do indeed exclude certain kinds of behaviour; but to describe them for that reason as repressive or life-denying implies a very narrow and individualistic notion of life. The crucial point, however, is that this openness of life to a greater variety of good can be achieved only if the rules in question are accepted as binding on all in all circumstances. Rejection of this principle by no more than a small proportion of the community in quite a small proportion of instances is enough to destroy all the peace, security, mutual trust, and freedom which would otherwise ensue.

Finally, we should not overlook the use of rules as one means of building up and safeguarding our identity – which is a large part of what we mean by self-respect. The rules by which a man chooses to abide in living his life are a kind of diagram of the person he wants to be and to whom he is constantly approximating. It is because of such rules that we can say with confidence of someone, 'He would never do such a thing', or, 'It sounds just like him'. These rules need not be admirable. A man may pride himself on never forgetting an injury or on never getting 'involved' in other people's lives. They may not even be explicitly formulated or consciously referred to, having become un-examined habits; on the other hand, they may be clearly enough framed and yet for good or bad reasons erratically obeyed. But they provide a person with that sense of individuality, lack of which leaves us an easy prey to dissolution and despair. The evils of intolerance and inflexi-bility, of living by narrow, mean, or vicious rules, or indeed by rules in which we ourselves do not really believe, are both great and obvious; the dangers of having none are also great but generally unnoticed. With evil rules we shall become an evil person. Without any we shall never become a person at all.

This reflection serves as a reminder of the close relation between this subject of general moral directives and another important aspect of the moral life, that of 'roles'. By 'role' is meant a particular function which a person fulfils in a clearly defined context. Within this context certain regulations are called for which will not necessarily apply anywhere else. The classic examples of such systems are the codes of professional ethics such as obtain, for example, in the Law or Medicine, on the general model of which codes of practice have been or are being drawn up for many other callings. A professional code may not always serve elevated purposes. It may be framed to embody restrictive practices or to ensure a high standard of living for those bound by it. In essence, however, it exists to protect the interests both of the practitioner and of his client by defining their relationships and mutual responsibilities. The need for such codes arises from distinctive circumstances, such as the need for a patient to disclose personal secrets to his physician, or from the special methods which the practitioner may have to employ, as in the case of certain drugs or surgical operations. Special abuses and temptations must be avoided, unusual opportunities for more common-place wrongs foreseen and forestalled – for example, in the field of the extortion or misappropriation of money. Consequently, it is common to find that such issues as confidentiality, undue influence, property rights, declaration of interest, segregation of personal and professional life, and the integrity of the person, are of especial concern.

Where the scope of a relationship is clearly defined, it is easier to set about the task of drawing up effective rules, even if their precise formulation may call for long experience and meticulous care. Never-theless, though the resulting regulations may be excellent within their context, they frequently cut across what to the ordinary person seem the more natural rights of life in general. Medical etiquette sometimes seems to the outsider to keep the doctor from action which common humanity would dictate – as in the matter of blood transfusions for minors whose parents have religious objections to the practice. Again, the punctilio of the law can be slow, artificial, and cruel. Provided, however, that a professional code is kept up to date, it normally gives the practitioner his best chance of successfully fulfilling his appointed role.

The question naturally arises: can the model of the professional role with its tailor-made code be extended to help with more general human problems? Might we move on, let us say, from the ethics of those who have the care of the young in teaching or the welfare services to say something about the ethics of the natural human state of parent-hood? In a sense books of advice to parents on the upbringing of children are precisely this; they arrive at concrete guidance for conduct by starting from the facts about a specific relationship and the demands and problems which these create. The same applies to marriage guidance or to advice on how to enjoy a happy retirement. Yet, as these three very obvious examples will at once suggest, any patterns of conduct developed with the needs of a particular role or relationship in mind will almost certainly clash at some point with those evolved for a different one. Any code for the role of a human being, therefore, is likely to be framed in the broadest terms. This does not necessarily imply that it is impossible to frame one at all.

This contrast between our particular roles and the general vocation to be human indicates the source of another serious issue in morality. Insistence on considering people in terms of a particular role may make it virtually impossible to think of them as persons. For small children all adults are predominantly role-figures – thought of as a 'father', or 'mother', or 'teacher', and so on – not as a human person, a concept which lack of experience puts outside their scope. Only other children are in practice if not in theory thought of as 'like oneself'. This is natural and excellently suited to the childhood situation, but when the child grows into a man or woman it will not do. One of the main problems of adolescence is the need for both parties to adjust the parent-child relationship so that it becomes also a relationship between people, thinking of each other in the round as people. Where there is a failure to do this, on either side, the results are always unfortunate and can be disastrous. The habit of thinking in such stereotypes appears in many aspects of ordinary adult life. Bogey-figures are created by the emotional over-simplifying of problems, and then real knowledge of some individual who happens to qualify for the role of bogey becomes impossible. He is not a human being but a 'foreigner', a 'black', a 'Jew', a 'capitalist', a 'Communist', a 'student', an 'establishment type', a 'Papist', a 'black Protestant', an 'atheist', an 'American', or a 'Limey'. In war we have the moment of shock, experienced by so many citizen-soldiers, when it comes home to them for the first time that the 'enemy' whom they have killed is a human being like themselves. In industrial disputes the conventions controlling the conduct of both sides, and designed to protect important rights or to achieve certain clearly defined objectives, are nevertheless too often conceived in terms of stereotyped roles for 'management' and 'wage-earners', 'bosses' and 'workers'. Many experts in industrial relations see no hope for radical improvement in this field until the old roles are scrapped and new ones evolved which will in turn generate new relations and conventions. Much the same can be said of international relations. The conventions of diplomacy are in some ways extremely effective and sophisticated rules; but unless they are supplemented by a personal element they may be effective only at inhibiting change and perpetuating problems.

Once again the facts of life are constantly prodding us towards certain practical compromises. Fully human relationships require time and mutual knowledge. It is impossible that any of us should have such relationships with more than quite a limited number of people; and for even that limited number to develop we need to live and work in small groups, communities on a 'human' scale. But the economic and governmental pressures of 'one world' force on us larger and larger interlocking organizations. More and more of us are compelled to have dealings with people who cannot ever be people to us but only representatives of a category, probably never encountered face to face. In such a situation it becomes ever harder not to fall into inhuman attitudes, into mere role-reactions. No doubt more personal contact, more openness to the personal ingredient in our mutual dealings, is essential; but where this cannot be had, or had in adequate amount, we need codes of behaviour which will do something to make us treat each other as if we knew each other as human beings. Such codes are the old *ius gentium*, the law of nations, or the eighteenth-century laws of war, or in our own day the Geneva Convention and the Declaration of Human Rights.

Such devices are all the more important since it is life in the mass, in which not men and women but cardboard cut-outs go through stylized motions, which is the locus of the demonic in our times. Just as a mob can be made to act in ways which its members as individuals would repudiate with disgust, so in ordinary life if men and women can be taught to think of themselves not as individuals but as examples of a type, they can be persuaded into follies and wickednesses which they themselves in a more reflective moment would agree to be such. They do, not what is best for their personal situation, but what is expected of the 'young' or the 'progressive' or the 'smart operator'. But it is not only people who can be taken out of the personal dimension in this way. Facts of life, which in reality are found only in a personal context, are first abstracted, then made into gods; and their creators bow down before them. Because money can be used by people to exercise power, Money with a capital 'M' becomes the source of power, and is pursued, envied, feared for this reason. Sex with a capital 'S' becomes as much a goddess as any Aphrodite, and quite as cruel and ruthless, a superhuman force by which men and women allow themselves to be coerced, quite forgetting that in this impersonal guise it is simply their own invention. All the distinctive truth of each human situation is obliterated by this habit of seeing everything in crude generalities, as though the world were peopled entirely by characters from strip cartoons.

It is because of the problems so far outlined that moralists today seek to develop the approach which is usually labelled 'situation ethics'. One may sympathize with their aims, and yet feel very considerable misgivings about its ability to provide an effective ethical method. These misgivings may be summed up under two heads.

First, this approach seems to ignore completely the nature of decision-making in general. Totally new experience is totally incomprehensible. Before we can do anything with it, we have to find some links with what we already know. Even in science, where radical discoveries constantly stretch the mind, we are helpless in face of new phenomena unless the theoretical formulations of mathematics have told us to expect them, or unless some appearance of similarity (perhaps quite misleading) with the already known gives us a start. So too with moral thinking. Certainly every human situation is in some respects unique. If, however, our response to it is not to be completely arbitrary, we have to see it in terms of some precedent or precedents. Otherwise we have no means of predicting whether what we do is likely to turn out well or ill. The process of moral decision-making may fairly accurately be described as follows. First, we identify the various elements in the situation from past experience; then we collect the relevant generalizations from that experience which tell us what to do for the best, that is, our rules; and finally, we arrange these rules in order of priority, if that is necessary. Hence the unique ingredients in the situation are precisely those of least use to us, for in so far as they are truly unique we are at a loss. (An excellent contemporary example of this from the sphere of professional ethics is the argument over the definition of death, in connection with organ transplants. Never before in human history has it been necessary to decide so rapidly whether a person is dead or not.) Fortunately, even though the characters involved often imagine that nothing of the kind can ever have happened before, most human problems are simply permutations of a number of familiar ingredients. The proportion and arrangement of these ingredients may be new, but this does not make the situation unique in the sense just described, and so does not preclude us from drawing on the help of experience. That is why the words of Moses, Buddha, Confucius, Job, or Aristotle, still make sense today; why not only the four hundred year old plays of Shakespeare, but the two thousand four hundred year old tragedies of Aeschylus and Sophocles, still illuminate our moral thinking. Situationism in its extreme form is the ideal method for dealing with a predicament that no one has ever encountered before, when indeed it is hard to see what else could be used. In any modified version it is indistinguishable from casuistry, which in its essentials goes back to the very earliest records of human civilization.

The second major misgiving about situation ethics is implicit in what has already been said about rules. By confining the basis for our decision to the particular situation we in fact beg the whole question. How is this? Because to do so is to take for granted that the upholding of a general imperative as such never can outweigh the demands of the immediate moment. Situationism may allow us to define a problem broadly, to draw on past wisdom; the one thing it will not do is to permit a rule to override other considerations simply because it is a rule. If, however, there is any validity at all in the contentions advanced earlier, then this may often be the most important factor in the case, since a rule does not begin to do its most creative work until it is taken for granted by all that it will be observed.

An adjunct of the situationist approach is the figure of the autonomous man. A heteronomous person is one who allows some external authority, human or divine, to decide for him what is right and what is wrong; an autonomous person decides for himself. The autonomous man may not disagree with traditional ideas of what is right in any given case, but he does not consider that his actions are truly and fully moral unless he makes up his own mind. Now we may agree that it is good, indeed that it is vital to think about morality, to have reasons for our actions, to criticize laws or conventions that seem to us to be bad. There are times for all of us when we have to make up our own minds, either because traditional dicta are inadequate or in conflict, or because the choice is between two seemingly equal evils. But if we have any humility or common sense we will ask to be excused from the task of being autonomous all the time, for the simple reason that we do not fancy ourselves that good, that wise, that honest. We need the distilled ethical experience of the race to guide us nine times out of ten, precisely because we are not good but wish to be better. We are suspicious of the hidden pressures – the fears, the buried resentments, the unacknowledged desires, the lack of imagination, the comfortable illusions – which all too probably warp our judgement. And if someone asks, 'But would it not be better for you that you should wrestle with moral problems rather than thus blindly, lazily hand over your decision-making to the traditions of the species?' we reply: 'My dear chap, you may well be right. Perhaps it would be better for me. But would it be better for my fellow-men? Might it not be better for them that I should lazily and blindly tell the truth, deal honestly in business, be faithful to my wife, and live peaceably with all men, than that I should hazard these good results by trying to work out for myself whether the rule was justified in this or that instance? And then too, you forget what life is like. You forget how few of our decisions can ever be taken after calm and adequate reflection. When we have to make up our minds *now*, it is the generally reliable rule, or that built-in rule we call habit, which increases our chance of doing what is best.'

The autonomous man is the dream-child of a most unfortunate intellectual liaison between Philosophy and Romanticism. One parent we have seen in various guises: in Greece as the true philosopher, in the Enlightenment of the seventeenth and eighteenth centuries as the Rational Man, in the nineteenth and twentieth centuries as the Progressive Humanist. The other parent is equally fictitious. She is the golden-hearted courtesan of romantic fiction, the person who breaks all the conventional rules but is 'better' than the Pharisee or the

Puritan, or some other propaganda bogey-figure, because she is some-how 'honest'. But however winningly these two fantasy-parents sum up Man's wishful thinking about himself, essential innocence and omnicompetent rationality are not marks of human nature as it is. The autonomous man remains a dream, and an idle one at that.

An attempt to escape from this difficulty has led to an increasing emphasis on creative principles or attitudes which we can bring to each and every situation. The three most commonly supported are: the fulfilment of the person; the minimization of pain; and love.

The trouble with the first two is that they break in one's hand as soon as they are applied to any solid problem. We have already seen in the earlier part of the present chapter that Man has a great variety of needs, many of which are in conflict with one another. Even for the individual it is impossible that he should find fulfilment in all possible ways at once, and moral problems have a habit of confronting us with a choice between particular fulfilments. We then have to have some scale of priorities; and if our decision is to be in any sense a rational one, this scale has to be constructed in the light of experience. When we go on to take into account the corporate good, which includes the fulfilment of all the other persons involved, fulfilment itself as a criterion ceases to be of any use whatever for answering our questions. The crux of the matter is that 'fulfilment' is either a rather grand term for good in general or it refers to a particular good. Either way it is not a concept of practical value for the task of arranging goods in order of importance or for working out how best they are to be realized.

The minimization of pain does not suffer from this disadvantage. It is at least the right kind of concept, logically. If, however, the remarks on pain in the previous chapter are borne in mind, the difficulties in the way of using it will become obvious at once. As regards the great bulk of the worst misery and suffering in the world men of good sense and goodwill are already in agreement. They do not need a formal principle to tell them what to do. Pain itself by its very nature drives us to eradicate it. The hard questions arise in cases or at levels of pain where there is a conflict between different possibilities of good. Perhaps the pain could be eased or even abolished altogether but only at the cost of forgoing some other benefit. If 'minimize pain' is taken as an absolute principle, then it certainly provides clear advice, but only by the expedient of begging the question; for it provides no method of com-paring one good with another. It simply assumes that pain, at any level, will always be a worse evil than anything else. This is highly question-able; but even if it were not, the principle itself would not show us how to come to that conclusion. If, however, the minimization of pain is taken to mean merely, 'Minimize pain as far as you can without sur-rendering anything else more important', then as a directive for conduct it is vacuous. It does not tell us the one thing we want to know.

The third principle, love, is in a different category again. It denotes an attitude of the person. Approach all problems in the spirit of love, and there is a better chance that the answer will come right than if you confine yourself within the rigidity of rules. But is this assertion borne out by experience? In the name of love, as in that of liberty, patriotism, and religion, some vile things have been done. In the name of love husbands have shot wife and family before committing suicide; parents and children, brothers and sisters, friends, have made each other's lives a misery; men and women have thrown away years of achieve-ment, despised loyal affection, wrecked homes, robbed and embezzled from the poor, betrayed their country, denied their faith. To this there are two possible replies. One might say, 'You call these things vile; but if they were what love demanded, then they were right.' Here the classic retort is that of Dr Johnson: 'If a man . . . pretends to a principle of action of which I can know nothing, nay, not so much as that he has it, but only that he pretends to it, how can I tell what that person may be prompted to do?' Unless love has some coherent meaning, which enables other people to know at least roughly what kind of conduct to expect from it, it is no use whatever as a basis for relationships. But it is relationships with which love is primarily concerned; hence any concept of love which leaves it entirely to be determined by the private wishes of the individual fails to measure up to the essential nature of love, and must be false. That is why the other reply is much the more usual, namely: 'The people you mention were insane or deluding them-selves; real love seeks the good of the one loved.' But good in whose opinion? The lover, the one loved, their well-wishing friends, the community? We know only too well how, say, a parent and a child can disagree violently about what is 'best' for the child, even after the child has reached years of some discretion. Unless there can be reasoned discussion about what is best in the circumstances, no progress is possible. We have reached deadlock. But such discussion implies other criteria than the motive of love for deciding what is good.

Love is of inestimable value, but it is not, and never can be by itself a guide to the content of the good. Why then are so many people convinced that it is? The answer is quite straightforward. If we have a strong affection for someone, two things commonly happen. First, we have more knowledge to work on, because we sense facts about them which others miss; and secondly, we are strongly motivated to certain kinds of action, for instance, to protect them, because not to do so causes us intense pain and anxiety. So it is that we form the impression that from an attitude of love we can 'read off' what is to be done.

In the kind of context just described, this is true. But it is hopeless to try to generalize this method. Even where intimate bonds exist it is only of limited effectiveness, and when we come to talk of 'loving our neighbour' it works with very erratic success. As for the entire sphere of public and international morality, it is hard, for reasons already discussed, to know there what concrete meaning to attach to it.[1]

The structure of close relationships between individuals at their best is no adequate model for all ethical thinking. That one tiny area of experience, albeit an important one, where rules, roles and conventions are least needed, where intuition and freedom are most intense, can never stand as the norm for the whole of human life.

In our examination of the ends and means of the moral good we have already seen clearly enough how easy, nay inevitable is the genesis of moral evil. Ignorance, stupidity, fear, unfulfilled needs, misunderstood desires, psychic fragility, involvement in the mass society with its impersonal views and quasi-demonic forces – all these factors and others, if realistically assessed, can be seen to place the truly good life in effect beyond our reach. Moreover, both the capacities with which we are endowed and the situation into which we are born are the product of an immeasurable history not simply of progress and achievement but equally of failure and mistake; and even such progress as there has been (and wonderful it is, in some aspects of life) is qualified by the fact that in some sense mankind must, in each generation and individual, start again. The twentieth century has shown with woeful clarity that it can be as greedy, cruel, and treacherous as any of its predecessors.

It would not be in the least adequate or honest to think of this situation in the traditional moralistic terms of free beings confronted at every juncture by a choice between right and wrong, good and evil. Where

[1] As Reinhold Niebuhr saw, when he made justice the true expression of love in social morality.

there are choices at all, they are often choices between evils, or, to take a more cheerful view, between partial goods; and in many instances it is doubtful whether such terms as 'choice', 'decision', 'commitment' truly fit the case. This whole question will occupy us when we come to consider freedom in the next chapter.

Perhaps even more significant, however, than the existence of these overwhelming pressures towards failure is the fact that the theoretic good as a universal condition is, it would seem, inherently unattainable. The very fact of life in community – and for us there can be no other – involves us in compromise and second-best. There are times when the needs and desires of two or more individuals can be simultaneously realized. Because this most frequently happens where love is strong, it is one of Man's favourite and recurring illusions that in a world of love everyone would have all the good he or she desired. But this is non-sense. Even the needs of one individual conflict to some degree, and the needs of numerous selves infinitely more so. If we are not to leave all to the arbitrament of force or chance, we have to use our reason to try to decide on priorities; and 'priorities' is another way of saying, 'who is to sacrifice how much of his own good'. This, however, at once confronts us with an insoluble moral problem. For how can we weigh one good for one person against another good for another? The calculation will always work out differently according as it is performed within one self or the other – and this not because of what we call 'selfishness' but because of the inescapable limitations of selfhood. There is no rational method by which it can be demonstrated that I ought to put someone else's good before my own. The heart of the moral perplexity of human life is to be found in this simultaneous necessity and impotence of reason. Reason is expert to show me the present possibilities of good for myself and for others, but tongue-tied at the point where I have to choose between them.

Our human situation, therefore, prevents even the best of men from realizing an unflawed good, and leaves most of us groping feebly and clumsily and with only intermittent resolve after a very corrupt notion of what is for the best. This is evil by default, the moral evil of our frailty and finitude. It is perhaps one way of describing what the old philosophers meant when they said that evil was a *privatio boni*, a deprivation or absence of good. But this is not the only form of moral evil. There is also a constructive or positive moral evil which is easily recognized, if difficult to define.

The person who does what is evil by default is not working of set purpose on evil principles. His moral ideas may be crude or vicious, but he is open to better guides and values, if he can once apprehend them. If he abandons such good rules and principles as he knows, it is because of the exigencies of the present. He does not in theory approve such conduct for all occasions, even if he would justify it now. He may be vague, weak, ignorant, narrow, or unstable; but he is in theory on the side of good against evil, of right against wrong. But there is another kind of person who has decided of his own motion to work on principles which he knows the common opinion of men to reject. He does not lie out of fear or vainglory, but with deliberate intent thus to achieve his ends; he is cruel not in a fit of rage, but because this is a successful method of bending others to his will; he defrauds, not because someone puts a 'good thing' in his way, but as a settled business technique; he murders, not from hate or for revenge, but as the most obvious way of removing rivals. When such a man rises to supreme power, we have a Napoleon, a Stalin, or a Hitler – and, compounding the horror, a thousand underlings who adopt torture, intrigue, and faithlessness as the natural way of behaving. Once men regard moral evil not as something into which anyone may lapse, but as the rule by which everyone of sense will live, a new dimension is introduced which can properly be called unnatural, inhuman, because if we are to cope with it, we have to suspend all the usual, spontaneous responses of human intercourse, and calculate with a studied detachment the motives and reasoning of what has become virtually an alien being.

And yet, if there is anything at all which can persuade us that there are indeed norms of moral conduct, it is when we see such lives systematically governed by their opposites. Then the niceties of this or that case, the legitimacy of such and such an exception take their small, proportionate place; and the broad outlines of the human role and of the code that must direct relationships between man and man begin to be visible.

Our purpose in surveying some of the problems that arise in the sphere of moral good and evil was to discover whether any progress could be made in constructing a hypothetical answer to the ultimate question, namely: If this question is to be answered in terms of a good God, what must that God be like if he is to answer the question adequately? As yet it is not possible to set out more than provisional findings; but it is interesting that a general affinity is beginning to emerge between the indications from this aspect of human life and those afforded by the fact of Man's sufferings.

Once again we are confronted with a world in which pursuit of the good absolutely demands the use of reason. Just as the reduction of suffering called for an exact, scientific knowledge of the nature of things, and the development of practical measures on this basis, so the direction of the moral life requires a precise understanding of Man's real needs, and careful and detailed planning of the best way to supply them. Once again, however, we find that at the point of decision reason forsakes us. It was not possible to provide a rational argument to justify one person's suffering in place or on behalf of another; it is not possible to prove by logical argument that in the moral compromises which the nature of things makes unavoidable there is any rational means of choosing between two possible courses, both right and good in the abstract and in moral theory, but here and now not only incompatible but favouring the interests of different people.

We have also found that just as there would seem to be an irreducible minimum of suffering, so we live in a world where at the very least the moral ideal can never be realized. We shall all of us always be in need of each other's tolerance. Moreover, the absence of any 'perfect' solutions in the quest for happiness is matched by the absence of any perfect rational answers to moral problems. If the good life is to be lived at all, this will be done not through the achievement of perfection but through the love which alone can resolve the moral problem, because it finds natural those sacrifices which reason can never commend.

5

Freedom, Guilt, Forgiveness

SO FAR our wide if cursory discussion of moral good and evil has been carried on with very little use of the language, or even of the idea, which is commonly thought to be central to the subject – that of 'ought', of moral obligation. The idea of 'ought' is something of a mystery. It cannot be derived logically from any other sort of statement. If we say that some course of action is wise or good or conducive to happiness, we still have not said that anyone 'ought' to adopt it. To move from one point to the other we need the bridge proposition that one 'ought' to do what is good or wise and so forth. And this again introduces 'ought' from nowhere, fully formed, by an arbitrary decision. The same difficulty attaches to an attempt to derive obligation from rules. It may be argued that it is good to obey the law of the land, or prudent, or dangerous not to, or that disobedience brings social stigma. But none of these observations is equivalent to the statement that we 'ought' to obey it. A rule as such says nothing about moral obligation; it issues an order, for example in a direct imperative ('Do as you would be done by'), or in what looks like a future tense ('All personnel will assemble in the canteen at 1400 hours'). The rule may be explicitly limited to a particular situation ('Anyone wishing to withdraw funds is required to give fifteen days' notice'). None of these types of sentence, however, conveys the idea of 'ought'; nor, conversely, can a rule be expressed by using the word 'ought'. 'Must', 'is to', 'is required to', 'will', 'shall', these and others will serve the purpose; but as soon as we introduce the word 'ought', what we say ceases to be a rule, and becomes at most an admonition or exhortation.

In our own cultural tradition we are so accustomed to the idea of 'ought' that we tend to assume that it is a general human characteristic. Many people, when talking about morality, seem to think that it is a part of Man's primordial equipment; and it is not infrequently spoken of as one of the features distinguishing him from the animals, closely linked with a supposedly innate capacity for what we call 'conscience'. It comes as something of a surprise, therefore, to discover in history whole cultures which have no word for 'ought', and arguably little interest in the concept. One example, which may be quite unexpected to most people, is the Hebrew Old Testament. Biblical Hebrew has no separate expression which can be used as we use the words 'ought', 'should' and their equivalents. In the English versions there are passages which seem to suggest such an underlying original (cf., e.g., *II Kings* 13:19; *Job* 11:2; 15:2), but such renderings, though defensible, run the risk of begging our immediate question.[1]

The moral utterances of the Old Testament are either couched in the language of descriptive approval ('It is a good thing to give thanks to Yahweh'), direct command ('Fret not yourself because of the wicked'), or legal enactment ('Thou shalt do no murder'). The variations on these basic forms are many and ingenious; and what they have to say can, of course, be transposed into the language of 'ought'. But the fact remains, and it is an interesting one, that such language was not available for them to use, and there is therefore no justification for assuming that the idea was available either; and the same holds good for numerous other cultures and languages of the ancient Near East. In the Greek New Testament the idea is common enough; but this makes it even more striking that there are very few instances of it in the recorded words of Jesus. The Aramaic which he spoke is, like biblical Hebrew, not equipped to express the concept unequivocally; and in fact, in the gospels of *Mark* and *John* Jesus is never represented as using it. *Matthew* has three cases, two peculiar to himself and one shared with *Luke*; the two of his own are significantly in passages where free composition by the evangelist or in oral tradition might be expected. *Luke*, apart from the one shared with *Matthew*, has only one clear instance (13:16), and this again could as easily

---

[1] In the *II Kings* example, for instance, the Hebrew would be literally translated, 'For striking five or six,' i.e., the arrows were for striking five or six times on the floor, not the three times which the king in fact struck them. It certainly cannot be said to be wrong to render in English, 'You should have struck . . .' (*RSV*), but the elliptical construction of the original does not demand it, and so provides no solid evidence for a distinct idea of 'ought'. In the *Job* passages 'should' is again interpretative; 'shall' would be more precise.

be the phrasing of the story-teller as strict reportage of original dialogue.[1]

This leaves us with one passage (*Matt.* 23:23 = *Lk.* 11:42), which is both strongly attested and part of a piece of ethical teaching, where Jesus is said to have used the concept of 'ought', and the phrase in question, if a genuine saying of Jesus, must have been elliptical in Aramaic. In short, not only does the oldest of the great ethical religions of the world manage without the idea of 'ought' in its sacred Scriptures, but there is no firm evidence that the man who is most widely respected, among people of all faiths and of none, as an ethical teacher ever used it either.

So far as European culture is concerned the idea of 'ought' makes its entry through Greek language and thinking. A basic notion of 'binding' is developed in two ways, for which there are parallels in English usage, that of 'must' ('it was bound to happen') and that of 'ought' ('I am bound to tell you . . .'). Here the concept connotes our being bound by something, some law or rule or principle of action. In English the same effect is arrived at through the idea of 'owing'; just as to owe money implies that the sum in question belongs by right to someone else and will therefore have to be paid back, so 'ought' implies the owing, and thus the necessity of paying, some duty or obedience. In both images, however, that of 'binding' and that of 'owing', there is the feature of an external norm or controlling factor. 'Ought' is quite inapplicable to a purely arbitary act of choice.

Nevertheless it is equally inapplicable to a situation in which we are constrained by some superior force either from within or without. If I am under constant surveillance by the police, it would be perfectly sensible to comment to a friend, 'I have to keep within the law; I am not given a chance to do anything else.' It would be nonsensical to say, 'I ought to keep within the law; I am not given a chance to do anything else'.[2]

The word 'ought' would be appropriate only in some such sentence as, 'I ought to keep within the law, because if I do not and I am arrested, then my wife and children will suffer.' The crucial point is not

---

[1] On the subject of the evidential status of various types of material in the Gospels cf. pp. 164 ff. below.

[2] There is, of course, the peculiar colloquial usage in English by which one can say, for example, 'I ought to be good at it; I've had enough practice.' But this extended idiom does not affect the main point of the present argument.

whether the law is a formal public regulation or an inward conscientious principle but whether I am in a position to break it or keep it as I choose. Again, we do not use 'ought' to describe the condition of being overmastered by some emotion or psychological compulsion. A man leaving his wife and family, with whom he has been happy, for some other woman whom he does not even like or respect, and a man leaving his wife to volunteer for some form of public service, may each say, 'This is something I have to do'; but only the latter could add, 'and something I ought to do'. The word 'ought' can be meaningfully used only by someone who in regard to this particular decision is a free agent.

The question of freedom, like that of pain, fascinates all kinds of people. This is hardly surprising, since it touches, with a directness that everyone can appreciate, the very stuff of Man's ordinary life. We are torn between two attractive opposites. On the one hand, we like to think of ourselves as free, masters of our fate and captains of our souls, able at any rate to aim at what we want once we have made up our minds to it; and furthermore, we prefer to think that this making up our minds is something done of our own motion, an act originating within ourselves after an impartial survey of the evidence. On the other hand, the indications borne in upon us from time to time that this picture of our situation may not be entirely true do not necessarily distress or horrify us. There are moods (and they may grow) when the responsibility which goes with our supposed freedom seems a wearying nuisance. Indeed, it may be doubted whether the man or woman lives who has not at some time used determinism to justify exemption from blame: 'I can't help it; I'm simply made that way.' This attitude is age-old; but there is no doubt that it has been spread and reinforced during the past hundred years by the growing corpus of careful investigation into the influence of social, economic, and psychological factors upon the individual and upon the group, as well as by the undiscriminating popularization of truths and half-truths, sound theories and quarter-baked generalizations, proceeding from these areas of research.

In discussions of morality it is often taken for granted that it is better for an act or decision to be 'free'. Sometimes this consideration is given supreme importance, an act which is not 'free' being regarded as morally worthless or indeed not a *moral* act at all; or behaviour which is cruel or self-indulgent but 'freely' chosen is seen as more truly moral than more generally acceptable behaviour which has been motivated purely by habit or social conformism or fear of the consequences of doing otherwise. When we talk in this way, however, of 'free' acts and decisions we may mean one or more than one of a number of different things.

First, there is freedom from limitations. These, of course, take many forms apart from the obvious ones of physical disability or coercion. In a primitive agricultural or pastoral society, for example, the work a man does is not his free decision. Each person's work is much the same, and he or she takes the part in it allotted by the community. If a man is born into a family where a special office is hereditary, then in due time he enters into that. When his self-contained community is opened up to contact with urban, industrial civilization, these old limitations are broken. Now he can at last take a free decision; he can choose to leave the village altogether, and travel hundreds of miles to the mines or the factories. Or again, a boy leaving school in the north-east of England may have to go on the dole. This is not his decision. There are no jobs. A change of national fortune or government policy may one day create jobs, and offer training facilities. At once he becomes to some extent a free man at last. The increasing variety of leisure activities is another example of the creation of this sort of freedom. The availability of theatres, cinemas, concerts, dance halls, television, bowling alleys, package holidays abroad, clubs for every kind of hobby – it is this which for many people provides one of the main areas in which they are effectively free agents. Finally under this head we may perhaps include freedom from ignorance. Only if we are aware what can be done in a given situation are we free to make a reasonable decision. The inadequate mother who does not know how to budget or plan or what foods to give her children is not free; the peasant who does not know how to combat soil erosion or cattle pest is not free – his ignorance is just as crippling a limitation as lack of the necessary materials or lack of physical strength through malnutrition.

Secondly, there is freedom from unconscious compulsion. Deepseated pressures within ourselves, arising sometimes from physical causes, sometimes from early or traumatic experience, restrict the range of possibilities open to us. Indeed, if a suitable vector pattern of forces is set up within the psyche, the individual may be reduced to total immobility. From such trivia as our choice of clothes, up through our sympathies or antipathies among our personal acquaintance to our attitudes on questions of race, politics, personal morality, or religion, these hidden forces may play a large part in dictating our decisions. The effects of such dictation may or may not be damaging in any particular instance; but if the decision turns out well it is more by good luck than good management. The psychologist Szondi once conducted an interesting experiment with patients suffering from various types of mental illness. He showed each patient a set of about twenty photographs of both men and women, some of whom were troubled in the same way as the patient himself, and asked him to say which of the faces portrayed most attracted him. In a statistically significant proportion of cases both men and women were decidedly attracted by the pictures of people with their own psychic disorder. Indeed, the choice of marriage partner among normally healthy people as well is probably one of the least free decisions anyone ever makes in our society. The compulsive quality of this choice has, however, some natural utility in helping to keep parents together while children are nurtured, and in securing marriage partners for those who might otherwise never get them; nor is it clear that in a matter so full of imponderables a purely cool and rational decision would more often produce a happier result, though a greater measure of freedom than commonly exists might indeed prevent some wretchedly unsuitable unions. But such freedom, in this as in all the other cases in this category, can be achieved only by self-knowledge, by uncovering and recognizing the bases within the self, often trivial but powerful none the less, of attraction or repulsion.

Such knowledge is indispensable if we are to be able to tell which of our arguments are rational and which mere rationalizations. Discerning this will not of itself necessarily enlarge the range of action of which we are capable. We may say, 'I know my attitude on this matter is not primarily a rational one, but I cannot help it.' A situation of this kind may arise, for example, where powerful character-forming techniques, such as deprivation-of-love punishments, have been used on an individual in childhood to secure obedience to particular rules or attitudes. The subject may then either be 'brainwashed' on the issue in question, and for the rest of his life never contemplate deviation from the line thus inculcated, or, if he does become aware later on that he has been conditioned in this way, this knowledge may still not be enough to release him to step outside the magic circle. Discernment does nevertheless create some freedom, because it enables the agent at least to consider seriously alternatives which beforehand, if they had ever so much as crossed his mind, he would have dismissed as worthless, ridiculous, or degraded.

Thirdly, there is freedom from unthinking conformism. This is the point at which the discussion in contemporary Western society is apt to become most heated. Is an action truly 'free' if it is performed in blind obedience to a conventional moral code? Such a question, common enough today, is really a whole battery of questions, some of which are skilfully masked. In one sense such an act may very well be termed 'free'. I find a wallet in the road, and hand it in at a police station. Of course, I could have put it in my pocket and kept it; perhaps if I had been sorely pressed for money I would have had a stern struggle not to do so. But my code tells me that such a thing is 'wrong', 'not done'. I do not stop to debate the justification for the code, or to ask whether it is applicable in this case; I simply follow its direction, confident that this will be morally for the best. Or perhaps someone at a party makes it clear that she is not averse to exploring the chance of an affair. I ignore the hint and break off the conversation more or less automatically, even though she is extremely attractive. My conduct can rightly be called free, because I am aware of other possible courses and I reject them. I may do so on the basis of a set of rules which have been taught me by others, and which I have accepted in a kind of package deal as the wisdom of many generations, and therefore probably right. I may have thought through the argumentation behind each of them, and assented to it; or again, I may not have done so for any of them. If, however, I am unaware of the moral implications of my actions, or of the principles on which they are based, I may be a 'free' agent, but am I free in respect of my morality? I have chosen my actions, but I have not chosen my moral reasons.

A fallacious line of argument not infrequently developed from this observation concludes that the person who is indeed morally free will not have any general rules at all. What has been said already on the subject of rules and situationism will have indicated why the present writer rejects this as a far from necessary entailment. The decision to abide by a general rule can perfectly well be a morally free decision; and if the person concerned is convinced after his best thought that there can be no case in which his rule does not apply, then there can be no possible reason for him to go through the argumentation every time a decision in this field is called for. An adherent of non-violence may be said to act unthinkingly when he is suddenly attacked and refuses to resist; but it would be grotesquely unfair to say that his behaviour is not based on a free moral decision. There are plenty of situations in life where he who hesitates in order to think is lost – not because his rules are exposed as inadequate but because hesitation forfeits the chance of obeying them. The moment has passed. It is too late now to speak the truth or to be loyal to a belief or a friend, to do that act of kindness or to avoid that corruption. What is mistaken and dangerous is to suppose that therefore our rules or general principles do not need to be kept under constant review as our own experience or the light shed by others changes our insight into life. The free moral decision we made twenty years ago may very well be a blind and insufficient conformism in us today. Moral freedom in this context means that we understand and assent to certain moral bases for our actions in accordance with our current knowledge and experience.

In the three categories so far considered one of the most important methods of enlarging freedom was the increase of relevant knowledge. There are, however, situations where information is so ample as to inhibit action almost altogether. This is especially liable to happen where complex predictions have to be made involving a large number of personal factors, as in the decisions of national and local governments, of military commanders, or of large corporate bodies. Here the foreseeable effects of any feasible policy may be so mixed, and the unforeseeable possibilities so manifold and hazardous that rational choice becomes impossible. In that event, if those in power are unable, because of their training and habits of mind, to commit themselves to any decision which cannot be clearly justified on balance by rational argument, then they may find themselves paralysed, incapable of taking any effective step until the situation has changed for better or worse, and so made the problem easier to solve. Ignorance in such a case would in one respect liberate. It is no accident that we read so frequently in history that some ruler was intelligent but indecisive; the impotence of rationality has at all times come to light in the marriage of power with knowledge and human imagination. In the contemporary international scene too consistency and decisiveness of action tend to be marks of those powers which, for good or ill, have some dogmatic end to justify their means, and which are thus to some degree spared the torment of facing the full human realities of their actions.

Such paralysis may, however, appear in the life of the individual as well. If, for example, justifiable self-assertion and proper self-sacrifice meet head-on, and the probable good or bad results of giving priority to either are fully and deeply pondered, then there may be no step to which the person can give himself heart and soul, and he may therefore fail to act at all. To fail to act is indeed in a sense also a decision, but if it ensues willy-nilly from a divided self and a divided judgement it cannot meaningfully be called free. Rules, as we saw, just because they are generalizations from human experience, are of no help here, since the conflict in question will certainly be reflected in correspondingly conflicting rules. Situationism is no better, for it is the situation which is morally equivocal. The only solution is to be found in an act of naked and arbitrary will, even one as crude as deciding to decide on the spin of a coin. Human existence being what it is, such a solution may be required of anyone at some time in his life; and the man or woman who cannot make the necessary act of will lacks what is perhaps the most essential freedom of all.

For all these reasons and in all these forms freedom is unquestionably one of the vital conditions of full human life. But this is very far from saying that all men possess it, even in a limited degree. Mightily re-sounding sentiments have a way of being silly; but of all those brayed to wild applause from pulpit or rostrum year after weary year surely the silliest is this – 'Man is born free'. The codicil, 'but everywhere he is in chains', does little to amend this essential silliness. Even if men nowhere tyrannized over each other, it would still be true that every human being is born a helpless slave. Freedom is something into which each one of us has to grow, which he has to attain. Indeed, it is a characteristic of freedom that it cannot be detected as a static condition; we can be confident of its reality only when we see it growing or shrinking. Increase of freedom is increase of the number of options we can use; its decrease is the reduction of that number. It is the fact that we become aware of enlargement in the scope of our options, whether for internal or external reasons, which gives us our assurance that freedom is not an illusion. (This may be even more true of the shrinking of our scope, let us say, with old age.) A fixed capability would be a slavery from which there was no escape.

There is, however, one circumstance which for many people would threaten to blight their life with the nightmarish conviction that even this modest sense of freedom is an illusion. That circumstance is the existence of a God. For if God, as is normally asserted, foreknows everything, including everything that I think or do, then how can I be said to choose, to be free? If it is known what I am going to do, then surely I cannot help doing it?

The theological problem of divine foreknowledge and its relation to human freedom is not quite the same as the problem of determinism. Let us be clear about one thing first: we are not talking about sheer brute predestination, a notion that God by supernatural force compels everyone to do whatever they do do, and that any impression they may have of choosing is pure illusion. Such a God would be a wholly vacuous one; the word 'God' would connote no more than 'Fate', and belief in him would simply be a poetic or primitive way of talking about total determinism. Moreover, the only grounds, as we have examined them, on which one might rationally believe in a good God point right away from such a concept.

Foreknowledge is another matter. We need to draw a distinction. If we say that God knows in advance everything that is going to happen, we may mean either of two things. First, we might mean that God, having complete knowledge of all the relevant information, could perform infallibly a scientific prediction which we cannot perform because of our limitations. This, however, rests on the assumption that human conduct is predictable in theory, if not in our practice. Such an assertion is of necessity unprovable, since the only way of proving that human behaviour is predictable is by doing so in practice, that is, by successful prediction over a significantly large statistical sample of cases. More immediately relevant, however, is the fact that it limits God's foreknowledge to the kind of certainty we can have by scientific prediction. If human nature is not predictable in this way, then God cannot know what is going to happen; and if it is predictable in this way, then God's foreknowledge does not in principle affect my situation, since what happens could still have been predicted even if God did not exist.

Secondly, we might mean not that God can infallibly predict the future but that he has a quasi-magical awareness of it, of a kind logically compatible with no predictive ability at all. This kind of foreknowledge might be envisaged in two ways. God might be imagined as having a ubiquitous Time-capsule, which enabled him to be present at all periods of history simultaneously. Or it might be compared to a preview of a film. God has, as it were, had a private advance showing of a film – except that we would have to make the film a newsreel, not a fictional story where the characters are manipulated by the author. The question then becomes: would awareness of events in these sorts of ways make my free choice a nullity?

To take the Time-capsule first, it would seem that this mode of awareness would not affect the issue at all. To see all moments at once is to abolish Time altogether; everything is telescoped into a single instant. It makes no difference whether we think of this as a still-shot, permanently held in an eternal 'Now', or as one infinitesimal flash. What matters is that process is destroyed. The movement and succession which are the essence of existence in Time have gone. But without process, movement, succession there can be no decision-making, no choice. To be aware of reality in this simultaneous way would thus mean that one could not be aware of choice or decision-making going on within it. A God with this kind of awareness could not affect my freedom to choose, if I had any, for the simple reason that to him all my choices would be in a kind of 'past'. Behind each moment of which he was simultaneously conscious the process that produced it would trail out into limbo. We meet here once more the sort of picture-thinking which we had occasion to criticize in talking of the logic of creation. Its only effect is to cut God off from reality, to attribute to him a wholly false impression of the way things are.

The other imaginative illustration, that of the newsreel shown in advance of the events, appears to avoid this defect. God has seen the show already; he knows that when I walk out of that door on to the corridor I shall turn right and not left, even though there is nothing to choose between either direction as a means of getting to a lift. To many people such an idea seems to entail that their behaviour is predetermined. The argument, however, is fallacious, and for the same reason that vitiated the Time-capsule approach, namely that it denies the reality of process. The event of my turning right or left depends in some way on preceding events; and these may or may not include an act of free choice. The question thus becomes: Is it possible to foreknow an act of free choice? In working out an answer it is necessary to remember, however, that the reality of foreknowledge cannot be experimentally verified, since there can never be any criteria to distinguish it from successful prediction. Hence this question can be tackled only in the form: Is there a logical incompatibility between an act of free choice and foreknowledge of that act?

The answer would seem to be, 'No, there is not'. Let us imagine a man who calls to see an acquaintance at his place of business, and is left unattended for a few moments in an outer office. Aimlessly ferreting around while he waits he opens a filing cabinet drawer, and sees a top secret folder, obviously put there temporarily in a hurry. The temptation to look at it is strong. How does a belief in divine foreknowledge affect his position? Not at all. It is equally logical for him to say either: 'God knows I am going to look at these papers, therefore I cannot help opening this folder,' or, 'God knows I am not going to look at these papers, therefore I cannot help leaving them where they are.' In short, the man has still to decide which of the two courses of action he 'cannot help' taking. Whatever he does, God will be right, for the simple reason that he has no idea what God has seen at the preview of the newsreel. The process which he has to go through is unchanged, and the concept of God's foreknowledge is therefore morally vacuous.

Would it make any difference if God's foreknowledge on the matter were communicated to the person concerned? – if, for example, an angel were to appear in the outer office at the crucial moment and say, 'Aha! God knows you are going to look at those papers, so hurry up and open the folder'? Here the situation has only to be imagined for its inherent impossibility to become clear. You cannot convey foreknowledge to a being in Time; you can only present him with a prediction. It makes no difference whether the form of words used is a strictly predictive one or pretends to being a statement of foreknowledge. To the recipient it remains a prediction. Not, it is true, a prediction of the scientific type, in which we evaluate certain facts about the present, and on the basis of our experience of similar cases describe how matters will develop in the future – but a prediction deriving from supranormal powers, where the claim is to know the future not simply to prophesy it, however rationally. Nevertheless, it is still open to the person concerned to say either, 'Oh dear! in that case I must,' or, 'Go to blazes!' He may do either, precisely because, seeing that he himself does not possess foreknowledge, the words come to him as prediction.

The ancients realized this long ago when they told of heroes whose doom was foretold by divine oracle. The hero believes in the divine source of the prediction and thus in its theoretical status as foreknowledge; but he behaves as though it were simply a fallible human prophecy. He uses every ingenuity to falsify it. But the event foreknown comes about whatever men do; indeed it is their very struggles to avoid the doom foretold which lead to the doom's fulfilment. So Oedipus kills his father and marries his mother.

Such an outcome can, however, be engineered only at a considerable distance in Time, and by deceiving the people concerned. Oedipus goes straight to his doom only because he does not know who his true father and mother are. Man's freedom of decision is thus left unimpaired, and it is this which in fact is the essence of the tragedy – the entanglement of the good, free Man in the net of Fate.

We have, of course, other occasions of observing the effects of communicating 'foreknowledge'. A clairvoyant who gives a sad forecast to a susceptible client, that is to say, one who is convinced that the seer does indeed have genuine glimpses of the future, and is not simply peddling more or less intelligent guesses for entertainment, may induce either disastrous inertia and depression (comparable to the despair of primitive people cursed by a witch-doctor) or an outburst of intensified life and energy. On the other hand, a forecast of exceptional good fortune may either give needed self-confidence or encourage reckless and regrettable decisions. It is hard, however, to see in any of these instances much evidence that the freedom of human beings is necessarily affected, even when they sincerely believe that they have been granted a measure of foreknowledge. What does happen is that quite often the predictability of their actions is reduced rather than increased. This accords with the principle, which has been experimentally verified, that the effect on human behaviour of predictions about that behaviour is itself unpredictable, and thus makes the behaviour less predictable than it would otherwise have been – a somewhat portentous way of generalizing scientifically what men have always known from their practice of bluff and double bluff. Once again we see that men generally react in much the same way to self-styled foreknowledge as they do to straight prediction. Reduced predictability is by no means the same thing as freedom, but it is certainly no ground for thinking that freedom has been impaired.

There is therefore no reason to suppose that God's foreknowledge, if it were communicated to me, must necessarily limit my power to take the kind of decisions that are actually within the scope of such freedom as I have. Since we have already seen that it definitely cannot affect that freedom if it is not communicated, the whole problem would seem to be as unreal as the torments with which it has afflicted souls are unnecessary.

Freedom, then, is something which human beings can attain to a certain degree within limits laid down by their inward and outward condition, and something therefore which can grow or shrink in the course of a human life. One mark of freedom, or so we have argued, is the ability to say genuinely, 'I ought', rather than 'I must', or, 'I cannot help it'. The free nature of 'ought' is confirmed by the frequency with which all of us have to confess, 'I know I ought to do this, but I just can't.' To think in terms of 'ought' is already to be free in some small way, but to act as we ought is real freedom.

Why then is the complaint so often raised today that moral obligations are a restriction on freedom? Coercion or incapacity, physical or psychical, may restrict freedom; an obligation can do so only in so far as I acknowledge it. The controlling force of moral obligation lies in the loyalty which the individual feels towards the relevant injunction. It is true that because all rules are matched to situations we may at any given time devote our loyalty to an inappropriate rule, and so lose the freedom to do what is really good. But why should moral loyalty as such be an intolerable bondage?

The answer to this question takes us into the subject of guilt. Guilt-feelings, as we experience them, are an anxiety-state, a condition of distress and tension induced by the transgression of some injunction regarded as binding. The occasion of these feelings may vary greatly. At one end of the scale the primitive who has broken some tabu may experience anxiety so desperate that it results in his death. When we talk of 'tabu-morality' in the context of our own society, we mean a system of absolute rules which people have been conditioned to accept at such a deep emotional level that any breach of them is accompanied by intense and irresistible feelings of fear, shame, and despair. Indeed, in most people's lives there is some quite trivial thing – a minor waste-fulness or carelessness, a social impropriety perhaps – about which they feel a wholly disproportionate guilt because of an impression made upon them in early years. At that level the matter is merely fit subject for light-hearted banter. It ceases to be so, when conditioning has imbued someone with a dangerous fixed idea, such as a class, national, or racial prejudice, or has made them, as we reflected earlier, in some way inflexible to the point at which they lose the capacity for certain goods. At the other end of the scale we have by contrast the distress of the person who has failed in loyalty to some obligation which had commanded his free allegiance.

Clinically the sensations of guilt are the same all along this scale. It is sometimes implied that an anxiety-state is incompatible with a truly moral guilt-feeling; but why? It is true that much the same symptoms may accompany the irrational reaction of the tabu-breaker, the immoralist's fear of detection and punishment, and the moral man's grief at wrongdoing; but to classify the inner condition of the person concerned we need to examine not the nature of his pain but the state of mind that has induced it. Nevertheless, the physical distress and tension do prompt us to analyse the fairly complex sources of the guilt-feeling in the truly moral person.

One, quite obviously, is the element of human sympathy. If what we have done has in any way injured other people or deprived them of the opportunity of some good, and if their suffering is brought home to us by our imagination, then we become unhappy to have been the cause of it. This effect of sympathy can extend very widely. Its most natural and frequent occasions are those on which we have done direct harm, physical or mental, to the living. But we may feel guilty even though those who would have been distressed by our action are dead and gone. We may sorrow simply because an object to which someone unknown had obviously devoted care and love has perished through us, or because the product of skill and artistry, even if in no way great or unique, has been lost. The waste of the thing is nothing much; the waste of a part of someone's life is everything.

Awareness and sharing of the suffering of others, however, contribute only indirectly to our guilt-feeling. Their service is to bring home to us what we have done. The person who asks, 'What are you making such a fuss about?' is unlikely to have severe feelings of guilt. But the characteristic distress of guilt springs not from what has been done but from the fact that we have done it. Here many factors play a part. In the first place we feel ourselves under condemnation. By some external norm what we have done is evil; and we, as the origin of that evil, are ourselves evil, and therefore in this regard something that should not exist. There can be no sense of guilt without this external standard of condemnation, because guilt does not say merely, 'This is a sad thing that I have done,' but, 'I ought not to have done it.' Secondly, to be under condemnation in this way is not painful only in itself but also by contrast, contrast with our ordinary evaluation of ourselves. The man who utterly despises himself, who is convinced that he is no good, cannot feel guilt. Indeed, this defeatist attitude is commonly an attempt to escape from the torments of guilt. Anyone who has sunk below self-respect has also sunk below moral responsibility – and this for some can be a blessed relief. Most people, however, rate themselves reasonably highly, and this good opinion is necessary to maintain the minimum self-confidence required for effective living. Hence to have done wrong is distressing precisely because, as we say, they have not been 'true to themselves'. They have betrayed not only the good but their own self which held the good in honour. Equally (and this is the third major factor) they have betrayed other people who shared that particular loyalty to the good. They have gone over to the evil against those with whom they enjoyed fellowship by virtue of rejecting that evil. This means that they are aware both of having damaged many who were not directly affected by their action, and of having put themselves outside the community to which they had belonged and which formed an essential part of their life. Fourthly, those who believe in a God of goodness will have a sense that they have offended against the author of their being by misusing the gift of existence.

It is hardly surprising, therefore, that even true moral guilt should bring with it acutely painful guilt-feelings, since by his action the person concerned has seriously impaired the satisfaction of some of his most fundamental human needs. He has damaged his necessary confidence in himself; he has alienated the community which, as we saw, he needs in a dozen ways for his own health and happiness. Moreover, he has failed in both self-assertion and self-subordination: in self-assertion, because he has abandoned the principles which he himself had freely and rationally chosen to govern the relation between his self and his world; in self-subordination, because he has caused others to suffer unjustifiably. It will be apparent at once, however, what a vital part is played in all this by communally accepted norms. Where there is no broad measure of agreement in the community concerning what is morally good and what is not, or where the only generally agreed principle is that of permissiveness, there can hardly be much feeling – or indeed much reality – of alienation from the community. At the same time each individual is entrusted with the task of fashioning his own approach to morality more or less from scratch, with one of two results. On the one hand, with no external norms to challenge his conclusions, a person's private code may tend to conform very largely to his own tastes and temperament; and then his self-assertion will find adequate expression in obeying this code, and will run far less risk of damage from failure to do so. On the other hand, the effect may be to fragment society into a multitude of sub-groups ('progressive', 'suburban', 'hippy', and so on), each consisting of those whose mores happen to coincide. Here the individual finds both confidence in his self-assertion and approval from his peers. In such circumstances the chance of developing guilt-feelings at all is minimal.

Moral obligations which are not, however, tailor-made to the shape of the individual or the sub-group, but represent the accumulated wisdom of society at large, tend to cut across personal preferences, and thus to increase liability to guilt-feelings. Because these feelings are painful, they are the means by which moral rules exert pressure on the individual. In other words, moral obligation in the traditional sense *is* to some extent coercive and restrictive, whether we freely accept it by the use of our moral reasoning or are conditioned into regarding it as binding. The only method of evading this coercion is to evade the guilt-feelings, usually in one of the ways just described; and it is against the pain of these feelings that those who inveigh against moral obligations as destructive of freedom are in fact protesting. But the only way of abolishing this pain altogether, and so obtaining the much-desired 'freedom', is to disintegrate human society to a molecular, perhaps even atomic level – which means in effect to disintegrate human personality as well. We saw in the previous chapter that men and women cannot hope to avoid moral wrongdoing; it is equally certain that they cannot dispense with moral obligation. The inevitable conclusion is that neither can they escape from guilt and the pain of guilt, nor would they be wise to try to do so. The sense of guilt is the mark of the free and human being.

Nevertheless, the fact remains that this sense of guilt can be a crippling burden, reducing the guilty person's capacity for living to a fraction of what it could be, and ought to be both for his own sake and for that of his fellows. Consequently men have always sought means to remove it, and these have taken three principal forms: expiatory sacrifice, punishment, and forgiveness. In the present context we need not discuss the first of these, though it will call for close attention at a later stage. A brief word must, however, be said about the role of punishment in this connection, and a rather fuller one about forgiveness.

Punishment as such is always retributive. The fact that the concrete penalty imposed by society may also serve the purposes of deterrence and rehabilitation does not affect the issue. In so far as prison or probation, let us say, are used to these ends they are not penal. The moral justification for punishment is based on such things as the conviction that a man ought not to profit from his wrongdoing and from the pain which he has caused – that indeed he ought to suffer loss for the egotism which dares to bend the essential structures of corporate human life for his own private advantage. On this basis the loss inflicted can be roughly balanced, in theory at any rate, against the damage which the offender has himself done; and when the account has been put straight, the matter can be regarded as settled. He has purged his offence.

What his punishment, however, can never affect is the fact of guilt. Moral guilt is a historical reality, an element in the life story of the guilty person, and as such is irreversible. A certain quantity of suffering may conceivably be set against another quantity of suffering. It can hardly be held to cancel a quantity of guilt, which is a reality of an entirely different order. Guilt cannot be eradicated. The question nevertheless remains: is there something else that can be done about it? Is there any way of enabling men and women to live with it, not as a crippling burden of fear and destruction, but as something that works for life and strength and good? The classic answer to this question is: forgiveness. But this is a subject so complex and so generally misunderstood that we shall have to examine it in some detail.

There are two quite different kinds of situation in which we may be required to exercise forgiveness. The first is one in which we have no contact with the person who has done us the wrong. We may be the random victims of an unjust or ill-considered directive issued high up in the system of power, the corporation, let us say, for which we work, or the government. We may suffer from the side-effects of war, civil disturbance, economic collapse; we may receive anonymous poison-pen letters, be injured by a hit-and-run driver who is never caught. In such circumstances the offender may have no sense of guilt, simply because he is quite unaware of what he has done; or he may be aware, and have a sense of guilt, but be beyond the reach of forgiveness because he is also beyond personal contact.

This does not mean, however, that there is no useful function for forgiveness in such a situation. The guilt of the offender is not the only evil involved; there is also the suffering of the victim. This latter evil will be compounded if the victim allows his own personality to become deformed or diseased by bitterness, either towards his unknown enemy or towards Fate. The refusal to add to the sum total of evil by entertaining such bitterness is essentially the same as the act of forgiveness, even though no personal recipient is available. For what is required is not just a momentary gush of warm and generous optimism. The stock advice, 'Forgive and forget', is thoroughly inadequate in a great number of cases, because it takes no account of the fact that the consequences of the wrongdoing may be long-lasting, even permanent. Bodily injury, unjust accusation or slander, waste or misappropriation of money, are but a few instances of the kind of act that can change a whole life. In such circumstances it is unavoidable that each new day, at least for a very long time, should bring back to mind what has happened. Forgetting is then far too negative an approach to succeed. The victim who has to live with the legacy of the evil simply has to do something positive with it. This means taking the changed circumstances as the new framework within which to create a good life, accepting their givenness as the world with which the self must be in constant and vital interplay if the person is to be healthy and not moribund. It is important to realize that this is not a mere transvaluation. It is not pretending that what is evil is in fact good. No one can hope to live on such a pretence, which is – however much it may appear in certain types of religious piety – a lie, and which can lead only to the sickening of the personality until all that is left is an empty shell of artificiality, a mere external pattern of gestures. If we seek a word for the living and honest approach, then perhaps a good one will be not transvaluation but transmutation – in the alchemist's sense of the changing of base metal into gold. The past has gone, and we have this present, and this present only, from which to create a glory. This is very hard; but it is no use pretending that anything less will do.

In the second kind of situation we do have contact with the offender; and here something can be done about him, and his burden of guilt. Forgiveness in this context is concerned with both parties and with the relationship between them and between the offender and the community at large.

The first thing to note here is that there is nothing in the concept of forgiveness which requires the victim to act as though nothing serious had happened. It is important for the offender that his guilt should be based on reality, that he should be aware of the truth. It is difficult to ensure that this is done in a way that does not drive him away from truth and on to the defensive, but the attempt must be made. This holds good not just in offences between individuals, but also in issues affecting whole groups and communities. There is nothing in the virtue of forgiveness which necessitates our enduring injustice in helpless silence. The very fact that human beings find it so difficult not to ignore or gloss over their own faults points to our urgent need for mutual help in discovering, facing, and correcting them, however unpleasant that may be. There can be no true, strong fellowship, either of individuals, families, nations, classes, races, or churches, unless people learn to give and take rebuke properly.

The second point – which should go without saying – is that nothing can be done for the offender's guilt if he will not acknowledge that he is guilty. If he falsely disowns responsibility, or if he insists that nothing of moment has happened, when in fact everyone else knows that great harm has been done, then the essential basis for human relationship is not present: there is no common ground of external reality, the parties are living in incompatible worlds.

Let us suppose, however, that the offender does face the truth and acknowledges his guilt. What can forgiveness do for him? One thing which it cannot do, as we said just now, is to change the facts. This is something which most people find it very hard to accept. The distress and tension of guilt-feelings are so unpleasant that when forgiveness is proffered and accepted men quickly feel at ease, and fluff out their feathers once more. But could anything be more false or absurd? The offender is still the same person who told the lie, broke the promise, perpetrated the cruelty. The evil has happened; it is there, in history, for ever. We like to delude ourselves that forgiveness rewrites the record, and makes us splendid characters once more; but it does not. What then does it do? First, it reaffirms a full human partnership with the guilty person. Not a partnership where he is watched and suspected and looked down upon, but one where he is trusted and accepted as an equal, thus restoring the satisfaction of one of the basic needs denied by guilt. Secondly, forgiveness takes the evil he has done, the consequences of his offence, and uses them, as we said just now, as the framework, the new givenness of the world, within which to create a good life. In each of these two ways forgiveness is really doing the same thing: making sure that the evil which has happened does not breed more evil, does not spread through time and space. This 'alone can break the entail of accumulated wrong, and set men free from the past to accomplish their present and future tasks' (Dunstan).

None of these effects of forgiveness is a thing which the offender can do for himself. He cannot eliminate the evil of bitterness from his victim's heart; he cannot force his way into fellowship; he cannot convert the damaged life into a good life. When, therefore, these miracles are performed, you would expect him to be overwhelmed with joy and gratitude at an event so far beyond anything which he had reason to hope for. But is this the common response? Do we not rather act as though to be forgiven were a right? Once the fault has been regretted and the guilt acknowledged, the injured party is considered to be under some sort of obligation to forgive, and there is indignation if this duty to ease the uncomfortable situation is not performed promptly. Or again, the wrongdoer may try to create the reconciliation himself, perhaps making reparation ('generously', as they say, should he be in a position to do so), perhaps inflicting some penalty on himself which by cancelling the injury entitles him, as he thinks, to immediate restoration. One thing, however, is clear: forgiveness can never be a right. We have no claim to it at all. If it comes, it is a free gift, an unearned bonus.

Yet there is some truth in this wrong-headed (and wrong-hearted) attitude. The injured party does, in justice, have a duty to forgive, because he too has incurred guilt at some time in his life, and has no business withholding from others a gift which he himself has needed and received. But it does not lie with the wrongdoer to say so; he has put himself out of court. Forgiveness can and should be asked; it cannot be demanded.

To all this there are three important corollaries. First, forgiveness is essentially a free act. It is a service which we all need from each other, but it has to be spontaneous and voluntary and, above all, inward. The determination to renew a full human relationship with the offender, and to take the circumstances changed by his act as the now given framework for the good life – just as if one had been born to them – has not even begun to exist if the injured party does no more than go through the outward motions of pardon. Reconciliation has to be 'created', not in the weak and colloquial sense of that word but in its full connotation; it has to be 'brought into existence' within the wronged person before it can be extended to the wrongdoer. Such an act of spiritual creation may well take a long time. Not for most of us the divine directness, 'Let there be light – and there was light.' But slow or sudden, one thing will always hold good: it cannot be compelled or done to order.

Secondly, forgiveness can be shown only by the victim. This is not quite as narrow as it sounds, since the effects even of a highly personal wrong done to an individual may spread to many. Strictly, however, we can forgive only for that particular share of harm which has come to us. I cannot forgive on behalf of others; I have not the right. Conversely, a wrongdoer can seek and receive forgiveness only from the person or persons whom he has wronged. Anything else must be in some degree unreal. Does this mean that a murderer, for instance, can never be forgiven? As regards his central act, as distinct from its effects on others, it does; and it is just this irreversible fact which gives rise to the uniquely poignant element in the remorse of the repentant killer, as life and literature have often testified. Whether this must be the last word is another matter. It is certainly, however, one of the strongest arguments in favour of the practice of expiation that where forgiveness is not to be had this may be the only means by which a tormented soul can find peace.

Thirdly, forgiveness is bound to be humiliating for the recipient. However harsh the lot to which the victim is called by the wrong done to him, he at least has a creative task. It is on him that the chief responsibility for treating the new circumstances as the given material of the good life rests. (It is worth bearing in mind, perhaps, the unenviable burden laid on the friends of the victim, for they must somehow both provide a right and needed sympathy and yet not by so doing put obstacles in the way of the victim's creating a new beginning.) The wrongdoer, however, has nothing to do but accept. If contrite, he cannot but be aware all the time how different things might have been, and that he is responsible; and the difficulty of believing that the miracle has been done, and that evil has indeed been transmuted into good, can prove insuperable, so that he in effect refuses to have his load of guilt taken away. The more genuine his remorse, and the more sensitive his awareness of the facts, the greater the temptation to cling to his guilt, to parade it, to insist on it. But, again, by what possible right does he do this? If the one on whom the evil has fallen has transmuted it into good, what justification has anyone else for asserting that this is not really so, that his forgiveness is a failure? None whatever. It is not for the offender to say. His views on the matter are utterly irrelevant. And why, after all, does he refuse to allow the reality of the miracle? Usually for one or both of the following reasons. The first is a misconception of the nature of forgiveness. If he thinks of it as no more than a refusal to be angry, a kindly making the best of what is nevertheless still felt to be a miserable business, then of course he will not see what has really happened. Such persistence is at the very least bad manners; for even if the person he has harmed is in fact only pretending that all is well, the least he can do is to fall in with the pretence. It may, however, be nothing more, and due to ignorance or lack of perception rather than perversity. The second reason is far more fundamental and malign, and perhaps more common; and this is nothing other than pride. He is trying at bottom to vindicate his own moral character by showing that he realises how dreadful is the result of his behaviour. He is not thinking of the victim at all – only of himself. Forgiveness can succeed only by humiliating, however much it may wish that it did not have to do so; and anyone who truly wants to be forgiven must be prepared to be humiliated.[1]

Let the last word on this subject, however, be a positive one. In a memorable passage from his great sermon *On Conversion* Bernard of Clairvaux has left us a classic description of the healing and reconciling effect of true forgiveness, which it will be worth while to quote at length:

> How shall my life escape from my memory? Suppose some piece of thin, poor parchment has absorbed the writing of a scribe, by what art can it be erased? The stain is not superficial, it is ingrained. In vain should I try to remove it; I should tear the parchment before the wretched writing was got rid of. For perhaps entire forgetfulness might destroy the memory itself, so that, my reason lost, I should no longer remember what I had done. It remains then to ask: What keen edge can effect the scouring of my memory without destroying it? Surely it is alone the word, living and powerful, . . . which puts away thy sins . . . Pardon blots out sin, not indeed so that the memory of it is destroyed, but that what formerly was wont alike to be in the memory and to defile the memory, henceforth is in the memory in such a way as not to defile it at all . . . Take away condemnation, take away fear, take away confusion – all of which does full forgiveness of sins – and not only will they not be against us, but they will work with us for good (*De Conversione* XV).

The time has now come to draw all these threads together. We said that the word 'ought' can be meaningfully used only by a free agent. Yet 'ought' binds us in a way that no other method of presenting the good can do. To say, 'This is good, but for such and such reasons that is better', is at most simply persuasive. The interior sense of right and wrong does not come into being until we have committed ourselves

---

[1] It would probably be more accurate to say 'humbled' rather than 'humiliated'. But 'humbled' is in piety such a cosy and virtuous thing to be that 'humiliated' seems to be necessary to convey the fact that *this is not pleasant*.

to the principle that we 'ought' to do whatever is best in the circumstances.

The idea of 'ought' is not concerned with the concrete content of any particular good. It is a way of expressing our loyalty to some ground or grounds for our choice between goods or goods and evils. When, therefore, we are told that we ought to do X, then we need first to ask whether X is a good, and if so, how important or universal a good, before we can go on to consider whether we ought to do it. But in the last analysis, when we have pushed back as far as we can go in determining the reason for our acceptance of obligation, we shall always find that the ultimate commitment is one that cannot be determined by rational argument. It will be a naked decision, an act of faith.

'Ought', then, not only expresses an internal attitude possible only to a free agent, but by its very logic rests on the freest of free acts, one springing purely from the inner resources of the self. By the same token so does the true moral sense of guilt which follows transgression of the 'ought'. And, as we have seen, the forgiveness which alone can deal with guilt is something essentially interior and free in the one who forgives, as well as being a free gift for the one who receives it, something which he himself can do nothing to procure.

Commands, however, which we noted as another traditional form of stating the pattern of the good life, are as such irrelevant both to the content of the good and to freedom. The fact that a course of action is enjoined in commandment form tells us nothing about its moral value, nor can we assess the moral quality of obedience to it without further information about the grounds on which such obedience was given. A command simply tells us how the one issuing the command sees his relationship with the one receiving it.

But moral obligation, our voluntary loyalty to what we believe to be the good, is wholly free. Freedom is its pre-condition, its vital air, its creative goal. Yet because Man is not born free, his life, if moral good is to have any place in it at all, must be a continual striving and pilgrimage towards freedom. For this he needs three things. First of all, knowledge, knowledge of himself and his world, knowledge which when handled by Reason will yield to him insight into the myriad possibilities of good. Secondly, he needs an ultimate commitment which Reason alone cannot give him, not because that commitment is irrational, but because it means choosing between the basic possibilities, which are all that Reason can reveal. Thirdly, he needs responsibility, with its consequences of guilt and forgiveness. The common opinion is that we cannot be responsible until we are free. This is an illusion. We become free by accepting that we are responsible. Only the man who is prepared to stand up and say of his life, 'This is my own doing,' however great the pressures that have conditioned and circumscribed him, has broken out of bondage and is on his way to freedom.

When, therefore, we ask, 'What kind of a God must he be – if he be – who stands behind the moral order as we see it?' our answer is clear. He will not be a God who thinks of perfection in terms of precisely defined acts and words and thoughts. The world which he has made will not admit of this; it allows us only a perpetual flux of compromises, in which every situation calls for both fulfilment and sacrifice in varying proportion. He will be a God who lays upon us the necessity of living in relationship; yet relationship not simply of mutual benefit but also of constant mutual forgiveness. He offers us a world not of pure goodness, nor of immutable quantities of good and evil, but of good on the one hand and on the other of evil which by sacrificial love can be transmuted into good. And above all he will be a God who makes it impossible to achieve any of these things except in freedom, creating them out of our own inner resources, assenting to them by a voluntary loyalty, realizing even through our necessary rules an environment of liberty; and thus he shows himself a God who requires not slaves, not machines, but partners. A God who is an adequate answer to our ultimate question must be one who holds these as the supreme values. Our contemplation of the moral order leads us to the same answer as our consideration of the world's sorrow, and confronts us with the same challenge. Only if these values are our values, only if we first believe that here is goodness to be found, can we rightly believe also in a God whom we can call good.

6

Love and the Nature of God

THE LAST three chapters have each brought us face to face with the same unavoidable challenge. The world's sorrow told us that the only believable kind of God is one for whom adventure, courage, disinterested goodness, loyalty, concern, sacrifice, and self-forgetting are the supreme values. We saw that by a strange similarity the happiness and beauty of life too can be experienced only by those who forget themselves and become absorbed in something or someone else. Our exploration of moral good and evil showed that however pragmatically the good is conceived, however carefully we seek it in the fulfilment of Man's needs, it cannot be had without sacrifice. The problems of the last chapter taught us that in a world of mingled good and evil there is a way in which evil can be transmuted into good, namely by the forgiveness which takes the results of evil, and uses them as the framework of a new good. But once again it is sacrifice which alone can write off the potentials of the past, not just to make life better and easier for ourselves, but to restore a full human relationship with those who have imposed evil upon us, and to rescue them from the desperate consciousness of a wasted and ruined existence.

Life is not all sacrifice, nor is all sacrifice painful or heroic or motivated by concern for others. In a sense self-discipline calls for sacrifice; but for many people it is something not only habitual, so that the self-denial is not noticed, but positively pleasant, giving a sense of direction and achievement. We deny ourselves in the short term for our own good in the long; we would regret it if we did not. Or again, the best all-round solution can often be secured by a compromise which demands only a slight sacrifice from everyone, far outweighed by the eventual gain. But there are times when the issue is beyond the scope of rational compromise or adjustment. The decision lies not between an evil which I desire and a good which calls for renunciation or self-control but between things all arguably good, of which some entail sacrifice on my part and others do not. In such a situation to think of the world as the creation of a good God means nothing less than this: *If my brother needs help which only I can give, and only at cost to myself, I must give it, and not let that cost hold me back. If the kind of life in which I could do most to meet men's needs can be lived only at cost to myself, I must live it, and not let that cost hold me back. If I do – then I am rejecting all that is highest in life, and blocking the purposes of the world.*

I cannot argue myself into taking this stand, for here all the arguments depend on each other. If I do not value this as the supreme law of life, I cannot rationally believe in a good God or in a coherent meaning to existence; and if I do believe in such a God and such a meaning, then I am already committed to this law. This is the point of naked choice, the leap in the dark of which men have spoken, the decision for which there can be no guarantees.

This fact ought to be rather daunting; but there is no evidence that it deters or frightens anyone. Parents find it obvious and natural to live in this way for their children, husbands and wives for each other, citizens for their country, friends for their friends, enthusiasts for their cause. There is no song and dance about it all, no great rhetoric or fuss. Most people would think the very word 'sacrifice' far too pompous for the self-denials they readily, almost automatically undertake.

And what makes this so – if not love? Maybe there is no argument which can prove to me that I ought to give up my own good in order to benefit someone else. To those who love, this fact is quite irrelevant, since love does not need arguments. If I love, I know that I must give up my own good, should the needs of those I love demand it; and if I cannot bring myself to do this, then I feel that somehow my love is imperfect.

Goodness is rational. What we like to call our 'conscience', and think of almost as a voice within us, independent of ourselves, is just the whole self – feelings, reason, training, intuition – passing its moral verdict on the situation. An informed and reliable conscience comes into being only if I am informed, and use my brains on the matter in hand, not allowing feelings alone to dictate to me. Love is not rational. This certainly does not mean that love is irrational. If love is genuinely to seek the good of the one loved, then reason has to come into play to present love with the various possibilities of good. But once this has been done, love goes beyond reason and makes its choice by an act of faith.

Goodness is equitable, love is partisan. Love cannot dispassionately say, 'My friend has done this wrong; he must be punished.' Love may have to stand by and see the one loved undergo the punishment of his crime or the consequences of his act. But this is always a terrible suffering, even when the offender himself accepts the consequences as right and as the means of expiation. Love, if it could, would always simply forgive and start again.

Goodness can be external, love is inward. There are many acts which love would do spontaneously which can also be done as a duty. We may nurse the sick, read to the blind, weed the cripple's garden, provide food and shelter for the destitute, because these things are good and right, and yet not be moved to them by love. Love is always and essentially free, a new creation from the inner resources of the self. It includes the doing of good; it is not exhausted by it.

What then is the unique character of love? Some have said, the desire to possess; but this can exist (often horribly) without love, just as love may involve not possession but the surrender of all claims, all contact. The same applies to the desire for union. These are nevertheless phenomena of love, and as such they direct us towards the heart of the matter. Why do we love this person or these people above all others? Surely because we value them most. But what do we mean by this? Not that those we love are objectively better or more worthy than anyone else. We do not have to think our children or our marriage partners or friends objectively superior to all others in order to love them. Indeed, if we did, then logically no one could love more than one person at a time, and most of us no one at all. Is the value we set upon them therefore quite arbitrary? Nonsense – that would be an immoral proceeding. What then?

Love affirms the absolute right of the beloved to exist. This is why one of the central concerns of love is to create 'a space within which the beloved can be himself' (Guardini), to enable those we love to be free as love is free. The truly free imposes no chains on anyone. It exacts no return, no gratitude, applies no moral blackmail; for, being free itself, it treasures only the response that is also free. Yet it does treasure that response, precisely because being free the response is truly part of the one who is loved.

Where the needs of the lover and of the one loved cannot both be satisfied, it is the latter which love would, of course, choose to fulfil, if it had its way. But the value which it sets on the response to love means that where love is mutual the desire to give may have to be renounced in order to receive. To be always giving is an egotism which, far from leaving those we love space to be themselves, in fact tyrannizes over them. Love, therefore, delights not merely in helping but in being helped, and values what is done for it more than what it is able to do for itself.

The absolute right of the beloved to exist is also the reason for the special sense of outrage at the death of someone we have really loved. This is not just the self-regarding pain of losing one who has been the very flesh and blood of all our joy. It is anguish that this unique being should cease. We cry, 'This ought not to be', not because we are deprived, but because they are what they are.

This absolute right transcends even the lover's own right to exist. In the limiting case, where it is a question of our life or theirs, there is no hesitation, no weighing of claims. Here, if anywhere, it is manifest that love has moved beyond reason into the realm of faith. Love is an option for the unprovable.

Love begins as love for one or for a few. But once we have caught it, once it has taken possession of us, and has set up its own values in the heart of the self, there are no limits to those it can touch, to the relationships which it can transform. The recognition of the absolute right of others to exist imbues all encounters, however casual, with true courtesy. It meets all offences with the forgiveness that changes evil into good. Love enters into all roles, because it inspires a new attitude to the specialist interests which bring men and women together in the varied sub-structures of society. Because love takes for granted the good faith of the other person, it removes fear and precaution, and so opens up a greater number of possibilities for achieving the good. And by thus adding to men's options it enlarges their freedom.

Yet there is no security in love. It is the most superficial of optimisms to think that love has only to be shown in order to evoke a like response. The parent who loves his child cannot be sure, even when his love has exercised the greatest wisdom, that that child will turn out well. Love knows perfectly that it may be cheated, laughed at, betrayed, vilified, tormented, even killed – or worse still, perhaps, ignored, never even noticed. Love does not say: 'I affirm your absolute right to exist so long as you come up to my expectations', but simply: 'I affirm your absolute right to exist.' Just that and nothing more. It acts by that affirmation in the help which it offers, the good which it seeks to do. But wherever a free response is possible, it will not compel. Of course love does not leave freedom to the infant which cannot take the simplest care of itself. But as the infant grows, so love steadily enlarges the area of freedom, makes over its own knowledge for the other to use (if he will), replaces compulsion with guidance, decision with advice. It knows there can be no guarantees. It suffers the mistakes and wrong-doings of all those whose right to be themselves it must respect or perish. That is why the relationship of the parent and child is the greatest of all the works of love. The parents have given the child its very existence; therefore, if they are normal people, it is bound to matter more to them than to anyone how that existence is used, and to hurt them more than anyone if it is used wickedly or foolishly. But, by giving existence to a person, they have created something which, when it comes to maturity, can be fulfilled only in freedom; and so their very act of creating is also a promise in due time to renounce their power over what they have created. At the heart of Man's deepest fulfilment lies his greatest sacrifice.

In the world as it is, therefore, we find at every turn the necessity of sacrifice. We find also that nothing can give sacrifice this supreme status except love. If there is any rationale to existence, if it is to make any coherent sense, love as we have defined it must be the fountainhead of all acts and attitudes. And if we ask what kind of a God would be an adequate answer to the ultimate question, it can only be a God who intends this to be so.

But we cannot stop there. The inner logic of love drives us on. For, if God's world makes sense only from the standpoint of this commit-ment which we call love, then this must be the standpoint of God as well. The creation cannot be a purely theoretical exercise for God, a dispassionate experiment in one possible way of doing things. For love is meaningless, inconceivable except to those who already love. It means something to us because we love by natural inclination. This natural love may be fitful and imperfect, but it gives us a basis from which to extend and deepen our understanding. A psychopath cannot even begin to understand. To him the word conveys either nothing or something totally false, and its true meaning cannot be communicated to him by description or argument. We are thus driven to suppose that if God made an environment for love, if he established the evolutionary process which endowed us with an innate impulse to love, then love must be an inner reality for him too. He must be freely committed to it. At the very source of things the naked choice has already been made.

If we take our definition of love seriously, then the implications of this are remarkable. For one thing it means that, though all owe to God their nature and existence, yet he has granted them an absolute right to exist, to be themselves. In this most fundamental of all senses God is the pattern of all parenthood; and creation itself is an act of love, a sacrifice, a self-denying. For another thing it means that God bares himself to suffering. To have created something for the achievement of that which we regard as supremely good, and then to see it misused, misunderstood, hated, slandered, destroyed – do we not suffer when this happens to us? Is it not the price of love, of having real values, that is, ones which we genuinely care about, that it makes us vulnerable? So too, by creating, God makes himself vulnerable. For the very values which he most cherishes, and for which he intends his creation to be the setting, all depend on freedom; and in the process of learning to share these values, to achieve this freedom, his creatures misunderstand and misuse his work with terrible consequences not only to each other, but, precisely because he loves, to himself as well.

It is when we begin to think of God in these terms that we also begin to see an answer to the dilemma which, as we noted in the first chapter, has baffled men since ancient times, and which may be summarized as follows: If God is responsible for everything, then he can have no clearly definable character. Because the sum total of things is morally incoherent, God must be morally incoherent too. He has no shape, no cutting edge. He is simply a poetic way of talking about Fate or Destiny or the All. If, on the other hand, God does have a definite character, then not all things (or not all things equally) are evidence about him; and in that case how can we hope to know what selection of things is the significant one? God is therefore either vacuous or unknowable. Because of this dilemma those who ascribed to him a clear moral character, as Israel did, were tormented by the intractability of the facts of life; and those who were content to fragment him into many gods or to accept his incoherence, in the pagan manner, found that they had no God worth worshipping. But now we see that the dilemma is false. In the universe God is creating not a realization of his own freely chosen values but an environment in which his creatures too may freely choose and realize them. The universe gives us a clue to its meaning, in that this is the only perspective in which its warring elements start to fall into a pattern. God does have a definite moral character, but it is indicated obliquely, by the appropriateness of the world for the development and exercise of that same character in free and understanding beings.

We have now come to the end of this particular road – the search for an answer to the ultimate question by observing and evaluating the way things are. Reason cannot prove that there is a God, and that he is good. What it does tell us is this. If there is a God who is responsible for these things, this is the only kind of God he can be.

Yet when we have said this, an ironic reflection remains. It may be that there is a higher wisdom than ours, a more profound logic than any constructed by the human mind, in the light of which love and its attendant sacrifices could be proved to be the only truly rational law of life. But if we are to talk about wisdom and logic as we know them, if we ask what rational human judgement has to say, then the verdict will always be the same. Throughout their history men have approved of love; they have never approved of making love absolute. And that the all-good who is also the all-powerful should renounce the exercise of power and allow goodness to be ground under the heel of evil may be magnificent – but it revolts our common sense. At the end of the most fundamental and significant of all its quests the wisdom of Man finds itself face to face with the foolishness of God.

PART TWO

Jesus of Nazareth

7

The Loss of the Christ

IF IT could ever be proved that the Gospels consisted throughout of completely accurate material for a biography of Jesus, the traditional Christian faith would collapse in ruins. This can hardly be stressed too strongly, especially to those Christians who are convinced that an orthodox faith rests on the factual reliability of the Bible in general and on the status of the Gospels in particular as precise records of the words and acts of Jesus, and of the incidents of his life. Such a conviction is very nearly the reverse of the truth. Every one of the systematic edifices of belief, both orthodox and heretical, which have marked the history of Christianity has depended in the last analysis on an edited, expanded, or artificially interpreted version of the Gospel text.

To illustrate this point, let us take three fundamental elements in traditional Christian belief about Christ. First, his sinlessness. The great Jewish scholar, C. G. Montefiore, once wrote that 'Jesus was not good enough to be God'. It is not hard for any reader to find incidents or passages in the Gospels which, if read without the presuppositions of faith, give colour to this charge. The fierce denunciations of the scribes and Pharisees (*Matt.* 23; cf. *Mk* 7:1–13; 12:38–40; *Lk.* 11:37–52; *John* 9:40–41) strike us as lacking in charity and understanding at least. Whether they are, as apologists for Judaism assert, also untrue in their allegations, it is difficult to decide in view of the shortage of contemporary evidence from first-century Palestine other than that contained in the New Testament itself. A similar violence marks the language which Jesus uses towards those Galilean cities that did not believe in him (*Matt.* 11:20–24).

Moreover, Jesus' attitude towards ordinary people is not presented as always conforming to the high standards of the pious sermon. Many a preacher has staggered and stumbled over the reception given to the

Gentile woman who appealed to Jesus to heal her daughter (*Mk* 7:24–30 = *Matt.* 15:21–28): 'It is not right to take the children's bread and throw it to the dogs.' 'Dogs?' Could the most bigoted and racially exclusive Jew of the time have been any more brutally rude? Of course, the Greek word is more like 'puppies' than 'dogs',[1] and this may suggest that the words were said in half-jest, with a look and in a tone of voice which made them an ironic reflection on the rules of Jewish exclusivism. After all, they did evoke from the woman that superb repartee: 'Yes, sir: but even the dogs under the table eat the children's crumbs.' Such psychological reconstructions, however, do not meet the point that really concerns us. Why should Jesus have wished even to give the impression that he was interested in doing good only to Jews? There was, as we would expect, a problem here for Christians from the start; for at a very early stage Gentiles were admitted into the Church on equal terms with Jews, and this became one of the main planks in the Christian platform. Mark clearly felt this difficulty; in his version Jesus prefaces the distasteful phrase with the words: 'Let the children first be fed.' This would allow the interpretation that Jesus was not excluding Gentiles from the people of God but simply deferring their entry until his mission to Israel was complete. Matthew makes the exchange a test of the woman's faith; when Jesus finds that she really does believe, he grants her prayer – a pattern sometimes found in other healing stories (cf. *Mk* 9:21–29; *John* 4:46–54). Strictly speaking, however, the woman does not show any more *faith* by her answer than was implicit in her coming in the first place. What she has done is to turn the tables on Jesus, defeat him in argument – as Mark realized when he presented Jesus as replying: '*For this saying*, go your way: the demon has left your daughter.' Nor does the woman desire any breach of the exclusivist principle, such as might constitute a precedent. She simply suggests one little miracle that no one will notice, perhaps not even Jesus – a scrap dropped by accident on the floor and gobbled up in a flash. In short, the incident leaves us with the impression of a Jesus who did not see men and women

---

[1] What the actual Aramaic word used by Jesus was we naturally cannot be sure, and the Greek itself may be a toning down in the process of translation. In all study of the Gospels it should be remembered that the minute details of the wording will at most tell us something about the mind of the particular Evangelist; as indicators of the mind of Jesus they will not bear the weight which expositors too often confidently place upon them.

primarily as human beings, equal before God, but as inside or outside the chosen people. No wonder Luke, who in his Gospel loves to look ahead to the inclusion of Gentiles as equals, has left this story out altogether.

Embarrassment can also be occasioned by Jesus' attitude to his own family. It jars upon us to read of his saying to his mother when they were guests at the wedding in Cana: 'Woman, what have I to do with you?' To argue, as many have done in defence, that 'Woman' is a perfectly acceptable form of address (no Scotsman ever supposed otherwise) is beside the point. It is perfectly acceptable, when used, for example, to a stranger like the Syro-Phoenician whose story we have just been considering. But there is no evidence that it was a proper way to address one's own mother. Nor is it intended to be. The remark stands in the same tradition as certain sayings in other Gospels: 'He that does not hate his own father and mother . . . cannot be my disciple,' or, 'If anyone love father or mother . . . son or daughter more than me, he is not worthy of me,' or the following episode recorded in *Mark*:

> And his mother and his brothers came; and standing outside they sent to him and called him. And a crowd was sitting about him; and they said to him, 'Your mother and your brothers are outside, asking for you.' And he replied, 'Who are my mother and my brothers?' And looking around on those who sat about him, he said, 'Here are my mother and my brother! Whoever does the will of God is my brother, and sister, and mother' (*Mk* 3:31-35).

Jesus fulfils his own demand; those bound by the closest natural ties are relegated to the same level as anyone else in the service of the cause. Sometimes this may be put the other way round; the man or woman who meets Jesus' demand will acquire new fathers, mothers, relatives, and friends by the score (*Matt.* 19:29). But whether the attitude is expressed as a downgrading of one's own flesh and blood or an up-grading of outsiders it is equally offensive to our normal scale of values; and even if we were prepared to reconsider these, we might still feel justified in taking exception to the harsh abruptness with which Jesus put his position into words.

Such difficulties can, of course, be accommodated in a variety of ways. We might wish to disagree with the assumptions on which Jesus is criticized. We might point out, for example, that there are many things in life to which we ought to react with violent anger, or that brutal frankness may on occasion be the only hope (even if a forlorn one) of bringing home to the persons concerned the moral quality of their behaviour. Or again, it could justly be pointed out that the Gospels are not interested in the psychological aspect of the stories they relate. There is no attempt in their skeletal style to convey the finer nuances of the interplay of personalities. This sort of truth, the truth of what it would have been like to be involved – a subject in which we take a great interest – is sketchily indicated in the simplest and most general terms: 'They were astonished'; 'he went away sorrowful'. Hence we are not really in a position to pass judgement.

Even if we were to take this line, however, it would be a waste of time, since Jesus himself would seem to have settled the question for us In *Mk* 10:17–22 (= *Lk*. 18:18–23) we have the story of the rich young man who came to Jesus to learn the secret of eternal life. Mark records him as saying: 'Good Teacher, what must I do to inherit eternal life?' To which he receives the dusty answer: 'Why do you call me good? No one is good but God alone.' The words are admittedly not unambiguous. Jesus might have meant: 'Don't use words without thinking what they really mean. Only God is good. If you do in fact think that I am good, then you are equating me with God' – hoping perhaps that the young man would draw this conclusion. It is quite obvious, however, that Matthew, who certainly did regard Jesus as divine, did not read *Mark* through these highly orthodox spectacles. When he incorporated Mark's story into his own Gospel, he altered the wording to tone down the offensive suggestion:

> 'Master, what good deed must I do to have eternal life?' 'Why do you ask me about what is good? There is One who is good. If you would enter into life, keep the commandments.'

Here Matthew has moved the question into the area of a stock Jewish discussion (as he also does in the dispute about divorce: cf. *Matt.* 19:3–9 with *Mk* 10:2–9), namely, which good works earn salvation from God? The statement that only God is good is retained, but given a different function in the argument. Now God's goodness is not blatantly contrasted with that of Jesus, but is the justification for referring the inquirer to the Ten Commandments: God is good, therefore his Law will give you the answer you want. This modification by Matthew is similar to one which he has introduced into the story of Jesus' baptism at the hands of John (cf. *Matt.* 3:13–17 with

Mk 1:9–11). Here again it is the implication that Jesus was a sinner, in need of a baptism of repentance designed to convey forgiveness, which worries him.[1]

The doctrinal purpose which *Matthew* serves by bending the tradition *John* achieves by intimations and even flat assertions put into Jesus' own mouth. 'Which of you convicts me of sin?' (*John* 8:46); 'I am the good shepherd' (10:11, 14); 'I am the Way and the Truth and the Life' (14:6). This is not the stage at which to consider the reasons for this approach by the Fourth Evangelist. All that is necessary is to observe the fact. The Jesus of the Fourth Gospel lays claim to a moral perfection which the Jesus of *Mark* and *Luke* apparently repudiates. The Christian dogma of the sinlessness of Christ could arguably be compatible with the historical veracity of either account. It certainly is not compatible with the correctness of both; for if both recorded actual utterances of Jesus, then his sincerity in one instance or the other would have to be called in question.

The second element in the traditional belief about Christ which would be undermined by the total historical accuracy of the Gospels is his infallibility. Importance has been attached to this in the past chiefly because the communication of truth has been envisaged almost entirely in terms of propositions accepted by the reason. On this basis it was vitally necessary that every verifiable recorded utterance of Christ should be demonstrably true, otherwise men could not have the absolute confidence in him necessary if they were to found their whole life on his teachings. Loyalty to this principle has, for example, led Christians to insist that Jonah was in very truth swallowed by a great fish, because Jesus referred to his being 'in the belly of the whale for three days and three nights' (*Matt.* 12:40; cf. *Jonah* 1:17). Others have maintained the authenticity of the book of *Daniel* as a composition of the sixth century B.C., because in *Matt.* 24:15 Jesus refers to 'the desolating sacrilege spoken of by the prophet Daniel'. It is difficult to have much patience with this kind of argument. No doubt it is overwhelmingly probable that Jesus did share the assumptions of his fellow-Jews, and thought of Jonah's story as an actual miraculous happening, and of Daniel as living when the book of that name said that he lived. If so, he was almost certainly wrong, though it will never be possible to provide conclusive proof of this on either count.

[1] He is also concerned to rule out any idea that John the Baptist was greater than Jesus.

But nothing could be more irrelevant to the points at issue. What Jesus has to say in each context is entirely unaffected, whatever the truth on this historical question. Indeed, if we are going to be absolutely rigorous, it cannot be demonstrated from Jesus' recorded words that he did not in fact hold a correct view of the book of *Jonah*, and think of it as what it was intended to be, namely an edifying piece of romantic fiction, something like an episode from a spiritual Arabian Nights. Moreover, even if he did, why should an exceptional talent for historical criticism make him a trustworthy guide on matters ethical or religious? The fact is that such anxieties about Jesus' infallibility derive from an unsatisfactory theory of incarnation, whereby Jesus' divine nature overrides his human condition and supplies him with the appropriate truth on every question. If that is what incarnation means, then of course any slip proves that Jesus was not God incarnate.

Dispute whether Jesus was ever wrong on a matter of fact may be futile and interminable; but there can be no doubt that the Gospels represent him as mistaken on matters of prediction. The reference to Jonah and the whale mentioned above occurs in connection with Jesus' prediction that the Son of Man would be 'three days and three nights in the heart of the earth' – a forecast clearly meant to apply to the period between his own burial and resurrection. In fact, the Gospels assert that Jesus' body was in the tomb for something between twenty-seven and thirty-nine hours. Another saying seems to anticipate God's final intervention in world history during the course of Jesus' own preaching ministry to Israel: 'Truly, I say to you, you will not have gone through all the towns of Israel before the Son of man comes' (*Matt.* 10:23).[1] By far the most notable example, however, is Jesus' prediction of the end of the world. Immediately before the Passion story in each of the first three Gospels stands a chapter (*Matt.* 24; *Mk* 13; *Lk.* 21) which presents substantially the same material in three variant versions. In all three Jesus unequivocally declares that the end of the world will come within the lifetime of those then living (*Mk* 13:30 = *Matt.* 24:34 = *Lk.* 21:32). Nor is this expectation of his confined to this particular set-piece (cf. *Mk* 9:1; ? *Lk.* 9:27). Attempts have been made to extricate Jesus from this position by pointing to his warning, inserted towards the end of two of the versions, 'But of that day or that hour no one knows, not even the angels in heaven, nor the Son, but only the Father' (*Mk.* 13:32 = *Matt.* 24:36). It is extremely

[1] On the meaning of the phrase 'Son of Man' here cf. pp. 147 ff. below.

unlikely, as we shall see, that Jesus ever made such a remark; but even on the assumption that the Gospel record is completely accurate, it still would not help. The plain sense of the words refers to the precise moment of the End *within* the general period already indicated. We cannot use it as an escape clause, as if Jesus were saying, 'Well, *I* think it will come in this generation, but of course I may be wrong.' Anything more out of character it would in any case be hard to conceive.

The third element in traditional belief is, however, far and away the most important. This is the assumption not merely that Jesus was God made Man but that he was conscious of himself as such. The difficulty here is to see how Jesus could have been genuinely human if he thought of himself in the way that his recorded words suggest that he did. Clearly this problem is at its most intractable in the Fourth Gospel. There is a passage in Chesterton's *The Everlasting Man* where the author asks why the sky did not crack and the birds cease to sing when a strolling carpenter casually remarked, almost over his shoulder, 'Before Abraham was, I am.' Chesterton was clearly reacting here with all the customary enthusiasm (and inaccuracy) of his generously romantic temperament to the sense of drama, the *frisson* which most readers or listeners experience at some time when they encounter *John* 8:58 in the Authorized Version. (The French, '*Avant qu'Abraham fût, je suis,*' is not quite so impressive.) But if these words really were said, it is hardly conceivable that anyone present could have taken them to imply what we know as orthodox Christian belief. There is an argument still used, unfortunately, by some Christian apologists that anyone who said such a thing must be either mad or speaking the truth. As a piece of logic this is distressingly incompetent to begin with. One may speak the truth and yet be mad, just as one may be lying and yet sane. Just as bad, however, is the way in which it misses the real point at issue. There are a number of reactions which one might have on hearing a man utter these words: (1) he is sane, but talking nonsense designed to make an effect on gullible people, and is therefore an ordinary man but a charlatan; (2) he is an ordinary man who is mad and talking nonsense; (3) he is sane and speaking the truth, in which case he is God (or a god) disguised as a man. The last of these three reactions is no doubt improbable from a twentieth-century audience in western Europe, but would have been perfectly possible for a pagan of the first century A.D., as the New Testament itself relates in *Acts* 14:11, where the crowd say of Paul and Barnabas, 'The gods have come down to us in the likeness of men.' The one reaction which would not be evoked is: 'This is an ordinary sane man like ourselves; nevertheless what he says is true.' It simply is not possible at one and the same time to share the common lot of humanity, and to be aware of oneself as one who has existed from everlasting with God and will continue to do so. If, however, the doctrine of the Incarnation does not mean that God fully and genuinely shared the common lot of humanity, then it is of no interest, it offers no world-shaking news. You cannot have both the Jesus of *John* 8:58 as a piece of accurate reporting and the doctrine of the Incarnation.

It is easy when reading the Fourth Gospel to form the impression that this view of Jesus as conscious of his divine origin and status is expressed again and again. There are, however, surprisingly few unequivocal examples. Such passages as 8:23: 'You are from below, I am from above; you are of this world, I am not of this world,' or 10:30: 'I and the Father are one,' are susceptible of more than one interpretation. Perhaps the only verse as decisive as 8:58 is 17:5:

> Father, glorify thou me in thy own presence with the glory which I had with thee before the world was made.

Nevertheless, it is clear from the hymn about the divine Word, which the Evangelist has used as the preface to his work (1:1–14), from his own explanatory comments such as 5:18 ('This was why the Jews sought all the more to kill him, because he not only broke the sabbath but also called God his Father, making himself equal with God'), or from words which he puts into the mouth of the Jews ('We stone you for no good work but for blasphemy; because you, being a man, make yourself God': 10:33), what he intends to convey. What is more, two other points are also clear from the fact that he describes Jesus' contemporaries as reacting in this way. First, he is not talking about hidden implications but about a direct challenge; this divine claim is one of the historical reasons why Jesus is rejected. Secondly, apprehension of the truth about Jesus is not open to natural human understanding, but only to faith. John is just as well aware as any modern questioner could be that there is an inexpressible paradox in the idea of a God who is genuinely Man. It is precisely because the truth is inexpressible that any honest statement by Jesus himself always leads to misinterpretation: 'No one can come to me, unless it is granted him by the Father' (6:65; cf. the whole passage, 6:35–69). This by itself ought to be enough to warn us that this Gospel is not working solely at the artistic level of straight historical narrative.

Whether John has also faced the paradox which this implies for Jesus' self-awareness is another question. Probably he has not. What light do the other Gospels shed on this problem, if any? Matthew, Mark, and Luke also mention hostility to Jesus on account of what his enemies take to be his superhuman claims:

> Now some of the scribes were sitting there, questioning in their hearts, 'Why does this man speak thus? It is blasphemy! Who can forgive sins but God alone?' (*Mk* 2:7).

Luke (5:21) heightens the implication by changing the first question to 'Who is this that speaks blasphemies?' In contrast, however, to the typical picture drawn in the Fourth Gospel, Jesus does not use the occasion to affirm or even to hint at any divine status for himself, but only to prove that 'the Son of man has authority on earth to forgive sins'. The complex ambiguities of this statement will occupy us in a moment; for the present it should simply be noted that it is in no sense a divine claim. In much the same way Mark tells how the Pharisees and Herodians were conspiring to destroy Jesus from the very first days of the ministry, because of his attitude of free authority towards the keeping of the sabbath, an institution not merely ordained in the Law but observed by God himself when he rested after the creation of the world (*Mk* 2:23–3:6). It is at least possible that in *Mark* we have implicit the interpretation which *John*, as we saw, makes explicit (*John* 5:16–18). Once more, however, Jesus' own comment is free of divine pretensions:

> The sabbath was made for man, not man for the sabbath; so the Son of man is lord even of the sabbath (*Mk* 2:27–28).

Such instances do not justify us in ascribing to Jesus anything more than a claim to be the human agent chosen to usher in the reign of God on earth:

> If it is by the finger (*Matt.*: 'spirit') of God that I cast out demons, then the kingdom of God has come upon you (*Lk.* 11:20 = *Matt.* 12:28).

The real problem presented by the first three Gospels in this context is linked not with any explicit claim on the part of Jesus to be in himself divine but rather with his utterances on two other topics – his

K

death and resurrection, and the Son of Man. The central difficulty as regards his predictions of his own death is that they also are regularly combined with a prediction of his own resurrection after three days (*Mk* 8:31; 9:31; 10:34; *Matt.* 20:19; *Lk.* 18:33; cf. *John* 2:19). In one instance (*Mk* 9:9–10) stress is laid on the fact that Jesus really did make such predictions by the Evangelist's comment that the disciples discussed among themselves 'what the rising from the dead meant'. We cannot therefore avoid facing a number of questions. Can a man who apparently knows that he is to be restored to life – eternal life – within a short period of his execution be said truly to experience death as the rest of mankind experience it? If not, what becomes of the claim made down the Christian centuries that Jesus 'tasted death for everyone' (*Hebrews* 2:9)? Many men, even before the time of Christ, have, it is true, died in a sure hope of eventual resurrection or immortality. Jesus' confident expectation could be understood in the same sense but for one thing – the insistence on 'after three days' or 'on the third day'. We need to bear in mind here the difference between the Judaistic concept of a future life, as held, for example, by the Pharisees, and that found in the mystery-religions and some philosphic sects of the Greek world. For the Greek, immortality was the survival of the soul in some environment other than the earthly; if the soul, as some thought, did return to the world of men, it did so through incorporation in a new physical organism, and after total oblivion of its previous existence. Some Jews (like the author of the *Wisdom of Solomon* in the Apocrypha) apparently shared at any rate the idea of an immortal soul entering and leaving the physical body, even if they did not envisage more than one earthly life for each individual. But the majority opinion among those Jews who did believe in a life after death (and not all did, cf. *Mk* 12:18) seems to have been that restoration to life called for the creation by God of a new body as well (cf. *II Maccabees* 7:28), a bodiless human existence being an unthinkable concept. It is this re-created physical existence to which the words 'resurrection', 'raised', or 'rise from the dead' refer; and the gift of resurrection was thus not unnaturally thought of as taking place at the end of the world, when God's new and eternal order was to be set up. The notion of a resurrection within some very short period, therefore, would seem to imply that Jesus was thinking along one of the following lines. It could be that he envisaged something rather like the events which the Gospels try to describe, that is to say, a personal reappearance in the ordinary course of the world by some visible and tangible presence. If so, then we would have to say at the very least that he regarded himself as uniquely exempt from the normal destiny of mankind. But there is another possibility. He may have believed that his death would in fact usher in the Last Days, and that his own resurrection would simply be the signal for the general resurrection of all the holy dead and for the Last Judgment. Such a belief would not necessarily imply any higher assessment of his own nature and vocation than the one already noted as typical of the first three Gospels, namely that he was the human agent chosen to usher in the final reign of God. Before we can decide one way or the other, however, we must look at the related topic of the Son of Man.

The problem here is complex, and scholarly debate continues in full flood. The central issue may, however, be summarized as follows. The Gospels bear witness to an expectation among some Jews that the Last Judgment and the end of the present world would be presided over by a heavenly being, destined by God for this purpose, a being who is given the title 'the Son of Man'. It is generally agreed that the extant antecedents of this idea are to be found in the 'one like a son of man,' to whom in the book of *Daniel* everlasting dominion is given by God at the Last Day (*Dan.* 7:9-13), and in a similar figure described in the apocryphal Jewish work known as *I Enoch*. Jesus is represented in the first three Gospels as referring on several occasions to the coming of this Son of Man (*Mk* 8:38 = *Matt.* 10:32-33, cf. *Lk.* 12:8-9; *Mk* 13:26 = *Matt.* 24:30 = *Lk.* 21:27; *Mk* 14:62 = *Matt.* 26:64 = *Lk.* 22:69; the differences of detail between the various versions of these sayings can be ignored for the moment). The crucial question is: Did Jesus identify himself with this heavenly being?

There are undoubtedly a number of passages in the Gospels where Jesus refers to himself as the 'Son of Man'. The Greek phrase of which this is a rendering may represent either of two phrases in Aramaic; each is an emphatic way of referring to a human individual, and this, in a religious context, may be the heavenly Son of Man. When, therefore, Jesus spoke the words which appear in our New Testament as 'the son of man has authority on earth to forgive sins', then it could well be that, whatever the sense the Evangelist put upon them, his original remark meant no more than that God had delegated to him as a man power to release others from the burden of guilt. Such a meaning would be an appropriate answer to the objection raised by the

Pharisees: 'Who can forgive sins but God alone?' A similar interpretation could be applied to Jesus' dictum, 'the son of man is lord
even of the sabbath', which would then be simply an extension of
the thought contained in the previous verse. Another possible example occurs in *Matthew*:

> Foxes have holes, and birds of the air have nests; but the son of man has
> nowhere to lay his head (*Matt.* 8:20),

where the contrast is primarily between the lot of the man who is truly
open to the will of God and that of the animals.

In addition to 'son of man' sayings which may refer simply to the
general human condition there are, however, others which quite
plainly do speak of the heavenly Son of Man, but which by no means
necessarily imply that Jesus identified himself with this figure. Thus,
the saying in *Mk* 8:38 —

> Whoever is ashamed of me and of my words in this adulterous and
> sinful generation, of him will the Son of man also be ashamed, when he
> comes in the glory of his Father with the holy angels –

could equally well imply either an equation of Jesus with the Son of
Man or a distinction between them. Indeed, the latter might even be
thought the more natural reading. The same is true of Luke's version
(*Lk.* 12:8–9), but it emphatically does not apply to Matthew's (*Matt.*
10:32–33), where the actual title 'Son of Man' is dropped, and Jesus
speaks in the first person as the dispenser of eternal judgement in the
presence of God. Another instance of the highest importance is the
reply of Jesus at his trial to the High Priest's question, 'Are you the
Messiah?' In *Mark* (14:62) Jesus claims the Messiahship, and goes
on:

> You will see the Son of man sitting at the right hand of Power (i.e.,
> God), and coming with the clouds of heaven.

In interpreting this we need to remember that there is no conclusive
evidence that the Messiah and the heavenly Son of Man were ever
identified in Jewish speculation at this period. Hence, *prima facie*, a
claim by Jesus to be the Messiah would imply that when he went on to
speak of the Son of Man he was *not* referring to himself. His meaning
would more probably be that the judicial murder of the Messiah by the
rulers of God's people would be God's foreordained signal for the final

judgement, to be executed by the Son of Man. Matthew's version is very close to Mark's. His substitution of 'You have said so' for Mark's 'I am' in answer to the question about the Messiahship sounds evasive, but is meant as an affirmation. The rest is virtually identical. Luke's wording, however, is drastically different. First of all, the High Priest's question is changed: 'If you are the Messiah, tell us.' Jesus' reply is simultaneously a refusal to accede to their command and an indication that if he did so the answer would be in the affirmative: 'If I tell you, you will not believe; and if I ask you, you will not answer' – they are not interested in the truth. The passage then goes on:

> 'But from now on the Son of man shall be seated at the right hand of the power of God.' And they all said, 'Are you the Son of God then?' And he said to them, 'You say that I am' (*Lk.* 22:67–70).

Certain points are noteworthy here. The mention of the imminent appearance of the Son of Man has been dropped. Furthermore, the court all take it for granted that in speaking of the Son of Man Jesus is referring to himself, otherwise there is no point in their next question. The assumption that the Son of Man is also the 'Son of God' may reflect an argument from two Old Testament texts, namely *Psa.* 2:7 and *Psa.* 110:1, which when taken in combination suggest that he who is to sit on God's right hand is his Son. This conclusion Jesus then accepts as applicable to himself. Here there can be no doubt at all that Jesus is represented as claiming for himself supreme honour next only to God.

This evidence suggests a possible answer to the question which we asked earlier, namely what did Jesus mean by his references to his own resurrection? So far as the Markan and Matthaean versions of the prediction are concerned, there is nothing in them incompatible with the view that Jesus thought of himself as God's human agent, whose death would usher in the end of the world and the resurrection of the saints with himself as their firstfruits. The primitive Christian expectation of an immediate arrival of the Last Day could certainly be reasonably explained, if they had at first supposed that Jesus' own resurrection heralded this event; and Paul in *I Corinthians* is still thinking of Jesus as the 'firstfruits of those who have fallen asleep' (*I Cor.* 15:20), and describing how those who are still alive at the Last Day will be transformed for life in the new heaven and earth (*I Cor.* 15:51–52). What may be a legendary distortion of the same theme is to be found in Matthew's story that at the moment of Jesus' death on the cross

> the tombs also were opened, and many bodies of the saints who had fallen asleep were raised, and coming out of the tombs after his resurrection they went into the holy city and appeared to many (*Matt.* 27:52–53).

In *Luke*, however, all has been accommodated to a long delay, with Christ in heaven and the Church on earth (cf. also *Lk.* 21:9, 24).

Finally, we may note a number of sayings in which 'Son of man' is used not simply to mean 'man' or 'generic Man', nor to refer to some distinct celestial being, but as a title of Jesus. These include particularly the prophecies of the Passion and Resurrection mentioned more than once already – for example, 'The Son of Man will be delivered to the chief priests and scribes, and they will condemn him to death' (*Matt.* 20:18), or, 'the Son of man came not to be served but to serve, and to give his life as a ransom for many' (*Mk* 10:45 = *Matt.* 20:28). Here, if the title is to mean anything at all, it must allude to some concept generally accepted but not defined in the context. It would in theory be possible that Jesus on occasion referred to himself with the Aramaic phrase meaning 'human being' as a way of expressing a vocation of an anonymous and representative kind; and that on other occasions he used the slightly different phrase to refer not to himself but to the heavenly Judge; and that the distinction has been obliterated in the Greek, which uses the same rendering for both. The picture conjured up by such a hypothesis is, however, artificial and precisian, not to say precious, to a degree impossible to associate with any man whose character even remotely resembled the Jesus portrayed in the Gospels. The only plausible alternatives are either that Jesus did say these things, and therefore did equate himself with the heavenly Son of Man, or that he did not say them, and they have been put into his mouth by the Evangelists. On the working assumption of the present chapter, namely that everything in the Gospels is accurate reporting, they would of course imply that Jesus thought of himself as a pre-existent heavenly being who would return after his death to judge the world.

The last of the 'Son of Man' sayings quoted above raises one further point about Jesus' attitude to his own death. Here and in the story of the Last Supper (*Mk* 14:24; *Matt.* 26:28) he is represented as describing his approaching crucifixion as an expiatory sacrifice to God for the sins either of all mankind or of all Israel. The question has been canvassed in recent discussion whether this too is not incompatible with a genuine sharing of the limitations of humanity. This objection does not seem to the present writer anything like so weighty as the ones already discussed. Any conclusions must take into account so many factors special to Jesus' situation but remote from our own experience that they can be properly formulated only in the context of a full reconstruction of him as a historical person. We shall therefore defer them until the next chapters.

The general conclusion, therefore, to be drawn about the relation of the Gospel record to the third vital element in traditional Christian belief about Jesus is as follows. In *John* Jesus is presented as aware that he is a perfect divine being who existed with God before the creation, and who will return to him after his work on earth is accomplished. In the other three Gospels the testimony varies. Jesus implicitly disclaims sinlessness; and the sayings attributed to him which demand to be understood as affirmations of near-divinity are very few, perhaps only one (*Lk.* 22:70). It is interesting in this connection to reflect that the story of the Temptation in the Wilderness (*Matt.* 4:1–11; *Lk.* 4:1–13) could perfectly well, in place of the more usual expositions, bear the interpretation that Jesus rejected as a diabolic evil the suggestion that the vocation to be God's 'son' entitled him to behave as if he were God's equal. Nevertheless the Gospels also show him as arrogating to himself the title of a heavenly being appointed by God from everlasting to execute final judgement on the world. (In *John*, as we would expect, the few references to the Son of Man describe Jesus as using the title in its celestial sense quite definitely of himself: 3:13, 14; 5:27; 6:62; 8:28; 12:23; 13:31.) Yet at the same time the first three Gospels at least contain other evidence which can quite reasonably be taken to mean that he did not identify himself with this supernatural Son of Man. As regards Jesus' statements about his own death and resurrection, it is not necessary to understand these as implying a sense of superhuman status.

It follows that any attempt to treat the Gospels as in their entirety an accurate factual record would both make it necessary to abandon any doctrine of true incarnation and at the same time render it impossible to resolve the contradictions of the texts in any rational manner. In fact the conflicts of evidence are such that the Gospels cannot be said to give united support to any view of Jesus, orthodox or heterodox. The total picture does not hang together; and unless we are prepared to believe in a Jesus who was both confused and confusing cannot be correct. This is the reason why all presentations of Jesus edit or gloss the record. The contemporary labelling of him, for example, as the 'Man for Others', as one who was free to give himself in sacrificial love for the needs of his fellow-men, is just as firmly rooted in the documents – and just as selective – as its more conventional predecessors.

It is this which makes the 'quest of the historical Jesus', the attempt to arrive at some firm conclusions about what he really was, absolutely imperative. We need to probe and to assess, not to prove or disprove orthodoxy, but to form any coherent picture at all. But there is another reason for pursuing this quest which is of equally critical importance.

We have already seen the various Evangelists moulding or elaborating the material to hand in order to express particular insights into Christian faith and life; and we shall note more of this as our investigation continues. They are trying by these methods to convey the significance of Christ to members of their Church, and so ultimately to the world. There can be no question that the Church must do this at every period of her history. She may, however, in carrying out this essential task convey a very diluted or distorted meaning. In England during the thirties of this century Dick Sheppard used to set out the heart of Christianity to the theme of 'God is my Pal' – a slogan which distilled the pure spirit of a certain kind of piety, and a piety which communicated to many. It was unfortunate that it proved so inadequate to real life. At the opposite extreme we might point to the crisis theology associated with the name of Karl Barth. This too spoke to the condition of its generation, and still does speak to some; but its denial that human reason is of any fundamental use in the discovery of God is ensuring that in the end it too will cease to communicate effectively. We can see the pattern clearly enough, as it repeats itself in recent and modern times; but we tend to be blind to it in the beginnings. The presentations of Jesus set out in the New Testament are better and more important than ours for obvious reasons. For one thing, they derive from the traditions of people who knew him personally, who moved in his world of thought, who used the same words and customs, who had that natural community with him without which sympathetic judgement and understanding are impossible. For another, without these presentations we would know nothing of Jesus at all. But they are presentations none the less.

Now we may take various attitudes to this fact. If the N.T. presentations are all we can have as our basic material, if we cannot start level with the Apostles, or even with such secondary authorities as Mark or Luke or John in constructing our own presentation, then there are two main ways of proceeding. The first is that known as 'demythologizing'. Here we take the N.T. presentation and translate it in terms of a contemporary world-view. The second might be called 'revelationism'. On this approach we attach supreme value to the actual words of the presentation, and find its saving efficacy precisely in the shock with which its folly and mystery challenge us. The former method is associated with the name of Bultmann, the second with the figure of Barth; and they might seem to be the most distant and diametric opposites. In fact, however, they belong very firmly on the same side of a fence much bigger than any that divides them.

That fence separates two radically different views of the vital principle of Christianity. One sees her life as a process of growth and development from a single creative root, the Gospel, a process which continues by her own God-given inner dynamic, so that her message in each generation is the message of Christ to that world. The other sees her life as a permanent living dialectic between two creative centres, one being the inner dynamic of the Church, the other the living fact of Jesus himself. On this view the Master and Founder of Christianity is not to be encountered solely and wholly in his Church and her current proclamation. She may witness to him, she may embody him in a contemporary presence and do his works – indeed, she is of value to God only insofar as she does so. But Christ and the Church are not interchangeable terms. He is not only present in her; he also stands over against her in permanent challenge and criticism.

We may almost say of these two views that the Church in its institutional self-interest always tends towards a version of the first view, while the ordinary man, whether inside the Church or outside it, thinks in terms of the second. The first offers an endless variety of simple solutions to the problem of faith. One form they may take is that of an ever-enlarging system of doctrine, in which each new teaching or definition is carefully constructed and phrased to be compatible with what has gone before. The more comprehensive such a system becomes, the more numerous and detailed the precedents, the less room there is for manœuvre, the less chance of any new fundamental insights. In such a system everything, even the words of the Founder, become part of the single utterance. If we are to listen to him it must be in the context of the system, because this is the organic, God-directed unfolding of his words. We must meet him here if anywhere, for nowhere else is he to be found. Another form, equally springing from this same vision, is that which disowns any need for continuity with the past. In each succeeding age the Church is stimulated by the basic datum of her tradition, or rather by whatever selection from that tradition seems meaningful at the time, and communicates this in whatever form the contemporary world-view makes possible. Here more than ever there is no chance of a genuine critique of the Church by Christ, because by definition everything which is not included in her current proclamation has no meaning or relevance for the present moment.

This last approach has been pressed almost, but not quite as far as it will go by the American school of Radical Theology – quite far enough anyway for us to see the logical conclusion. Thomas Altizer, in an essay entitled 'Word and History',[1] writes:

> Increasingly there is the recognition that to the extent that we imagine Jesus in his traditional Christian form we are closed to his contemporary presence. The Gospel portraits of Jesus are inseparable from modes of belief that long since have become impossible for us ... To cling to these traditional images of Jesus is to pose an insuperable barrier to the appearance of Jesus in our flesh.

The images to which Altizer refers here (*RT* p. 125) are explicitly stated to be not only the apocalyptic Son of Man, the eternal Son of God, the cultic Christ, and the cosmic Logos, but also the historical Jesus. There is no 'possibility of mediating the New Testament Jesus to our time and space'.

One naturally asks then, what does Jesus contribute to the radical theology? Ironically, the concept of Incarnation. This at first sight seems odd, but in the system of Altizer and Hamilton it is perfectly logical. Their thesis is that the Church has refused to accept the logic of the incarnation-concept, which is simply that the old transcendent God

[1] Cf. Thomas Altizer and William Hamilton, *Radical Theology and the Death of God*, to which the page numbers given in the text refer.

has gone for good, and that all that he stood for has passed into the world. 'The death of God (is) a final and irrevocable event . . . (and) the horizon of our history (is) the full arena of faith' (*RT* p. 126). 'The original form of Jesus has disappeared from view, transcendence has been swallowed up by immanence, the events of our salvation history have passed into the dead and lifeless moments of an irrevocable past, no heaven can appear above the infinite stretches of a purely exterior spatiality, and no grace can appear within the isolated subjectivity of a momentary consciousness' (*RT* p. 128). What effect then can Jesus be said to have on us, what continuing difference entitles us to call ourselves his followers? Simply this: the rejection of the typical 'religious' attitude of attachment to the past and the attempt to recover it, and the living of a truly 'eschatological' attitude which seeks only the future. 'Only by a continual process of negating its own past expressions can the Word be a forward-moving process' (*RT* p. 133). The essence of Christian faith is a 'meditation between faith and history', and if the past has ceased to be meaningful in the present, then faith *must* abandon that past and seek something new.

Another contribution of Jesus is stressed by Hamilton (*RT* p. 49). Jesus seems to have taught that good done to others in his name was good done to him; Christianity, following the Pauline formulation, has found Jesus in its own members; we must find Jesus in all men. Note, however, that this will not be the Jesus of the past, but men in themselves. The phrase, 'finding Jesus in your neighbour', does not imply a mystical identity between the neighbour and the historical Jesus. It refers to the fact that 'our way to our neighbour . . . is mapped out not only by the secular disciplines, (but also) by Jesus Christ and his way to his neighbour'. Correspondingly, the Christian can talk about 'becoming Jesus in and to the world' (*RT* pp. 48–49).

Here the link with Jesus seems at first rather stronger. In Altizer's presentation it amounted to little more than this: that Jesus was not afraid of radical change in Man's understanding of his existence, nor must we be. We are most fundamentally untrue to him, when we cling to what he was once considered to stand for, even though this is no longer viable. In such a context the search for new understandings of existence (in Oriental mysticism, for example) is natural enough. But if so, what is the significance of retaining even a nominal link with Jesus? There is nothing specific to Jesus in the attitude which says, 'If it doesn't work, drop it.' On this basis a truly 'radical' theology would, one might think, drop Jesus too, and say, 'He was wrong; let's move on.'

Hamilton, by contrast, wishes to use Gospel material about Jesus to guide us in our new existence. But there seems to be an underlying uncertainty in his method. If we model our lives on Jesus' 'way to his neighbour', we may do so on one of two assumptions. The first is that the real-life Jesus was this sort of man, that the stories to this effect are true. To be rational, this assumption demands that we prosecute our 'quest of the historical Jesus' with care, and have good reasons for believing that Jesus actually was like this. Hamilton, however, offers no such reasons. He cites the 'Great Assize' parable of *Matt.* 25:31–46, with its famous saying, 'Inasmuch as you did it to one of the least of these my brethren, you did it to me.' It is probable that this particular saying, like the parable in which it is set, is in fact a product of Church piety rather than an original utterance of Jesus. Even if it is not, however, even if it is a genuine word of Jesus, it tells us nothing about his own behaviour; and what is, from Hamilton's standpoint, more serious still, it does not express the attitude we want. It supports not an openness to all men but to Christians only. Hamilton's other main reference, the story of the Good Samaritan, does by contrast commend an attitude of generosity to all, whether inside or outside one's own group. But again it tells us nothing of Jesus' practice, only of his theory.

It would seem then that Hamilton is not basing himself on a 'Jesus of history', even so minimal a one as the 'good man from Nazareth', stripped of all his outmoded religious beliefs and of the mythical trappings which his followers have hung upon him. Equally, however, he is not taking his stand – how could he? – on any of the total pictures of Jesus as presented by the faith of the N.T. writers. He is appealing to one or two fragments of the mosaic that is the Christ of faith, the fragments which seem to him most attractive. These may be morally admirable fragments; but the vital point to notice is that any principle by which we choose these, and not those more problematic fragments which, for example, provoked Montefiore's comment quoted earlier, cannot be derived from Jesus himself. It is no longer Jesus, either as he was or as he is made out to be, who shapes our life, but some quite independent scale of values by which Jesus like everything else is to be assessed. The frame of mind in which Hamilton approaches the Gospel (and the same may be said of John Robinson) is the same as that which causes us to be moved or excited by one or two features in the hero of a story. It makes no difference whether the hero is real or fictitious, whether his character is consistent or inconsistent, whether the account of him is accurate or biased. Moreover, if the same ideals were embodied in the different hero of another story they would do just as well. In fact, though there appears to be a closer link to Jesus along this line, it turns out not to be a link with *Jesus* in any coherent use of that name.

This theology leaves us with one inheritance from traditional Christianity, the concept of Incarnation; and this is given a sense the exact opposite of its former one, namely not 'taking of the manhood into God' but 'conversion of the Godhead into flesh' – a fair summary of the theme of Altizer's essay, 'William Blake and the role of Myth' (*RT* pp. 171–91). The link with Christianity is simply that a Christian word has stimulated a completely contrary line of thought. In the result, therefore, the only surviving apparently Christian element must be adjudged either otiose or un-Christian. The reader is left with the feeling that this position would be much more clearly and correctly stated without the use of inherited relic-words like 'eschatological', 'incarnation', and 'God', which bring over to the new cause no detectable meaning but something of great practical value: emotional associations. Likewise the name 'Jesus' is retained for much the same reasons as one might retain the name of an old-established firm after a takeover. It attracts a certain amount of goodwill, and looks well on the notepaper. But where the self-propagating thought of the Church, unchecked by any other criterion, is its own justification, how can it possibly be said that such a development is wrong?

Not only Barth and Bultmann, therefore, live on the same side of our main fence, but also Catholicism and the 'Death of God' movement. Such an assertion may at first sight seem merely perverse; or perhaps it suggests that there is no 'other side' of the fence to be on, that some version of this position is the only one that can be adopted. One might indeed think so, were it not for the regular appearance throughout Christian history of proof to the contrary in the form of endless ordinary people who have rejected the contemporary Church because it seemed to them to have betrayed Jesus as he actually was. Early monasticism, the Franciscans, the Brethren of the Common Life, the Protestant Reformation, John Wesley, the Christian Socialist movement – these and many others are marked by one common feature, the appeal to Jesus against the Church. In comparison with this, any other traits or motives, the question whether they remained and worked inside the Church or outside, whether they were loyal members or revolutionaries, is of minor importance. And in their tradition stand all the young people and outsiders who point to our ecclesiastical institutions and say, 'What has this to do with Jesus of Nazareth?' This is the only critique of the Church's institutional self-interest which has ever been creative and effective, the only true reformation.

How continuously this critique has to be exercised can be seen, to cite a modern example, from the oecumenical movement. This too began as a return to Jesus of Nazareth and his vision of unity. Soon, terribly soon, it has been perverted into yet another expression of institutional self-interest. On the one hand, unity is sought in order to build a more powerful and durable organization, and to impress the world. A sure sign of this is the tendency to treat outward reunion in itself as an absolute value to which the stuff of true unity – truth, ideals, spirituality – is sharply subordinated. On the other hand, unity is postponed and resisted in an effort to ensure that the combined church-to-be will to the greatest possible extent resemble one's own present spiritual home, and be as little as possible modelled on that of the other parties to the merger. Here the critique of the existing Church by Jesus is accepted in theory, but is in practice respected far less than certain trivial incidentals of Christianity which, because of men's fears and prejudices, can be used as powerful counters in a piece of political bargaining.

In apparent contrast to these attitudes we have that of the radicals who boldly declare, 'The Church as we know it must die.' It may seem ludicrous to suggest that such people are actuated by institutional self-interest, but they may be so more than they themselves realise. To condemn the existing Church because its ruinous state proclaims it a non-viable organization, and to look for a new structure which will function successfully, is to give higher priority to survival than to truth. Changes just as cataclysmic – perhaps more so – might in fact follow from a reverse priority, from applying the proven principle of Christian reformation; and it is part of the purpose of the present work to suggest that they would. But we must start from the question, 'What is Christ's truth?' – not from the seemingly more realistic question, 'What will work?'

It would, however, be harshly unjust to pass such strictures on current Church attitudes without admitting that their proponents have been given very little alternative. They have been deprived of the traditional basis of reformation by the effect of one hundred and twenty years of New Testament criticism, which has finally convinced almost everyone that Jesus himself is unknowable. This has destroyed the second creative centre of Church life, the fact of Christ, and therewith the tension by which the Church's inner dynamic was constantly directed, transformed, and overruled. There being no grace to perfect nature, nature has had to do duty for both. The only remedy there can be is that this second centre should be restored. It cannot be restored by a return to a fundamentalism which treats the whole Gospel text as direct evidence about Jesus as he was. We have seen the insuperable problems there. Today there is happily a growing feeling that it is possible to take account of all the objections of negative criticism honestly, and yet build up a usefully complete and reliable portrait of the man Jesus, a portrait no doubt in some respects impressionistic but veracious none the less. In the next chapter we shall see whether we cannot, even in a necessarily brief compass, find a way to touch at least the hem of his garment.

8

The Recovery of Jesus:
(1) The Method

OUR PURPOSE in the present chapter is to see whether by taking the principles of historical investigation seriously we can build up a picture of Jesus as he was, a picture which even if not a detailed biographical portrait in the modern style will be more solid than a mere list of generalities. We shall proceed not by chipping away at the Gospel portraits, removing first the outrageously impossible, then the highly suspect, then the improbable material – a process which seems all too often to leave one at the end with nothing at all. We shall begin by assuming that certain elements in the tradition, which given all the circumstances are probable, are in fact true; and moulding them together will hope to see the shape of a man emerging, a form and character which may in their turn make new sense of other material and suggest where and what its proper place in the whole may be.

The first question to ask and to answer – and, however silly it may seem it has been asked, and answered in the negative – is this: Did Jesus really exist? That he did is now acknowledged as beyond reasonable doubt. The chief evidence, of course, is the fact that 'in the early days it never occurred even to the fiercest adversary of Christianity to doubt the historical existence of Jesus' (Bornkamm). Outside the Bible we have testimony to his existence from both Jews and Romans. The Roman evidence is the earlier; the historian Tacitus writes of 'Christus, who was sentenced to death by the procurator, Pontius Pilate, during the reign of Tiberius' (*Annals* XV, 4). Though close to the events in time this may not, however, be genuinely independent evidence, since its most probable source is the interrogation of Christians by the authorities; the mistaken assumption that Christus is a proper name tends to confirm this.[1] By contrast the references in the Jewish Talmud, asserting that Jesus was a sorcerer who led the people astray, are much later, but less likely to be a distortion of the Christian story than a lineal descendant of the attitude mentioned in the N.T. itself: 'He is possessed by Beelzebul, and by the prince of demons he casts out demons' (*Mk* 3:22; cf. *Matt.* 9:34; 10:25). Both the Talmud and the Romans confirm Jesus' execution by the State. These are small enough scraps of information, it is true, but they do at least concur in attesting two cardinal facts – that Jesus lived in Palestine around the dates usually assigned to him and that he was executed 'under Pontius Pilate'.

For the rest we have to go to the New Testament. The sayings and incidents recorded in orthodox or heretical Christian writings outside the canon of Scripture help us hardly at all, since their plausibility has to be assessed by comparison with the New Testament before they can be laid under contribution. Furthermore, within the New Testament our information is virtually confined to the Gospels. References to the resurrection constitute a special class of statements, and will have to be dealt with separately. For the public ministry of Jesus we have little to add to the Gospel record. In the *Acts of the Apostles* Jesus' life and work is briefly characterized by Peter in a speech to the household of Cornelius at Caesarea:

> You know the word which he (sc. God) sent to Israel, preaching good news of peace by Jesus Christ (he is Lord of all), the word which was proclaimed throughout all Judaea, beginning from Galilee after the baptism which John preached: how he anointed Jesus of Nazareth with the Holy Spirit and with power; how he went about doing good and healing all that were oppressed by the devil, for God was with him. And we are witnesses to all that he did both in the country of the Jews and in Jerusalem. They put him to death by hanging him on a tree. . . . (*Acts* 10:36–39).

Here succinctly we already have the typical account of Jesus as cherished in the hearts of Christians down the centuries. It mentions certain key points – that Jesus began his work soon after the mission of John the Baptist, or perhaps overlapping with him; that he worked outwards from Galilee; that he was a preacher, healer, and exorcist; that his activities took him to Jerusalem; and that he was crucified. This is

[1] As in the other Roman reference (Suetonius, *Claud.* XXV, 4), where it is mis-spelled 'Chrestus'.

effectively a summary of the picture in the first three Gospels, as we would expect in a book written, at least in part, by the same author as *Luke*. It may be, however, that the Gospels are accounts which, though on a larger scale, yet retain the traditional plan used in the preaching of the first Christians. In that case both this speech and the Gospel books witness to a stage of the tradition earlier than either; but it cannot be said that its evidence has much independent value, nor does it add anything to our other sources. Elsewhere in *Acts* the apostle Paul in a farewell speech to the elders of the church of Ephesus quotes as a saying of Jesus words not found in any of the Gospels: 'It is more blessed to give than to receive' (*Acts* 20:35). In his own writings Paul refers to Jesus' teaching on divorce (*I Cor.* 7:10–11; cf. *Mk* 10:2–12) and to his words at the Last Supper (*I Cor.* 11:23–26; cf. *Mk.* 14:22–25; *Matt.* 26:26–29; *Lk.* 22:14–20). Despite differences in detail all these passages are in broad agreement on the incidents or teaching of which they speak. Other N.T. information, such as the allusion to the Transfiguration in *II Pet.* 1:17–18, adds little weight to the Gospel's own version; though an exception to this assessment may perhaps be made for the Gethsemane reference in *Hebrews* – 'In the days of his flesh, Jesus offered up prayers and supplications, with loud cries and tears, to him who was able to save him from death' (5:7) – since it mentions a detail, that of the tears, not found in the closest Gospel version, that of *Luke*.

Of the passages just discussed those by Paul are probably earlier in date than any of the written Gospels; the rest are later. In certain instances, notably Paul's account of the Last Supper, it is stated that the information given has already been conveyed to the readers by the apostle in the course of his teaching. It is clear therefore that some historical detail was included in the instruction of converts from the first, and this, implying as it does a continuous chain of tradition, increases the chances of preserving accurate and authentic memories.

Historical proof is very hard to attain. We know how complicated a task it can be to unravel the true course of events in matters of great moment which have taken place within the lifetime of people still living, and for which ample documentary and eye-witness evidence is available. We know that a correct evaluation of even the most honest and circumstantial narrative from more distant periods depends on a sound understanding of the conditions and culture of the society to which it relates; and what a labour it can be to achieve such an understanding, what minute and widespread research is required even in the case of so recent a past as that of nineteenth century England. In the ancient world our background information is fragmentary; we are fortunate if we have two independent accounts of the same events. Historical reconstruction more often than not is a matter of trying to work a huge jig-saw with but the roughest idea of the picture and only one tenth of the pieces. In these circumstances all historians are compelled to rely to some extent on intelligent conjecture, unless they are content to stop at a bald catalogue of the clues and a list of perhaps many possible alternative interpretations. It is no use pretending that anyone can write a scenario of the life of Jesus; it cannot even be done for a heavily documented figure like Julius Caesar. But where a complete narrative is out of the question, a portrait may be a much more feasible task.

One other warning is called for, before we turn to building up the portrait of Jesus from the Gospel material. In any portrait we assume that there will be coherence. Because one person is the subject there will be an inner unity, an essential organic form, for that after all is what we mean by a person. Hence we start with the presupposition that where words or actions of the person concerned seem inconsistent with one another there may be some perspective in which they are not inconsistent. Only when we fail to find such a perspective do we feel reasonably sure that some of our information may be inaccurate or fictitious. But we have to base our reconstruction, find our key, fix our viewpoint, on something; and it makes a great difference which of the facts provided we select for this purpose. In the case of Jesus there is the added complication that faith, not historical assessment may supply that key. The fundamentalist will take it for granted that he can begin from statements such as those questioned in the previous chapter; and will insist that other statements which appear to clash with these must be interpreted in a sense which will make them fit. 'Why do you call me good?', for example, must be understood in a sense which will accord with 'Before Abraham was, I am.' But why, historically speaking, should we start from the latter, and not from the former? Why should we not take the recorded sayings in their natural sense? The portrait which we are about to build up also has a theological presupposition, as has already been made clear: that Jesus was fully and completely human, a man in essence like ourselves. It is no use pretending that this does not beg the question; it does. But there is this justification for choosing to beg this question rather than the other. We know that Jesus was a man by the most decisive of all criteria. He died. A man who was a man in this definitive sense, and who was also aware of himself as the eternal God, would not be a unity, and no coherent portrait of him could ever be made. Without our assumption we would have to give up Jesus as unknowable. Surely it is worth finding out whether such a disastrous surrender is really necessary?

Turning now to the Gospel material, it will be as well to bear in mind certain points about its texture, nature, and probable evolution. In *John* the characteristic unit of construction is a long address by Jesus, following on and expounding some especially significant act on his part, or prompted by an inquirer (cf. *John* 3; 4; 5; 6; 7:14–8:59; 9–10; 12:20–36). The Passion narrative (in the present form of the Gospel, at any rate[1]) is prefaced and interpreted by four long addresses and answers to questions and an extended prayer. Moreover, these discourses are not only closely woven in an almost poetic, spiral treatment of their topics, but are packed with significant allusions to other parts of the Gospel. For these reasons many have seen the Fourth Gospel not just as a piece of reporting, but as the product of long reflection on the life and work of Jesus, in which Jesus himself explains to the Christian reader the true significance of what happened, in the light of its eventual fulfilment in his resurrection. If this evaluation is correct, as the present writer believes it to be, then clearly we must exercise great care in calling upon this Gospel for historical testimony. That it contains some facts, however, which are not supplied by the other three is now generally accepted.

By contrast, Matthew, Mark, and Luke share a different kind of texture, being composed for the most part in short sections with a minimum of connecting material. The linking phrase, 'And immediately', of which Mark is so fond in his account of Jesus' public ministry

---

[1] There are considerable reasons for thinking that the discourses of chh. 13–17, at present allocated to the night before Jesus' crucifixion, were originally written as teaching given by Jesus to his disciples after his resurrection: cf. esp. *John* 14:1–6, 18; 16:4b, 7–8; 17:2, 4 (with which cf. 19:30), 6–10 (the readiness of the apostles for their mission), 11–12 (Judas apparently already dead), 13, 18 (cf. *Matt.* 28:19; *Mk* 16:14; *Lk.* 24:48; *Acts* 1:8), 19 (cf. *Hebrews* – the 'eternal High Priest'), 24 ('where I am'). Those who wish to pursue this interesting possibility further are referred to an article by Boyd, *Theology*, 1967, pp. 207 ff., which also explains the reasons why the discourses might have been moved to their present position.

(cf. e.g., *Mk* 1:10, 18, 20, 21; 2:2; 3:6 etc.), and which gives his narrative a naïve but effective air of dramatic urgency, does little to disguise the lack of any necessary order in the various incidents. There may be a theological or artistic reason for his arrangement, but in some instances the Evangelist does not even claim that his story is continuous, or that a particular event has to come exactly where he has put it (cf. *Mk* 2:23: 'One sabbath'). In *Matthew* and *Luke* there is more 'setting the scene'; a story may more often be introduced with some circumstantial details. On the other hand, there is perhaps less definite connection with the preceding material than in *Mark*.

This overall effect can be illustrated from modern European literature. In Boswell's *Life of Johnson* there is one period, that of Boswell's early married life, when for a considerable time he had no contact with his hero even by letter. To supply this deficiency in his own diary and notes Boswell incorporated into his work a memorandum 'furnished ... by the Rev. Dr Maxwell, of Falkland, in Ireland, some time assistant preacher at the Temple', who was much in Johnson's society during the time in question. The memorandum, which may be found under the year 1770, though it covers several years from 1754 onwards, presents phenomena remarkably alike in some respects to the texture of the first three Gospels. The whole is made up of unconnected units. Some are very short, consisting only of a saying introduced by 'He said' or 'He observed'; others are given a context; others again are longer, and contain several sayings arranged in a connected paragraph. There are also general notes on the Doctor's manner of life. But of a sequential narrative, giving even an outline of the period, there is nothing. Yet it would be absurd to deny such a memorandum all accuracy or biographical value. Even if the original wording of some sayings has been blurred, or lost altogether, so that only the sense is retained; even if sometimes a witticism or opinion has been ascribed to Johnson which in fact originated with someone else; nevertheless from comparison with the rest of the work it is clear that the material thus supplied has the stamp of authenticity, and brings us reliably into contact with its subject. And yet we know that this memorandum must have been compiled for Boswell by Dr Maxwell some twenty years at least after the incidents which it records. No doubt in the meanwhile Maxwell had told and re-told many of the anecdotes, and this, while helping to fix them in his mind, had probably also modified, stereotyped, or even improved their phrasing. (We all know how we edit, abbreviate, heighten, and generally polish up our own favourite stories over the years.) Much the same must have happened to the units of the Gospel record during the not dissimilar gap of time before they were written down.

There are, of course, significant differences between the two cases. Far more people will have had a hand in the shaping and re-telling of the Gospel contents; and it is widely believed that behind *Matthew* and *Luke* lies another written document which has not survived. Fundamentally, however, we are dealing at this point with an *oral* tradition; and it will be as well to bear in mind what oral tradition is, and how in broad principle it works. It is not at all the same thing as the memorization of a written text. In true oral tradition the material is composed in the head, spoken to one or more people, remembered by them, and passed on by word of mouth. This procedure sets a premium on those stylistic methods which create an easily and quickly assimilated unit. The ideal technique is to have a striking pattern which can be picked up at once, preferably one with which the hearers are already familiar. In *Luke* (6:20–22), the shorter version of the Beatitudes, we have an excellent example of this:

> Blessed are you poor
>> for yours is the kingdom of God
> Blessed are you that hunger
>> for you shall be satisfied
> Blessed are you that weep
>> for you shall laugh
> Blessed are you when men hate you
>> for great is your reward in heaven.

The form, 'Blessed are . . .', is familiar to the Jew from the Old Testament. There, however, the blessedness usually resides in some virtue or piety for which the blessed one will be rewarded (cf. *Psa.* 1:1). Here the familiar form is given a shatteringly unexpected content. 'Happy are you who are poor – for the greatest of all kingdoms will be yours.' Not 'poor and good'; just poor. This simple pattern is repeated four times. Each time blessedness is said to consist in some wretchedness: poverty, hunger, mourning, rejection. And the reason for the blessedness is equally simple, a straightforward reversal of each misery when God's kingdom comes. As the starting-point of a chain of oral transmission this little unit is well-nigh perfect. The shock which rivets attention comes at once. What has preceded it is so traditional that the mind has picked it up automatically, and in any case it is to be repeated three times more. The shock then concentrates the mind on the pattern of future reversal; we have to know why this man thinks the poor of all people blessed. Hence when the second sentence begins with the same traditional formula we can guess that something unusual is coming, but we are intensely interested none the less to see what new shock it may be that awaits us; and, if we are sympathetic, we listen for it eagerly. Moreover, the subject-matter of all four sayings is part of the experience of anyone, however humble or uneducated. Poverty, hunger, mourning, pain, rejection – the ingredients of all the world's sorrow. Anyone, provided that he was not drunk or asleep or hopelessly preoccupied, could go home and tell you exactly what the speaker had said. And that is the essence of good oral tradition.[1]

Many of the utterances of Jesus display these characteristics. In the original Aramaic some were probably poetry (cf. e.g., *Matt.* 12:41–42). In such cases we may expect a high degree of verbal accuracy. But, of course, it is not always important to preserve the precise original wording. If the material is a story, then what matters is that the story-line should be correctly retained. Many of the stories in the record of Jesus' teaching are in fact barely more than outlines:

A certain creditor had two debtors; one owed five hundred denarii, and the other fifty. When they could not pay, he forgave them both (*Lk.* 7:41–42).

Such a bald summary would hardly be used as it stood by the early missionaries of the Church in their preaching; it represents rather the product of a memorizing technique, and would provide the basis for a more picturesque re-telling, expanded with the speaker's own artistic detail. A very good example of such expansion is the much longer and more dramatic version of the same story in *Matt.* 18:23–35, where it is used to point a slightly different but related moral. There is also no reason to suppose that Jesus himself did not use the same basic illustra-

[1] In the light of these criteria it is interesting to compare the records of the teaching of two other great religious leaders. The Koran simply is not credible as a piece of genuine oral tradition. The various sections are too long, too shapeless. Uttered rather than written by Mohammed they may have been; but if so they were almost certainly taken down by disciples and transmitted in writing. By contrast, the texts of the Buddha's teaching display all the marks of pure oral tradition. The famous passage about the Noble Eightfold Path is a classic example of the technique.

tion in different contexts; but on occasion we can detect in the incidental embellishments the special interests of the Evangelist himself, or of the community from whose teachers his material came. A good instance of this is the Parable of the Wedding Feast (*Matt.* 22:1–10 and *Lk.* 14:16–24). The reader will find it instructive to compare these for himself. Suffice it to say that Matthew has used the story as an opportunity to refer in allegorical form to the fate of the Jewish nation, seeing the sack of Jerusalem by Titus in A.D. 70 as God's punishment of the Jews for their rejection of Jesus (cf. v. 7), a rejection which is but the climax to a long history of persecuting the prophets and servants of God (v. 6). Luke, however, besides the purely narrative expansions of vv. 17–20, which serve to make the story more entertaining, has duplicated the excursions by the servants to find new guests, one to the city streets, the other to the countryside around the city. This reflects his special interest in the history of the Church, whose first mission was to the Jews, and then later to the Gentiles. The stress on the sorry condition of the new guests symbolizes another of his favourite themes, Jesus as the friend of sinners. It is interesting that he does not have the incident of the man who was ejected for not having a wedding-garment (*Matt.* 22:11–14), which may be an elaboration from Matthew's own local church, stressing the need for formal Christian initiation. Nevertheless, behind both we can recognize clearly the same story, which may with confidence be attributed to Jesus.

What is true of the stories told by Jesus in his teaching can apply also to accounts of incidents in the life of Jesus. Some are very simple indeed:

> And immediately he left the synagogue, and entered the house of Simon and Andrew, with James and John. Now Simon's mother-in-law lay sick with a fever, and immediately (!) they told him of her. And he came and took her by the hand and lifted her up, and the fever left her; and she served them (*Mk* 1:29–31).

No dialogue, no details about the illness or how long it had lasted, about the patient, how weak she was or how old. Luke tells the same story just as briefly, but with two changes of detail (*Lk.* 4:38–39); he says that it was a 'high fever', and he describes the healing differently, making it into the exorcism of a demon – 'he rebuked the fever' – rather than the communication of strength by touch which we have in *Mark* (cf. *Mk* 5:41). Matthew, however, has tinkered with the story tendentiously. Here there is no need for the family to ask Jesus' help (*Matt.* 8:14–15); he himself notices the sick woman. Moreover, when she is cured, she does not carry out the hospitable duties of attending to the whole party; she serves 'him', the Lord, as any pious churchgoer would (though not necessarily any true disciple – cf. *Mk* 6:37!). With longer stories there is naturally more scope. *Mk* 5 contains two examples of this. The first is the dramatic detail in the tale of the Gerasene demoniac (n.b., esp. vv. 3–4), the second comes in the account of the healing of the woman with a haemorrhage (v. 26). Luke says nothing of the woman's having spent all her money on doctors to no effect (which has convinced some that he himself was indeed a doctor!), and has shortened the whole passage considerably. Matthew has compressed it even more, but he throws in a picturesque touch – there are flute-players to accompany the ceremonial mourning for the little daughter of the synagogue official (*Matt.* 9:23). But to speak of Matthew and Luke 'compressing' or 'shortening' the complex of stories may not be the whole truth. The evidence that both of them had *Mark* to work from is certainly convincing; but this does not necessarily imply, as it is sometimes assumed unthinkingly to do, that all differences from *Mark* in either Gospel are purely alterations of *Mark*. Thus, Matthew may have been indebted not only to Mark's written text but also to 'outline' versions of the same tradition as employed by teachers and missionaries of his own church. If so, the flute-players may have been included for one of a number of reasons – as an incidental embellishment from some point along a different line of transmission, as a historical detail accidentally preserved along this line, or as a feature put in by Matthew to express the distaste of an austere Jewish Christian for the hellenistic customs cultivated by some Jews.

It will be as well at this point to say a word about a type of biblical study which has been of great importance for both Old and New Testaments in this century, namely that known as Form Criticism, or, more correctly, the study of the history of forms. The aim of this technique is to generalize from the individual pieces of Gospel material in order to show the basic patterns to which they conform. The hope is that once this has been done we may have a clearer idea of the situation in the life of the Early Church to which each of the general types of tradition-unit, and also the variations upon a given piece of material in the individual versions, are relevant. The best service of this study has been to provide solid confirmation for the theory of a stage of widespread and intensive oral transmission behind the written Gospels, since the evidence for this does indeed reside specifically in the *form* of the material. When, however, we go on to compare *content*, the results are far less convincing, and some of the conclusions decidedly dubious, as the following example will show.

Especially prominent among the types of unit in the Gospel record are miracle stories, and in particular miracles of healing. Analysing the structure of these stories, form-critics detected a pattern on these lines: (1) description of the sufferer's illness, emphasizing its severity, often with the comment that all attempts at a cure had failed, or that it had lasted many years, perhaps even from birth; (2) the encounter between the healer and the victim or an intermediary, often including a brief dialogue to elicit information or to evoke faith; (3) the actual healing, with stress on its immediate and complete character; (4) the astonishment and praise of the onlookers. They then went on to point out that the same pattern could be found in many pagan healing-miracle stories, such as those connected with the wandering Greek wonder-worker and popular sage, Apollonius of Tyana.[1]

This is hardly surprising, since it is virtually impossible to write the story of a miraculous healing without using all or most of this pattern.[2] If the illness was not serious, and had not resisted the efforts of ordinary medical practice, neither would there be an appeal to the wonder-worker nor would the cure be worthy of comment. An encounter with either the victim or an intermediary is, to say the least, more probable than not. If the cure were not swift, it would be hard to attribute it with certainty to the healer; and if it were not complete, it would hardly count. Finally, if miracles happen, people are likely to be amazed. The 'form' detected with such care is simply the way any account of such an incident will probably turn out, whoever writes it, and whether it is true or fictitious. The early form-critic might have seen this for himself, if he had been rigorous in his methods, and, instead of including notes of content in what should have been an abstract account of form, had kept to the kind of terms appropriate to his purpose. In that case the

---

[1] It might with equal justice be said that it occurs in the Old Testament – for example, in the account of Elisha's healing the leprosy of Naaman the Syrian (*II Kings* 5).

[2] One of the first to make the criticism set out in this paragraph was the Jesuit scholar McGinley in his monograph, *Form Criticism and the Synoptic Healing Narratives*.

analysis would read: (1) description of context and circumstances; (2) introduction of the principal characters; (3) account of the incident; (4) reactions of those concerned. This, however, is hardly informative. It could serve as a structure for any piece of narrative writing.

There is here a methodological dilemma which form-criticism in all fields has never managed to avoid. Either its analyses are so general that they cease to be useful for purposes of classification, or they become analyses of content, not of form. Comparison of content is, as we have already seen, an extremely useful exercise; but it should not be called form-criticism. The comparisons between the Gospel stories and those concerning Apollonius or the cures effected at the various healing sanctuaries in the Mediterranean world are comparisons of content. The similarities led many scholars to argue that because they believed the healings credited to the pagans to be bogus, those attributed to Jesus were probably bogus too. They were all equally pious fictions, generated by religious enthusiasm. This ignored two points: first, the point of theory already mentioned, that whether a miracle were actually performed or merely invented, the accounts would come out very much the same; secondly, the point of fact, that spiritual and faith cures, if not so common as some maintain, are nevertheless well enough attested to make it probable that incidents of this sort did occur not only with Jesus but with Apollonius and the rest as well.

The purpose of raising these objections, however, is to warn against rushing to conclusions by non-viable methods. It is not intended to suggest that the interests of the Early Church have not left their mark on the tradition. This they manifestly have done; and in using our evidence to build up the picture of Jesus we have to be on guard against overlooking this influence, which can seriously alter Jesus' message while the authors believe that they are bringing out the truth implicit in his words. A striking example occurs in *Matt.* 18:15–17. This is one of only two passages in the Gospels (both in *Matthew*) where Jesus is alleged to have used the word 'church'; and these particular verses purport to give Jesus' instructions how to deal with an obdurate sinner in the congregation. The giveaway phrase, however, comes in v. 17: 'If he refuses to listen even to the church, let him be to you as a Gentile and a tax-collector.' That Jesus, who 'ate and drank with tax-collectors and sinners' (*Lk.* 5:30; cf. *Mk* 2:16; *Matt.* 9:11) should ever cite either of them as an illustration of total ostracism is simply incredible; and it would be a highly artificial interpretation to say that he meant, 'let him be to you as tax-collectors and Gentiles are to the average Jew'. By far the simplest explanation is that this is a story, perhaps elaborating some piece of tradition now lost to us, which certain early Christians told in order to show what they thought Jesus' guidance on the subject of sinners in the congregation would have been. The use of the word 'Gentile' suggests that they were members of a Jewish Christian congregation. It is, moreover, likely that the passage had reached its present form by the time it came to Matthew's hand, since this Gospel as a whole is not exclusivist, and does not seek to deny Gentiles a place within the Church. But when we have said this, we must go on to face the implications, namely that at a very early stage in the history of the Christian church there were people who could in all sincerity misunderstand and misrepresent Jesus as drastically as this. Here we have palpable evidence from the very origins of Christianity of the need for that permanent critique of the Church by Jesus which was argued in the last chapter to be so essential.

The other Gospel passage in which the word 'church' appears (*Matt.* 16:13–20) illustrates a slightly different type of church influence on the Gospel record. This is the section in which occur the famous words:

> Blessed are you, Simon Bar-Jona! For flesh and blood has not revealed this to you, but my Father who is in heaven. And I tell you, you are Peter, and on this rock I will build my church, and the powers of death shall not prevail against it. I will give you the keys of the kingdom of heaven, and whatever you bind on earth shall be bound in heaven, and whatever you loose on earth shall be loosed in heaven (*Matt.* 16: 17–19).

Matthew contains other instances of a special relationship of Peter with Jesus. One is the story of Peter's walking on the water to go to Jesus (14:28–32), and the other the fascinatingly silly little story of the shekel in the fish's mouth (17:24–27), a version of a tale familiar in folk-lore all over the world, but here used to show Peter's special intimacy with Jesus, and also perhaps to provide a setting for a saying about paying tribute, the original context and point of which has now been lost. This interest in Peter is one indication that the home church of Matthew's Gospel may have been the Christian community at

Antioch in Syria.[1] What seems to have happened, therefore, is that a story of basic importance in the tradition, found also in *Mark* (8:27–30) and *Luke* (9:18–21), has been embellished to give prominence to a Christian hero held in special honour by this particular church. In all the forms of the story Peter plays a key part (cf. *John* 6:66–69). Here he receives a personal grant of the disciplinary and absolving authority which elsewhere, even in *Matthew*, Jesus is shown as bestowing on the apostles or the disciples as a whole (cf. *Matt.* 18:18; *John* 20:23), thus singling him out for a primacy of honour.

Consideration of these peculiarly Jewish Christian interests leads on naturally to another type of modifying influence, namely an assimilation to the ideas of Judaism itself. Here some care is needed. Jesus was a Jew, and it would therefore be very surprising, and indeed suspicious, if his teaching did not have features in common with the Judaism in which he was brought up. The fact that a saying can be paralleled in Jewish writers surely does not mean that it cannot be an authentic utterance of Jesus. This may be illustrated from an incident described in each of the first three Gospels (*Mk* 12:28–34 = *Matt.* 22:34–40 = *Lk.* 10:25–28). Jesus is asked to state which is the supreme commandment of the Jewish Law. This was a question debated by the Rabbis themselves, and Jesus in his answer agrees with one authoritative school of thought on the subject:

> The first (sc. commandment) is, 'Hear, O Israel: The Lord our God, the Lord is one; and you shall love the Lord your God with all your heart, and with all your soul, and with all your mind, and with all your

---

[1] Peter's connection with Antioch is recorded by Paul in *Gal.* 2:11–14, a passage which, though it puts Peter in the wrong, yet bears eloquent testimony to the powerful influence of the conservative Jewish Christian party at Antioch. Other hints of a link between *Matthew* and Antioch come in his story of the birth of Christ. The motif of the Star of Bethlehem and the homage of the Magians points to Syria, where the latter were active and influential. They are described in the story as bringing to Jesus well-known materials of their occult sciences, gold, frankincense, and myrrh, and they were, of course, famous in the ancient world for their skill in astrology. The Star was still an important focus of theological speculation in Antioch a generation later, when its bishop, St Ignatius writes of the birth of Christ: 'A star shone forth in the heaven above all the stars; and its light was unutterable, and its strangeness caused amazement ... From that time forward every sorcery and every spell was dissolved, the ignorance of wickedness vanished away, the ancient kingdom was pulled down, when God appeared in the likeness of man unto newness of everlasting life' (IGNATIUS, *Ephesians* 19:2–3).

strength.' The second is this, 'You shall love your neighbour as yourself'
(*Mk* 12:29–31).

In another famous instance Jesus agrees in substance with a well-known
dictum of Jewish teaching but expresses it in a form of his own. This is
the case of the so-called 'Golden Rule'. Rabbi Hillel had formulated
this in the words, 'That which you hate do not do to another', a saying
which we find echoed in the N.T. in Paul's letter to the *Romans*: 'Love
does no wrong to a neighbour; therefore love is the fulfilling of the
law' (*Rom.* 13:10). Jesus expresses the same thought in its positive
form: 'Whatever you wish that men would do to you, do so to them;
for this is the law and the prophets' (*Matt.* 7:12). The fact that Jesus
does put it this way round, setting out a creative principle for action
rather than a precautionary principle for the avoidance of wrongdoing,
is no doubt significant. As regards authenticity, the combination of
teaching known to belong to the Judaism of the period with a distinctive new way of stating that teaching must create a very strong presumption that this is the voice of Jesus himself.

There are, nevertheless, passages where the differing versions of an
incident in different Gospels show up an assimilation to Judaism which
is tending to obscure or distort the original teaching. One such
example, Matthew's treatment of Jesus' question, 'Why do you call me
good?', has already been noted;[1] another is the same Evangelist's
additions to the story of Jesus' ruling on the admissibility of divorce.
In *Mark*, *Luke*, and by inference St Paul (*I Cor.* 7:10–11) Jesus'
teaching is clear and unqualified: marriage is for life, and therefore
divorce followed by re-marriage is adultery. In *Matthew* (19:3–9) the
question which evokes the guidance from Jesus has been changed to
conform with a current Jewish ethical dispute: Is it lawful to divorce
one's wife for any cause?' - that is 'Are there any grounds for divorce
and if so, what are they?' Jesus' answer in this Gospel appears to
allow the possibility of divorce on the grounds of persistent immorality
in the wife. Many difficult questions of detail surround this passage,[2]

[1] Cf. chap. 7 p. 140 above.

[2] One possibility is this: a Jewish woman who was divorced had either to marry
again or become a prostitute, if she were not to starve. This may be the meaning of
the saying attributed to Jesus in *Matt.* 5:32, that every man who divorces his wife
'makes her an adulteress'. Clearly, however, this would be both untrue and unfair,
if she were by her own act an adulteress already. Hence the words 'except for
unchastity' in this passage. This may have induced the legally minded Matthew to

but one thing is clear; the effect is to tone down and 'judaize' Jesus' line on a matter where he was at variance with his Jewish contemporaries.

Another area in which, of recent years, Jewish colouring has become apparent is in the language of the Fourth Gospel. The discovery of the scrolls from the Qumran community, about which so much has been written, has shown that some of the basic concepts in *John* – notably those of the supernatural power of evil as 'the prince of this world' (*John* 12:31) and of the recurring contrast between 'light' and 'darkness' – were also favourite motifs of the Qumran sect. It is hardly possible at this distance of time to decide whether Jesus used this terminology or whether the Evangelist used it to express his faith about Jesus; and the ideas involved are, in any case, such fundamental religious commonplaces that they prove virtually nothing. What is certain is that the Jesus of the Gospels is at the opposite pole from the Qumran sect with its fanatical addiction to complex rules of ritual and moral purity and its self-righteous withdrawal from contact with the world; and if Jesus did use these images, as in the phrase 'sons of light' (*John* 12:36 and the 'War Scroll' from Qumran), he is also represented as giving the whole concept a completely new dimension in such claims as 'I am the Light of the World' (*John* 8:12). On the whole, this new information does little to help us in our present inquiry.[1]

Another criterion which is sometimes of use is that of attempting to translate sayings of Jesus back from the Greek in which they have come down to us into the Aramaic which he must have used. Where this cannot be done, the exact form of words will naturally be ruled out of court; but if the remarks made earlier about the methods of transmitting material by word of mouth for missionary preaching are borne in mind, the fact that this does happen will hardly cause much surprise.

There is no need to recapitulate here the questions discussed in the previous chapter about the influence on the record of the doctrinal interpretations of Jesus arising from the faith of the early Church.

[1] *Matthew* and *Luke* also attribute a 'light and darkness' saying to Jesus (*Matt.* 6:23 = *Lk.* 11:35), so it is probable that he did use this imagery. But this, as remarked above, is such an ethical and religious commonplace that it would be far more remarkable if he had not.

---

add the same exceptive clause to the other section about divorce in chap. 19, the alteration to the inquirer's question then being made to fit. But this must remain pure conjecture.

These clearly have introduced into the record elements which as history must be suspect. As we develop our positive portrait, however, it will appear that evaluating them is not always the simple matter which sceptical scholars like to make it.

One possible influence which, if frequent, might present peculiar difficulties is that of Christian prophecy. It is certain that prophets were a prominent feature of church life in New Testament times. Paul gives instructions to regulate their conduct at meetings of the congregation (*I Cor.* 11:4–5; 14:29–33; *I Thess.* 5:19–21); and 'false prophets' constituted a serious problem (*I John* 4:1–6; *Rev.* 2:20; cf. *II Pet.* 2:1). In what did the activity of these prophets consist? *Acts* gives the impression that they predicted future events (*Acts* 11:27–28; 21:9–11). Paul, however, implies a rather wider scope. In *I Corinthians* we have some hints of this: prophets might be men or women (11:4–5; cf. *Rev.* 2:20, but also *I Cor.* 14:34–35), and their utterances were intelligible, not the ecstatic ravings of those with the 'gift of tongues' (*I Cor.* 14:1–5, 6–9, 13–19, 22–25), which were of lesser value. The fact that 'prophecy' and 'teaching' are listed as two separate gifts of the Spirit in the Pauline church (*I Cor.* 12:28) suggests that their contributions differed.[1] It is likely that teachers were concerned primarily with expounding the written tradition and the Old Testament scriptures, while prophets gave new and direct 'revelations'. This, at any rate, is one possible explanation of the terms used by Paul in *I Cor.* 14:26–31:

> When you come together, each one has a hymn, a lesson, a revelation, a tongue, or an interpretation (v. 26).

The context suggests that 'interpretation' means 'interpreting an ecstatic utterance' (i.e., a 'tongue'). 'Lesson' may then denote the work of the teacher, 'revelation' that of the prophet; and vv. 29–31 tend to support this. What were these 'revelations'? Vv. 24–25 of the same chapter suggest one kind, namely telling people unknown to the prophet the secrets of their thoughts and past life, and so convicting them of sin and converting them. Another kind of revelation may well have been that of which we have an extended example in the book entitled the *Revelation of John the Divine*. This work explicitly refers to itself as the 'prophecy' (1:3; 22:18–19). Of special interest to us are the first three chapters, which contain messages from the 'Spirit' to seven principal churches of Asia Minor. These utterances are in the true

[1] Cf. p. 341 below.

tradition of Old Testament prophecy, in that they combine prediction with moral censure and exhortation; but, more to the immediate point, though communicated through the prophet by the Spirit they are also words of Jesus himself, who appears in heavenly glory at the beginning of the visionary experience (1:12–18). The words

> Fear not, I am the first and the last, and the living one; I died, and behold I am alive for evermore, and I have the keys of Death and of Hades (1:17–18)

establish the identity of the speaker beyond doubt. One at least of the sayings of the glorified Jesus in this book has passed into common Christian tradition as on a par with the sayings in the Gospels:

> Behold, I stand at the door and knock; if any one hears my voice and opens the door, I will come in to him and eat with him and he with me (3:20).

The general principle behind such sayings is expressed in 19:10:

> The testimony of Jesus is the spirit of prophecy.

Furthermore, it seems from comments on 'false prophets' in the letter known as *I John* that prophets sometimes included in their revelations assertions on what we would call 'doctrinal' points, such as Jesus' supernatural status and nature:

> Beloved, do not believe every spirit, but test the spirits to see whether they are of God; for many false prophets have gone out into the world. By this you know the Spirit of God: every spirit which confesses that Jesus Christ has come in the flesh is of God, and every spirit which does not confess Jesus is not of God. This is the spirit of antichrist (4:1–3).

Possibly Hymenaeus and Philetus, who threw their congregation into turmoil by declaring that the resurrection had already taken place (*II Tim.* 2:17), were prophets of this kind.

Our examples so far have all come from *Acts*, the Epistles, and *Revelation*; but concern about false prophets is also expressed in the Gospels. Thus, in the Sermon on the Mount Jesus warns his disciples:

> Beware of false prophets, who come to you in sheep's clothing, but inwardly are ravenous wolves (*Matt.* 7:15).

A reference to misleading revelations about the return of Jesus and the end of the world is to be found in a chapter often called the 'Little

M

Apocalypse' (*Mk* 13 = *Matt*. 24 = *Lk*. 21), in which Jesus is presented as foretelling the future to his disciples before his death:

> And then if any one says to you, 'Look, here is the Christ!' or 'Look, there he is!' do not believe it. False Christs and false prophets will arise and show signs and wonders,[1] to lead astray, if possible, the elect. But take heed; I have told you all things beforehand (*Mk*. 13:21–23; cf. *Matt*. 24:11, 23–26).

The question therefore inevitably arises: is some of the material attributed to Jesus in the Gospels the work of Christian prophets, inspired like the writer of *Revelation* by the spirit of Jesus, and speaking in his name? It may well be that the Little Apocalypse itself falls into this category. There are other sayings of Jesus in which he apparently rejects the idea that the coming of the end of the world can be inferred from signs and portents:

> Being asked by the Pharisees when the kingdom of God was coming, he answered them, 'The kingdom of God is not coming with signs to be observed; nor will they say, "Lo, here it is!" or "There!" for behold, the kingdom of God is in the midst of you' (*Lk*. 17:20–21; cf. also vv. 22–37).

Moreover, the central theme of his preaching was that the kingdom of God had already broken in upon men, that the time was short and decision urgent. The exhortations to his disciples to be vigilant and prepared at any moment (*Mk* 13:34–37; *Matt*. 25:13; *Lk*. 12:37–39) make the same point. There is obviously a discrepancy here, and it is reflected within the Little Apocalypse itself (cf., e.g., *Mk* 13:32–37). It may therefore be that the tradition behind this chapter, which has been differently edited by each of the first three Evangelists, originated with a Christian prophet who (possibly in opposition to false prophets) tried to provide an official and orthodox prediction of the End, combining known words of Jesus with popular Jewish apocalyptic ideas.

The importance of the question is obvious. Are we at the mercy of these prophets? For the more truly such a man was governed by the 'spirit of Jesus', the harder it would be to distinguish his contribution from the authentic words of Jesus himself. To ask the question, how-

---

[1] This phrase suggests that some of these prophets may have come from the class of popular wonder-workers. Note the implication of the closing words of the passage: Jesus is the true prophet *par excellence*, and other true prophets speak by his spirit and in his name.

ever, is to have already a fair idea of the answer. For one thing we must not forget that there *is*, as we saw, a tradition of the actual words of the Lord, and it is this tradition which forms the mind of the Early Church. If, as *I John* urges, the pronouncements of the prophets are to be 'tested' (4:1), this can only be by checking them against what is known about Jesus in his human life. For another, if we are concerned to create a portrait and not a biographical record, then a prophetic saying which is so true to the human Jesus as to pass convincingly for authentic will distort our result hardly at all. Finally, so far as the N.T. evidence indicates, the revelations of the prophets, when not concerned with personal and congregational matters, seem to have concentrated on utterances of the Risen Jesus,[1] and disclosures about his divine status and nature – precisely those matters, that is, which the material of his earthly life did *not* supply. To this extent, therefore, the possibility of their influence would help rather than hinder us, since the kind of passage we might feel most inclined to attribute to them is exactly that which, as we argued in the previous chapter, creates the most awkward problems for our investigation into his historical likeness.

Lastly, we can detect some of the peculiarities of the Evangelists themselves as creative writers. Sometimes these have large-scale effects on the arrangement of the Gospels. Matthew, for instance, presents Jesus as a Second Moses, giving a new Law to Israel from the mountaintop,[2] and in carrying through this theme arranges Jesus' teaching in five main blocks to match the five books of the Law (*Genesis* to *Deuteronomy*). Since his grouping of the various pieces of teaching is not paralleled in any of the other Gospels, and since we can detect a symbolic reason behind it, working itself out not just in one small tradition-unit but throughout a lengthy literary work, the conclusion that this is indeed part of the Evangelist's own creative presentation is probably correct. The Moses theme may also be responsible for numerous minor details and emphases – such as the massacre of the

---

[1] One is tempted to speculate whether this kind of prophecy may not lie behind the form at least of the speeches of Jesus in the Fourth Gospel, especially those which include the famous 'I am' sayings.

[2] The Sermon on the Mount (*Matt.* 5:1) with which we are so familiar is, in *Luke*, the 'sermon on the plain' (*Lk.* 6:17). Since the latter setting in its turn may be a symbolic allusion to O.T. precedent, it is obviously impossible to decide which (if either) is correct.

Innocents (*Matt.* 2:16) and the flight of Jesus and his parents into
Egypt (2:13–15) to escape the wrath of Herod, followed by their
eventual return to Palestine (2:19–23), which are intended to remind
the reader of Pharaoh's slaughter of all the Israelite male children
(*Exod.* 1:15–22), and Moses's survival, only to flee later from
Pharaoh's anger (*Exod.* 2:15), and then return years afterwards to save
his people from oppression. Nevertheless, it is significant that the
details of the two stories do not correspond; the resemblance is in the
broadest terms only. Moreover, Matthew himself seems more interested
in pointing out how these incidents in the life of Jesus fulfil various
prophecies from quite different parts of the Old Testament, *Hosea*
(*Matt.* 2:15) and *Jeremiah* (*Matt.* 2:18). This suggests that perhaps the
stories, together with their echoes of the Moses drama, were already
fixed in this form by the time Matthew came to work on them; and if so,
then the whole Moses symbolism was probably already in the tradition,
and he was simply being obedient to the tradition in developing it on
the grand scale. We see, therefore, that while awareness of motifs of
this kind makes it impossible to be certain about the historical value of
any given details, even so systematic a treatment cannot wholly conceal the awkward shape of the hard facts with which it has had to
produce its effects. Other examples of the same kind of systematic
symbolism include Luke's reshaping of the post-resurrection stories to
make Jerusalem the scene of Jesus' ascension into heaven and the
birthplace of the Christian Church, and, of course, John's thoroughgoing attempt to make explicit in the narrative all the truths which, as
he sees it, were present but hidden at the time.

The matter just mentioned of the awkward shape of the hard facts,
which do not really fit the symbolic structure into which the Evangelist
wishes to build them, brings us at last face to face with the supremely
important truth which this perusal of critical methods and criteria will
already have made clear, and which gives us our real basis of confidence
for the task of recovering the portrait of Jesus. It is a truth so simple
and obvious, so irreducible and inescapable, that it is really ludicrous
that it should so often be ignored; and it is this. It was Jesus with whom
it all began. If we ask why Christianity turned out as it has done, or
why the New Testament writers developed their particular religious
ideas and not some quite different ones, or why their own notions and
inclinations are often quite clearly struggling with some very refractory
material, then the answer is: Jesus. Because he was the man he was,

because he said the things he said and did the things he did, the whole story was pointed in a particular direction and endowed with certain specific potentials. The books of the New Testament are like the pieces of a puzzle; when we have put them all together, however, they do not fill the whole space provided; at the centre a piece is missing which locks in to every single one of the other pieces ranged around the outside, and, because it will lock into them only in one particular way, determines their position. The missing piece is Jesus as he was in his historical reality. But though we do not have the piece, we do have the gap which it has left; and the shape of that gap gives us our exciting certainty that we can know him, in all essential points and qualities, for the man he really was.[1]

[1] This illustration, like all illustrations, is too simple. One ought to say, at the very least, that some of the outside pieces are damaged or defective, and some of them missing altogether (after all, the New Testament is only a selection of early Christian writing). But the principle involved is, it is hoped, clear enough

9

The Recovery of Jesus:
(11) The Portrait

JESUS, THEN, lived; and he died, died by public execution. It is true that many innocent men and women have suffered the same fate, swept up in a purge, or taken as hostages, or simply by a tragic case of mistaken identity, judicial error, or corruption. But it is not claimed for Jesus that his innocence was of that kind. Both his enemies and his friends agree that he brought his death upon himself. His life, therefore, must have been, at least towards its end, one of conflict and confrontation with those who had the power to secure his death by judicial means. Whether what they did was just or unjust is at the moment irrelevant. He did or said something which they considered either dangerous enough or criminal enough to warrant his removal.

The only authorities whom he could have offended were either the native leaders of the Palestinian Jews or the Roman occupying power. If we accept that he was crucified, then the sentence was carried out by the Romans, because this was a Roman, not a Jewish method of execution. And the reasons for accepting that he was crucified are overwhelming. Crucifixion was a disgraceful fate, meted out to rebels, brigands, pirates, slaves, and suchlike. Freeborn Roman citizens were not executed in this way, nor was it thinkable that any good and respectable man would come to such an end. Yet when they came to preach their message to the pagan world, the early Christians insisted on this fact, shouted it aloud with exultation in the face of every prejudice:

> We preach Christ crucified, a stumbling block to Jews and folly to Gentiles (*I Cor.* 1:23).

It was the Romans, it would seem, who executed him. But was it the

Romans whom he had antagonized? The Gospels say no. They are unanimous that it was his own countrymen who got rid of him by denouncing him to the Romans on a charge that would ensure this penalty, namely sedition. This is explicitly stated only in *John* (19:12-16), though it would seem to be implicit in *Mark*, for example, in the way that the trial before Pilate is made to turn on the repeated phrase, 'the King of the Jews' (*Mk* 15:2, 12, 18, 26, 32). The tradition that Pilate was reluctant to pass sentence has been played up, notably by Luke, who likes to take every opportunity of stressing that both Christ and his followers are exemplary citizens, but also by Matthew in order to underline the guilt of the Jews for the murder of the Son of God (*Matt.* 27:23-25). It may, however, rest on an actual vagueness in the accusation or insufficiency of convincing evidence; and this would be understandable, if the real bone of contention was a religious quarrel between Jesus and the heads of Judaism.

Seen from this angle, an explanation suggests itself for a small historical puzzle that has provoked some argument. In the Fourth Gospel there is the following exchange between Pilate and the Jews:

> Pilate said to them, 'Take him yourselves, and judge him by your own law.' The Jews said to him, 'It is not lawful for us to put any man to death' (*John* 18:31).

There has been a good deal of discussion whether the Jewish reply is historically correct. Did the Jewish authorities have the power to inflict the death penalty? Later they did not; but there is some evidence that in the time of Jesus they may have done so. It does not really matter, for one simple reason. Nothing would have been easier than for the rulers to have Jesus dragged outside the city and stoned to death by the same mob whom they paraded before Pilate; the Romans would have neither intervened nor taken proceedings, any more than they did in the case of Stephen (*Acts* 7:54-60). If we ask why they did not do so, but involved themselves in the complicated rigmarole with the procurator, the answer must be that they particularly wanted Jesus to die in the way he did; and for that their most probable motive is to be found in the declaration of the Jewish Law, that every one who is hanged (a term taken at this period to include crucifixion) is accursed of God (*Deut.* 21:23). They wanted to make it clear to everyone for all time that this man's teaching and pretensions were utterly rejected by God.

The passage in the Fourth Gospel is thus probably an attempt to explain their devious process in the light of the legal position after the fall of Jerusalem in A.D. 70, and to show how this difficulty contributed to fulfil Jesus' own purposes. Its interest is that it shows the query to have been raised. That the true motives of the Jewish leaders were the ones suggested is given some support by the fact that Paul has to wrestle with the problem of the curse in *Deuteronomy*, and indeed uses it to mount a positive counter-interpretation of his own (*Gal.* 3:13–14). Moreover, it is likely that to a considerable extent their policy was successful. Stoning was compatible with innocence (*II Chron.* 24:20–21), and might therefore have laid the foundation for a cult of Jesus as a martyr; crucifixion could, it would seem, carry no such peril. The large proportion of Palestinian Jewry who remained impervious to the preaching of the Gospel may possibly testify to the correctness of this calculation.

A theory which crops up from time to time in modern discussion of Jesus holds that his aims were in fact political. He saw himself as the Messiah, he gathered nationalistic enthusiasts around him, and aimed to oust the current national leaders and free his country from the Romans. All this was combined with an eschatological expectation: the liberation of Jewry would usher in the Last Day when, as promised in the Old Testament Scriptures, God's elect would reign in glory. The charge against him was, therefore, in substance true, and was brought by the chief priests and scribes either to protect their own ruling status or to save Judaism from the disastrous consequences of such a rebellion. That such an interpretation was in fact put forward in the first century by Jewish apologists may perhaps be inferred from *John* 11:47–53, and the decided rebuttal of its implications in the account of the trial before Pilate. The former passage purports to tell of the debate in council when the chief priests and the Pharisees were wondering what could be done to check Jesus' growing influence:

> So the chief priests and the Pharisees gathered the council, and said, 'What are we to do? For this man performs many signs. If we let him go on thus, every one will believe in him, and the Romans will come and destroy both our holy place and our nation.' But one of them, Caiaphas, who was high priest that year, said to them, 'You know nothing at all; you do not understand that it is expedient for you that one man should die for the people, and that the whole nation should not perish' (*John* 11:47–50).

On arraignment before Pilate Jesus expressly counters this suggestion:

> Pilate entered the praetorium again and called Jesus, and said to him,
> 'Are you the King of the Jews?' Jesus answered, 'Do you say this of
> your own accord, or did others say it to you about me?' Pilate answered,
> 'Am I a Jew? Your own nation and the chief priests have handed you
> over to me; what have you done?' Jesus answered, 'My kingship is not
> of this world; if my kingship were of this world, my servants would
> fight, that I might not be handed over to the Jews; but my kingship is
> not from the world.' Pilate said to him, 'So you are a king?' Jesus
> answered, 'You say that I am a king. For this I was born, and for this I
> have come into the world, to bear witness to the truth.' (*John* 19:33–37).

This latter incident is unlikely to be historical, since the other Gospels
maintain steadfastly that Jesus made no attempt to defend himself to
Pilate (*Mk* 15:1–5; *Matt.* 27:11–14; *Lk.* 23:1–4, 9; cf. *I Pet.* 2:21–23).
It is much more likely to be the Evangelist's refutation in drama form
of a contemporary anti-Christian version of the facts.[1] But it does
suggest that the 'revolutionary' theory of Jesus is nothing new.

Any candid historian will admit that, where evidence is as dis-
connected as it is in this matter, and where many vital data will never be
known, any reconstruction is bound to contain a good deal of conjecture, and many detailed points have to be decided simply by personal
judgement. This is especially necessary when dealing with pieces of
information which could find a place in several widely differing syn-
theses, and would take on a different colour in each of them. The one
fatal, if seductive approach is to argue like this: '*p* is a possible and
interesting interpretation of datum A; let us assume it to be correct. If
it is correct, then *q* could well be the right explanation of datum B; and
if *q* for B, then *r* for C; and if *r* for C, then *s* for D, and so on.' The
trouble is that one has only to make a slight error in the initial choice of
interpretation *p*, and the whole structure becomes pure fantasy. While
it is true that human character and human affairs never run with complete consistency, yet on the whole it is safer to explain minor incidents
in the light of more broadly established features. The relevance of this
to our immediate problem will soon become clear.

Quite a number of small points in the story of Jesus lend themselves
to a revolutionary interpretation. Galilee, his native district, was a

---

[1] In a recent study by J. L. Martyn, *History and Theology in the Fourth Gospel*,
the author traces many instances of the influence of controversy between church
and synagogue on the Evangelist's presentation of his material.

centre of unrest. He had among his closest disciples a man called Simon who, in the Lukan version, is referred to as 'the Zealot' (*Lk.* 6:15), and 'Zealots' was the name given to the militant supporters of national independence among the Jews at this time. It has been suggested that the name 'Iscariot' is a corruption of *sicarius*, the term used for the assassins who made it their business to kill Romans and collaborators. It is said in *John* that after the feeding of the five thousand the people wanted to take Jesus and make him king by force (*John* 6:15). Above all, Jesus' visit to Jerusalem at Passover time, which ended in his death, is marked by puzzling and perhaps sinister details. The entry in triumph on Palm Sunday, which Matthew sees as fulfilling an old prophecy of the king's coming to Zion (*Matt.* 21:4–5; cf. *Zech.* 9:9), was accompanied by scenes of dangerous popular enthusiasm. Moreover, there seems to have been some prior arrangement for the ass used in the entry to be available (*Matt.* 21:1–3; *Mk* 11:1–3; *Lk.* 19:29–34); and similar carefully laid plans for the room used at the Last Supper (*Matt.* 26:17–18; *Mk* 14:12–16; *Lk.* 22:7–13). Could it not be, for example, that the message which, according to Matthew, Jesus sent in the latter instance: The Master saith, My time is at hand (*Matt.* 26:18), implied that the moment for the *coup d'état* had arrived? – a plot which was frustrated only by the treachery of Judas?

No doubt it could. But every one of these pieces of 'evidence' is suceptible of quite different interpretations. Simon could just as easily have been a nationalist Zealot who found in the personality and teaching of Jesus a more worthy cause for his enthusiasm. Iscariot is a name for which other derivations are equally plausible; and even if this one is correct, we still have to reckon with the possibility that he was for a time attracted to Jesus' different methods, and then abandoned him in disgust. If the people did try to make Jesus king, then it is clear that he did not allow them to do so. The entry on an ass, if it had royal symbolism (as it may well have done), nevertheless represents a coming in peace not in war or to conquer. The arrangements for the upper room can just as well have been a precaution to ensure that Jesus had time for a last meeting with his followers before the arrest and execution which he saw to be inevitable. If we are to judge between these interpretations, it must be done on the basis of our general assessment of Jesus and his purposes.

It can be said, of course, that to accept the second set of interpretations rather than the first is to succumb to the Gospel picture, and that this picture is false. It is the little details which give the truth away. Our judgement on this point will be controlled to a great extent by our attitude to the resurrection story. The complex problems attaching to these narratives will have to be discussed in the next chapter; but they will not hinder us from a decision on this matter now. For whatever view we take of the historical question, namely, what, if anything, happened at the first Easter, the result is an overwhelming argument against the revolutionary picture of Jesus. Let the actuality behind the narratives be that of unique phenomena interpreted as convincing evidence that Jesus was alive, or that of hallucinations induced by grief and intolerable disappointment, or that of a brief and macabre resuscitation of someone who had never really died, or that of total fabrication without any experience, objective or subjective to support it. It makes no difference. On any of these hypotheses the effect – and therefore, where a plot was involved, the intention – was to vindicate Jesus and his cause, to show that he had been not defeated but glorified, and that that glory would soon be manifest to the whole world. In such a conviction, whether honest or simulated, one would expect his followers to continue his work as they understood it. In that case a political revolutionary Jesus ought to have left behind a group of militants even more fanatically confident of eventual success. What we find, however, is the exact opposite. Instead of activist freedom fighters, we discover men and women dedicated to non-violence and inculcating obedience to the civil authorities, whether Jewish or pagan; instead of Jewish nationalists, a readiness to break down racial barriers as never before. On any plausible historical assessment of the events connecting them there ought to be some affinity between the ethos of Jesus and that of the early Church, not complete reversal. It is in the light of what is known of the first Christians that the revolutionary portrait of Jesus can be seen to suffer from a basic incoherence which no amount of argument about details can disguise.

It may be concluded, therefore, that the charge against Jesus before Pilate was not a true bill. Whether it was made under a sincere misapprehension, or was to a greater or lesser extent perjured, we can hardly hope to decide; but either way, it is clear that there was much more to the quarrel between Jesus and the Jewish leaders than this one topic. Thus, when we find that the Gospels present them as at variance on a number of points from an early stage – Mark even asserts that the Pharisees plotted his death from the very first days (*Mk* 3:6) – there is nothing *prima facie* suspect in such a picture. It could, of course, be a distorted version of the facts, inspired by the hostility between church and synagogue which grew up so rapidly in the first decades of Christianity. One way of trying to resolve this doubt is to ask whether anything in Jesus' teaching and behaviour would have been likely to create such violent enmity. Here it will not be sufficient to point to passages in which Jesus denounces the Pharisees and others, since these themselves may have been heightened by the Evangelists in the atmosphere of later bitterness. We need to look at some of the main positions which Jesus upheld, in order to see whether they were indeed such as to arouse anger and condemnation in orthodox Jews.

There is no reason to question that one of the most prominent themes in Jesus' preaching was that of the kingdom or sovereignty of God.[1] The phrase occurs thirteen times in Mark's record of his words, and far more often in *Matthew* and *Luke*. This kingdom is at once something active, which draws near to Man and impinges on his life here and now and specifically in the activity of Jesus, and also a goal which men seek, an order into which they strive to enter. It is said that John the Baptist also proclaimed the imminence of the Kingdom (*Matt.* 3:2); and as the fact of God's ultimate sovereignty over all creation it was a concept familiar to the Judaism of the time. Jesus, however, saw the implementation of this sovereignty with eyes rather different from those of his contemporaries.

First, he seems to have rejected the idea that God showed his sovereignty by intervening in the details of life to reward or protect the good and to punish the wicked. It was a feature of his picture of God that 'your Father who is in heaven . . . makes his sun to rise on the evil and on the good, and sends rain on the just and on the unjust' (*Matt.* 5:45). He rejects the idea that the victims of tyranny or of natural disaster were by their fate shown to be worse sinners than other men (*Lk.* 13:1–5). He clearly regarded the poor, the bereaved, the hungry, and the persecuted as God's special favourites (*Lk.* 6:20–22).[2] In taking up these positions he was to some extent expressing his own

[1] Or 'of heaven', following Jesus' distinctive custom of substituting conventional alternatives or circumlocutions for the actual word 'God'.

[2] On the particular reasons for thinking the latter passage authentic cf. p. 166 above. That similar formulations have been found in the Dead Sea Scrolls, referring in that instance to the members of the Qumran community, does not affect the question.

mind, to some extent voicing attitudes found in sectarian Judaism, but he had little or nothing in common with the official and orthodox assumptions of his time.

Secondly, he put forward a radically different doctrine of God's forgiveness. He repeatedly taught that only one condition was necessary to obtain forgiveness from God, and that was a readiness to forgive other people. This principle is set out in the Lord's Prayer,[1] and in many other passages (*Matt.* 6:14–15; 18:35; *Mk* 11:25–26; *Lk.* 17:3–4). The views of Judaism on this subject were both more complicated and more restrictive. Forgiveness could be secured by expiatory sacrifice, or by good works undertaken as a kind of penance to cancel out the guilt which had been incurred.[2] At the Last Judgment God would forgive the unexpiated sins of those who on balance had lived a good life, keeping the divine commandments. Moreover, when God did forgive a man's sins here and now, this fact would be confirmed by manifest signs of his blessing.

This last point is the key to a story found in all the first three Gospels – the healing of the paralytic whose friends let him down through the roof of the house where Jesus was teaching, because they could not make a way through the crowd (*Mk* 2:1–12; *Matt.* 9:2–8; *Lk.* 5:18–26). Jesus' first words to the paralytic are: 'My son, your sins are forgiven.' When the scribes sitting in the audience take exception to this, Jesus goes on:

> Why do you question thus in your hearts? Which is easier, to say to the paralytic, 'Your sins are forgiven,' or to say, 'Rise, take up your pallet and walk'? But that you may know that the Son of man has authority on earth to forgive sins (he said to the paralytic) I say to you, rise, take up your pallet, and go home.' And he rose, and immediately took up the pallet, and went out before them all (*Mk* 2:8–11).

The point here is not just that anyone can say, 'Your sins are forgiven,'

---

[1] It has recently been argued that this prayer was not composed as a set piece by Jesus himself, but is a compilation by the Church from his teaching. The present argument is not affected either way, but the suggestion seems on balance improbable, and to be based on a misunderstanding of the purpose of the Prayer. It is not a fixed formula for individual or liturgical use, but a guide to the kind of praying men should do: 'Do not heap up empty phrases ... pray like this ...' (*Matt.* 6:7, 9).

[2] Expiation or atonement sacrifices in the Old Testament are themselves to be understood as in part acts of penance: cf. pp. 301f. below.

and that, since there is no means of verifying that this has really happened, therefore something difficult, a healing miracle, is added to provide visible proof that Jesus' words are indeed effective. There is an organic relationship between the two. The cure of the paralysis is the divine blessing which proves that God has in fact pardoned the man's sins.

This, however, brings us to the true stumbling-block which was scandalizing the devout Jews. Jesus claims to cure the man by God's authority delegated to him. Since the scribes' objection to his declaring the forgiveness of sins was that no one can forgive sins but God alone (*Mk* 2:7), and since the miracle is Jesus' answer to that objection, it is clear that he is also claiming divine authority in the matter of forgiveness as well. Indeed, any pretension to be empowered to forgive sins must be a claim to divine authority. As we saw in an earlier chapter, a man can properly forgive only those sins which are committed against himself, or sins in general insofar as they affect him. God may be said to have a right to forgive all sins, because in addition to their being an offence against particular people they must all affect him as the one who has created life for the attainment of the good and not for misuse. Whoever the specific victims may be, he always suffers. Jesus had not personally suffered from the paralytic's sins, yet he takes it upon himself to announce that they have been pardoned. This he can do only on the assumption that he is the appointed mouthpiece or agent of God, with a commission to absolve which is either general or particular to certain cases. And he proceeds to verify this assumption by giving proof of God's favour towards the cripple.

At the natural level we may see an explanation of the actual healing in the possibility that the paralysis was a psychosomatic one, induced by some extraordinary guilt feelings deeply repressed. The authoritative forgiveness then produces a corresponding physical release, for forgiveness was what the man really needed. This makes no difference whatever to the point at issue. That Jesus did claim this authority to release men and women from their sins in God's name is confirmed not only by the passages already quoted, but also by the fact that the early Church believed that this authority had been passed on to them (*Matt.* 16:19; 18:18; *John* 20:23); and this belief has characterized Catholic and Orthodox Christianity ever since. More striking still, however, is the consideration that such a claim could not but be repugnant to Judaism. If we are looking for ways in which Jesus may have deeply antagonized his fellow-Jews on matters of profound principle, then here is an obvious candidate. The hostility of which the records speak and the pretensions attributed to Jesus match and confirm one another; and, what is more, precisely because the views of Judaism on this subject were so clear and so strong, the chances that the first Christians themselves invented this feature are small.

A counterpart in practice of Jesus' general doctrine of forgiveness is to be found in his association with the outcasts of society. The note sounded early in *Mark* by the Pharisees' question to his followers:

Why does he eat with tax-collectors and sinners? (*Mk* 2:16)[1]

recurs (*Lk*. 15:1). The tax-collectors have even supplied the 'hero' of one of the most famous passages in the Gospels, 'the Pharisee and the Publican' (*Lk*. 18:9–14). This story is one which could almost have been written by a conventional Jew (or by a conventional early Christian) – almost, but not quite. In a Jewish version or in one, let us say, by the Evangelists themselves (cf., for possible material, *Matt*. 23 or *Lk*. 11: 37–41) the Pharisee's unacknowledged faults would have had to be made explicit in order to show why the tax-collector was the better man. The greater penetration of the present version suggests that here we have a good tradition going back to Jesus himself. It is true that faults on the part of the Pharisee are implied; but then the tax-collector will have had serious faults too. The crucial difference does not lie here at all, but in the attitude of mind. The Pharisee cannot even cast a mental glance around to see whether he has any faults; he is lost in admiration of his own rectitude, while the Publican can only beat his breast and say, 'God be merciful to me, a sinner!' This, and this alone, is why the latter is accounted righteous by God (*Lk*. 18:14a).[2]

To be *accounted* righteous, however, is not the same thing as to *be*

---

[1] As is well known, the tax-collector was ostracized as a 'collaborator', a renegade agent of the occupying power. Moreover, under the Roman system of tax-farming the collector guaranteed a certain sum to the authorities out of his own pocket, and then had to recoup this by his exactions from the people. The unscrupulous had ample scope for rich profits (hence Zacchaeus's words to Jesus, *Lk* 19:8). Accordingly the right to collect taxes was itself sold to the highest bidder, which in turn increased the rapacity of those successful. It is hardly surprising that Jesus' conduct should be criticized by some, and should strike even his friends as remarkable.

[2] The tag about humbling and exalting oneself (v. 14b), which is found in other contexts also, may here have been added by the Evangelist.

righteous. It is noteworthy that Jesus never expresses the sentimental view that the tax-collectors, prostitutes, and other undesirables with whom he associated were 'good at heart', or 'not such bad sorts after all'. When he flays the devout with the warning:

> The tax-collectors and harlots go into the kingdom of God before you
> (*Matt.* 21:31),

he means to shame them. It is because the woman who weeps over him *is* a sinner that his respectable host ought to be all the more conscience-stricken over his lack of proper courtesy (*Lk.* 7:36–50).[1] The reference to the interest shown by the same class of people in John the Baptist (*Matt.* 21:32) uses the same technique of censure by contrast. This link with John the Baptist is illuminating in another way. John, like Jesus, turned no one away from God's forgiveness, provided that they were penitent; and he too demanded reform of life. The difference between him and Jesus lies simply in the fact that Jesus did not scruple to be friends with such people in the context of ordinary daily living; and this is an attitude so distinct from that of everyone around him – scribes, Pharisees, John, the common people – that it must have a basis in fact.

The same two elements – the 'tax-collectors and sinners' and John the Baptist – reappear in a delightful passage deriving from the non-Markan source common to *Matthew* and *Luke*, in which a wry allusion is made to Jesus' non-ascetic manner of life:

> But to what shall I compare this generation? It is like children sitting in
> the market places and calling to their playmates,
>> 'We piped to you, and you did not dance;
>> we wailed, and you did not mourn.'
>
> For John came neither eating nor drinking, and they say, 'He has a
> demon'; the Son of man came eating and drinking, and they say, 'Behold,
> a glutton and a drunkard, a friend of tax-collectors and sinners!' Yet
> wisdom is justified by her deeds (*Matt.* 11:16–19; *Lk.* 7:31–35).

Ascetic practices as a rule of life came late to Judaism. Fasting, sackcloth and ashes, abstention from wine and sexual intercourse, are all to be found in Old Testament times, but only for use on special occasions or for limited periods, and for particular reasons – public or private

---

[1] Note how Luke has intuitively coupled this incident with the quarrel over the forgiveness of sins (vv. 48–50).

days of mourning and repentance, vows, and so on.[1] Later, fasting as a regular devotional discipline became a mark of certain groups (cf. *Lk.* 18: 12, 'I fast twice a week'); and some Rabbis carried mortification to extremes. Neither John the Baptist nor Jesus, however, fit easily into any of these categories. John is an example of the desert hermit (*Lk.* 1:80),[2] whose manner of life is devoid of every pleasure and comfort which the average person enjoys. Jesus moves in ordinary society, but is celibate and has no home of his own (*Lk.* 9:58). His life is hard and exhausting to a degree (*Mk* 3:20, Jesus and his disciples cannot find time even for a meal; cf. also *John* 4:6–8); but this is due to the demands of his mission, not to any voluntary disciplines undertaken for self-improvement. Nothing could be more absurd, therefore, than to see in the passage we are considering evidence that Jesus was a *bon vivant*. The humorous exasperation with which he rebukes the detractors is aimed at the narrow conventionalism which will allow only one strictly defined way of life to be appropriate to the good and pious man, and which, because it never stops to think that different vocations may call for different patterns of conduct, condemns people for utterly superficial reasons. The incident may well have been seen in the early Church as relevant to the variety of rules among Christians. James, the Lord's brother, head of the Jerusalem church, is traditionally reported to have been an ascetic; and very severe ideals of life were put forward in some Syrian churches. Equally, however, a more relaxed tone is discernible in Pauline congregations, and in stories of Peter and others. But though the Christian situation may have been the reason for preserving the story, just as it has made Jesus refer to himself as 'the Son of Man' (*Matt.* 11:19; *Lk.* 7:34), the nuances and the delightful comparison taken from the games of children in the streets have the distinctive ring of Jesus' own words, and make it another reliable glimpse of him as he was.

We must return to the question of Jesus' authority as the agent of God's coming kingdom. His claim to forgive sins is but one example of a general attitude detectable in the narratives. Another is his approach

---

[1] In a late historical romance in the Apocrypha the heroine Judith, who is in no way 'professionally' involved in religion but simply a pious and wealthy widow, fasts and wears sackcloth next to the skin for more than three years after the death of her husband (*Judith* 8:5–6).

[2] It has been suggested, not implausibly, that he may have been trained in his youth by the community of the Dead Sea Scrolls.

N

to the question of sabbath observance. Judaism developed a most elaborate code of regulations relating to the sabbath, following her practice of putting 'fences round the Law'. The basic principle here is that the best way to ensure that scriptural commandments are not broken is to allow a margin for error. How, for example, is the command to do 'no manner of work' on the sabbath to be obeyed? What constitutes 'work'? Some things have to be done, unless one is to remain in complete immobility for twenty-four hours. By establishing a maximum of permitted activity, both in quantity and in kind, which is well below the amount that might still be within the spirit of the Law laid down by God, one can make doubly sure that no offence is committed. Thus, harvesting is work; but what constitutes harvesting? Jesus' disciples, walking through a cornfield on the sabbath, pluck some ears of corn, husk them, and eat them – is not this an offence (*Mk* 2:23–24; *Matt.* 12:1–2)?[1] There was also a strict limit on travel, about two miles (cf. *Acts* 1:12, Olivet is a 'sabbath day's journey' from Jerusalem), and even such journeys should be undertaken only if strictly necessary. When sick people come on the sabbath to the synagogue where Jesus is, in order to be healed by him, their journey is not strictly necessary because they could equally well have visited Jesus for that purpose on some other day (*Lk.* 13:14). The narratives are unanimous in their picture of Jesus' indignant impatience with this kind of pettifogging. If David's men could appease their hunger by eating the holy bread set out in the sanctuary (*Mk* 2:25–26, cf. *I Sam.* 21:1–6), could not Jesus' followers pick a few grains of corn in the open field? Which was the greater invasion of the rights of a holy God? If the rules allowed one for humanity's sake to untie an animal and to lead it out to feed and water it on the sabbath, why was it wrong to do the even more humane act of healing the sick, and for the sick themselves to make a journey for that purpose?

But is there a hint of more to the matter than just moral priorities?[2] It seems at times to be Jesus' very act of healing on the sabbath which is the chief offence, not such incidentals as unnecessary travelling. A

[1] Luke's version implies a further breach of regulations in the act of husking the corn; they were 'rubbing them in their hands' (*Lk.* 6:1). Such preparatory work for sabbath meals should have been done the day before.

[2] Cf. *Matt.* 23:23: 'Woe to you, scribes and Pharisees, hypocrites! for you tithe mint and dill and cummin, and have neglected the weightier matters of the law, justice and mercy and faith; these you ought to have done, without neglecting the others.'

story in *Mark*, which has been incorporated by Matthew and Luke, raises the question:

> Again he entered the synagogue, and a man was there who had a withered hand. And they watched him, to see whether he would heal him on the sabbath, so that they might accuse him.[1] And he said to the man who had the withered hand, 'Come here.' And he said to them, 'Is it lawful on the sabbath to do good or to do harm, to save life or to kill?' But they were silent. And he looked around at them with anger, grieved at their hardness of heart, and said to the man, 'Stretch out your hand.' He stretched it out, and his hand was restored. The Pharisees went out, and immediately held counsel with the Herodians against him, how to destroy him (*Mk* 3:1–6; cf. *Matt.* 12:9–14; *Lk.* 6:6–11).

There were indeed rules about how much medical assistance might be given to the sick or in an emergency on the sabbath; but is this the point? Is a miracle 'work' anyway?

The answer, phrased somewhat flippantly, is that it may not be work for Man, but it certainly is for God. Although, it is true, the Evangelists sometimes express the view that the healings were effected by a power in Jesus himself,[2] the relevant recorded words of Jesus himself offer no such explanation. In his view the power resides in God.[3] In *Mk* 3:22–30 he scornfully exposes the weak argument of those who attribute his cures to the Devil, and claims that the Holy Spirit, that is, the spirit of God, is responsible (cf. *Lk.* 11:20). If, however, this was his conviction,

---

[1] In *Matthew* the trouble-makers provoke the collision by asking Jesus, 'Is it lawful to heal on the sabbath?' (*Matt.* 12:10).

[2] *Lk.* 6:19 comments that 'power came forth from him', and healed all the crowd who managed to touch him. (In *Acts* the apostles radiate power even more dramatically: Peter's shadow – 5:15 – or handkerchiefs that Paul had touched – 19:12 – cure all kinds of afflictions.) In *Mark* the Evangelist explains Jesus' awareness in a milling crowd that some sick person had touched him, with the comment, 'perceiving in himself that power had gone forth from him'. This presumably interpretative observation Luke changes into a statement by Jesus himself (8:46). If Luke was, as tradition has it, a doctor, then he may be putting his own convictions about spiritual healing into the mouth of Jesus.

[3] Jesus' statement to certain sufferers that their 'faith' has been responsible for the cure, it would be anachronistic to understand in modern 'mind over matter' terms. 'Faith' in this historical setting must be faith in something or someone, presumably either God or Jesus. If the latter, then, it does not help us with the question whether the healing power is thought of as God's mediated through Jesus or as belonging to Jesus in his own right. Cf. *Mk* 5:34; 10:52; *Matt.* 9:22; 15:28; *Lk.* 7:50; 8:48; 17:19; 18:42.

then clearly he thought it right to call on the help of God on the sabbath, even though God had not merely ordained a sabbath rest for men but had himself rested on the seventh day from all his work in creation (*Gen.* 2:2; cf. *Heb.* 4:10). Trained theologians, therefore, might be pardoned for suspecting that Jesus, by performing miracles on the sabbath, was pretending to dictate to God in direct opposition to God's own revealed intentions. (The argumentation seems strange to us, but it is entirely in the spirit of the times.) Such a man was a blasphemer, and obviously any apparent good he did was really the work of the powers of evil.

The Fourth Gospel makes this conclusion explicit:

> The man went away and told the Jews that it was Jesus who had healed him. And this was why the Jews persecuted Jesus, because he did this on the sabbath. But Jesus answered them, 'My Father is working still, and I am working.' This was why the Jews sought all the more to kill him, because he not only broke the sabbath but also called God his Father, making himself equal with God (*John* 5:15–18; cf. 10:32–33).

– and *John*, as we have already seen, is often good evidence for Jewish anti-Christian polemic. In view of the belief of the early Church about the identity of Jesus such stories would clearly be regarded as of signal significance; but it is notable that Jesus' own understanding of the matter, as recorded, does not demand a developed doctrinal interpretation. For him, healing was a work of divine mercy, and was in season at any time. To restrict it by appeal to regulations of human invention showed a totally perverted scale of values which no one who, like himself, was the appointed agent of God's kingship could adopt for one moment. In this essential standpoint we may take it that the Gospels faithfully reflect his historical attitude.

His freedom in respect of the minutiae of sabbath observance does not, however, seem to have extended into a disregard for the traditional forms of Jewish worship. Quite a number of stories are given a synagogue setting,[1] and there are general statements to the effect that Jesus regularly taught or preached in the synagogues.[2] This is, of

---

[1] Cf. *Mk* 1:21–28; 3:1–6 = *Matt.* 12:9–14 = *Lk.* 6:6–11; *Mk* 6:1–6 = *Matt* 13:53–58, cf. *Lk.* 4:16–30; *Lk.* 13:10–17; *John* 6:59.

[2] *Mk* 1:39, cf. *Matt.* 4:23 (Galilee); *Lk.* 4:44 (Judaea, according to some MSS), *John* 18:20, where Jesus claims his practice in this respect as proof that he has given no esoteric teaching. In *Lk.* 7:5 the Jewish elders at Capernaum solicit

course, good ammunition for Christian propaganda, as underlining the fact that the Jews, and especially their religious leaders, had every opportunity to hear Jesus, and even so rejected him. But it also indicates something else, which does not easily fit the overall impression of hostility on the part of these leaders which the Gospels seek to give. Jesus could not have spoken in a synagogue except at the invitation or with the permission of the synagogue president and his elders (*Lk.* 4:16–17; cf. *Acts* 13:15). If this feature of the narrative is accurate, it suggests that some responsible and religiously trained Jews were ready to give Jesus a hearing, even if they sometimes heard more than they bargained or cared for (*Lk.* 4:23–28). In the same vein there are stories of Pharisaic interest (if not courtesy, *Lk.* 7:36–50), and of scribal approval (*Mk* 12:28–34, though here the scribe finds disconcertingly that Jesus is the one who does the approving!). This mixture of reactions[1] seems historically the more plausible picture, and makes it virtually certain that Jesus did participate in the ordinary religious life of his fellows. Similarly we find references to his attendance at the Jerusalem Temple for the major festivals. Since the first Christians were so emphatic that all these old rites and occasions had now been superseded, Jesus' practice in this matter was of no teaching value to them; and so there are no pressures to distort the record. In fact it would be more true to say that there was pressure, but in the opposite direction, namely towards suppressing this detail; and the Fourth Evangelist, anxious to avoid misunderstandings, portrays Jesus as predicting the time soon to come when men will no longer worship either at the Temple or with its schismatic rivals (*John* 4:21–24).

One thing that cannot rationally be doubted is that Jesus did teach, anywhere and everywhere. What kind of a teacher was he? Can he, for example, be classified as a rabbi on the contemporary Jewish model?

Jesus' interest on behalf of the centurion whose servant is sick by mentioning that 'he built us our synagogue'. The early Christian missionaries frequently began their work in a town by a sermon in the synagogue (cf., e.g., *Acts* 13:14–16), which may have given rise to additional stress on this practice by Jesus himself; but it is hardly evidence that he avoided the synagogues, a step which would have been so pointed that it might well have prompted the Church to do the same.

[1] Note in this connection Nicodemus's visit to Jesus (*John* 3:1–2) and later attempt to defend him (*John* 7:50), and Joseph of Arimathea, said to be a member of the Sanhedrin, whose tomb received the body of Jesus (*Lk.* 23:50–53; cf. *Matt.* 27:57–61; *Mk* 15:43–46). In *John* Nicodemus also assists at the burial (*John* 19:39).

In this respect the language of the Gospels is interesting. Mark has three instances of Jesus' being addressed as 'Rabbi,' using the actual Aramaic word transliterated into Greek (*Mk* 9:5; 11:21; 14:45), and in each of them the speaker is one of Jesus' inner circle of disciples. Matthew follows the same principle.[1] Luke never uses the actual Aramaic preferring the Greek word for 'teacher'. This may simply be meant as a translation of 'Rabbi' for Gentile readers, not an avoidance of it on principle; but it is interesting that only one out of his six instances coincides with those of *Mark*. Again, all are in the mouths of Jesus' closest disciples. John uses it only slightly more often, and makes it a form of address from interested Jews as well (3:2; 6:25; 9:2). How far he is, however, from giving it a strict technical sense may be seen from the fact that he has John the Baptist's disciples using it to their own master – and anyone less like a conventional Rabbi than the Baptist it would be hard to find. So far as Jesus is concerned, it may safely be said that the only feature which he had in common with the true rabbi was a circle of personal disciples. There is no evidence that he had ever received the essential qualification of an academic religious training as the pupil of another rabbi; indeed, the Fourth Gospel flatly excludes such a thing (*John* 7:15).[2] The essence of the rabbinic calling was to develop and hand on the tradition that one had received, taking scrupulous care to name one's authorities; of this, Jesus' method is the exact opposite. When, therefore, we find the title accorded to him in the earliest sources only by his own equally unprofessional followers, it is hard to resist the impression that this is another accurate element. Amateur Galilean enthusiasts may have liked to think of him as 'Rabbi'; the authorized leaders of Judaism would never have dreamed of doing so. On the whole, it suited the early Church to leave it at that.

---

[1] *Matt.* 23:8 is striking in this connection. It is clearly an instruction to the Church that no Christian is to be given the title 'Rabbi', because it belongs uniquely to Jesus. This may be a rejection of developments among Palestinian Christians, who in the later years of the first century trained a kind of Christian rabbinate for expounding the scriptures.

[2] One point of the story in *Luke* about the boy Jesus at the age of twelve astonishing the learned doctors in the Jerusalem Temple with his knowledge and understanding of the scriptures (*Lk.* 2:46–47) may be to prove that he never needed such a training. The 'questions' which he is said to have put to the doctors (v. 46) are to be taken as hard problems, testing and even defeating the learned, not as requests for information.

If Jesus was not a rabbi, what then was he? One of the most unexpected, and therefore intriguing features of the Gospel portait is his considerable indebtedness to what is known as Israel's 'wisdom tradition'. This tradition runs back more than a thousand years before the time of Jesus, and contains a great variety of material – the philosophic pessimism of *Ecclesiastes*, the existential *Angst* of *Job*, the cultivated commonsense of *Ecclesiasticus*, the popular commonsense of *Proverbs*, Greek speculation in the *Wisdom of Solomon*, theories of cosmogony, and practical hints on commerce, agriculture, and table manners. There were specialists in wisdom all over the ancient Near East, and Israel had its exponents of the art. Their method was to combine, in whatever proportions the individual sage's talents might suggest to him, the collecting and polishing of the wisdom of earlier masters and the adding of their own, based on their personal observations of life and nature. They were by no means exclusively 'religious' in their approach – today we might be inclined to call them 'humanists' – but they undoubtedly left their mark on religious teaching, and the records of rabbinic Judaism contain ample evidence of this. In earlier centuries they supplied many of the civil officers of state; but by the time of Jesus they were private and academic, men of sufficient means to have the leisure for study. Not, it may be thought, very much like Jesus. But in three characteristics especially he was one of them: first, in the pith and point of a telling epigrammatic style; secondly, in a reliance on free, personal thinking, based on observation; and thirdly, in a fondness for illuminating comparisons drawn from life and nature.

The recorded words of Jesus testify to his use of the proverb type of utterance: 'If salt has lost its taste, how shall its saltness be restored?' (*Matt.* 5:13); 'Where the carcase is, there the vultures will be gathered together' (*Lk.* 17:37); 'Leave the dead to bury their dead' (*Matt.* 8:22). Furthermore, it seems that he had read some at least of the wisdom writings of the Old Testament. For example, his ironical advice to take a humble seat when invited to a feast, and so gain the respect of the other guests by being asked to move higher up the table (*Lk.* 14:7–10) derives from *Prov.* 25:6–7. His comment on the contradictory criticisms of John the Baptist and himself[1] – 'Wisdom is justified by *all* her children' (*Lk.* 7:35; but 'her deeds', *Matt.* 11:19) – may therefore be in substance authentic.

But it is in perhaps the best known feature of all his teaching, his use

[1] Cf. p. 192 above.

of parables, that his debt to and original creative use of the wisdom method is most apparent.

> With what can we compare the Kingdom of God, or what parable shall we use for it (*Mk.* 4:30)?

he asks. To convey the truth by some analogy from ordinary life was a staple technique of the wisdom schools. In the Old Testament the book of *Proverbs* provides abundant examples, many of them simply popular commonplaces, others striking, humorous, or beautiful. In general the comparison is not elaborated; one, or two verses at the most, is the standard; and great thought has clearly been given to the phrasing of some of the finer specimens, which no doubt have been improved over generations to make them as telling and succinct as possible. The Gospels attribute some comparisons of this type to Jesus:

> He told them another parable. 'The kingdom of heaven is like leaven which a woman took and hid in three measures of meal, till it was all leavened' (*Matt.* 13:33; cf. 13:44, 45).

In other contexts, however, the Old Testament contains 'parables' of a different kind. These are symbolic word-pictures (sometimes loosely termed 'allegorical') which represent historical realities in a code of images. Thus, the prophet Ezekiel is said to have foretold the last days of the kingdom of Judah in a strange story about an eagle which cropped the highest twig from a cedar, and carried it to a distant land to plant it (*Ezek.* 17:1–6). The principle is straightforward. Each symbol corresponds to a person or community, and the interaction of the symbols represents the historical events – in this case the exile of king Jehoiachin and the chief citizens of Judah to Babylon. Other instances of the method occur in *Zechariah* (4:1–5, 11–14; 5:5–11). It later became one of the major techniques of the apocalyptic[1] writers (cf. *Dan.* 2:31–45; 4:9–27; 8.)

---

[1] 'Apocalyptic' is the name given to a class of literature concerned largely, though not completely, with the 'revelation' (Greek: *apokalypsis*) of secrets about existence or the future known only to God or to heavenly beings. In the Bible and Apocrypha it is represented by *Daniel, II Esdras*, and *Revelation*. Though having affinities with prophecy, apocalyptic is nowadays increasingly recognized to be a special branch of wisdom writing. The popular use of the word 'apocalyptic' to describe a scene of spectacular and wholesale destruction is secondary, and derives from the presence in some apocalyptic works of imaginative descriptions of the end of the world (cf., e.g., *Rev.* 16).

In the Gospels Jesus makes use of this method also;[1] and in one passage, which is clearly intended to be definitive, he is presented as teaching that all parables are to be interpreted in this way. The occasion is the parable of the Sower (*Mk* 4:1–20; cf. *Matt.* 13:1–15, 18–23; *Lk.* 8:4–15):

> And he said to them, 'Do you not understand this parable? How then will you understand all the parables?' (*Mk* 4:13.)

Luke keeps the disciples' question which called forth this generalization (*Mk* 4:10; *Lk.* 8:9), and indeed makes it less ambiguous; but he omits the generalization itself. Matthew both omits the generalization and changes the introductory question to read: 'Why do you speak to them in parables?' (*Matt.* 13:10). For him, it is already accepted that all parables are 'allegories', and that Jesus' followers must have been aware of this. He therefore alters *Mark* to remove, as usual, the apparent imputation of stupidity to the disciples. But we must ask whether this generalization about the nature of Jesus' parables is true.

There are two good reasons for thinking that it is not, or at any rate not always. First, in the very case of the parable of the Sower itself, the interpretation, supposedly given by Jesus, is internally inconsistent. Taking Mark's version as the earliest, we start with the statement, 'The sower sows the word' (*Mk* 4:14). If this decoding were followed through, then the various classes of people would be represented by the various kinds of ground. This line is kept up for the first category (4:15); 'along the path' represents certain people who receive the seed, that is the word, but Satan, symbolized by the birds, swoops down and takes it away. But when we come to the second category, the code changes. The seeds are now the people – 'they that are sown' – and these spring up quickly, but having no root in themselves, do not persevere when times are dangerous (4:16–17). The first code still persists in the comment that initially 'they receive the word with joy', but it is being overborne. With the third class of people this confusion persists. The ground is the circumstances of affluence in which they live: 'others are the ones sown among thorns; . . . they are those who have heard the word, but the cares of the world . . . choke the word, and it proves unfruitful' (4:18–19). Finally, 'those that were sown upon

---

[1] *Matt.* 13:24–30 and 36–43, 47–50; *Mk* 12:1–12 = *Matt.* 21:33–46 = *Lk* 20:9–19.

the good soil . . . hear the word, and accept it and bear fruit' (4:20). One thing is perfectly clear: the interpretation has not been carefully thought out. Two incompatible schemes of symbolism have been attempted simultaneously. It is highly improbable that any man as lucid as Jesus would have made such a muddle of interpreting a story of his own composition. We must attribute it, therefore, to the church tradition, and with it the introductory generalization (4:13). This does not, of course, prove that Jesus never used allegorical parables, nor even that the Sower is not one of them; only that, if it is, we do not have his decoding of it. These considerations do, however, remove the evidence for thinking that Jesus authorized this approach for all parables.

It is therefore no surprise, when we turn to the second reason, namely that some of the parables simply will not tolerate this treatment. The Seed growing Secretly, for example (*Mk* 4:26–29), defies all attempts at consistent decoding. These brief comparisons are intended to form in the hearer an approach to life (cf. the Treasure in the Field, *Matt.* 13:44, and the Merchant seeking Pearls, *Matt.* 13:45–46). The probable truth about the Sower is that it asks us to look at experience on the assumption that God's action is by human standards wasteful and random, very far from one hundred per cent effective, but that when it does succeed it succeeds miraculously. This can perfectly legitimately be illustrated from men's response to the preaching of the gospel, but it could equally well apply to any revelation of God's nature or to the distribution of his gifts and blessings in creation. A man who has this parable built into his way of looking at things will have a very different attitude from that of, say, the Judaism of Jesus' day, which tried to find the precise execution of a specific divine intention in all kinds of individual incidents (cf. *Lk.* 13:4). This may help us to understand the ominous threat of *Mk* 4:12, a quotation from the call of Isaiah (*Isa.* 6:9–10) in which that prophet is summoned to hasten the doom of his people:

> so that they may indeed see but not perceive, and may indeed hear but not understand; lest they should turn again, and be forgiven (*Mk* 4:12).

Those who cannot absorb a radical change of attitude miss the point of Jesus' teaching completely. This use of the parable method to create new attitudes is, so far as we know, unique, and is therefore probably a hard historical fact about Jesus.

Comparisons used in the ordinary manner to illustrate (the Lost Coin and the Lost Sheep, *Lk.* 15:1–10) are natural enough, and need no discussion. But did Jesus ever employ the allegorical story? As we have seen, it was available to him in the teaching armoury of Judaism, and so there is no general reason for doubting it; but before deciding, it is as well to bear in mind how many subtly different uses there are of the parabolic method. Matthew, for example, records an illustrative anecdote which Jesus is supposed to have used in argument with the chief priests and elders:

> What do you think? A man had two sons; and he went to the first and said, 'Son, go and work in the vineyard today.' And he answered, 'I will not'; but afterward he repented and went. And he went to the second and said the same; and he answered, 'I go, sir', but did not go (*Matt.* 21:28–30).

Then, employing a device attributed to him also by Luke in connection with the story of the Good Samaritan (*Lk.* 10:36–37), Jesus puts a question to them; and when they give the only possible answer follows it up with a judgement on them out of their own mouths:

> Which of the two did the will of his father? They said, The first. Jesus said to them, Truly, I say to you, the tax collectors and the harlots go into the kingdom of God before you (*Matt.* 21:31).

Now, the anecdote could stand by itself as a moral illustration without any specific reference, but as soon as it is used in the dispute the characters come to stand for people in the contemporary situation, namely the pious Jews who paid lip-service to God but did not obey his commands as revealed to them (possibly by Jesus himself),[1] and the sinners who had despised the Law, but now repented. Indeed, if the story is to have any effect on any hearer, he must compare it with his own condition, and decide whether or not either of the caps fits himself, thus converting it at once into a simple symbolic piece. Immediately following it in *Matthew* we have another rather more elaborate example of the same technique, the parable of the Wicked Husbandmen (*Matt.* 21:33–41 = *Mk* = 12:1–9 *Lk.* 20:9–16), which is pointed in such a way that it clearly symbolizes the history of Israel. The picture of this history as a saga of disobedience and apostasy is nothing new; it is

---

[1] The further interpretation in terms of John the Baptist might be the editorial work of the evangelist, setting the passage in the context of the preceding section (*Matt.* 21:23–27).

already found in the Old Testament itself.[1] In turn it is taken up by the early Church.[2] Here the verses about the sending of the Son at first seem to be expansion by the Church (*Matt.* 21:37–39). But the rest is still symbolic, and any attempt to remove this character can succeed only by demolishing the parable altogether. The evangelists comment that the Jewish rulers saw clearly that the parable was aimed against themselves; and certainly it is not a general moral tale which might be applied by any man to his own condition, but is tailored to fit a specific historical situation. Since it fits the state of antagonism between Jesus and the religious leaders which must have existed if his death is to be explained, and also Jesus' consciousness of himself as the final agent and emissary of God,[3] there is nothing implausible in his having given this traditional critique a special contemporary application.

Did Jesus then empoly this symbolic form of parable to teach about such matters as the Last Judgement (*Matt.* 13:24–30 and 36–43; 13: 47–50)? Clearly he could have done so. Our verdict in any instance must be based not on the presence of this particular method but on the content of the parable, and the strength of the attestation for it. In the two cases just cited, while there is nothing incompatible with other recorded teaching by Jesus, there is also nothing which could not be an expression of conventional Jewish or Christian thinking of the time. They are found only in *Matthew*, and only Matthew goes in for these scenarios of the Great Assize (cf. *Matt.* 25:31–46). It is impossible to be certain, but we may be inclined to doubt whether they are authentic.

One more remark on the subject of parables is necessary in order to exclude a long-standing misuse of the word, and to draw attention to something which undoubtedly does bring us close to the historical Jesus. From an early stage in the history of the Church it became customary to apply the term 'parable' to stories which are nothing of the kind. Under the influence of *Mk* 4:13 it was assumed that even such long and relatively complex pieces as the Good Samaritan (*Lk.* 10:25–37) and the Prodigal Son (*Lk.* 15:11–32) were also symbolic narratives, and to be interpreted accordingly. In fact they are examples of a quite

---

[1] The great history of the early Hebrew nation which runs in our bibles from *Judges* to *Kings* is based on this pattern; cf. also such passages as *Jer.* 7:21–29; *II Chron.* 36:15–16.

[2] Cf., e.g., Stephen's speech in *Acts* 7, especially the concluding verses (51–53), and such passages as *Rom.* 10:19–21.

[3] Cf. pp. 223–239 below.

different genre of teaching material common in Judaism, the edifying tale. There is, of course, nothing devotionally objectionable in reading the Good Samaritan, as Origen did, in terms of Christ rescuing Man wounded by the powers of evil, nor in understanding the Prodigal Son's father as God forgiving the penitent sinner. The original purpose of this kind of story, however, was to present the hearer with a personal moral challenge. Whether Luke, therefore, has the correct setting for the story of the Good Samaritan or not,[1] he sums up the spirit behind it in the closing dialogue:

> 'Which of these three do you think proved neighbour to the man who fell among robbers?' He said, 'The one who showed mercy on him.' And Jesus said to him, 'Go, and do likewise' (*Lk.* 10:36–37).

Similarly, though the elder brother in the story of the Prodigal Son could be taken to refer to the devout Jews as opposed to the disreputable, the narrative is not so framed as to demand it. Any good person is open to the temptation of self-righteously excluding and penalizing the repentant sinner. The father's gentle rebuke (*Lk.* 15:28–32) is in fact more likely to be Christian admonition to the Church's self-righteous members than one from Jesus to the Pharisees and their ilk, whom he usually castigates with severity. If Luke's own mildness is here responsible, we might assume a story by Jesus which has been told by the evangelist in his own way, thus pointing once again to an original intended to be taken to oneself wherever the cap fits, and used freely by the Christian writer in this spirit.

---

[1] It has been argued that he has not, on the grounds that neither the story itself nor Jesus' closing remarks fit the scribe's question which was their alleged occasion. The scribe asked, 'Who is my neighbour?', meaning, in terms of Jewish casuistry of the period, 'Do you take this word to denote pious Jews, Jews in general, or Jews and resident aliens?' The story Jesus tells assumes the question, 'Who is *a* neighbour?', and gives the answer, 'He who helps anyone in need' (cf. *Lk.* 10:36–37). Even so, this could be Jesus' way of correcting the radically wrong outlook of the scribe. Moreover, the argument obscures the fact that the scribe's question really is answered, and with telling dramatic irony. The hero is a Samaritan, who might be assumed to hate orthodox Jews as much as they hated him. Nevertheless, he treats the wounded Jew as his neighbour in the sense of the scribe's question. The implication is obvious: if a Samaritan can include a Jew in the category of neighbour, surely a Jew is not going to be less generous than that? – which means, in effect, having no restrictions at all on the 'neighbour' as the object of our help and concern. If this interpretation is correct, then Luke's closing remarks catch the spirit of the story, but not its original setting.

In addition, however, to such plainly edifying tales, presenting good characters in an attractive light, there are others which are of a very different sort. These are amusing anecdotes of people as they are, behaving in a far from exemplary way. In the Tale of the Dishonest Steward (*Lk.* 16:1–8) we have a brilliant vignette of a man in a position of trust who has been cheating his employer, and, when detection is imminent, cooks the books in such a way as not simply to cover up his defalcations but also to benefit his master's debtors, thus ensuring a *quid pro quo* for himself after his dismissal. If this is treated as an allegorical story, the results are positively scandalous. The master who expresses his admiration for the march which the steward has stolen on him can only be God – and where do we go from there? What then is the 'moral'?[1] The story ends with a rather cryptic saying:

> For the sons of this world are wiser in their own generation than the sons of light (*Lk.* 16:8b).

Does this mean that the sons of light ought to be more energetic and ingenious in pursuing their good and eternal interests than the worldly-wise are in prosecuting their criminal ones, though in fact they are less so (cf. *Matt.* 10:16: 'Be wise as serpents and innocent as doves')? Or that in this generation the sons of light must be content to seem foolish by this world's standards since they pursue charity not gain? Luke may have thought the latter, since it provides a connection of thought with the secondary moral which he has attached to the story (cf. n. 1 below). But the former makes fuller use of the point of the tale, and is more likely to be the right interpretation. The application of such 'unedifying' tales is therefore an *a fortiori* one; if people like that

---

[1] V. 9: 'And I tell you, make friends for yourselves by means of unrighteous mammon, so that when it fails they may receive you into the eternal habitations', can only mean: 'Use your money for good works – that is the wisdom of the sons of light – for this will get you to heaven.' The phrase 'unrighteous mammon' would seem to imply, in the context of the tale, money obtained by fraud, like the steward's; but in Jesus' mouth it would be more likely to have meant money in general, as something which tends to exercise an evil tyranny over men (cf. the saying, 'You cannot serve God and Mammon', *Lk.* 16:13 = *Matt.* 6:24; also *I Tim.* 6:10, 'The love of money is the root of all evils'). *Lk.* 16:9 is thus a somewhat self-regarding piece of conventional Jewish morality, which did not originate with Jesus at all, but is a desperate effort to extract an improving meaning from the tale, the ironic slant of which has not been understood.

act in such a way, then how much more . . . ? This certainly is true of another good example, the Unjust Judge (*Lk.* 18:1–8). Here, however, Luke (who, it will be noted has almost exclusive copyright in stories of this and the preceding type) has missed the point (18:1). Jesus is not saying, 'If it is worth the trouble to badger a venal judge, how much more worthwhile to badger God.' The moral is rather one of imminent judgement: if even such a judge gets round to doing justice in the end for grotesquely unworthy reasons, how much more quickly and thoroughly will not God execute his justice (18:6–8)? The purpose of these anecdotes is to catch the hearer's attention by a satirical recognition of what really does go on in life, and then to use the resultant mood of sympathy and openness to push home a message to which there might otherwise be considerable psychological resistance. They are not without parallel in Judaism, but are far from common. Their shrewdness and humour do not seem likely to be the product of Luke's own mind, to judge from his other contributions, nor indeed to be that of Christian piety in general. They bring us face to face with a man who could bring an ironic sense of humour to bear on life, and who no doubt had a laugh behind his eyes to go with it.

A student once remarked to the writer that he was disturbed by the fact that there was no mention in the Gospels of Jesus' having ever laughed. This omission is not in itself surprising. The Gospels are not biographies in the modern sense; and Jesus could have laughed a thousand times at all sorts of things – the antics of children or animals, good-humoured chaff round the table[1] – without the fact's standing a chance of inclusion, because it was irrelevant to his mission and message. But we can say more than this. It is interesting to see how little mention of laughter from pleasure or happiness there is in the Bible as a whole. Laughing in contempt, triumph, or disbelief accounts for twenty-six instances; the vacant guffaw of the fool for one or perhaps two more. Laughter from joy comes eight times in the Old Testament, and three of these passages express the view that it masks sadness or is unjustified. In the New Testament happy laughter occurs only three times. One instance is in the *Epistle of James*, where it certainly carries a suggestion that the joy is that of heedless and sinful people (*Jas* 4:9). The other two occur in Jesus' teaching, in the Lukan form of the

[1] The nickname Boanerges, 'sons of thunder', which he is said to have given to James and John (*Mk* 3:17), is sometimes cited as an indication of this latter kind of fun.

Beatitudes, which was cited in a previous chapter as a model piece of oral tradition,[1] and therefore quite possibly original. In short, Jesus is the only person in the New Testament whose recorded words contain any reference to laughter as the justifiable expression of true joy and release. This is a small fact, but when seen against the background of a society and a religious literature which so rarely mentions laughter approvingly in this context, it may be a significant one. When we combine it with the hint supplied by the stories just considered, it seems fairly certain that Jesus was a man who could and did laugh, though not in the vicious or vacant ways to which people are often inclined. Nor should it be forgotten that his clear-sighted awareness of the real urgency and seriousness of the human predicament must have meant that his constant preoccupations were sombre ones; and it is in contrast with this that our evidence needs to be evaluated.

To return at last to the point from which this lengthy examination of Jesus' distinctive teaching methods began, it is clear that Jesus is a wisdom teacher, but one of an unusual kind. Though he may on occasion use popular proverbs, he is in no sense an academic collector of traditional sayings. He does not improve them, nor teach them to a circle of pupils, nor organize them into a system. He is a wisdom teacher in principle rather than in detail, basing his instruction on observation of the facts of life and on insight into the essentials of the human condition. An openness to reality shows itself in his aesthetic appreciation of natural beauty (*Matt.* 6:28–30 = *Lk.* 12:27–28). He argues directly from experience; and for this very reason his analogies from daily life are to be understood as pointing to an underlying principle – not with exact literalism. For example, he talks of the employer who returns unexpectedly to find his major-domo tyrannizing over the other slaves and getting drunk on his master's cellar, and who accordingly has him beaten and demoted (*Matt.* 24:45–51 = *Lk.* 12:42–46). Such an incident would have been familiar enough to his hearers, and he uses it to awaken them to the kind of consequences to be looked for if men do not live in such a way as to be ready at any moment for the coming of God's judgement. Matthew is so conscious of this that he imports into the illustration words which strictly are appropriate only to the religious reality obliquely indicated: the master will 'punish him and put him with the hypocrites' (*Matt.* 24:51), a phrase which clearly has in mind the frequent condemnations of the scribes and Pharisees.

[1] Cf. p. 166 above.

Jesus is no more pronouncing in favour of slavery and corporal punishment than he is suggesting that God's relationship with Man is adequately described as that of owner and slave (a view which from other sayings it is clear he did not hold), or that God will flog those who disobey him. Jesus undoubtedly taught that to reject or ignore God's will for men would bring pain and misery and exclusion from all joy;[1] but the details of the illustration from life are there to open the mind, not to draw an exact picture of supernatural reality. In this again he is in tune with the general method of Old Testament wisdom. His originality lies in the fact that he thinks for himself, and chooses his own analogies.

This throws light on the distinctive way in which he fulfils another role which men are said to have applied to him, and which indeed he may have accepted for himself. This is the role of the 'prophet'. This term does not connote simply one who predicts the future, important (and currently underestimated) though this is in the work of Israel's traditional prophets. For a Jew the fundamental characteristic of a prophet was that he brought a direct message from God, a message which might be a prediction or a moral warning or a word of encouragement and advice. The common feature of each was that it came from God, and had been communicated to the prophet expressly for him to pass on. The communication might be in words 'heard', in a flash of insight prompted by some event or object, in dreams or visions. In Jesus' day there had been no prophets in Israel for perhaps as much as three hundred years, but expectation of their revival remained (cf. *I Macc.* 4:46), kept alive by the promise said to have been made by God through Moses: 'I will raise up for them a prophet like you from among their brethren' (*Deut.* 18:18). As the veneration of Moses increased, giving him unparalleled status as the communicator of the Law and therefore the greatest of all the prophetic messengers of God, so this expectation became harder to fulfil; but the equally intense worsening of the oppressed predicament of the nation made it even harder to forego. It is this situation which underlies the question of the 'priests and Levites from Jerusalem' to John the Baptist in the Fourth Gospel: 'Are you the prophet?' (*John* 1:21), that is, *the* prophet *par*

---

[1] The sayings which Luke attaches to this section (*Lk.* 12:47–48) also imply that the pain will be proportionate to the degree of moral responsibility; but this kind of detailed qualification is not generally typical of Jesus, and the words may therefore be Christian commentary.

excellence, the predicted prophet. In the same Gospel the crowds after
the Feeding of the Five Thousand decide that Jesus is this prophet
(*John* 6:14); and it has recently been argued that the evangelist is
presenting Jesus throughout his book in this light.[1] In the other three
gospels, however, Jesus is hailed simply as 'a prophet', or as one of the
Old Testament prophets returned to life (*Mk* 8:28; cf. *Matt.* 16:14;
Lk. 9:19). Mark is perhaps inclined to play this point down – it may
have seemed to sort ill with his hammering emphasis on Jesus as 'Son
of God' or 'Holy One of God' right at the start of his narrative (*Mk*
1:1, 11, 24; cf. 5:7). He has two allusions to the popular estimate of
Jesus as a prophet (*Mk* 6:15; 8:28); apart from these he admits the title
only once, but that, in view of his opening presentation, is, as we shall
see, especially significant. In *Matthew* we find Jesus referred to as 'the
prophet ... from Nazareth of Galilee' (*Matt.* 21:11) by the Palm
Sunday crowd; and the authorities are unable to arrest him because the
mass of the people 'held him to be a prophet' (*Matt.* 21:46). In *Luke*
the citizens of Nain, after the raising of the widow's son, declare, 'A
great prophet has arisen among us!' (*Lk.* 7:16); and Simon the
Pharisee finds his scepticism confirmed, when Jesus does not turn away
the prostitute who was weeping at his feet, because 'if this man were a
prophet, he would have known who and what sort of woman this is
who is touching him' (*Lk.* 7:39). Such incidental details may be due to
the writer of the Gospel as much as to the tradition, but even if so, it
would seem that neither evangelist thought them implausible. What is
more, such views are quoted not to glorify Jesus, but to show how far
short the people fell of a true assessment of him – which may be a small
point in favour of their general historical accuracy. Much more important, however, is a tradition in *Mark,* taken over by both Matthew and
Luke. The people of Jesus' home town, unlike the rest of Galilee,
have no time for him – they know all about him, and are offended at his
presuming to teach them. He is no one extraordinary, a mere working
man! (The reference to his mighty works is either sceptical or ironic,
because, the evangelist assures us, 'he could do no mighty work there
... because of their unbelief': *Mk* 6:5–6).

And on the sabbath he began to teach in the synagogue; and many who
heard him were astonished, saying, 'Where did this man get all this?
What is the wisdom given to him? What mighty works are wrought by

[1] J. L. Martyn, *History and Theology in the Fourth Gospel*, 1967.

his hands! Is not this the carpenter, the son of Mary and brother of James and Joses and Judas and Simon, and are not his sisters here with us?' And they took offence at him (*Mk* 6:2–3).

Jesus' reply is revealing:

And Jesus said to them, 'A prophet is not without honour, except in his own country, and among his own kin, and in his own house' (*Mk* 6:4; cf. *Matt.* 13:57; *Lk.* 4:24).

This famous saying could be an already existing proverb, but this is unlikely since it runs counter to the prevailing self-satisfaction of Judaism on the subject of its own piety and religious insight, a self-satisfaction evinced throughout the Gospel story. On the other hand, it fits well with Jesus' own estimate of the true situation, both past and present, as expressed for example, in another celebrated utterance where he again includes himself, this time by implication, among the prophets:

O Jerusalem, Jerusalem, killing the prophets and stoning those who are sent to you! How often would I have gathered your children together as a hen gathers her brood under her wings, and you would not! (*Matt.* 23:37; cf. *Lk.* 13:34).

Luke underlines the point by prefacing this with the words: 'I must go on my way today and tomorrow and the day following; for it cannot be that a prophet should perish out of Jerusalem' (*Lk.* 13:33). The evidence, therefore, is strong both that many Jews regarded Jesus as a prophet and, what is more important, that Jesus was himself prepared to accept the title.

Nevertheless, even here the matter cannot be left at that, for Jesus is not the only man of his time in Jewry of whom this estimate was made. The people held John the Baptist also to be a prophet (*Matt.* 14:5; *Lk.* 20:6). Where this impinges upon the record of Jesus' own sayings, great care is needed because of the later rivalry between Christians and the disciples of John, who also seems to have left a 'sect' behind him.[1] It is probable, for example, that John did take to himself the words from *Isaiah*: 'The voice of one crying in the wilderness, Prepare the way of the Lord, make his paths straight' (*Isa.* 40:3). It is connected with him in *Mark* (1:3), and also by Matthew and Luke (*Matt.* 3:3; *Lk.* 3:4) – in Matthew's case in a section which preserves a sketchy but plausible account, from an independent source, of some of John's

---

[1] Traces of this rivalry can be seen in *Acts* (18:24 – 19:7) and in *John* (3:25–30).

teaching. The Fourth Gospel supports the association of this prophecy with the Baptist (*John.* 1:22–23). But this is far from implying that it had its Christian significance when first used by John or of him. In Christian eyes the Lord for whom John was to prepare the way was Jesus; in the eyes of John's followers it was certainly God, whose Last Judgement was imminent:

> Even now the axe is laid to the root of the trees; every tree therefore that does not bear good fruit is cut down and thrown into the fire (*Matt.* 3:10).

John's task was to bring people to repent and to obtain God's pardon, symbolized or guaranteed by the purificatory rite of baptism, so that when the Day of Judgement came they would be saved from the fires of hell. The urgent, short-term nature of his work is clearly indicated by his ethical teaching. This essays no radical reforms or re-orientations; it merely calls on men to do their present duty justly and with compassion.[1]

It is certain that Jesus had a high estimate of John, and regarded him as genuinely sent by God. Otherwise it is inconceivable that he should have gone to John to be baptized himself – an incident which is one of the best attested facts of Jesus' life, for not only has it left traces in all four gospels (*Matt.* 3:13–17; *Mk* 1:9–11; *Lk.* 3:21–22; *John* 1:29–34), but in three of them it is regarded as an incident to be either played down (*Luke*) or explained as liable to give a wrong impression (*Matthew*) or skated over altogether (*John*). In all four, moreover, the central feature of the event is not that Jesus was baptized, but that on this occasion he was marked out as the Son of God by the descent of God's spirit and by a divine voice from heaven. Thus the evangelists ensure that Jesus does not receive anything from John, but rather bestows on him and on his rite a dignity greater than it would otherwise possess. The beginning of Jesus' own ministry in their view is not his baptism by John – we may note the evasive phrase in *Acts* 10:37, 'beginning from Galilee *after the baptism which John preached*' – but his proclamation by God as the Son in whom he is well pleased (*Mk* 1:11; *Matt.* 3:17; *Lk.* 3:22), and who therefore by implication does not need the forgiveness of sins conveyed by the rite. The Fourth Gospel carries the diminishing process

---

[1] Cf. *Lk.* 3:10–14. It is, in fact, to use the well-known phrase, a genuine example of 'interim ethics'. Jesus' teaching, though it has been called this, is nothing of the sort: cf. pp. 229f. below.

to the limit by omitting any statement that Jesus actually was baptized, and by making the purpose of John's whole baptismal ministry simply one of preparing the setting for this revelation (*John* 1:31).

All this is certainly a distortion. Sayings of Jesus preserved in other contexts give a truer picture of his own view:

> Truly, I say to you, among those born of women there has risen no one greater than John the Baptist; yet he who is least in the kingdom of heaven is greater than he (*Matt.* 11:11).

The second part of the verse is not a disparagement of John, but an attempt to convey the surpassing glory of the kingdom of God. The meaning is clear: John is the greatest man who ever lived, but when God's sovereignty is finally established everyone who enjoys the blessings of that age will be even more magnificent than he. It is worthy of note also that Jesus is said to have used reaction to John as a touchstone of men's response to God (*Mk* 11:27–33; *Matt.* 21:23–27; *Lk.* 20:1–8; *Matt.* 21:28–32).

One other comment on John ascribed to Jesus is relevant here. Jesus, addressing the crowds, asks them what this man was whom they had flocked the weary miles into the wilderness to see:

> Why then did you go out? To see a prophet? Yes, I tell you, and more than a prophet (*Matt.* 11:9).

'A prophet – yes, and more than a prophet.' John is the messenger who, as prophesied in *Malachi*, would prepare the way for God's coming (*Matt.* 11:10, quoting *Mal.* 3:1; cf. *Mk* 1:2). The quotation has been altered to fit the Christian conception that it was Jesus for whom the way was prepared; but there is no reason to assume that Jesus himself made this adjustment – he was at all times far too taken up with focusing men's attention on God to be tinkering with the Old Testament to make it refer to himself. John and Jesus, then, are both 'prophets', and Jesus himself said so. But they are both more than prophets, because of the unique roles which they have been given to play in the drama of salvation. How this affects Jesus' view of his own position we shall consider shortly.

Even if, however, Jesus is content to be classed as a 'prophet' (as at least a not too misleading title), in one respect he does not act as though he were fulfilling the traditional prophetic role. He does not claim to act as God's messenger or spokesman The application of the prophecy of Malachi just mentioned to John the Baptist is appropriate, because whether or not John used the Old Testament prophet's traditional messenger formula, 'Thus saith the Lord,' or an equivalent, yet by declaring himself God's outrider he gave his words much that kind of force. Jesus is never represented as using this kind of language about himself; and in one important respect he made it quite unsuitable, replacing it with a far more extraordinary claim.

The aspect of his authority in question here is that which he took upon himself to improve the Old Testament Law. The most clear-cut examples of this come in *Matthew* only, in the course of the Sermon on the Mount (*Matt.* 5:17–48). The section opens with a declaration by Jesus that the Law is valid for the whole of human history, that not one ornament of a single letter can be allowed to vanish, and that the only means of entering God's kingdom is by a perfection of conduct which exceeds that of the scribes and Pharisees (vv. 17–20). He then gives six examples of his meaning. The Law said, 'You shall not kill,' but this is not enough; we are not even to insult our brother, nor lose our temper with him (vv. 21–22). The Law said that men were not to commit adultery, but even this must be extended to condemn lustful looks as being the same sin committed in thought (vv. 27–28). The Law allowed legally witnessed divorce, but remarriage after divorce is equivalent to adultery (vv. 31–32).[1] The Law forbade one to perjure oneself; Jesus forbids the use of any oaths at all (vv. 33–37). The Law confined revenge to the infliction of an equal loss; Jesus excludes any revenge, replacing it with non-resistance or even active beneficence (vv. 38–42). The Law confined the scope of love to one's fellow-Jews or other members of one's own community; Jesus enlarges it to take in enemies and persecutors. Men are to be as perfectly impartial in their goodness as God himself (vv. 43–48).

The passage is interlarded with other relevant sayings, some of them found in other gospels as well, and forms a brilliantly sustained composition. That it represents the supreme ideal of Matthew's Judaeo-Christian piety is unquestionable – note the tell-tale v. 47: 'If you salute only your brothers, what more are you doing than others? Do not *even the Gentiles* do the same?' The refrain, 'You have heard that it was said to the men of old . . . but I say to you,' cannot be definitely assumed to be Jesus' own. It is too tailormade for the role of Jesus as 'second

[1] On this passage cf. pp. 174f. above.

Moses', so dear to Matthew's heart.[1] But the attitude of which this is the epigrammatic summary is not attested only by Matthew; it occurs in other sources as well.

A striking example is Mark's tradition of Jesus's teaching about divorce (*Mk* 10:2-9; *Matt.* 19:1-9). The Mosaic law permitted a man to divorce his wife by a simple, unilateral legal act, differing from Muslim practice only in the additional requirement of a written document. Jesus states that this system was a concession to human 'hardness of heart' (*Mk* 10:5). God's design in creation was that man and woman were meant for each other (v. 6), that the marriage bond should take precedence over every other natural tie (v. 7), and that in it the partners should become a single organic unity (v. 8). Since this is God's intention, to frustrate it by divorcing those united in marriage is wrong (v. 9). This piece of teaching is especially important as evidence, because we have confirmation earlier than any of the gospels that the rule upheld by this argument was indeed recognized by the church as the teaching of Jesus himself:

To the married I give charge, not I but the Lord, that the wife should not separate from her husband (but if she does, let her remain single or else be reconciled to her husband) – and that the husband should not divorce his wife (*I Cor.* 7:10-11).

To understand the implications of this incident in *Mark* for our present concern we need to note certain points. The teaching given here is in response to a question from the Pharisees intended, says Mark, to catch Jesus out. This immediately prompts us to ask, 'Why did they choose this topic? Had they already reason to think Jesus heretical on

---

[1] It will not do, however, to be too dogmatic here. The phrase, 'I tell you . . .', or 'I say to you . . .' is characteristic of Jesus in other streams of tradition: cf. p. 218 below. Even the remark about the Gentiles is historically plausible, when it is remembered that Jesus concentrated his ministry on Israel, and was seeking to train his fellow-Jews for a special role in God's universal purpose: cf. pp. 238f. below. There are other instances of his trying to shame Jews into a better frame of mind by comparison with heathen nations (an approach he could have learned from the Old Testament prophets); cf., e.g., from the healing of the centurion's servant, his comment: 'Truly, I say to you (!), not even in Israel have I found such faith. I tell you, many will come from east and west and sit at table with Abraham, Isaac, and Jacob in the kingdom of heaven, while the sons of the kingdom will be thrown into the outer darkness; there men will weep and gnash their teeth' (*Matt.* 8:10-12; cf. *Lk.* 7:9).

the subject?' There is some evidence that they had. Mark appends to this section a separate saying about divorce:

> And in the house the disciples asked him again about this matter. And he said to them, 'Whoever divorces his wife and marries another, commits adultery against her; and if she divorces her husband and marries another, she commits adultery' (*Mk* 10:10–12).

This is unlikely to be the original form of the saying, because it presupposes a situation where the wife could divorce her husband, which was possible in Roman law but not in Judaism. A very similar pronouncement without this adaptation for the Gentile church occurs, however, in *Matthew* and *Luke* (*Matt.* 5:31–32; *Lk.* 16:18). It is improbable that they altered Mark's revised version back to an older form; hence we conclude that it was in their common source, not used by Mark. If so, this is a very strongly supported piece of teaching, present in two separate lines of tradition – and, be it noted, in the form of a bald statement, backed by no scriptural authority. It seems probable, therefore, that the Pharisees knew that Jesus held this view, and that they seized on it because it seemed to contradict Moses's directive so flatly that they could see no way in which on this point Jesus could escape the charge of altering the Law. This explains why Jesus now moves to defeat them on their own ground, by appealing to *Genesis*, a book held to be by Moses himself.[1] The passage in *Genesis* in fact says nothing obviously relevant to divorce. The moral injunction as such is Jesus' own. This confirms the view that he had already laid down this principle on his own authority. He can, if required to do so, support its underlying assumptions by Scripture; he did not derive it from Scripture.

Another important piece of evidence for this approach on the part of Jesus we have already examined in a different connection – his teaching about sabbath observance.[2] Once again we find this practice of arriving at clear and simple ethical directives by thinking for himself of the world

---

[1] Jesus outmanœuvres the Sadducees in a similar way (*Mk* 12:24–27). The Sadducees rejected belief in resurrection, partly on the grounds that there was no authority for it in the Law, the only part of the Old Testament which they recognized as authoritative scripture. Jesus shows by correct rabbinic exegesis that the Law does imply such a belief. But note that he does not make this the sole ground for believing: 'Is not this why you are wrong,' he asks, 'that you know neither the scriptures *nor the power of God*' (*Mk* 12:24)? Cf. also *John* 10:34–36.

[2] Cf. pp. 194ff. above.

as the sphere in which the good God exercises his kingship. Again, he can justify his conclusions by Scripture (*Mk* 2:25–26); but not by any stretch of the imagination could he have arrived at them from Scripture. We have here a principle of cardinal importance. If you are thinking on the right lines and with the right values, you will find that your conclusions have already been adumbrated in essence somewhere in Scripture; but you will never find the right answer simply by asking, 'What does Scripture say?' and then attempting to work out from that what to do and how to live. In this respect it is interesting to compare the ways in which two different sources show Jesus handling two closely related points. In the Sermon on the Mount we read:

> You have heard that it was said, 'You shall not commit adultery.' But I say to you that every one who looks at a woman lustfully has already committed adultery with her in his heart (*Matt.* 5:27–28).

Here we start from a biblical command, and then extend and intensify it. In *Mark* there is the following incident:

> And he called the people to him again, and said to them, 'Hear me, all of you, and understand: there is nothing outside a man which by going into him can defile him; but the things which come out of a man are what defile him.' And when he had entered the house, and left the people, his disciples asked him about the parable. And he said to them, 'Then are you also without understanding? Do you not see that whatever goes into a man from outside cannot defile him, since it enters, not his heart but his stomach, and so passes on?' (Thus he declared all foods clean.) And he said, 'What comes out of a man is what defiles a man. For from within, out of the heart of man, come evil thoughts, fornication, theft, murder, adultery, coveting, wickedness, deceit, licentiousness, envy, slander, pride, foolishness. All these evil things come from within, and they defile a man (*Mk* 7:14–23).

The ethical consequences in each passage are the same – among others, lustful desires and thoughts are condemned, not just lustful actions. But what a world of difference in the approach! In *Mark* we have a Jesus who has observed and reflected on the facts of human nature, and who crystallizes his conclusions in a challenging and enigmatic saying – and in so doing, almost as an incidental bonus, abolishes for good and all the Jewish ritual preoccupation with regulations about clean and unclean foods, a point which the evangelist is anxious that his readers should not overlook. In *Matthew* we have the new lawgiver developing a new moral demand from the initial data of Scripture. Matthew is not wrong as regards the content of Jesus' ethical teaching, nor does that teaching contradict the scriptures. But we have seen enough to realise that Mark gives the historically more convincing picture of the way in which he arrived at it.[1]

It is this fundamental approach by Jesus to the task of teaching which was new and refreshing, and which made a vivid impression on those who heard him:

> And when Jesus finished these sayings, the crowd were astonished at his teaching, for he taught them as one who had authority, and not as their scribes (*Matt.* 7:28–29).

What he said was clear, comprehensible, and patently his own conviction. But that was not all. He presented his teaching as God's will for men, but at the same time he never attributed it to a direct communication from God like that given to Moses or to the prophets.[2] It is significant that one of the most characteristic mannerisms of his speaking style, attested in all the sources, is the phrase, '*I* tell you,' often given special solemnity by the introductory word, 'Amen', 'Truly', or 'Indeed'. The authority with which he speaks rests not on training, qualifications, or position as rabbi or sage, not on direct prophetic inspiration, not on the ultimate authority of Scripture, but on himself; and yet what he speaks comes to the listener with the authority of God.

This quality in Jesus is not confirmed only by an examination of his teaching, such as we have just made, and by the fury which he aroused in the orthodox religious leaders. It also explains more convincingly than anything else another feature of the Gospel portrait, his refusal to differentiate between himself and his message. His call to his first disciples (with the affectionately remembered and surely authentic

---

[1] Some modern commentators have gone astray at this point. Because they see rightly that Jesus did not operate in the scribal and legalistic way suggested in *Matthew*, they have gone on wrongly to allege that Jesus did not lay down universally binding rules on such ethical questions as sexual conduct. Even if, however, the long list of defiling things in *Mk* 7:21–22 owes something to conventional lists of vices in moral teaching of the period (cf., e.g., *Rom.* 1:29–31; *II Tim.* 3:2–4), inserted here by the evangelist, the implication is clear, and there is ample other evidence of Jesus' views on this particular subject: cf. p. 192 above, and *John* 8:11.

[2] Cf. in this connection the Jewish objection in *John* 9:29: 'We know that God has spoken to Moses, but as for this man we do not know where he comes from.'

joke, 'I will make you fishers of men') is a personal one, to follow him (*Mk* 1:17, 20; 2:14). The rich young man is told to give all his wealth to the poor and to follow Jesus (*Mk* 10:21). In Matthew and Luke's common source there was a story that John the Baptist, when in prison, sent two of his followers to Jesus to ask whether he was indeed 'the one who is to come', and received from Jesus the following reply:

> Go and tell John what you hear and see: the blind receive their sight and the lame walk, lepers are cleansed and the deaf hear, and the dead are raised up, and the poor have good news preached to them. And blessed is he who takes no offence at me (*Matt.* 11:4–6).

The preaching of the Gospel and the mighty works that accompany it are inseparable from the person of Jesus; response to them must include acceptance of Jesus. He himself is part and parcel of the good news.

How far is this tradition authentic? One or two incidents suggest very strongly that it is. It has often been remarked that a unique trait of Jesus was the value which he set upon childhood and the innocence of children. This is, so far as we know, unexampled in the ancient world. In paganism a child was essentially something immature, valuable only for what it might become. The practice of killing unwanted infants by exposing them at birth was widespread and taken for granted.[1] Judaism had always valued and cherished children as a precious gift of God (as it does to this day), but it did not see in the state of childhood any special quality which would be desirable in an adult. Nor, to judge from the frequent references in the New Testament to immature Christians as 'babes', did the early church. We may therefore take it that Jesus's idiosyncrasy in this respect is a genuine historical memory. This gives especial interest in our present context to such passages as the following:

> And they were bringing children to him, that he might touch them; and the disciples rebuked them. But when Jesus saw it he was indignant, and said to them, 'Let the children come to me, do not hinder them; for to such belongs the kingdom of God. Truly, I say to you, whoever does not receive the kingdom of God like a child shall not enter it' (*Mk* 10:13–15).

[1] This was something which both Jews and Christians regarded with abhorrence; but it was Christianity, spreading as Judaism never could, which educated men's consciences and finally brought about its suppression.

Or again:

> And he took a child, and put him in the midst of them; and taking him
> in his arms, he said to them, 'Whoever receives one such child in my
> name receives me; and whoever receives me, receives not me but him
> who sent me' (*Mk* 9:36–37).

Trust and innocence like that of childhood are needed if men are to
be open to the kingdom of God, and are the mark of those who are at
home in it. Care for those who supremely embody these qualities is
acceptance of God – but it is also acceptance of Jesus, and this element
is too deeply embedded in such stories to be excised by any critical
scalpel.

It would be nothing very extraordinary, indeed, that the preacher of a
new gospel should couple loyalty to that gospel with loyalty to himself;
but this is not quite what Jesus would seem to have done. In the case,
let us say, of a prophet, the hearer might respond to the message without
needing to pay any particular attention to the messenger; the inhabitants of Jerusalem could have repented at the preaching of Isaiah or
Jeremiah, and then forgotten about these men as such, without in any
way impairing their repentance. But in the Gospels an attitude to
Jesus in person is an integral part of the right response. This comes out
in a different way in another saying:

> And I tell you, every one who acknowledges me before men, the Son of
> man also will acknowledge before the angels of God; but he who denies
> me before men will be denied before the angels of God (*Lk.* 12:8–9;
> cf. *Mk* 8:38).

It will be remembered from our earlier discussion of this verse[1] that,
while the early Church undoubtedly took this as identifying Jesus with
the heavenly 'Son of Man' who was to judge the world at the Last Day,
the phrasing could perhaps more naturally be held to distinguish
between them. If the original meaning was the second, the saying
could easily be authentic, and would testify to the point in question:
the great criterion by which men will be judged is their attitude to
Jesus. Mark whose additional clause, 'when he comes in the glory of
his Father with the holy angels', indicates his version as secondary,
has included a reference to the teaching – 'ashamed of me and of my
words'. But the simpler form concentrates on Jesus himself. How are
we to interpret this?

[1] Cf. pp. 148f. above.

There is no need to recapitulate here arguments already set out in detail in a previous chapter.[1] A summary of conclusions will be sufficient. Jesus thought of himself as God's human agent whose death would usher in the end of the present age and the resurrection of the saints, with himself as their firstfruits.[2] He did not identify himself with the heavenly Son of Man. This is an equation which has been retrojected on to the tradition by the faith of the early Church, stimulated by certain sayings ('The son of man is lord even of the sabbath', 'The son of man has power on earth to forgive sins') which were originally statements about the privileges of all men who chose to live truly under the sovereignty of God.

In the light of these conclusions a number of factors in the story take on a new significance. We must take seriously the tradition that Jesus supplemented his own ministry by sending out his followers to preach the news of the coming kingdom of God (*Matt.* 10:5–23; *Lk.* 9:1–6; 10:1–20). These accounts have been considerably elaborated to make them models for the behaviour of missionaries in the early Church. Luke, moreover, with his special interest in the preaching of the gospel to the Gentiles, has foreshadowed this by having two such missions. In the first, the Twelve are sent out, symbolizing the preaching

[1] Cf. pp. 147–150 above.

[2] The sayings in which he gives his own rising again a precise deadline – either 'after three days (and nights)', or 'on the third day' – probably arose as follows. There are several passages in the Gospels where Jesus refers to the 'sign of Jonah'. In *Lk.* 11:30 this is explained on the lines that just as Jonah came preaching imminent judgement to the Ninevites, so is Jesus doing to Israel; in *Matt.* 12:40, the solution is that as Jonah was three days and nights in the whale's belly, so will Jesus be that length of time in the grave. The discrepancy suggests that there was no agreed tradition of Jesus' own explanation of the cryptic phrase, if indeed he gave one at all. That he did not is supported by the occurrence of the crucial words yet again in a small separate paragraph of material (*Matt.* 16:1–4), in which Jesus is flatly refusing to comply with the request for an authenticating miracle:' "An evil and adulterous generation seeks for a sign, but no sign shall be given to it except the sign of Jonah." So he left them and departed' (*Matt.* 16:4). They are left to make of it what they can! After Easter, however, the interpretation of the words as a hidden allusion to the resurrection may have encouraged a natural tendency to make Jesus' actual predictions of his return to life more precise. 'After three days' would then be the nearest to the Jonah story (*Jon.* 1:17), 'on the third day', the final stage of the process, in exact accord with the facts (starting in the ancient manner by counting the Friday as the first day). On the whole subject of the historical nature of the resurrection cf. chap. 10 below.

to the twelve tribes of Israel; in the second, seventy disciples are engaged, in accordance with the Jewish belief that the population of the
world was divided into seventy nations. But behind all this it is
not unlikely that there is a hard fact. The reason for this step on the
part of Jesus can be glimpsed in *Matt.* 10:23, a prediction which
was falsified in the event, and may for that very reason be regarded as
authentic:

> When they persecute you in one town, flee to the next; for truly, I say to
> you, you will not have gone through all the towns of Israel, before the
> Son of man comes.

How did Jesus react when this expectation was disappointed?[1] Did
he become convinced that something more was required of him than
simply to preach? — that he had to die as well?

We are now approaching the heart of the historical problem of Jesus.
We may note or deduce with some certainty any number of characteristics about him: the carpenter, son of a carpenter, with the quick and
powerful intellect, the commanding personality, the unforgettable
speech, the urgent compassion for the suffering, the eye for natural
beauty, the tough physique coupled with abnormal psychological capacities for endurance. Here was a man who deliberately identified with
the poor and the oppressed, who without compromising his own
standards made the weak and the sinful feel that there was no barrier to
friendship between him and them, but who demanded above all that
men be open and genuine. There is the shrewd sense of humour, the
reverence for children, the gift of poetry, the devastating anger, and yet
the rejection of solutions imposed by force.[2] We then begin to feel as if
we 'know' him, in the way that we might know a great figure of our
own times whom we have heard and seen on television or in the papers,
perhaps in the flesh, or whose biography we have read. We observe
that he apparently possesses exceptional gifts, such as the power of
healing. We can go on to study his ethical teaching and his belief about
God, to note its simplicity, its radical demands, its coherence, its
insight into human nature; and we begin to know him a little better,

---

[1] Albert Schweitzer, in *The Quest of the Historical Jesus*, saw this as the decisive
turning-point in Jesus' life.

[2] That he did not absolutely rule out physical action is clear from the havoc he
made of the desks of the Temple profiteers (*Mk* 11:15–17). But this was in
no sense a 'solution imposed by force'.

in rather more depth. We come to understand how he was able to inspire loyalty in his friends, but at the same time intense and enduring loyalty only in a few, and that even these might at times find the relationship almost too demanding, though once they had enjoyed it, everything else might seem insipid by comparison. Finally, we can watch and marvel at his bearing under persecution and injustice, his noble endurance of a cruel death, and feel that this was all of a piece with his life. It is what we would have expected of him. But at the very heart of him there is a mystery, one queston of absolutely overriding importance to which we must have an answer, for as yet he has eluded us. We may have a fair idea what we think of him, but our final verdict will depend on something much more significant: what did he think of himself?

It is obvious that Jesus did have a clear vision of his own role in history, and that he believed it essential for others to understand what this was. As we turn to examine the evidence on this crucial issue, we have some general guidelines already laid down to help us as a result of our examination of the various facets of his public presence. We are not dealing with a neurotic, or with a man whose moral values are perverse. He is not someone, for instance, who would try to force the hand of God or man by virtual suicide. If he walks straight up to death, it is because he is following the path of his duty, and death has chosen to bar his way. He is not someone who prides himself on one hundred per cent moral perfection. He does not 'thank God that he is not as other men are', for he is more interested in other men than in himself. He joins the crowd to receive a 'baptism of repentance for the remission of sins', and when an enthusiastic admirer calls him 'good' he takes him to task. Yet he sees his own mission as unique, and specifically as a unique work for God.

His own relationship with God is the best starting-point in the search for an answer to our vital question. Fortunately, we have here a rock-hard piece of evidence, the word *Abba*. In his letter to the Christians at Rome Paul writes:

> You did not receive the spirit of slavery to fall back into fear, but you have received the spirit of sonship. When we cry, 'Abba! Father!' it is the Spirit himself bearing witness with our spirit that we are children of God, and if children, then heirs, heirs of God and fellow heirs with Christ, provided we suffer with him in order that we may also be glorified with him (*Rom.* 8:15–17).

The retention by the Greek-speaking church of this Aramaic word (which the New Testament writers feel it necessary to translate on each occasion) requires an explanation; and this is not far to seek. The word is sacred to Christians because it was the form of address to God in prayer used by Jesus himself:

> And they went to a place which was called Gethsemane; and he said to his disciples, 'Sit here, while I pray.' And he took with him Peter and James and John, and began to be greatly distressed and troubled. And he said to them, 'My soul is very sorrowful, even to death; remain here, and watch.' And going a little farther, he fell on the ground and prayed that, if it were possible, the hour might pass from him. And he said, 'Abba, Father, all things are possible to thee; remove this cup from me; yet not what I will, but what thou wilt' (*Mk* 14:32–36).

Luke's version of the Lord's Prayer does not begin, as Matthew's does, '*Our* Father' (*Matt.* 6:9), which is an adaptation for Christian liturgical use, but simply 'Father' (*Lk.* 11:2) – undoubtedly presupposing this term used by Jesus himself. In view of these facts we may feel that another tradition of Luke's, which claims to record Jesus' last words on the cross, is also reliable. The Psalmist had written: 'Into thy hand I commit my spirit' (*Psa.* 31:5). Jesus said, 'Father,' – *Abba* – 'into thy hands I commit my spirit' (*Lk.* 23:46).

It is therefore not really surprising to find the title 'Son of God' attached to Jesus.[1] The Fourth Evangelist has it that Jesus claimed this

---

[1] At this point it is worth commenting on the mysterious figure of Barabbas in the Passion story. The problems are many; for one thing, there is no good evidence for the practice of granting an amnesty to a prisoner at Passover time (*Mk* 15:6–8; *Matt.* 27:15; *John* 19:39–40; Luke omits the assertion that there was a general custom). More immediately relevant, however, is the name 'Bar-abba', which means 'son of the father'. We know no other contemporary instances, but the name is quite often found in later periods. Moreover, this is only a second name, and needs one to precede it in order to identify the person properly. There is some MS evidence to the effect that the text originally gave this first name as – Jesus: Jesus Bar-Abbas. Jesus, the Greek form of the Aramaic: Yeshua, Hebrew: Yehoshua (= Joshua, cf. *Acts* 7:45; *Heb.* 4:8 in the A.V.) was a common Jewish name: cf. *Col.* 4:11, 'Jesus who is called Justus'. Barabbas's first name was presumably omitted by later scribes out of reverence, misplaced since it destroys the drama. But the drama lies not just in the choice between two men called Jesus, but in the fact that this other was also 'Jesus, son of the "father"'. How much of all this is legend it is hard to say; but it must have originated in the Palestinian church, for the irony would have been apparent only to Aramaic speakers. If there was a nationalist revolutionary called Jesus Barabbas around this time, perhaps the reflection that the Romans had executed Jesus of Nazareth at the instigation of the

title – indeed, it is a major theme of his gospel – and that this was one of the things that infuriated the Jews (*John* 10:31–39); and a passage similar in content, though not in actual wording, to John's material on this subject occurs in Matthew and Luke's common source (*Matt.* 11:25–27; *Lk.* 10:21–22). In Luke's account of the cross-examination of Jesus before the council the decisive question put to him is: 'Are you the Son of God?' (*Lk.* 22:70; but cf. *Matt.* 26:63; *Mk* 14:61).[1] The story of the Temptation in the Wilderness hinges on the same point (*Matt.* 4:1–11: *Lk.* 4:1–13). The devil's words, 'If you are the Son of God', may mean: 'Since you are the Son of God, use your power in the following ways', or they may be a temptation to doubt: 'You think you are the Son of God – all right then, prove it by doing this or that.' In *Matthew* Peter declares, 'You are the Christ, the Son of the living God' (*Matt.* 16:16), and the disciples confess Jesus as such after the stilling of the storm (*Matt.* 14:33). The voice from heaven at the Baptism and the Transfiguration proclaims Jesus as 'my Son' (*Matt.* 3:17; *Mk* 1:11; *Lk.* 3:22 – *Matt.* 17:5; *Mk* 9:7; *Lk.* 9:35). The demons, with their supernatural knowledge, cry out this secret (*Mk* 3:11; 5:7). The same ascription is implied in the present version of the parable of the Wicked Husbandmen (*Matt.* 21:37–38; *Mk* 12:6; *Lk.* 20:13). After Jesus' death on the cross, the centurion in charge of the soldiers says, 'Truly, this was the Son of God' (*Matt.* 27:54; *Mk* 15:39). Finally, in *Luke,* the angel Gabriel tells Mary that the child she is to bear will be the Son of God (*Lk.* 1:35).

The striking point about all these passages (except the reply of Jesus at his trial, which, as we shall see, is a special case) is their very low value as historical evidence for Jesus' own views. In *John*, and in the kindred passages in *Matthew* and *Luke*, a developed theology is being read back into the story; the Temptation narrative must be regarded as an imaginative attempt to reconstruct what happened during Jesus' retreat into the wilderness (recorded in *Mk* 1:12–13 without details), since the only alternative – to suppose that Jesus himself related this intensely personal spiritual experience to his

---

Jews themselves but that Barabbas had never met such a fate would be enough to start the legend-making process. The theory of the amnesty would then have been invented to account for the story. But whatever the explanation, in a roundabout way this tale testifies to a very early belief that Jesus of Nazareth was in a special sense 'son' of that Father whom he addressed as 'Abba'.

[1] Cf. p. 149 above.

P

disciples – is utterly out of keeping with everything else that we know about him.[1] Matthew has inflated Mark's Caesarea Philippi story, where Peter simply says, 'You are the Messiah' (*Mk* 8:29); and in Mark's storm scene the disciples are baffled, and do not draw the conclusion mentioned in *Matthew* (*Mk* 6:51–52, cf. 4:41). The supernatural voices, divine or demonic, are 'not evidence'. As for the parable, we have seen indisputable proof of the way in which these can be rewritten to express a church viewpoint. Whether the centurion or the angel Gabriel used the words attributed to them is irrelevant. In short, there is no solid reason in the first three gospels to hold that Jesus ever thought or spoke of himself as the 'Son of God'. Indeed, other material suggests that Jesus saw it as every man's potential and vocation to be just as much a son of God as himself. The fact that he taught his disciples to pray with his own form of address to God is the strongest testimony on this side. The implications of another piece of teaching on prayer (*Matt.* 7:7–11 = *Lk.* 11:9–13), and the instruction in the Sermon on the Mount to 'love your enemies ... so that you may be the sons of your Father who is in heaven' (*Matt.* 5:44–45) are not so significant; but they certainly do not tell against this idea.

The one exception is Jesus' answer to the High Priest and the council at his trial; and here the case is particular in a vital respect. In *Mark*, the earliest account, the question runs, 'Are you the Messiah, the Son of the Blessed?' (*Mk* 14:61), and Matthew agrees: 'I adjure you ... tell us if you are the Messiah, the Son of God' (*Matt.* 26:63). Luke, as we saw in an earlier chapter,[2] has modified the dialogue, but in the respect important for our present purpose, his version comes to the same thing: Jesus accepts the title 'Son of God' in apposition to the term 'Messiah'.[3]

That the expected Messiah (literally, the 'Anointed One') would be God's son was a well-established belief in Judaism, based on such Old

[1] The only comparable passages are two in which Jesus implies supernatural knowledge about Satan (*Lk.* 10:18; 22:31), but both refer to the frustration of Satan's plans against others, in the former case mankind, in the latter, Peter. Except for the incident in Gethsemane the inner spiritual life of Jesus is a blank to us, a point on which he is markedly different from other great religious figures such as the Buddha or Mohammed. The most obvious reason for the blank is his own reticence.

[2] Cf. pp. 149f. above.

[3] Matthew's version of Peter's confession, therefore, though an elaboration, is not a falsification in essence (*Matt.* 16:16).

Testament texts as *Psa.* 2. But this phrase conveyed different things to different people. Some thought of the Messiah as a supernatural being who would come from heaven; others envisaged him as an earthly ruler, descended from the tribe of Judah, and within that tribe from the line of David.[1] Jesus, therefore, could perfectly well have believed himself to be the Messiah, without thinking that he was anything more than an ordinary human being. But was he really of Davidic descent?[2] Here an incident in *Mark* is of great interest. During the controversies of the week before his crucifixion, we are told, Jesus while teaching in the Temple asks:

> How can the scribes say that the Messiah is the son of David? David him-
> self, inspired by the Holy Spirit, declared,
> > 'The Lord said to my Lord,
> > Sit at my right hand,
> > till I put thy enemies under thy feet.'
> David himself calls him Lord; so how is he his son? (*Mk* 12:35–37; cf.
> *Matt.* 22:41–46; *Lk.* 20:41–44.)

What is the point of this passage? The early Church no doubt saw it as a claim by Jesus to be from heaven, and thus existing before David and infinitely greater than he. But in Jesus' mouth the words could well have had a very different import, questioning the necessity of Davidic ancestry for the Messiah. And why are the people so pleased (*Mk* 12:37: 'the great throng heard him gladly')? It might be that they saw in this dialectical victory a hint by the prophet from Nazareth that he himself was claiming the role of Messiah. Again, as we have seen, in the oldest form of the Caesarea Philippi story, when Peter declares simply, 'You are the Messiah', Jesus accepts the role, but charges the disciples

---

[1] A school of thought in the community of the Dead Sea scrolls apparently expected two Messiahs, one Davidic, the other from the priestly tribe of Levi and family of Aaron.

[2] The New Testament insists that he was – by adoption, *Matt.* 1:1–17; *Lk.* 3:23–38; by blood, *Acts* 2:30–31; *Rom.* 1:3, cf. 9:5; *II Tim.* 2:8; cf. *Heb.* 7:14; *Rev.* 5:5; 22:16. The birth of Jesus in Bethlehem (*Matt.* 2:1; *Lk.* 2:4–7), David's native city, also serves to fulfil the prophecy of *Micah* (5:2), traditionally applied to the Messiah (*Matt.* 2:6). In *John* 7:42 some of the Jews doubt whether Jesus can be the Messiah, because he comes, as they believe, from Galilee, not from Bethlehem, and is not of Davidic blood: cf. *Matt.* 12:23. Jesus is sometimes addressed by the people as 'Son of David', a title associated with the nationalist independence movement: *Mk* 10:47–48; *Matt.* 9:27; 15:22; 20:30–31; 21:9, 15; *Lk.* 18:38–39.

to keep this a secret (*Mk* 8:27–30). There may have been good reasons for this reticence. Nothing whatever in the portrait of Jesus leads us to suspect that he was ready to engage in the kind of military and political activity which the people would have demanded of an aspirant to this title. In this connection, the story of Palm Sunday is instructive. Jesus' entry into Jerusalem on an ass, accompanied by wildly excited crowds, is given in substantially similar form in all the gospels; and the church *later* (as *John* carefully emphasizes: 12:16) saw this as fulfilling the prophecy in *Zechariah* (9:9) of the king coming to Zion. The event was so obviously planned by Jesus (the ass was in readiness, and the disciples who fetched it used a message agreed beforehand: *Mk* 11:3; *Matt.* 21:3; *Lk.* 19:31) that we are forced to conclude that he intended to demonstrate some claim of this kind. But – and this is the significant thing – he deliberately lets the moment of popular enthusiasm slip away. He leaves himself in an exposed position, daily more helpless. The simplest explanation is that he meant to declare his Messiahship (cf. *Lk.* 19:39–40), but to fulfil it in his own way, not by the violent policy hoped for by nationalist enthusiasm and alien to the will of God as he had always understood and taught it.

If we accept this as a working hypothesis – and there is nothing very new, improbable, or revolutionary about it – does it help to make sense of other evidence in the gospels, which we have not as yet incorporated into our portrait? It will now be argued that it does, though not in the way commonly supposed. Here it will be only fair to give the reader a warning. Right from the start we had to face the fact that in the opinion of quite a number of well-qualified scholars the whole of this lengthy investigation would be built on sand, that it is in fact impossible to know the historical Jesus to any significant extent, and that even the reductionist conclusions here put forward will be purely subjective. The present writer is inclined to think that there is no way of refuting such people except that of trying to do the impossible thing, and then asking the customer, 'Well, what do *you* think? Can it be done or not?' The prime difficulty has always been the mystery of Jesus' own sense of his vocation – can we find a unified conception of this which will accommodate not just all the evidence of one type concerning his ideas, or all the evidence of another type, apparently incompatible with the first, but, in principle at least, the bulk of all types? So far not a great deal of success has attended the various efforts to do so; perhaps it will not attend the theory which is now to be put forward. The justification for attempting it, however, is that some fresh comprehensive hypothesis is needed; and there is no hope of progress without offering hypotheses for criticism. But the reader should remember that, whereas what has been said hitherto could summon up a fair amount of support among New Testament scholars for its various component parts, what follows is more largely, though again not entirely, the personal theory of the writer.

We start from one crucial question. It will be remembered that we earlier drew a distinction between John the Baptist's ethical teaching, which laid down no new rules or principles, and that of Jesus, which made far more absolute and radical demands. The former, we suggested, can rightly be called an 'interim ethic', for it was intended not to be the framework of a permanent human society but simply to tide the baptized over the brief interval until the coming of the end of the world. Jesus too, as we have seen reason to believe, looked for an imminent divine judgement:

> As it was in the days of Noah, so will it be in the days of the Son of man. They ate, they drank, they married, they were given in marriage, until the day when Noah entered the ark, and the flood came and destroyed them all . . . I tell you, in that night there will be two men in one bed; one will be taken and the other left (*Lk.* 17:26–27, 34).

There is to all intents and purposes to be no more 'history' – not at any rate in this dispensation. *What then was the point of his new ethical teaching? When would there ever be a chance to put it into practice?*

The view has been put forward that Jesus's ethic was so high-strained, so heroic and superhuman, that it can have been intended only for a brief period. Human nature could not have stood it for longer. That Christian conduct could be regulated on such a basis did occasionally cross the minds of the New Testament writers themselves, as may be inferred from a remark like this of Paul to the Corinthians:

> I mean, brethren, the appointed time has grown very short; from now on, let those who have wives live as though they had none, and those who mourn as though they were not mourning, and those who rejoice as though they were not rejoicing, and those who buy as though they had no goods, and those who deal with the world as though they had no dealings with it. For the form of this world is passing away (*I Cor.* 7:29–31).

There is a superficial similarity between this passage and one attributed to Jesus, the unvarnished directness of which may mark it as authentic:

> For there are eunuchs who have been so from birth, and there are eunuchs who have been made eunuchs by men, and there are eunuchs who have made themselves eunuchs for the sake of the kingdom of heaven. He who is able to receive this, let him receive it (*Matt.* 19:12).

In fact, however, Paul's view is basically different, and lacks the realism and sanity of Jesus' own balanced but decisive teaching. Jesus is commending vocational celibacy, that is, celibacy undertaken because the particular service of God to which a man feels himself called cannot be performed without this sacrifice. This is a way of life to be adopted only by those who are convinced that they can shoulder its burdens; it comes under the general rubric of sitting down and counting the cost before beginning a major project (*Lk.* 14:28–32). Paul is commending this kind of sacrifice to everyone (even to the married if they can stand it), for the doing of God's work certainly, but on the grounds that they will not have to keep it up for long anyway. Jesus is clearly thinking in terms of a minority vocation against a general background of normal life. Indeed it is hard to resist the impression that all his ethical teaching is seeking to set out the permanent basis for right human living, a view confirmed by the reaction which this teaching evokes today, and has always evoked – that human life would be immensely finer, freer, and happier if only his principles were put into practice. This is the response not just of religious believers, perhaps not always so much of them as of others who find the ethic attractive where the religion repels. But why did Jesus bother to give this teaching, if he foresaw no earthly society in which it would be needed? And an earthly society it must be, for by no stretch of the imagination can it be supposed relevant to heaven (cf., e.g., *Mk.* 12:25).

It could, of course, be argued that the teaching is not his, that the demands for forgiveness, for love of enemies and persecutors, for purity, for kindness to all afflicted fellow-humans, for absolute truthfulness, and the rest, were formulated by the church when they realized that the end was not yet. But quite apart from the fact that there is nothing and no one in the history of the early Church to make this plausible, we have the evidence of the New Testament that these moral demands were already known and recorded and applied to the life of the Church at a time when the expectation of an imminent Last Day was still very much alive. We are driven therefore to conclude that Jesus himself did envisage a future settled society to which his ethic would be relevant. And if, as surely we must, we hold also to our opinion that he looked for an immediate coming of the Son of Man, then he can have foreseen this society only on the far side of that coming. In short, we say that Jesus expected that judgement would be followed by the setting up of the kingdom of God *on earth*.

This was by no means an unprecedented view. There is a good deal in the writings of Judaism around the turn of the eras to show that others too had such an expectation. Moreover, it is significant that the commonest designation of this future society was the 'age' or 'kingdom of the Messiah'. When we bear this in mind, a new light falls on such promises by Jesus to his disciples as the following:

> You are those who have continued with me in my trials; as my Father appointed a kingdom for me, so do I appoint for you that you may eat and drink at my table in my kingdom, and sit on thrones judging the twelve tribes of Israel (*Lk.* 22:28–30; cf. *Matt.* 19:28).

(We should note here the motif of the so-called 'Messianic banquet', a standard piece of contemporary imagery to express the joy and fulfilment of the new order; it will appear again shortly.)

The choice by Jesus of an inner group of twelve disciples has always been recognized as a symbolic act, the foundation of a 'new Israel', which would have its twelve leaders just as the old Israel had its twelve patriarchs at the head of twelve tribes. The intriguing point about the tradition on this point, however, is that the names of the holders of these twelve places have been imperfectly remembered. The lists vary (*Mk* 3:14–19; *Matt.* 10:1–4; *Lk.* 6:13–16); and in the first three gospels Peter, the two brothers, James and John, and Judas Iscariot, are the only ones who play any effective part. In the Fourth Gospel, Philip, Andrew, Thomas, and possibly 'Bartholomew' (if the Nathaniel of *John* 1 was his first name) have important supporting roles. But in the early history of the Church, as recorded in *Acts*, which has a special veneration for the Twelve, only Peter figures prominently. New men, such as Paul and Barnabas, come to the fore. Nevertheless, *Acts* records that the very first business of the disciples after Easter was to choose by lot a man to fill the gap in the Twelve left by the defection and suicide of Judas. Luke presents the Twelve here as men who, having known Jesus intimately throughout his career, could give convincing witness to the reality of his resurrection (*Acts* 1:21–22) – the distinctive task of an 'apostle'. In his gospel, therefore, the Twelve are designated as apostles by Jesus (*Lk.* 6:13); but this is not supported by the other gospels. It is more probable that the real reason for the immediate replacement of Judas was to make sure that when the Lord returned to set up the Messianic kingdom, as he might do at any moment, the required twelve patriarchal princes would be available.[1] As things turned out, however, they were not needed. They remained faithfully in Jerusalem, even under persecution (*Acts* 8:1), and all, save Peter, passed into oblivion except under their corporate title, the 'Twelve', a no longer comprehended, and therefore historically weighty testimony to the intentions of Jesus himself.[2]

Several other pieces of teaching by Jesus find their natural setting in this vision of the future – his admonitions, for example, that those who are rulers must be servants of all. The Messianic kingdom will turn upside down the ordinary attitudes of human society; in the nations of the world those in authority lord it over their fellow human beings and are adulated in return, 'but it shall not be so among you' (*Mk* 10:42–44; cf. *Matt.* 9:33–36). Luke places this instruction in the context of the Last Supper (*Lk.* 22:24–27), which, as we shall see, is a not inappropriate setting for it. Again, it is this earthly kingdom to which James and John are looking forward, when they ask Jesus for the places of honour beside him (*Mk* 10:35–40; in *Matt.* 20:20–23, it is their mother who presses their claim).

During this latter incident Jesus asks the brothers:

> Are you able to drink the cup that I drink, or to be baptized with the baptism with which I am baptized? (*Mk* 10:38b).

When they declare that they can, he grimly assures them that they will indeed be required to do so. The reference is clearly to his coming sufferings, and recalls a very interesting passage in *Luke* which contains a similar saying:

[1] It should be noted that the method of selection by lot is used to ensure that the new member will be supernaturally chosen by 'the Lord' (*Acts* 1: 24–26).

[2] In the second century A.D. an extensive series of religious romances was written, purporting to give the later doings of these men; but these are devoid of historical value.

I came to cast fire upon the earth; and would that it were already kindled!
I have a baptism to be baptized with; and how I am constrained until it
is accomplished! (*Lk.* 12:49–50).

Here Jesus indicates that his own death is a necessary prelude to the
fulfilment of his purpose; and to this question we must now turn.

Of all the acts and sayings of Jesus none have more precisely dictated
the conduct of men than those of the night before he suffered. Day
after day, week after week, among nine hundred millions of human
beings throughout the world, the words he then spoke, translated into a
hundred tongues, the ceremony he there performed, are repeated. This
ritual is not an impersonal symbol of general truths and values; it is
focused directly on Jesus himself:

> For I received from the Lord what I also delivered to you, that the
> Lord Jesus on the night when he was betrayed took bread, and when he
> had given thanks, he broke it, and said, 'This is my body which is for
> you. Do this in remembrance of me.' In the same way also the cup, after
> supper, saying, 'This cup is the new covenant in my blood. Do this, as
> often as you drink it, in remembrance of me.' For as often as you eat
> this bread and drink the cup, you proclaim the Lord's death until he
> comes (*I Cor.* 11:23–26).

Here we have the earliest record of this act, quoted by Paul from the
oral tradition of the community as he himself was taught it, and passed
it on to his converts at Corinth, a tradition which is not just the words
of others about Jesus, but the words of Jesus himself transmitted down
an unbroken line: 'I received *from the Lord.*'

What Jesus did, taken in its entirety as a single complex of act and
meaning, is without analogy in the known history of men. The blessing
and distributing of food and drink as a symbol and realization of
spiritual fellowship, and the idea of sacrifice, both are universal. But the
fusion of these elements by an individual as a presentation of his own
imminent death is unexampled. These general considerations create a
strong presumption that we are here in touch with historical truth.
Strangely enough, however, we cannot be sure what Jesus' exact
words were. Those over the bread are the most uniformly attested in
all the accounts; and, there being no Aramaic word for 'is', nor a true
equivalent for 'body', we can be reasonably sure that in this case the
original ran: 'This (sc. is) my flesh for you.' The saying over the wine
is more difficult. It has come down to us in two main forms: 'This is

my blood of the (new) covenant' (*Mk* 14:24; *Matt.* 26:28), and: 'This cup is the new covenant in my blood' (*I Cor.* 11:25; *Lk.* 22:20). It would be an unjustifiably lengthy exercise in this context to set out all the points to be taken into account in assessing the historical value of these two versions. On balance, in the view of the present writer, the Mark–Matthew form is the more plausible. But even this has its problems. As it stands it cannot be translated back into Hebrew or Aramaic, since you cannot say 'my blood of the covenant' in these languages. When, therefore, we reflect that nowhere else in the recorded words of Jesus is there any reference to 'covenant', the best solution is perhaps to see this element as theological elaboration by the Church, and to make the saying parallel to that over the bread: 'This (is) my blood for you.' The distinction here drawn between 'flesh' and 'blood' strongly recalls Jewish sacrificial terminology; and the words, 'for you', 'for many', 'poured out' (*Mk*, *Matt.*, *Lk.*), and 'for the forgiveness of sins' (*Matt.*), simply underline this connotation. Are all these extra phrases original? There is nothing in them intrinsically improbable in Jesus' mouth; but one point suggests that some of them may be elaboration. The disciples clearly did not understand even now that Jesus intended to accept death. In Gethsemane they were still ready to fight. If Jesus' words earlier had been incapable of interpretation in any way other than that of a martyr's sacrifice, then this confusion is hard to explain. If, however, Jesus said, 'This is my flesh for you,' and 'This is my blood for you (and for many)', then his words could have been taken, by those wishfully disposed to do so, as a pledge of total loyalty to the messianic cause in the imminent combat. Afterwards, the disciples realized that his meaning had been very different, and in the story they made this clear by the various additions to and rephrasings of his words.

That the relation of the bread and the cup to the terrible realities was symbolic is certain. No Jew, since the drinking of blood was forbidden to him by the Law, would have thought for a moment that the wine *was* now blood, or to be drunk as if it were the blood. No human being but one utterly perverted would eat the bread as if it were the body of the man standing before him.[1] In this way we move right

---

[1] It is significant that in *John* 6, which is a discourse by Jesus on himself as the true bread from heaven, and in which eucharistic language is frequent, the Jews object to the stark and seemingly literal imagery: 'How can this man give us his flesh to eat?' (v. 52). When Jesus then repeats his statements, even more

outside the common forms of sacrifice; with the legacy of this ritual act Jesus puts into the hands of his followers the means to write *finis* once for all to the whole apparatus of animal slaughter on which the religions of the ancient world, Judaism included, were based.

But this was not all that Jesus is reported to have said. In the first three gospels there is another declaration at this point:

> Truly, I say to you, I shall not drink again of the fruit of the vine until that day when I drink it new in the kingdom of God (*Mk* 14:25; cf. *Matt.* 26:29; *Lk.* 22:18).

These words never found their way into the liturgies of Christendom. How could they? It was impossible to fit them into the pattern of history which the Church came to accept as normative. The kingdom of God would not come until Jesus himself came again in power to judge the world; the time when Jesus would return to share the bread and wine with his followers was in the future, and could only be longed for, not thought of as present. But is this what Jesus himself expected? Surely not. The natural sense of the words fits exactly into the vision we have suggested: that the Last Judgement by the Son of Man would come after his death, and the Messianic kingdom be established in which he, raised from the dead by God, would join once more with his disciples in the fellowship meal. That the words are there, even though they very soon became a problem, witnesses forcefully to their authenticity.

This is why we can say that Luke is right in spirit, and may be so in the letter, when he places in this context the promise to the disciples that they are to judge the new Israel. But that particular passage raises one more point which we need to consider. It begins with the words, 'You are those who have continued with me in my trials' (*Lk.* 22:28). But the time is coming when they will be able to hold on no longer; even Peter, the most confident of them all, will follow at a cautious distance and perjure himself in panic at the first hint of danger (*Lk.*

---

emphatically, bewilderment becomes outright rejection: 'This is a hard saying; who can listen to it?' (v. 60). Jesus' reply is important: 'It is the spirit that gives life, the flesh is of no avail; the words that I have spoken to you are spirit and life' (v. 63). John seems to be saying that to concentrate on the physical act of eating and drinking, as a kind of magical salvation, is to miss the point; what saves is the life and death of Jesus in its innermost meaning. Perhaps some Christians were tending to take 'This is my flesh' in the former way.

22:31–34; cf. *Mk* 14:66–72; *Matt.* 26:69–75; *Lk.* 22:56–62). Jesus is to go on alone. Yet earlier we saw him predicting to James and John that they would have to undergo sufferings like his own. But when? In the Messianic kingdom? This seems wildly improbable.

The answer is probably to be sought in another belief of contemporary Judaism which went with the expectation of the Messianic age. This was to the effect that the new dispensation would be preceded by a period of great distress, the Messianic 'woes', which would fall with crushing force on God's chosen people. If the words of Jesus to the two brothers are historical, as we have argued, then they represent a stage when Jesus thought that his friends would necessarily be involved with him in the sufferings of this dark hour before the dawn, and would probably die with him. He then came to believe that it was his duty to protect them, and as the Messiah, hidden but the Messiah nevertheless, to take all the woes upon himself – a conviction which the Fourth Evangelist has expressed in some of the most famous words in the New Testament:

> Greater love has no man than this, that a man lay down his life for his friends. You are my friends . . . (*John* 15:13–14a).[1]

It has often been suggested that Jesus owed his sense of this particular aspect of his vocation in large part to meditation on the Suffering Servant of God, described in *Isa.* 52:13–53:12 – the 'man of sorrows' with whose stripes the sinful people were to be healed. That the passage was seized upon by Christians from the earliest days as a prophecy of Jesus is unquestionable; the relatively large number of quotations from it which appear in the New Testament in one connection or another shows how thoroughly they had sifted the whole section. But there is not one clear, evidentially impressive allusion to it in all the recorded words of Jesus himself. *Lk.* 22:37 is the only certain example, and this comes in a short paragraph which is notoriously one of the most baffling and obscure in the gospels. It is, of course, intrinsically probable that Jesus would have pondered this famous passage – all the more so, perhaps, as his view of the Messiah's role was so radically different from that of most Jews. But we must beware of distorting the influence of scripture on Jesus by supposing that he found a role in the Old

[1] Cf. *John* 17:12: 'I have guarded them, and none of them is lost but the son of perdition': cf. also 18: 8.

Testament, and then proceeded to act it out, a spiritually hollow approach. As with his general attitude to scripture mentioned earlier, we may be sure that he saw the role first in the facts of his own situation and their setting within the values and sovereignty of God, and then drew courage and confirmation from finding it adumbrated in scripture.

If, however, Jesus' death was to usher in the kingdom, what about the phrase, 'Do this in remembrance of me', which we have not so far discussed? Two preliminary points need to be made. First, the words, 'Do this', do not (indeed cannot, if read naturally) mean, 'Repeat the formula, "This is my body" – "This is my blood".' The latter were words that could be used once only, by Jesus himself, to indicate the meaning of what he was about to do. The command refers to the acts of breaking and distributing the bread, and of passing the cup, with their accompanying prayers of blessing and thanksgiving. Secondly, the word 'remembrance' is to be understood not in our modern sense of 'commemoration', when we remind ourselves of some great event, but in its Jewish cultic sense of 'reminding God', that is, either claiming from God some promised blessing or acknowledging one already given. These two points help us to understand both what Jesus intended and what actually happened. He commanded that in the kingdom his followers should in this symbolic way celebrate before God the sacrifice by which the kingdom had been made possible. In the event, the Church used the prescribed action to 'remind' God of Jesus' death, and to claim the kingdom which this had won for them but which did not come. In either case two things are true which will be of paramount importance, when we come to discuss the Christian Eucharist in Part Three. The ritual is still a symbolic re-enactment of history's most significant event: the Cross. But now it is carried out on the far side of the Cross. It does not effect the vital change in Man's situation; it celebrates the fact that the change has already happened.

We must now draw to a close our search for Jesus as he was. Long though it has been, it has not been long enough to do justice to all the amazing complexity of the evidence. Yet the present writer believes that in the interpretation here set out we have a key conception which enables us to draw a coherent portrait, doing more justice to the documents and to their special characteristics than any other.

But there is also a reverse confirmation of this theory. Wherever we have reason to believe that extant traditions have distorted the historical process, reconstruction of the facts needs to take account of two main points. It is not enough to use as many of the details as possible, arranging them in a theoretically feasible pattern. There must also be at least a plausible explanation how events which are presumed to have happened in one way came to be presented so differently. It is important to realize that these are not two separate questions, but aspects of the same one. For if a conjectural reconstruction is even approximately correct, then it gives the actual historical situation; and it is from *this* situation that the process of distorting the tradition must have started, and in this situation that the seeds of distortion must lie. Failure to produce a probable account of the process of distortion on this basis must therefore tell against the reconstruction.

In the case of Jesus, the picture we have tried to present is this. He was convinced that God, the Father for whom he had absolute love and trust, and whose will he took as the absolute directive of his own life, had called him to be the Messiah of Israel, and so eventually to establish and rule in the Messianic kingdom on earth. But this kingdom lay on the far side of a time of crisis and distress culminating in a divine judgement of the whole world, to be carried out by a heavenly being, the Son of Man. His immediate task, therefore, was not to proceed directly to the setting up of the kingdom. In the prevailing circumstances this could be done only by means of force, propaganda, and political intrigue, which was as much as to say that it could not be set up at all, since God's sovereignty could never be implemented by anti-God methods. In the meantime, therefore, he could only prepare, by enlisting men who as the servants of mankind were to head the new order, by training them in those values and principles of God on which the kingdom was to be built, and by preparing them for the coming period of crisis, which they were to meet in that same spirit and with that same perfection of human conduct. This meant first of all that his Messiahship had to remain a secret to all except those who had been initiated into its new and revolutionary ethical nature. It could not be revealed to the generality of men, who would interpret it in terms of their own violent, nationalist, and anti-God aspirations. It also meant, however, that he was bound to criticize and challenge the assumptions of Israel at large, and to confine himself to Israel, since it was Israel, purged and converted, which would have to be the central, foundation community of the new world order. It could not be otherwise, since they were the only people who knew that human life must be based on total love for the one universal God and for all men as his children. This challenge to Israel was therefore a recall to the basic principles of her own heritage,[1] and a critique of the ways in which they had perverted it. As such it inevitably meant hostility, danger, and death for himself and his friends. Hence he finally decided if possible to draw down all this enmity on himself, and as the hidden Messiah to take the full brunt of the Messianic woes, thereby opening the way for the divine judgement and for the resurrection which would usher in the kingdom of God on earth.

After the crucifixion and resurrection the Church proclaimed the imminent fulfilment of this plan:

> Let all the house of Israel therefore know assuredly that God has made him both Lord and Christ, this Jesus whom you crucified (*Acts* 2:36).

They set up in Jerusalem a community of complete sharing and brotherly love (*Acts* 2:44-45; 4:32-35), attracted many converts (*Acts* 6:7) and widespread admiration (*Acts* 2:46-47; 5:12-13). But this only brought down upon them increasing persecution, first of the Christian leaders (*Acts* 4:1-22; 5:17-42), and then of the whole body (*Acts* 7:54-8:3). This, by dispersing the new sect, helped the spread of their gospel (*Acts* 8:4). But it must also have led to a re-assessment of the point they had reached in God's programme. Clearly the time of the Messianic woes had not yet passed. Jesus' predictions of danger and persecution for his followers, therefore, were now seen as applying to their present stage,[2] and his instructions on the subject of missionary preaching were also expanded and adapted to guide the Church's current activities.

---

[1] Principles which have unfolded themselves over the centuries in the immense corpus of Jewish ethical teaching, which is one of the greatest creations of the human mind and heart: for an introductory survey cf. I. Epstein, *Judaism* (Pelican Books).

[2] C. F. D. Moule has made the very illuminating suggestion that the passage in *Col.* 1:24, where Paul speaks of himself as completing in his own flesh 'what is lacking in Christ's afflictions', may refer to the Messianic woes. The leaders appointed by Christ (of whom Paul insists that he is one) must follow him in taking on themselves as much as possible of the perils of this time of crisis. Note also Paul's constant insistence on the role of the apostles as 'servants' of the Church.

Likewise, the judgement by the Son of Man must be still in the future; and here what is perhaps the most crucial creative change is made – the identification of the Messiah with the Son of Man. The Fourth Evangelist has recorded this identification as clearly as anyone could wish:

> For as the Father has life in himself, so he has granted the Son also to have life in himself, and has given him authority to execute judgement, because he is the Son of man (*John* 5:26–27; cf. also 12:34).

The effects of this change on the wording of the tradition have already been studied in some detail; all that we need to remark here is the naturalness of it. In the first place, there were, as we have seen, sayings of Jesus which could spark off the identification; secondly, Jesus had spoken of his earthly mission, with its criticism of the existing order, in the imagery of judgement and division:

> Do not think that I have come to bring peace on earth; I have not come to bring peace, but a sword (*Matt.* 10:34).[1]

Thirdly, having 'ascended to his Father' after the resurrection,[2] he must return if he was to reign in the Messianic kingdom; and if that kingdom was to be preceded by the judgement, then the conclusion shouted for acceptance that the return of Jesus and the judgement by the Son of Man would prove to be one and the same event.[3]

---

[1] The parallel passage in *Lk.* 12:51 has 'division' instead of 'a sword', thus leading more naturally into the prophecy quoted from *Micah* (7:6) to the effect that members of families will be set one against another by their response to or rejection of the Gospel. For the sword as an image of spiritual judgement cf. *Heb.* 4:12.

[2] On this subject cf. pp. 251, 259 below.

[3] There are a number of sayings attributed to Jesus which stress that the judgement will come suddenly, without warning signs, and will take men unawares; hence they must be constantly on the watch and in readiness. One has already been quoted (cf. p. 229) above); others include *Mk* 13:33–37; *Lk.* 17:20–21; cf. also *I Thess.* 5:2–4; *II Pet.* 3:10, which testify to the presence of these sayings in the tradition, and the importance attached to them. It would seem likely therefore that the saying, 'This generation will not pass away before all these things take place' (*Mk* 13:30; *Matt.* 24:34; *Lk.* 21:32 – which, it has been suggested [cf. p. 178 above] may be the work of a Christian prophet – and cf. *Mk* 9:1) is the result of combining the expectation of the end with the promise of Jesus that his principal followers would be the leaders of the Messianic kingdom. For an adjustment of this belief in the light of events cf. *John.* 21:21–23.

In this connection it is interesting to note the wording of another passage in one of Peter's early speeches in *Acts*, where he is referring to the return of Jesus:

> Repent therefore, and turn again, that your sins may be blotted out, that times of refreshing may come from the presence of the Lord, and that he may send the Christ appointed for you, Jesus, whom heaven must receive until the time for establishing all that God spoke by the mouth of his holy prophets from of old (*Acts* 2:19–21).

Here we have, on the present hypothesis, a very early form indeed of the Christian hope. The ultimate vision is of the setting up of the Messianic kingdom on earth, predicted (as it undoubtedly was) by the Old Testament prophets. In preparation for this, the believer is to repent, to receive God's forgiveness, and by his new manner of life to hasten the return of the 'Messiah appointed for you, Jesus', for citizenship of whose kingdom he will now be fitted. No identification here of Jesus with the coming Judge – indeed, no mention of the latter at all. Other passages in these chapters seem to imply a judgement of some kind (*Acts* 2:40; 4:12), but the allusion is oblique, and this element clearly not a primary concern. The purpose of Jesus' exaltation to heaven is to make repentance and forgiveness freely available (*Acts* 5:31).[1]

This sunny and hopeful atmosphere did not, however, last long. Rejection of the Gospel and persecution of its messengers made it clear that the battle was far from over; and the continuing vigour of the evils which Jesus had denounced brought into prominence his sayings about the seriousness of decision, the inevitability of an ultimate separation of wheat from tares, of the children of the kingdom from the hypocrites – and with these sayings, of course, the role of the Son of Man. It was beneath the louring skies of conflict and persecution that the vision of judgement, and of Jesus' part in it, came to the fore – sometimes, alas, from motives of bitterness and revenge (cf. *Rev.* 18) but sometimes from a sad but accurate realization of the power in men of those evil forces which were personalized in popular myth as the ape and enemy of the Messiah: the Antichrist (*I John* 2:18; 4:3; cf. *II Thess.* 2:1–12). Not unnaturally in such circumstances, Christians

---

[1] It will be clear that the present writer sides with those who do regard these chapters of *Acts* as providing genuine evidence for the beliefs of the very earliest Christian community in Jerusalem. This is further supported by the contrast with some later passages, which equate Jesus with the Judge (e.g., *Acts* 17:31).

gradually ceased to believe in the possibility that the times of the Church might be the Messianic age.[1] Jesus had not returned, the apostles were dead (*II Pet.* 3:4). The hope of future blessedness now moves wholly into an other-wordly existence in the eternal presence of God.

In seeking to recover the portrait of Jesus as he was, we have made no attempt in the currently fashionable way to indulge in generalized ethical assessments, or to highlight only those pieces of evidence which can be easily distilled into abstract principles – 'freedom to give oneself in sacrificial love', 'the Man for Others', and so forth. It is not that such phrases are false to Jesus; indeed, they are necessary and useful. But they are also dangerous, because they disguise the fact that he was a distinct and distinctive individual, with specific beliefs and hopes and values expressed in the thought and imagery of a particular time and society, and that it is this historical man to whom we are asked to respond, and who stands over against all the generations of those who seek to follow him, as a challenge, a judgement, and an eternal inspiration. Jesus did not see himself just as Everyman, nor as the Saviour of the World, even less as a divine pre-existent being from heaven. His whole life was directed to the task of bringing men to see that their only Saviour was God, who was in very truth their Father in heaven. But he did see himself as the Messiah of Israel, appointed by God to bring in his kingdom on earth through service, suffering, and death. This, in the classic phrase, is the 'scandal of particularity' in the faith that proclaims him also as universal Lord. How such a man can justly be accorded supreme and saving significance for all men in all times will be the

---

[1] There is some evidence from sources outside the New Testament that in the churches of Asia Minor there were some Christians who did think of themselves as living in the Messianic age, but who took this to mean, following certain hopes of a popular and enthusiastic type of Judaism, that men now had complete liberty to enjoy themselves without restraint – wine, women, and song, in fact! Nevertheless, that they should have believed this is significant. In the New Testament itself other solutions of the problems can perhaps be discerned here and there. In *Revelation* there is the expectation of a Messianic kingdom of one thousand years on earth after Jesus' return in judgement (a very obvious adjustment which may support the reconstruction of Jesus' own view here put forward): *Rev.* 20:4–6. It is from this source that the recurrent phenomenon of Christian millenarianism derives, as in the sect of Jehovah's Witnesses. In the Gospels themselves, it may be that the nature miracles of Jesus and the stories of the feeding of the multitudes represent an interpretation of Jesus' life on earth as the Messianic age. This being past, a further series of woes is now ushering in the final judgement and the translation of all the righteous to a heavenly existence.

subject of the next chapters. Our final thought here must be simply this: that even though faith has hailed him as in the deepest sense both Son of Man and Son of God, it is in the end the role to which he himself felt that he was called by which he and his followers have been and will always be known – 'Messiah', the 'Anointed One', in Greek, 'Christos', the Christ of the Christian Church.

10

The Lord's Doing

WHEN JESUS of Nazareth died, his secret perished with him.

If we find that hard to believe, let us ask one question: who else knew that secret? Not the authorities who executed him. It is doubtful whether the Romans knew very much about him at all, and what they did know was almost certainly inaccurate. In the eyes of the High Priest and the Jewish Council Jesus was a blasphemer in league with the devil, one who taught men to break the law of God and was leading the nation headlong to destruction. What then of his followers? Mark, at least, is at pains to stress how little even they had grasped of what he was trying to tell them; and in this he is more likely to be right than the later, more reverential evangelists:

> And he began to teach them that the Son of Man must suffer many things, and be rejected by the elders and the chief priests and the scribes, and be killed . . . And he said this plainly. And Peter took him, and began to rebuke him. But turning and seeing his disciples, he rebuked Peter, and said, 'Get behind me, Satan! For you are not on the side of God, but of men' (*Mk* 8:31–33).

As the ministry progressed, and popular success seemed within their reach, they must have been more and more baffled and perturbed by such predictions, and probably found it easier to repress them out of conscious attention. The more convinced they were that Jesus was the saviour-hero appointed by God, the less were they able to envisage an ending in terms of failure and defeat. Indeed, the very fact that they could see death for God's cause solely as an ending, a failure, and a defeat, was the clearest possible proof that they had not even begun to understand. The panic-stricken flight of Jesus' closest friends and helpers at the moment of his arrest is the classic illustration of the thesis which we have tried to argue throughout the present work: that no man can believe in God deeply and unshakeably unless he has first accepted the moral primacy of sacrifice and of disinterested loyalty to love and its demands as the absolute and universal law of life.

As for the Jewish people at large, we catch glimpses during Jesus' public career of ordinary folk thrilled by a new note, by something strong and convincing, but inevitably unable to penetrate very deeply into its meaning. Some were grieved at the way things turned out; but the comment

We had hoped that he was the one to redeem Israel (*Lk.* 24:21)

suggests that their expectations had been primarily political. Others, like the crowds at the trial and execution, either cared nothing or had been whipped up into active hostility.

All the indications are that Jesus had not succeeded before he died in communicating his secret to anyone.

He himself was well aware of this. He knew that his judges were wilfully blind to the truth, that his disciples were missing the point and in the end would abandon him. Seeing then that his secret had been entrusted to him for the good of his fellow-men, was it not irresponsible and wrong of him to walk into a trap and allow himself to be killed before it had been handed on?

Was he trying to further his cause by martyrdom? It hardly seems likely. By sacrificing life itself for a cause or an ideal we may indeed induce others to take that cause more seriously; but it is first necessary that they know what that cause is. Jesus' death was not going to win anyone to his cause, for that cause was opaque to them.

Jesus was no fool. These obvious arguments cannot have escaped him. He knew that to all appearance the only way for him to save his secret was to save himself. But he also understood something men tend – or prefer – to forget: the logic of the Good. To anyone for whom love is the absolute and universal law of life the Good which love would choose in any given situation is the object of total loyalty. It may happen, indeed it often does, that there is some particular good to which we are devoted which we shall not be able to carry out unless we are prepared to compromise, to abandon another demand of love at some other point. But if we do compromise in this way, we prove that, however faithful we may be to some particular good thing, the Good in general, the absolute and universal principle of choosing the good course which love requires, does not command our total loyalty. To step outside the goodness of love, even for the sake (or the alleged sake) of that goodness, is to confess that love is not the supreme law of one's life.[1]

To the average person such an attitude seems strained, quixotic, absurd. It seems so even to the millions of Christians who daily pay lip-service to the Cross. They praise it, but they have never grasped what it is about. This means that they have failed to grasp not only what Jesus' death is about, but his life also. He could have interested the pious Jews in his theory, if love had not compelled him to speak the truth, truth so alien to them that they were inevitably antagonized. He could have interested the common people, if he had been prepared for them to take no notice of his theory in practice, and had allowed them to make him a revolutionary leader. He could have interested even the Gentiles, if he had been willing to set up a philosophical school in which the merits of such an ideal could have been discussed and its implications analysed. He might have persuaded his friends to take it seriously, if the urgency of love, which changes life so drastically, so recklessly that there is no time for the slow of heart to catch up, had not left them far behind, bewildered and afraid. He could have done all these things; and in the eyes of sober common sense it would have been better to have done them. For then people would have been brought gently to understand his secret – and in good time to accept it? Never. It would have remained for always what in fact it would have been, a theory.

For if we step outside the law of love in order to commend that law, to interest men in it, then we make certain that its power will never be revealed, that it will remain for ever nothing more than an abstract ideal. The real power is in our own wisdom, our pragmatic sense of tactical expediency, which claims to do for love something that we are sure love could never do for itself. If there is any power in the law of love, then that power can be manifested only in those who are loyal to that law, who believe in the power and do not imagine that they can do

[1] For the most profound of all modern treatments of this subject the reader is referred to the short work by Søren Kierkegaard, *Purity of heart is to will one thing*, the first of the *Edifying Addresses* which appeared in 1847 (English language edition, translated by Douglas V. Steere, published New York 1938, London 1961.) The present writer's own debt to this work is too great either to assess or describe.

anything for it which it cannot do better for itself. Hence, if obedience
to the law of love, loyalty to whatever good love willed to choose in the
given circumstances, meant that Jesus had steadfastly to set his face
towards Jerusalem and certain death, to have evaded that death would
have been to make irreparably sure that the power of love would be
sealed off, would have no chance to make itself felt. To have sought, by
human wisdom, to serve the cause to which his life had been devoted
would have been to throw that life away:

> Whoever seeks to gain his life will lose it, but whoever loses his life will
> preserve it (Lk. 17:33).

Jesus strikes us today very forcibly as a man who was free: free from
conventional restrictions and prejudices, free to follow truth and goodness to the full, free to give himself in love to the real needs of other
men. Such freedom emphatically indicates as its psychological basis a
complete and unshakeable confidence. Jesus never made any mystery
of the source of that confidence, since it formed the constant and central
theme of all his preaching: that God is sovereign over all men and all
things at all seasons, and that his sovereignty is that of a good and
loving Father.[1]

It would be easy to misunderstand this, to misrepresent it as no more
than a blind assurance that despite all appearances to the contrary he
was, as we say, 'on the winning side'. But, if we remember what has
just been said, it should be clear that this was not possible for Jesus.
God's victory depended on the planting of the secret, the word of life,
in the hearts of men. But it had not been planted. It had been scattered,
but it had not taken root. If he died at this juncture, there seemed no
reason why it ever should take root. And yet, if he did not die, it was
certain that it never would. How, in such circumstances, could there be
any arrogant or complacent assurance? Worldly idealists are fond of
assuming that if you sow love people will respond. Sometimes, thank
God, they do. Often they do not. It is one of the marks of wickedness
that it returns evil for good, sees good as an opportunity for evil. We

---

[1] There is a very sad passage in Paul van Buren's book, *The Secular Meaning
of the Gospel* (p. 133), where for one crucial moment he entertains the possibility
that this affirmation by Jesus might be true. 'It might be argued,' he writes, 'that
Jesus was "free" because "he trusted in the God of love".' But to take this
seriously would make nonsense of everything else in the book, and so, without
ever countering that argument, this trained logician escapes in total disorder
behind a smokescreen of incoherent verbiage.

cannot ensure that men will be good by doing good to them; in the world of goodness there are no such laws of cause and effect. It is indeed precisely because the good man cannot know what effect he will have that he is truly free. He is free to do good for its own sake, free to be crucified, daily and then finally, to lose all, to be deceived, to be a failure. If he is this, he is free; he is free to be this.

This freedom, however, has a paradoxical effect. The truly good man does not triumphantly accept his failure and defeat. It is failure and defeat which break his heart, because he really loves. The man who says, in exultation of spirit, 'I do not care that I have failed, I have done what was right and good,' demonstrates only that he is fundamentally self-centred. The good man does not care about his own goodness, because he cares for all the men and women for whom truth will be hidden, hope destroyed, and love discredited by his defeat, for all those who will see his 'Here I stand' as mere egotistical obstinacy, as a foolish and futile betrayal of the good, for God who suffers in the evil and perversity of his children. He cannot take comfort in the thought that sacrifice is the most 'effective' way of converting others, because he more than anyone knows how shallow and false such a notion is. He of all men knows the difference between genuine sacrifice and moral blackmail.

Why then should we be surprised, when we read that best attested of all the words of Jesus from the cross, the only one indeed which Matthew and Mark record, the cry of dereliction?

> And at the ninth hour Jesus cried with a loud voice, 'Eloi, Eloi, lama sabachthani?' which means, 'My God, my God, why hast thou forsaken me?' (*Mk* 15:34.)

It really is inconceivable that the church should have invented this tradition. The narratives do indeed suggest a certain confusion as to what was said (*Mk* 15:35–36; *Matt.* 27:46–49); but this only confirms one's feeling that someone must have been sure of the words, for otherwise here was a ready-made way of avoiding them. Luke and John leave them out; each has a completely different set of three sayings from the cross.[1] Most of these are historically perfectly possible, and

---

[1] *Luke*: 'Father, forgive them; for they know not what they do' (23:34); 'Truly, I say to you, today you will be with me in Paradise' (23:43); 'Father, into thy hands I commit my spirit' (23:46). *John*: 'Woman, behold your son! – Behold your mother!' (19:26–27); 'I thirst' (19:28); 'It is finished' (i.e., achieved, accomplished: 19:30).

are certainly in character; but by this very quality they throw into bolder relief the rugged factuality of the one which at first sight seems out of character, and which has of choice been avoided. How are we to understand it?

First, we need to remember the Old Testament background. In old Israel the righteous who are in affliction constantly question God and pray for deliverance, on the grounds that in their defeat God himself is defeated; and an attentive reading of *Psa.* 22, of which Jesus' cry is part of the opening phrase, will show that this is the context of these words also. But, it may be asked, if Jesus, as we have argued, was convinced that it was God's will for him that he should bear in his own person the Messianic woes of Israel, why should he at this juncture think that God had forsaken him?

Secondly, we must be careful not to read into the words extravagant conclusions about Jesus' spiritual state at the time, conclusions which go well beyond anything which the actual words justify. It is still on God and on the dialogue with him that his being is centred; and the word, 'why?' at least does not exclude a reason behind what has happened. Moreover, we can be fairly certain that it was not his own personal fate that was worrying him. His belief in resurrection for all men, quite apart from any question of his own unique role, and his lifelong conviction of God's mercy and forgiveness tell against this. Relevant here may be Luke's story of the penitent thief. We should perhaps think of this man as one brought up on the stories of the martyr-heroes of his nation who fought the religious wars of independence against the Greeks in the second century B.C. If so, then he will also have believed that God would grant the prayers of such faithful men (as well as those of the earlier patriarchs and prophets), and here at his side was one like them, the prophet and healer from Galilee, falsely condemned. Surely this man would enter into the inheritance of the kingdom of heaven, laid up for the saints? Perhaps if he asked his prayers, Jesus would intercede with God and win forgiveness for him. 'Sir,' he said, 'remember me when you come into your kingdom.' 'Truly, I say to you,' came the reply, 'today you will be with me in Paradise.' The incident is found only in *Luke*, but as we have said, there is nothing in it which is historically impossible.

Our real difficulty with the cry of dereliction is that we cannot help seeing it from our side of the resurrection and the subsequent history and faith of the church. If we assume, as the evangelists did, that Jesus envisaged events exactly as they did in fact turn out, then of course it is incomprehensible. Everything was going according to plan, and there was no reason to think in terms of failure and defeat at all. But if we consider the situation in the light of the expectation which we have argued in the previous chapter that Jesus did hold, then matters look very different. On all sides he was surrounded by mockery and abuse and the triumphant taunts of his persecutors (*Mk* 15:29–32; *Matt.* 27:39–44; *Lk.* 23:35–38). Not one in all this chosen people of God, maybe not even the friends whose lives he had managed to save, had caught the spirit and message of the Messianic kingdom of which they were to be the citizens. Once during his work of preaching he had asked, 'When the Son of man comes, will he find faith on the earth?' (*Lk.* 18:8). Now it seemed terribly plain that the answer would be 'No'. This was the anxiety that haunted him; and now there was no time left to do anything about it. God had apparently allowed him to fail. Judgement would come, and find God's kingdom unpeopled. Whether he died with the agony unresolved, or, as Luke's tradition suggests, in a recovered peace (*Lk.* 23:46), we cannot tell. In either case, the vindication of the truth, the survival of the secret of true human life, had finally passed out of his hands into the hiddenness of God.

The implications of this for an understanding of Jesus' permanent significance, of his liberating and transforming effect on our own existence, must wait for the next chapter. We shall then have to come to terms with the fact that his own picture of God's plan was wrong, and begin to learn not simply that this does not matter but that it is an essential element in the whole divine plan for remaking our lives in accordance with the truth. But first we must ask how it was that Jesus was vindicated, and that his fundamental vision did survive.

There is a phrase which has had some currency as a taunt against Christians on the run in a scientific age. They are said to believe in a 'God of the gaps', the gaps in question being the ever-closing gaps in our scientific knowledge. This is in fact, as we saw early on, the exact reverse of the truth, since God is Creator, and therefore the more we know about his world, the more, one way and another, we know about him. But in another sense Christians do most definitely believe in a 'God of the gap', one particular gap. This is, of course, the gap of about thirty-six hours between 3 o'clock on the afternoon of a certain Friday and dawn on the following Sunday. What happened in that gap is hidden from us beyond our knowledge. But that Jesus did rise from the dead as his friends affirmed is attested by the resurrection of that secret which went down into the grave with him, the secret of the sovereignty of God.

The stories in the Gospels about the resurrection of Jesus present their own peculiar problems. Opinions differ to what extent it is possible to put together a connected narrative of the appearances of the risen Jesus, or to reconstruct what 'happened' when he did appear. Since as events they are utterly without analogy in the experience of mankind, we can have no criteria to help us decide. The accounts speak of mingled terror and joy, of difficulty at first encountered in realising who it was who had come among them. All agree that after not too long a period the encounters ceased, but – and this is the significant point – that their cessation did not give rise to doubt or regret or an attempt to regain the experiences but to a sense of mission and a certainty that from the glorious and triumphant Jesus nothing could ever separate them again.[1]

Because the stories are, as regards their content if not their literary interrelation, difficult to handle with the techniques of criticism, they fall short of providing decisive evidential reasons for belief in the resurrection of Jesus. Readers tend to find them convincing or otherwise according to their presuppositions. This is nothing new. When Paul preached the Gospel in Athens, *Acts* records the reactions (which must have been typical of the experience of most Christian missionaries):

Now when they heard of the resurrection of the dead, some mocked; but others said, 'We will hear you again about this.' (*Acts* 17:32).

Others have found a difficulty in the relatively small number of people who are said to have experienced the Risen Jesus. Even if we accept the Pauline tradition that on one occasion he appeared to more than five hundred 'brethren' – and this raises some puzzling questions[2]

---

[1] This, and not any 'return to the sky', is the central meaning of the various versions of the 'Ascension' (*Lk*. 24:44–53; *Acts* 1:6–11; *John* 20:17–18; *Mk* 16:14–20; *Matt.* 28:16–20).

[2] 'Brethren' presumably implies 'Christians' in some distinctive sense; if so, five hundred seems a very large number for the period traditionally associated with the resurrection appearances. *Acts* puts the full muster of the original Jerusalem church at one hundred and twenty (1:15). *Matthew* and *John*, however, place some resurrection appearances in Galilee, the scene of Jesus' early ministry

– the number is not large, and was made up entirely of disciples. Why no appearances to his enemies, or to the world at large?

In *Luke* there is a comment on this aspect of the matter which is sometimes overlooked. It comes at the end of the so-called Parable of Dives and Lazarus (*Lk.* 16:19–31), which is not a true parable but rather an edifying tale. The hard core of the story seems to be that reversal of earthly fortunes in the age to come which we have seen as an element in Jesus' teaching. There is a rich man, Dives, who lives in the greatest luxury, and there is a beggar outside his house, covered with the sores of malnutrition. The dogs come and lick the sores of this wretched, helpless hunk of humanity, but the affluent man never notices, never cares.[1] In time both die. The rich man goes to hell, the beggar to paradise. The dwellers in one realm can see those in the other,[2] but are kept apart by the great abyss. So, when Dives asks Abraham to allow the beggar to do for him that which he in his lifetime never bothered to do for the beggar – give him a drink of water – it is impossible as well as unjust to grant his prayer. Dives then asks that Lazarus be sent back to earth as a supernatural visitant to warn the rich man's five brothers of the fate in store for the uncharitable. So far there is nothing in the story which could not be simply Judaistic, but the ending has acquired a Christian twist:

> But Abraham said, 'They have Moses and the prophets; let them hear them.' And he said, 'No, father Abraham; but if some one goes to them from the dead, they will repent.' He said to him, 'If they do not hear Moses and the prophets, neither will they be convinced if someone should rise from the dead' (16:29–31).

The ideas are still those of Judaism; the Law and the Prophets command love of neighbour, there is no need for miraculous intervention.

[1] The callousness of the man is not contrasted with the 'kindness' of the dogs – perhaps our natural western way of reading it. The detail is meant to emphasize the man's weakness; he cannot even keep the scavenger dogs away. If the reader reflects for a moment, he may conclude that he would not find the attention mentioned particularly kind.

[2] A theme which reappears in some Christian speculations about heaven and hell.

(*Matt.* 28:16; *John* 21). It may be that there were more professed followers of Jesus in that district, or even that Jesus' following was more coherently organized even in his lifetime than the Gospels indicate, or simply that the figure is inflated. But such speculation will not get us very far.

If goodness does not commend itself to them for its own sake, or as God's revealed will, then no amount of signs and wonders will make any difference. The Christian adaptation, however, is to be seen in the words 'rise from the dead'. The implications have now gone far beyond those of the original idea, and clearly have the resurrection of Jesus in mind, and the refusal of the Jews as a whole to pay heed to this event. This in turn gives new meaning to the reference to Moses and the prophets; for it is a constant motif of Christian preaching in the New Testament that the resurrection of Christ was predicted in the Old Testament Scriptures.[1]

The general point now, therefore, is closely akin to the one we have been so often considering. If Jesus cannot be accepted as the true revelation of God in his life and teaching, then his resurrection carries no weight. The moral challenge comes first. In his lifetime Jesus had constantly refused to perform supernatural conjuring tricks in order to impress. This still holds good. The resurrection is not there to bludgeon into submission those for whom the Gospel of the sovereignty of God exercised through the absolute and universal law of love is a closed book; for it is a vindication of this sovereignty, and of Jesus as its agent and manifestation. To everyone else it is meaningless and therefore incredible. Appearances to his enemies or to the pagans would thus convey nothing, or, worse still, the wrong thing. Only to those who have already caught the spirit of Jesus' love will Easter bring the true joy, for this joy is precisely that Love reigns at the heart of the universe.

Another difficulty of rather a different kind is felt by some over the nature of the resurrection appearances; for the stories in the Gospels steer a middle course between two possibilities, either of which would have been more the kind of account one might 'expect' – if that is not too bizarre a word to use of something wholly unexpected. The matter may perhaps be put this way. If we think of the mental and religious background of the earliest Christians, and then ask how they might have framed a story of Jesus' return from the grave, had they been inventing one, two possible versions suggest themselves. The most likely is that they would have described him in terms of a heavenly being, someone of transcendent light and glory. We know, for example, that some Jews thought of resurrection in these images. At the

---

[1] This has passed into the Creed: 'and the third day he rose again *in accordance with the Scriptures*' (cf., e.g., *I Cor.* 15:4; *Lk.* 24:25–27, 44–47; *John* 5:39, 46).

close of the book of *Daniel*, a work which in its present form dates from the middle of the second century B.C., the writer speaks of the celestial radiance of the righteous sages of Israel, after God has raised them up at the last day:

> And those who are wise shall shine like the brightness of the firmament and those who turn many to righteousness, like the stars for ever and ever (*Dan.* 12:3).

A similar picture is painted by the *Wisdom of Solomon*, a book which may belong to the period immediately before or just after the life of Christ:

> But the souls of the righteous are in the hand of God . . . and . . . they shall shine, and run to and fro like sparks among the stubble (*Wisd.* 3:1, 7).

The convention arises no doubt from conforming human beings in the enjoyment of eternal life to those other inhabitants of heaven, the angels, who were customarily portrayed in terms of dazzling brightness. That there was certainly no bar to describing Jesus in this way is apparent from two passages in the New Testament. The first is John the Divine's vision of the heavenly Jesus:

> I saw . . . in the midst of the lampstands one like a son of man, clothed with a long robe and with a golden girdle round his breast; his head and his hair were white as white wool, white as snow; his eyes were like a flame of fire, his feet were like burnished bronze, refined as in a furnace, and his voice was like the sound of many waters; in his right hand he held seven stars, from his mouth issued a sharp two-edged sword, and his face was like the sun shining in his strength (*Rev.* 1:12–16).

The second is the story of the Transfiguration:

> And after six days Jesus took with him Peter and James and John his brother, and led them up a high mountain apart. And he was transfigured before them, and his face shone like the sun, and his garments became white as light (*Matt.* 17:1–2).[1]

---

[1] Matthew's version is quoted as being the more typical of this kind of imagery. Mark (9:2–3) is less conventional. Luke (9:29) says simply that 'the appearance of his countenance was altered, and his raiment became dazzling white'. The sense is the same in all three cases.

We shall have occasion to consider the significance of the second passage later.

The other possibility for the resurrection appearances is that Jesus should have been restored to his normal human state. This would have had no exact precedent in Jewish tradition, though it would require only a slight adjustment of an already existing type of miracle story.[1] That the possibility of presenting the conquest of death in these terms was available to the early church is clear, for example, from the accounts of the raising of the widow's son at Nain (*Lk.* 7:11–17) and of Lazarus (*John* 11). Jesus' subsequent departure to heaven would provide no problem, since the idea of a bodily assumption of especially favoured friends of God was already firmly embedded in Jewish thinking. Thus, Elijah is taken up to heaven in a chariot of fire (*II Kings* 2:11–12); and Enoch, one of the patriarchs before the Flood, was also said to have been translated while still alive (*Gen.* 5:24). The reference to this latter story in *Hebrews* (11:5) shows that Christians were just as conscious of this tradition as were other Jews.

Either of these approaches would have served excellently to convey all the obvious implications of Jesus' resurrection. In the light of the religious thought of the time we would certainly expect one or other of them. In fact we find neither. The Risen Jesus falls into neither of these ready-made formats. This faces us straightaway with the following question: if the disciples were inventing the story that Jesus had come back to life, or if they were simply trying to convey an inner certainty that his soul, like that of John Brown, went marching on, is there not a probability that they would have used, albeit with minor variations, a convention recognizably akin to those already current in their world of thought? We have, after all, noticed how easily and how often they succumb to the influence of that world; and generally speaking it is only the distinctive individuality of Jesus himself, preserved in the tradition, that saves them from it. Is there not, then, a *prima facie* case to consider, that they did in fact have distinctive experiences, which have affected the story they had to tell?

There is a tendency today, even among those scholars who conclude that there was an objective resurrection (not merely a mystical experience on the part of the disciples), to say that we cannot hope to

---

[1] In the O.T., cf., e.g., Elijah and the widow's son (*I Kings* 17:17–24) and the similar story of Elisha (*II Kings* 4:8–37). In *II Kings* 13:21 a dead Israelite is revived by contact with the bones of Elisha.

know anything of what actually 'happened'. The record is so over-
grown with legend, so elaborated with fanciful detail, and so full of
divergences and inconsistencies, that any inquiry of this sort is
doomed to failure. The change in the disciples makes it clear that
something happened to change them; and with that we must be content.
But this approach is unnecessarily timid. It ignores the important
principle which we considered in the last chapter: that there must be
some reason, when every allowance has been made for legendary
accretion and for assimilation to current thinking, why the Gospel
took this particular form and not some other; and that this reason must
ultimately be sought in the facts about Jesus himself. If this is applied
to the question of the resurrection, its relevance is obvious. Precisely
because the stories, for all their legendary and conventional elements,
do not fall into a standard pattern, do not present a series of purely
traditional episodes and images, we have *prima facie* grounds for
inquiring whether certain hard facts have not determined the overall
shape of the narrative, and whether we may not make a reasonable
guess what these facts were.

One disadvantage which makes this task harder than it might otherwise have been must be mentioned. As a glance at any modern translation of the New Testament will show,[1] Mark's Gospel ends abruptly,
and various alternative postscripts have been supplied in the ancient
manuscripts. The main body of the text tells how three women
followers of Jesus went to the tomb on the morning of the first day of
the week to anoint the body and prepare it more decently for permanent
burial than had been possible in the haste of Good Friday. They find
the rock tomb open and empty, and see a young man in white who
gives them the news of the resurrection:

> And he said to them, 'Do not be amazed; you seek Jesus of Nazareth,
> who was crucified. He has risen, he is not here; see the place where they
> laid him. But go, tell his disciples and Peter that he is going before you
> to Galilee; there you will see him, as he told you.' And they went out
> and fled from the tomb; for trembling and astonishment had come
> upon them; and they said nothing to any one, for they were afraid (*Mk*
> 16:6–8).

Two possibilities are open: first, that this is all that Mark intended to
write, and that later hands, feeling this to be bald and unsatisfactory,

[1] E.g., the Revised Standard Version, the New English Bible, or the Jerusalem
Bible.

rounded the narrative off with selections from the tradition; or secondly, that the text is incomplete. The latter seems to most scholars the more likely solution. The Greek (though this does not show in the English renderings) almost certainly breaks off in mid-sentence; the young man's prediction seems to demand some account of its fulfilment in a meeting between the Risen Jesus and his followers, such as we find in other Gospels. If so, then either the text was damaged at a very early stage – for example, the final column of the scroll may have been torn off before any copies had been made – or Mark was prevented from finishing it.[1]

The point is of some importance. If Mark really had finished at the words '. . . for they were afraid', then he had no appearance stories to include; if he had not finished, as seems more probable, then he had at least one, and presumably one fulfilling the promise: '. . . he is going before you into Galilee; there you will see him.' This must make a difference to our attitude to the appearance stories in the other three Gospels. All are later than *Mark*, perhaps by as much as thirty years in the case of *John*. If we had to assume that *Mark* told of no encounter with the risen Jesus, and that such tales had needed fifty to sixty years to find a place in the written records, then we might well feel more hesitant about using them. As it is, such complete scepticism is not called for. We need only make due allowance for the longer period of elaboration.

This much said, the next point of interest is that Matthew's account of the appearance of the risen Jesus to his followers is in substance largely what *Mark* leads us to expect, but does not provide. Matthew has inserted a note of his own to counter the allegation by the Jews that the empty tomb was due to nothing more than the theft of Jesus' body by the disciples (27:62–66; 28:4, 11–15). There are other brief additions which we shall examine shortly. The Gospel ends with the following words:

Now the eleven disciples went to Galilee, to the mountain to which Jesus had directed them. And when they saw him they worshipped him; but

[1] It is now widely held that *Mark* was composed in Rome for the use of the church there. If one were writing a romance of the early Church in the manner of Lloyd C. Douglas, this would provide a fine opportunity for a dramatic scene: Mark writing furiously in the middle of the night to finish his work; then the hammering on the door, and Nero's soldiers burst in and arrest him, the manuscript just hidden in time. There have been less plausible theories.

R

some doubted. And Jesus came and said to them, 'All authority in heaven and on earth has been given to me. Go therefore and make disciples of all nations, baptizing them in the name of the Father and of the Son and of the Holy Spirit, teaching them to observe all that I have commanded you; and lo, I am with you always, to the close of the age' (*Matt.* 28:16–20).

The threefold formula of baptism (still used throughout Christendom today), and the expectation of a lengthy if indeterminate history for the Church, may be attributed to Matthew's later date and to his church-centred attitude, of which we have already seen evidence. If, however, we leave aside for the moment the question of presentation, the fact remains that the heart of Matthew's Easter story is a single major appearance in Galilee. We have here either an echo of Mark's lost ending or of tradition like that which he intended to use.

Two other features of Matthew's account must be mentioned. The first is his elaboration of the scene at the tomb: the rolling back of the stone at the door is now seen by the women; moreover, it is the work of an angel, and is accompanied by an earthquake. In *Mark* the women found the tomb open and empty, and it is not made clear whether the 'young man' in white, whom they found inside, is meant to be human or angelic. But such changes are the natural result of pious dramatization. The second feature is of more interest. On leaving the tomb, in *Matthew*, the women

departed quickly . . . with fear and great joy, and ran to tell his disciples. And behold, Jesus met them and said, 'Hail!' And they came up and took hold of his feet and worshipped him. Then Jesus said to them, 'Do not be afraid; go and tell my brethren to go to Galilee, and there they will see me' (*Matt.* 28:8–10).

Was there anything in *Mark* corresponding to this appearance? One small clue makes it highly likely that there was some episode between the proclamation to the women and the encounter in Galilee which we have conjecturally reconstructed. This is the phrase, 'and they said nothing to any one' (*Mk* 16:8). If the evangelist was to arrange for Jesus' message to reach the disciples, then a further incident was necessary to bring this about; and following the hint afforded by the verses from *Matthew*, it would seem that it was a meeting with Jesus himself. On the other hand, it is unlikely to have been a meeting between Jesus and the women, as it is in *Matthew*. It may have been with Peter[1] – though obviously we cannot be sure. Be the details what they may, we have therefore good reason to think that the Easter narrative in *Mark*, like that in *Matthew*, consisted of three basic elements: the news of the resurrection given to the women at the empty tomb; a meeting between Jesus and one or more individuals immediately afterwards; a subsequent major and decisive appearance to all the disciples in Galilee. If *Matthew's* outline is to be trusted as a guide to the lost passage of *Mark*, then this last encounter serves the same purpose as the 'Ascension' stories in *Luke* and *Acts*, namely to mark the end of the resurrection appearances, and yet to leave the disciples with a sense of mission and of permanent fellowship with their exalted Lord.[2] What is more, though the appearances are only two in number, yet significantly they are divided between Galilee and the neighbourhood of Jerusalem.

When, therefore, we come to consider the two Gospels in which the resurrection experiences are treated at much greater length, *Luke* and *John*, it is vital to begin by noting that this same basic pattern is still discernible: proclamation to the women (*Lk.* 24:1–11; *John* 20:1, 11-13) encounter with a few individuals (*Lk.* 24:13–35; *John* 20:14–18); final and decisive meeting with the principal disciples (*Lk.* 24:36–53; *John* 20:19–23, 26–29). The distribution between Galilee and Jerusalem remains a potent factor, but in a more complex way.

The final chapter of *John* may be a supplement to the original form of the work; certainly the closing verses of the last chapter but one (20:30–31) read like an ending to the whole story. This supplementary chapter is devoted entirely to the record of an appearance of Jesus to seven of his closest followers in Galilee, on the shore of the Lake of Tiberias. Like every other part of the book this chapter is densely packed with hints and allusions of profound interest, but only a few will concern us directly. The first is the symbolism of the haul of fish (21:11). The number of fish, one hundred and fifty-three, is deliberately chosen. According to some Jewish sages there were this number of different species of fish in the world; the implication here is that the

[1] An early appearance to Peter is attested by Paul (*I Cor.* 15:5), where it would seem to be the first of the appearances; the exact phrasing should be noted: '. . . he was raised on the third day in accordance with the scriptures, and . . . he appeared to Cephas, *then* to the twelve'. The same order of events appears to underlie *Lk.* 24:34. Tradition makes Mark a close friend of Peter (cf. *I Pet.* 5:13).

[2] Cf. p. 251 above.

disciples, called by Jesus according to the traditional story to be 'fishers of men', would, in Matthew's phrase, 'make disciples of all nations'. In other words, this is John's version of the sending of the Church to the Gentiles, which, as we have seen, is an important aspect of the decisive resurrection encounter in other versions also. In *Luke* and *Acts* (which as companion volumes may be regarded for our present purposes as one work) this mission charge is again prominent (*Lk.* 24:47; *Acts* 1:8). But Luke has no appearance of the risen Jesus in Galilee; indeed, he stresses that the twelve apostles, whom he consistently treats as the heart of the Church, never left Jerusalem – in fact that they were explicitly commanded by Jesus not to do so (*Lk.* 24:49–53; *Acts* 1:4–5). In keeping with this presentation he has omitted all reference to the saying, given so special a place in the *Mark* and *Matthew* narratives, 'I will go before you into Galilee' (*Mk* 14:28; 16:7; *Matt.* 26:32; 28:7, 10, 16). Since he knew Mark's Gospel, he must have known of this tradition; hence his treatment is quite deliberate. The most probable explanation is this.[1] Galilee, with its mixed pagan and Jewish population, referred to in the Old Testament as 'Galilee of the nations' (*Isa.* 9:1),[2] was understood by Luke as a symbol of the whole Gentile world.[3] Jesus' prediction was fulfilled not in one resurrection appearance, but in the whole history of the church, led by Jesus on its worldwide mission radiating from Jerusalem.

Is it possible to decide between these two presentations? Did the disciples return for a time to the district which for most of them was home (cf. *Matt.* 26:69–73)? Is Luke idealizing in view of the undoubted fact that for more than thirty years Jerusalem was revered by Christians as the mother congregation of the whole Church? Or are Matthew and John giving a literal interpretation to a saying of Jesus, remembered in the tradition, the original meaning of which had been lost? If we had Mark's own actual (or intended) ending, we might be in a better position to say. On balance the present writer is inclined to think that from a variety of motives – partly because Jerusalem was too dangerous (*John* 20:19), partly because Jesus' own mission had begun from Galilee and his memory commanded more allegiance there, and

---

[1] Brilliantly set out by C. F. Evans in an article in the *Journal of Theological Studies*, April 1954.

[2] A passage quoted in *Matt.* 4:15–16.

[3] It is possible that it may fulfil a similar role in *John*, Judaea there standing in a similar way for Jewry.

partly, it may be, under the influence of the 'Galilee' saying, whether understood or not – there was a temporary move to Galilee, and that this may have been one of the jumping-off points for the spread of the Gospel; but that the principal leaders very soon returned to Jerusalem, and some indeed may never have left there. What is absolutely clear, however, from all the versions, is that the disciples received from the Easter experiences not merely the conviction that Jesus had been vindicated as God's appointed Saviour and that he was alive for ever-more, but that it was their duty to carry the news of his teaching and of this confirmation of it to a wider circle of people. And this conviction grew not just out of the experiences of one or a few individuals but chiefly out of something we have called the 'decisive' encounter between Jesus and his principal followers in a body.

One other very striking feature of the basic pattern of the Easter narratives should be mentioned. This is the agreement about the role of the women. The hard core of this tradition is quite precise: the women who went to the tomb were given not a meeting with Jesus but an in-timation that he was alive. In the formal summary of resurrection appearances cited by Paul (*I Cor.* 15:3–7) they are not mentioned. Paul's list is not a narrative; it is very nearly a creed. But in fact, even as narrative, it concurs with the basic pattern; it does not conflict. For this is a list of encounters with the risen Jesus in person; it does not include hints, messages, or intimations. That before too long the tendency to elaborate had not only created an appearance to the women (*Matt.* 28:9; *John* 20:14–18), but had begun to bring the apostles into this early stage is shown by the episode in *John* (20:3 10), where Peter and the beloved disciple run to the empty tomb and inspect it for themselves. But alongside this the earlier version remains (20:1–2); and that it should be these devoted but humble and relatively insignificant followers who are given the credit for the discovery in every gospel is historically impressive. It is not, one may think, the kind of detail anyone would have thought or wished to invent. *John* and *Matthew* (but not *Luke*) say that they also met Jesus; but Mark's closing words tell against this, as they also suggest that the story of their taking the news to the menfolk may be a later tidying of the narrative. If indeed they kept their discovery to themselves – perhaps out of distress which at first they had no wish to communicate to the rest – and only revealed their secret after the first appearances, then this strengthens rather than weakens one's feeling that this incident has all the awkward corners of a piece of fact. What then did they see? Was there, as *Mark* relates, a young man at the tomb already, who had found it empty and broke the news to them? Possibly. In any event we may think that it was the empty sepulchre which best explains both their silence and the later recognition of their importance as witnesses.

Moreover, this surely is the correct approach to the question of the empty tomb. In modern times Christians have been prone to place too much emphasis on this feature of the story. It is a tendency which springs, whether consciously or not, from the desire to avoid any appeal to the 'supernatural'. An empty grave and a dramatic change of heart and character in once frightened and uncomprehending men – these, it is felt, are solid facts which even the most earthy sceptic must respect. Hence it is best to argue from these, and to avoid the dubious ground of the miraculous and unexampled. But, of course, it is precisely in so far as they are ordinary and everyday (even assuming what is not at all necessary, that a non-believer will be prepared to accept the emptiness of the tomb without question) that they are insufficient. Nor is the importance accorded to the empty tomb in the New Testament itself such as to justify our giving it a pre-eminent place. Paul never appeals to it, but always to the evidence of those who had met the risen Jesus – among whom, as we must consider later, he includes himself. And in the gospel narratives themselves the tomb plays a restricted, if definite, part, namely to disturb, to arouse wonder, fear, conjecture. The evangelists themselves make this point. In *Luke* the depressed disciples walking to Emmaus are quite clear that the tomb was empty, but they are no more convinced by this than by angelic messages:

> Moreover, some women of our company amazed us. They were at the tomb early in the morning and did not find his body; and they came back saying that they had even seen a vision of angels, who said that he was alive. Some of those who were with us went to the tomb,[1] and found it just as the women had said; but him they did not see (*Lk.* 24:22–24).

But him they did not see. That is the crucial point, as the evangelists very well knew, even if their modern apologists have forgotten it. In the end everything hinges on the actual encounters with Jesus. Having clarified some of the problems concerning the setting, structure, and nature of the narratives as a whole, it is to this central question that we must now turn.

[1] Cf. the comment on *John* 20:3–10 at p. 261 above.

When we do, however, we find that the empty tomb does indeed have a special significance, though not the one that contemporary Christians of a traditionalist turn of mind usually ascribe to it. It is of no special moment as evidence for the bare fact of a return to life of the man who had been laid in it thirty-six hours before; but if it had not been empty there could never have been the particular kind of resurrection of which the Gospels try to tell. For another strange conviction in which the narratives are at one is that the risen Jesus was in some sense still using the body which had hung upon the cross.

It will be remembered that Mark and Matthew tell us nothing relevant to this aspect of the question. Mark, it is true, might have done; but it is improbable that he did. Matthew certainly does not. We have to rely therefore entirely on *Luke* and *John*. Luke brings out the physical nature of the risen Jesus in two incidents. In the house at Emmaus Jesus takes a piece of bread in his hands, breaks it, and gives the pieces to his hosts. Later the same evening the same point is made even more strongly:

> As they were saying this, Jesus himself stood among them. But they were startled and frightened, and supposed that they saw a spirit. And he said to them, 'Why are you troubled, and why do questionings rise in your hearts? See my hands and feet, that it is I myself; handle me and see; for a spirit has not flesh and bones as you see that I have.' And while they still disbelieved for joy, and wondered, he said to them, 'Have you anything here to eat?' They gave him a piece of broiled fish, and he took it and ate before them (*Lk.* 24:36–42).

The passage has some puzzling features. One, however, is clear enough. The crucial test of recognition, the surest of all signs that this is indeed Jesus, is the marks of the nails of crucifixion in the hands and feet – 'See my hands and feet, that it is I myself.' Moreover, these are not merely a visual illusion: 'Handle me and see; for a spirit has not flesh and bones as you see that I have.' The same ingredients reappear in a story in *John*. The disciple Thomas had not been present on the occasion of Jesus' first appearance to the assembled disciples (20:24), and he refuses to believe their story except on one condition:

> Unless I see in his hand the print of the nails, and place my finger in the mark of the nails, and place my hand in his side, I will not believe (*John* 20:25).

A week later Jesus visits them again, and Thomas is present. Jesus invites him to carry out the test, to feel the nail-marks and the wound of the spear-thrust given to ensure that the victim had really died (19:32–37). Whether Thomas availed himself of the invitation is not made clear; but this is unimportant. Here, as in *Luke*, the invitation is given, and is meant to be taken seriously.

The other main element in the story in *Luke* is strange and ambiguous. Is it implied that Jesus really needed or desired to eat food for its own sake? Or is this simply another way of demonstrating the genuinely 'physical' nature of the risen body? Since, in the context, the incident is followed very quickly by the ascension to heaven, the former implication would have something ridiculous about it; but the latter is equally unsatisfactory in a different way. For the risen body manifestly is not physical in the same sense as the bodies of the disciples, or of Jesus before his crucifixion. It vanishes and appears at will (24:31, 36). There is moreover something unworthy about such a performance. If Jesus did not need to eat, then it smacks of a supernatural conjuring trick of the very kind he had abjured in life; and to anyone who had caught his spirit might seem to cast doubt on his identity rather than confirm it. Yet there is no question but that this particular piece of tradition was considered of great importance in the Lukan circle; it is included in Peter's speech at Caesarea, when he gives a summary of the Gospel to the Gentile household of Cornelius, as an outstanding proof of the resurrection:

> God raised him on the third day and made him manifest; not to all the people but to us[1] who were chosen by God as witnesses, who ate and drank with him after he rose from the dead (*Acts* 10:40–41).

Are there any other details which may throw light on it?

The motif of eating with the disciples occurs also in the supplementary chapter to *John*. The seven disciples fishing on the Sea of Tiberias find, when they get to land, that the risen Jesus has prepared a meal of fish and bread on a charcoal fire for them after their long night's work (*John* 21:3–4, 9–13). Here, however, though he serves them with food, there is no mention of his eating any himself. The same applies to the Emmaus story in *Luke*; it is the gesture of blessing, breaking, and giving which completes the episode (*Lk.* 24:30–31). At the very least, therefore, it looks as though Jesus' own eating is a rather inept legendary intensification of a tradition which began with a story of the

---

[1] Cf. pp. 251ff. above.

risen Jesus presiding over a meal with his disciples, as he had so often done in their ordinary life together. Moreover, it is clear that this resurrection meal is presented with very particular associations. These are brought out in the closing words of the Emmaus story:

> Then they told what had happened on the road, and how he was known to them in the breaking of the bread (*Lk.* 24:35).

In *Acts* this same phrase, 'the breaking of bread', is used to refer to the communal meal characteristic of the early Christians (*Acts* 2:42; cf. 2: 46; 20:7; *I Cor.* 10:16), from which grew up the sacrament of the Mass, Eucharist, or Holy Communion. This from the first recalled the Last Supper, shared by Jesus with his disciples on the night in which he went to his death; and the New Testament writers express this link by using the standard sequence, 'bless – break – give' (*Matt.* 26:26; *Mk* 14:22; cf. *Lk.* 22:19). Thus, when Luke writes of the dramatic moment in the house at Emmaus—

> When he was at table with them, he took the bread and blessed, and broke it, and gave it to them (*Lk.* 24:30)—

it is this association which is evoked. The same is probably true of the lakeside meal in *John*; though here the near-technical sequence of terms is not used (*John* 21:13). Finally, it should be pointed out that this latter story is composed of echoes of incidents during the ministry of Jesus: the miraculous draught of fishes (*Lk.* 5:1–11) and the feeding of the five thousand (cf. esp. *John* 6:11).[1] This inclines one to think that it is therefore a symbolic narrative in a long tradition rather than one directly deriving from a resurrection appearance.

On inspection, therefore, the theme of Jesus' eating with his disciples after his resurrection appears to have only slight foundation in actual reminiscence. But it does lead us to one last feature of these narratives which must be considered. The two disciples from Emmaus recognize Jesus for the first time by his characteristic gesture of blessing, breaking, and giving:

> Their eyes were opened and they recognized him (*Lk.* 24:31).

During the walk together a strange excitement had possessed them, but they had not realised why (*Lk.* 24:16, 32). A similar feature occurs in

[1] In *John* this incident and the subsequent discourses are full of indirect allusions to the Eucharist.

John. When Jesus hails the disciples' boat from the shore, they do not know him; it is the sudden extraordinary catch of fish which awakens them to the truth (*John* 21:4, 7). There may even be a suggestion that his appearance was still unfamiliar after they had joined him on the shore; but this is now no difficulty to them. They know it is he (21:12). How seriously are we to take this feature?

There is no hint of it in *Matthew*;[1] and this suggests that there was none in *Mark* either. The most likely origin of the idea is that the resurrection appearances at first caused terror and incredulity – a note which survives here and there in the Gospels (*Matt.* 28:17; *Lk.* 24:37–38) – and that it was only certain unmistakable personal signs and tokens which brought home to them what was happening. In the developed tradition this has been given theological significance. The risen Jesus assures men of his presence not by mere appearance but by the continuance of his acts of love and power – his miracles, the wounds of his crucifixion, the breaking of the bread, for ever hallowed by its association with his sufferings.[2]

Significantly, moreover, these are not just the phenomena of Easter. They accompany the history of the Church. Once again we find the conviction expressed that the resurrection is not simply the end of one story but the beginning of another, a story of an unbreakable fellowship between the living Jesus and his followers.

At the end of his letter to the *Galatians* Paul writes:

> But far be it from me to glory except in the cross of our Lord Jesus Christ (*Gal.* 6:14).

This theme of glorying in the cross, boasting about the fact that the founder of the faith had been executed as a criminal, is the common property of all the New Testament writers. The words are so familiar that we do not grasp how extraordinary they are; for in the context of the resurrection they immediately pose the question: 'Why glory in the cross, when Easter is the really "good news", the true heart of the

---

[1] The words, 'but some doubted' (*Matt.* 28:17), are too vague to require this explanation rather than any of a number of others.

[2] It is possible that the tradition of his eating and drinking with his disciples after his resurrection was also stimulated by the story of the Last Supper, as a fulfilment of the strange prediction made by Jesus on that occasion: 'I shall not drink again of the fruit of the vine until that day when I drink it new in the kingdom of God' (*Mk* 14:25). Cf. p. 235 above.

Gospel?' Or conversely, does this emphasis on the cross not suggest that Easter is not to be regarded as a separate event at all, but simply as a symbolic story embodying the conviction that the cross was indeed a victory, that Jesus' loyalty to the law of love even unto death was his supreme triumph, the fact about him which his followers must try to emulate, and of which they could be most justly proud?

The answer to these questions falls into two parts. The first is to be found in the observation with which the present chapter began, namely that when Jesus died his secret perished with him. The fact that this secret is now proclaimed to all the world, not merely as the secret of human life but as the power and wisdom of God (*I Cor.* 1:23–24) calls for some adequate explanation. This is not provided, if the assurance given to the disciples is simply an assurance that Jesus has won the last round. Jesus' followers were quite capable of seeing victory in the fact of resurrection without any help from anyone. This is precisely what would have come naturally to them. That of which they were not capable, that which (to judge from all their previous performance) was not natural to them, was to see victory in the cross. If there had been no resurrection at all, they certainly would never have come to see the cross in this light. But equally, if the resurrection had been purely one of transcendent glory, there would also have been nothing to make them see it. We are therefore under strong pressure, to say the least, to infer two things: first, that the resurrection events did give them experience of an independent, objective reality, since it was this reality which changed their whole outlook and scale of values, and no other event intervened which could have done so; secondly, that there was something about this event which was particularly adapted to open their eyes to this specific truth rather than to any other. When, therefore, we find in the accounts of the risen Jesus an insistence that in his restored and triumphant life the actual wounds of his Passion are retained as the badges of glory, we realise that this is not some dispensable piece of pious fiction. If this did not happen, then the New Testament and the whole story of the Church is inexplicable. The event may be unique, mysterious, supernatural; but every principle of historical argumentation demands that it be true. The purport of the resurrection events was not just to vindicate in a general way a man and his life and teaching; it was to specify the crucified human body as the means by which that vindication was fully and finally won.

For this reason the present writer cannot agree with those who regard the Transfiguration story mentioned earlier,[1] as a post-resurrection appearance which has somehow been moved back into the account of the ministry. Whatever led to the emergence of this story in its present form – and it would seem hopeless to conjecture – its basic meaning is not that of the Easter narratives. The divine radiance which shines from Jesus, like the voice from heaven and the figures of Moses and Elijah conversing with him, attests him the heavenly Messiah, the Son of the Most High. The note appended to the story in all three Gospels (*Matt.* 17:9; *Mk* 9:9; *Lk.* 9:36) to the effect that the disciples either did not, or were ordered not to, tell anyone about the occurrence until after the resurrection accords with the general standpoint of the Evangelists that Jesus' true identity was not understood till then. Luke alone uses the incident to point obliquely to the crucifixion as the event in which the will of God through his appointed saviour was finally achieved:

> Moses and Elijah . . . appeared in glory and spoke of his departure, which he was to accomplish at Jerusalem (*Lk.* 9:31).

Here the truth made plain by the resurrection experiences is hinted in advance. The theme of this story is eventually given full development as one of the strands running through the Fourth Gospel, where the 'glory' of Jesus is perfectly manifested on the Cross.

One more resurrection appearance remains, that which led to the conversion of Paul, the persecutor of the church, on the road to Damascus. Paul was in no doubt that he had encountered the risen Jesus, and that it was this which made him a witness to the resurrection, and therefore entitled to rank as an apostle:

> Last of all, as to one untimely born, he appeared also to me. For I am the least of the apostles, unfit to be called an apostle, because I persecuted the church of God. But by the grace of God I am what I am (*I Cor.* 15:8–10).

In Paul's own letters we do not have a description of this experience; we have to rely on the thrice-told tale of it in Luke's *Acts of the Apostles* (9:3–9; 22:6–11; 26:6–18). The three versions show a certain elaboration, the final account considerably expanding Jesus' words to Paul. As regards the actual manifestation, however, they are

[1] Cf. p. 254 above.

in agreement, mentioning with various degrees of emphasis only one outstanding phenomenon – an intense and dazzling light. We might suspect that this owed something to Luke himself, since he stresses in his story of the Ascension that the resurrection appearances properly so called have by now ceased, and this therefore would be a manifestation of Jesus from heaven. Nevertheless, there is one feature in Paul's own letters which suggests that his experience may well have been of this sort. He writes to the *Philippians*:

> But our commonwealth is in heaven, and from it we await a Saviour, the Lord Jesus Christ, who will change our lowly body to be like his glorious body, by the power which enables him even to subject all things to himself (*Phil.* 3:20–21).

The same idea seems to underlie his attempt to answer the question from Corinth, 'How are the dead raised? with what kind of body do they come?' (*I Cor.* 15:35–55). Paul apparently envisages that all men will enter into eternal life with bodies like that of Jesus, and the characteristic of this body is 'glory' – in biblical imagery an intense radiance, like that in the story of the Damascus road. Since there can be no reasonable doubt that something very remarkable did happen to Paul to cause his sensational conversion, it is fair to assume that it did in fact also have this character. If so, however, it differed from the resurrection experiences of the other apostles; for, as we considered earlier, one of the remarkable features of their story is precisely that the risen Jesus does not have this rather conventional appearance of a visitant from the heavenly world. This might suggest that Paul's enthusiastic emphasis on the Cross as the scene of God's triumphant power and wisdom came rather from his meditation on the tradition into which he entered than from his direct vision of the risen Lord. But the fact that in later years he apparently developed the stigmata of Christ in his own body (*Gal.* 6:17) may indicate that to him too Jesus had appeared with the wounds of the crucified.

This then is the first fundamental element in a proper assessment of the resurrection story. The risen Jesus is still the crucified Jesus, and the resurrection is not regarded as correcting, reversing, or cancelling the cross. This would have been a very natural way of taking it. The cross had been a scandalous injustice, a monstrous disgrace. As such, a good God ought to have stricken it from the record. It was an agony of mind and body which in a heavenly order ought to have been healed and forgotten, all traces erased. If the martyrs of Judaism were to shine like stars in the firmament, transfigured and glorious, showing no mark of their humiliation and torture, all the more should this man have been glorified. And the good news proclaimed to the world ought to have run that even the cross had not been able to frustrate the God who makes all things new, and whose salvation had been conceived by the Old Testament writers as the setting up of a kingdom where sorrow and sighing would be done away. The preaching of the early Church should by rights have been the preaching of the resurrection alone, with the cross merely setting the scene, a sad but defeated evil. Instead of this, however, Easter brought home to the disciples the truth that it is the 'word of the cross' which

> is folly to those who are perishing, but to us who are being saved . . . is the power of God . . . For since, in the wisdom of God, the world did not know God through wisdom, it pleased God through the folly of what we preach to save those who believe. For Jews demand signs and Greeks seek wisdom, but we preach Christ crucified, a stumbling block to Jews and folly to Gentiles, but to those who are called . . . Christ the power of God and the wisdom of God (*I Cor.* 1:18–24).

Many Christian writers today rightly emphasize this aspect; but their desire to avoid the scandal of the supernatural leads them to make two mistakes. First, they fail to see that it is only as an event in its own right that Easter achieves this result. It is not a mythological comment on the cross.[1] Hence, in the New Testament, the cross is never the whole heart of the Gospel. This consists of the Cross-and-Resurrection as a complex unity to which both elements are indispensable. Secondly, as an inevitable consequence of this they overlook the fact that this vindication of the cross is not the whole message of Easter. It has a further meaning which the cross by itself would never have been sufficient to convey.

In the New Testament there are two ways of referring to the resurrection. One is the form familiar to us from the Creeds and the developed language of Christian teaching, namely that 'Jesus rose from the dead'. This is found most often in the predictions of the resurrection attributed to Jesus by the Evangelists. The other, and more frequent form is to say that 'he was raised' or that 'God raised him' Thus, with classic simplicity, Peter declares to the crowd at Pentecost:

[1] This, in substance, is the view put forward by Bultmann in his *Theology of the New Testament*.

This Jesus God raised up, and of that we all are witnesses (*Acts* 2:32).[1]

A 'low' christology, that is to say, a view of Jesus as simply the human agent of God's salvation, even if later exalted by God to eternal glory, is more sympathetic to many people today than the traditional Christian presentation of him as God made man.[2] Appeal has therefore been made to the more frequent New Testament phrasing of the resurrection belief, in which Jesus is the passive object of God's action, to show that such a view is found in Scripture, and was the one held by the very first Christians. This may be true – though it should be remembered that this form of words is used freely by writers such as Paul who very definitely regarded Jesus as a divine being who became man. Whether true or not, however, it is quite beside the point. Our assessment of Jesus turns, as we shall see later, on other and more fundamental issues. The true importance of this evidence is to direct us to the second vital element in the resurrection story, the affirmation that it was indeed God who was at work in this event.

In the *Acts of the Apostles* Paul, who has been invited to make his defence before the Roman governor Festus and king Agrippa, asks:

Why is it thought incredible by any of you that God raises the dead? (*Acts* 26:8.)

Once more it must be stressed: the idea of resurrection is not new with Christianity. Easter does not open men's minds for the first time to the thought that death might be overcome in this way. What was unexpected about the resurrection of Jesus was its happening when it did; and what was new, as we have seen, was the character of the event, so different from any of the forms under which it had been envisaged in theory. In itself, however, simply as resurrection, it was but the realization of a possibility already entertained, discussed, and disputed. Paul, arraigned on another occasion before the Sanhedrin in Jerusalem, is able to throw his judges into dissension by declaring himself a Pharisee, and averring that the true grounds for his arrest and trial are not his particular membership of the Christian sect but his Pharisaic

[1] Similar phrasing occurs in Paul's letters, in the pseudo-Pauline *II Timothy*, and in *I Peter*.

[2] Cf., e.g., John Knox, *The Humanity and Divinity of Christ*, and W. Pannenberg, *Jesus, God, and Man*, who attaches great importance to the argument mentioned here.

belief in 'the resurrection of the dead' in general (*Acts* 23:6). The same line of argument, but running in the opposite direction, comes from Paul himself (not just from Luke's presentation of him) in *I Corinthians*:

> Now if Christ is preached as raised from the dead, how can some of you say that there is no resurrection of the dead? But if there is no resurrection of the dead, then Christ has not been raised; if Christ has not been raised, then our preaching is in vain and your faith is in vain. We are even found to be misrepresenting God, because we testified of God that he raised Christ, whom he did not raise if it is true that the dead are not raised. For if the dead are not raised, then Christ has not been raised (*I Cor.* 15:12–16).

But there is never any question, either for Christians or for those Jews who believed in resurrection, that this was an act which only God could perform. For those who, under the influence of Greek ideas, held that there was in each human person a spiritual entity, his soul, which was inherently immortal, there was no need for a new divine action to overcome death. But where the physical body was taken seriously as the essential medium of genuine human existence, death could not but be seen as fatally decisive, the end, irreversible by natural means, of the individual's identity, except in so far as he might live on in a different sense in his descendants, his works, or his remembrance. On an estimate of death so hardily realist any hope that it might after all not prove the end of everything must be a hope in God and no other; for where the human person has dissolved into nothingness only a new creation, in the strict sense of that word, can bring him back. And to create is something no one but God can do.

The resurrection of Jesus is thus stamped from the start as 'the Lord's doing'; and, working backwards from this indisputably divine act, all the rest of Jesus' story is now seen as approved and even arranged by God, not only the cross but the whole public career as well:

> 'Men of Israel, hear these words: Jesus of Nazareth, a man attested to you by God with mighty works and wonders and signs which God did through him in your midst, as you yourselves know – this Jesus, delivered up according to the definite plan and foreknowledge of God, you crucified and killed by the hands of lawless men. But God raised him up, having loosed the pangs of death, because it was not possible for him to be held by it' (*Acts* 2:22–24).

In the end, as everyone knows, this reappraisal in the light of the resurrection extends to the birth and very conception of Jesus.[1] There are other considerations – there were indeed for the early Church, notably in the fulfilment, as they saw it, of predictions in the Old Testament – which confirm this judgement. But it begins with the resurrection, the event which must be from God. Jesus' disciples did not assess his life, ministry, and death as morally incomparable, and then express their evaluation in a 'myth' of his divine origin and rising from the dead; it was the unmistakable hand of God in the objective fact of his resurrection which confirmed for ever their intuition of that same hand in all that had gone before.

But the light of the resurrection did not shine only backwards, to transfigure the past. It also lit up the future. Jewish thinking, working on Old Testament ideas, looked forward, as we have seen, to a final consummation of the history of the world, in which God's sovereignty would be fully and perfectly established in a new created order. It was on this Day of the Lord, the Last Day, that among other things the dead would rise to reward or retribution. There can be no doubt that in the earliest years of the Church Christians expected this Day to come at any moment; and this belief was unquestionably bound up with the fact of Jesus' resurrection.

> But in fact Christ has been raised from the dead, the *first-fruits* of those who have fallen asleep (*I Cor.* 15:20),

writes Paul; and he is of the mind that the Last Day may come so soon that some of those whom he is addressing will still be alive:

> Lo, I tell you a mystery. We shall not all sleep, but we shall all be changed, in a moment, in the twinkling of an eye, at the last trumpet. For the trumpet will sound, and the dead will be raised imperishable, and we shall be changed. For this perishable nature must put on the imperishable, and this mortal nature must put on immortality (*I Cor.* 15:51–53).

A picture slightly different in detail, but to the same effect, occurs in his first letter to the Thessalonians:

[1] Anyone who has engaged in arguments about Christianity knows how quickly and regularly the question of the Virgin Birth, that is, essentially the virginal conception of Jesus is mentioned. All that is asserted here is that the Easter conviction about Jesus has occasioned a supernaturalist interest in his birth and human origin which, to judge from its absence in *Mark*, was fairly slow to develop.

S

For this we declare to you by the word of the Lord, that we who are alive, who are left until the coming of the Lord, shall not precede those who have fallen asleep. For the Lord himself will descend from heaven with a cry of command, with the archangel's call, and with the sound of the trumpet of God. And the dead in Christ will rise first; then we who are alive, who are left, shall be caught up together with them in the clouds to meet the Lord in the air; and so we shall always be with the Lord (*I Thess.* 4:15–17).

The resurrection of Jesus is the beginning of the End, the prelude to the general resurrection and consummation of world history. It is because the one is so solid a fact, that the other seems to them so certain and immediate an expectation. They are the ones

upon whom the end of the ages has come (*I Cor.* 10:11).

In the life and work, the crucifixion and rising again of Jesus the end is already here, and once set in train cannot but run its course. Our own perspective of cosmic history is so incomparably more vast than theirs that the actual timing of the end ceases to concern us, and we look instead to the personal implications of the belief.[1] But the fact that their expectation was disappointed does not mean that the experience on which it was based was an illusion.[2] On the contrary, the intensity with which the first Christians looked for the dénouement of history in their own lifetime testifies to the reality of the resurrection which they inevitably understood as raising the curtain on the final scene.

[1] We might, of course, be wrong.
[2] Cf. the comments on the disappointment of Jesus' own, rather different expectation, pp. 249f. above and 297ff. below.

The World's Joy

THE TIME has come to ask: what difference has all this made? What are the permanent, essential, and universal changes which the advent of Jesus has effected in the condition of Man? The answers to this question all stem from the two fundamental truths about the resurrection – first, that it was an act of God, and secondly, that it was a vindication of Jesus.

There is not, there never could be any method of observing the process of miraculous divine intervention. With 'ordinary' events we can build up a fair, though never exhaustive picture of the way in which they came about. We can, as it were, write a scenario of the process. If there were such an event as a miracle, this scenario could never be composed, since the most important part of its supposed causation, God himself, is not accessible for us to observe. The results, certainly, can be investigated. The food eaten by the Five Thousand presumably had taste, satisfied hunger, was indistinguishable from ordinary bread and fish – in short, it was ordinary bread and fish. If it had been unusual, it could have been studied, and such study might in the end have been able to fit this food into the general pattern of our knowledge of the universe. Even if it failed to do so, yet, so long as there was something to observe, we would be justified in assuming that the difficulty lay in the limitations of our own understanding. When, however, we get back as far as the question: Where did the food come from? – then, if we assume for the moment that the traditional story is factually correct, we are baffled. There is nothing to observe, and there-fore our normal methods of investigation are useless. In the case of the resurrection appearances, again we have certain observable realities – a particular individual who is known to have died, but who is now alive; the wounds of his crucifixion; his presence at one moment, his absence at another, and so on – but the energies which produce these phenomena are not observable, in particular the power that made him alive when he had once been dead. He comes out of an impenetrable silence, an opaque order of existence; and all that we have is the result. We cannot, therefore, proceed by observation and comparative description. But this does not mean that we cannot proceed at all. Since, by everything we know of the universe, physical death is absolutely irreversible (indeed, irreversibility is the principal criterion for establishing death), the alleged result is in naturalistic terms impossible. If, nevertheless, this is what happened, then we are forced to supply a hypothetical explanation; but a hypothesis is no use unless it is adequate to the result it is required to explain. In this instance, no hypothetical cause will do except one which is not limited in its activity by the conditions of the universe, that is, it must have the attributes of the only being not included in the sum total of things, their hypothetical Creator, God.

The position, therefore, may be summed up like this. In the first part of the present work we argued as follows: there are several different types of answer to the ultimate question. One of them is an answer in terms of a Creator God, a good and personal being. If this particular answer is to be adequate to the facts of existence as we know them, then we must think of him in such-and-such a way, as a being with certain values and purposes. Only some such God as this would be credible, or, to put it the other way round, if there is a God, then this is roughly the kind of God he must be. But this particular vision of existence, even if it has been worked out carefully to make it adequate and consistent, is still only one among a number of basically diverse total explanations; and there is no valid way of choosing between them.

In the second part we have attempted a detailed historical critique, aimed at determining which aspects of the story of Jesus of Nazareth could reasonably demand our assent to them as historical realities. It has been argued that among these we must include his resurrection, not just as an inner spiritual conviction but as an objective event. But such an event, when accurately considered, will fit into only one of our various total explanations of existence, the one based on the hypothesis of God. And by the normal processes of reasoning, where out of a number of hypotheses there is only one which will accommodate *all* the evidence, this hypothesis is the one we adopt as the truest and best available.

The first and most obvious effect, therefore, of the resurrection of Jesus is a verification. *By a unique event, explicable in no other way, it confirms that there is a God, and that he designates Jesus as the one true Man.* The implications of this statement, however, need to be developed in some detail.

To begin with, it is important to remember that in certain respects the resurrection does 'confirm' rather than 'reveal'. The primary information which this event implies is not some entirely new conception, which never had nor ever could have entered anyone's head before. What does happen is that a total vision of existence, which hitherto had been confined to the realm of the conjectural now receives startling and specific support in human experience. A hope long cherished, sketched tentatively by various hands, and finally given classic definition in the teaching and life of one particular individual, now becomes more than a hope – something happens which pointedly singles out this as the right answer. This is, to be sure, a 'revelation' in a perfectly proper sense of that word. But the effect of the revelation is first of all rather to change the status of certain insights than to grant new ones, transforming them from hypothesis into faith. This could be done only by introducing something unprecedented, but this something was not an idea but a verification.

'Verification' is, admittedly, not an ideal word for what we need to say at this point. It implies too strongly the idea of proof through observation leading to 'knowledge'. This, in the nature of the case, we cannot have; as already considered, where God is involved this kind of proof is out of reach, because observation is impossible. Equally, however, it would be seriously underplaying the effect of the resurrection to speak of it as simply one more event, on a par with all others, and as amenable as they to all the various types of fundamental explanation. One of the first things that the resurrection does, therefore, is to define for us with a new precision the meaning of the term 'faith'. We are thinking of faith here not in its sense of personal trust but in its other religious aspect of conviction concerning the truth of what is believed. The way in which the word is commonly used in this latter context is to express the idea of holding to the truth of a particular but unprovable vision of reality. If, however, faith is understood simply in terms of this wide definition, it fails to do justice to the new factor which enters with the resurrection, and which for Christians gives faith a quality hitherto unknown. To represent the more general notion just described we may prefer to reserve the terms 'hope' or 'hypothesis'. The object of faith, however, may be defined as that which is *rationally but not empirically certain*. It is rationally certain, because it is the only total picture which co-ordinates all the facts in a satisfying way; it is not empirically certain, because it involves a reality which cannot be verified by direct observation. It is this concept of faith which the New Testament writer to the *Hebrews* is seeking to convey when he declares:

> Now it is faith which gives reality to what we hope for, and makes us certain of things we cannot see (*Heb.* 11:1, NEB version).

It underlies the pugnacious words of Paul, when he writes that

> the god of this world has blinded the minds of the unbelievers to keep them from seeing the light of the gospel of the glory of Christ, who is the likeness of God (*II Cor.* 4:4).

The Gospel of the Resurrection asserts that men now have sufficient evidence to arrive at certainty on the ultimate question, provided that they will reason by the ordinary canons of sound thinking. No special illumination is needed, no question-begging procedures. Reason and faith are not two distinct methods of arriving at truth; faith is a rational commitment to the demands of the evidence. And this conception of faith receives strong support from the significant circumstance that those who wish to controvert the faith, or to argue that it does not have this kind of certitude, are compelled at some point to reject or to try to demolish the Gospel account of the resurrection as objective event.

The thesis which the resurrection confirms might seem, as we stated it above, to have two separate components – 'that there is a God *and* that he designates Jesus as the one true Man'. But these are not two distinct matters; they are two aspects of one indivisible reality. For the nature of existence is such that the only credible God is one whose values are those exemplified in Jesus. If Herod the Great had risen from the dead, this would not have been tolerable to reason as a testimony to God. For a God who ratified monstrosity might explain the evil in the world; he could never satisfy us as a source of goodness. But the God who ratifies the values incarnate in Jesus can, we have argued, be seen as having a good purpose which gives meaning to the evil in the world. The vindication of Jesus alone supplies the crucial testimony. Conversely, if Jesus had not been vindicated, and in a way which demanded a divine action as its cause, the glorious hope would not have been refuted, but it would have remained – a hope.

This means that what is vindicated is Jesus in his life and death. Easter is not the correction of a ghastly mistake, nor the completion of an unfinished story. It sets the seal of truth on a story which is already complete and correct as it stands. Hence the prime effect of the Resurrection Gospel is to present a moral challenge: do we accept this life of absolute and universal loyalty to the Good in love, issuing in total failure and defeat, as the supreme ideal for Man? Certainly, not every life lived in such loyalty will necessarily end in failure; but are we prepared to accept that such failure, if it comes, is less important than to be thus loyal?

To see that this is the issue is of overriding importance,[1] for this alone preserves the integrity of the moral order. To interpret Easter as meaning that everyone who follows Jesus will in the end receive a reward to compensate him for all the suffering involved is to misconstrue it fatally, and indeed to go beyond what the event warrants. Jesus alone rose from the dead. There is here no necessary implication that we too will live again. By confirming a God who can, if he chooses, intervene to enable men to transcend death, it makes such a life a real possibility. Equally, by tying this confirmation to the resurrection of a uniquely good man it offers no guarantee. The hope of eternal life continues to rest, as it had done both for Jesus and for many others before the first Easter, on something quite different. This is the reflection that a God who cares and forgives and loves as God obviously must do, and who has brought joy into the lives of his human creatures by taking them as his partners in the cause of love, may well wish to save the person who has known such a partnership from falling into nothingness:

Whom have I in heaven but thee? And there is nothing upon earth that I desire beside thee. My flesh and my heart may fail, but God is the strength of my heart and my portion for ever (*Psa.* 73:25–26).

To have felt this is very naturally to feel also that this God whom we

---

[1] As the reader will realize, it also means that the resurrection finally confirms the thesis we have presented throughout the present work, that the moral question is the primary one. If we reject the supremacy of this moral ideal, then Easter does not bear witness to the only credible God. It remains a total enigma. You can have God only on these terms; if you refuse the terms, you cannot have God.

have come to know may show his love by the final and decisive blessing of welcoming us to his own eternity – and what can Man want more?

Is there not, however, a puzzling contradiction here? Does not the prospect of reward inevitably exclude true moral integrity? How can we possibly be loyal to the good for its own sake, if we know that God can give us a life beyond death, if we think that he may, and hope that he will? One possible answer is that nevertheless we do not demand that he should. We might put the matter this way: 'I have no confirmation from God of life after death for myself comparable to the confirmation he has given that in Jesus the true life of Man is to be found. Whereas my hope that there is a God, and that he is Love, has been given the certitude of faith, my hope of personal immortality remains a hope. If then I knew that this hope was to be disappointed, would it make any difference? Surely, to choose God's values as found in Jesus means to decide that it would not. If the joy of being God's partner in this life is all there is to be, then that is enough. On no other basis can I be free; and by refusing to assure me of an eternal reward, even when he could do so, God gives the last and greatest proof that for him my chance of free allegiance to the good is the most important gift he has to bestow.' If such an argument is sound, then it would appear that it is by this road that Jesus offers men liberation from the fear of death – not by guaranteeing another life, but by transforming this one. For if I truly care about the Good, then surely the knowledge that there is goodness at the heart of things, and that in serving this I am finding the one true fulfilment for which I was made, will provide my life here with a sufficient satisfaction?

Indeed it would, were it not for one thing – my own manifest and grievous failure to realize my loyalty in practice. As Paul wrote with exact insight: 'The sting of death is sin' (*I Cor.* 15:56). The more genuinely my first concern is for the good and not for myself, the more grieved I shall be at the intermittent and imperfect presence of the Good in myself. With slow and painful struggles my life comes to the point where I begin to see what the issues are, to face the fundamental moral challenge of existence, and to find in a partnership with God the beginnings of a worthwhile response to it – and then all is over. Is goodness, is love never to be truly incarnated in me or in any of us? Was the purpose of Jesus' life and sufferings solely to produce one true human being, so that this world might not be a total loss? If this were really so, then the Resurrection would certainly be no Gospel, no good news. It would be the deadliest bringer of despair, for it would mean that there was a God but that, having achieved his end, he had written off his own creation.

To such a conclusion our whole argument hitherto gives a peremptory dismissal. The Good to which our allegiance is claimed by the conjectures of reason and the confirmation of the resurrection is above all else the Good that regards others, and will suffer for their sake. Once again, the resurrection forces us to an important clarification, this time by posing the problem of reward. The phrase, 'to do good for its own sake', sounds so obviously the more free, the more morally pure. But it is not. It simply expresses a shallow concept of goodness. To think of goodness-in-love as the supreme fulfilment of personal life at once involves us, if we think clearly, in wanting everyone to find this fulfilment not just for goodness' sake but for *their* sake, since it is part and parcel of the nature of true goodness that it cares about other people in themselves. To be really good means to desire passionately not merely that good should be lived and done but that each individual person should live it and do it. *Their* good and *the* Good are indissolubly interfused. And this must include ourselves. To be zealous for the universal triumph of good but not for its triumph in myself is simply nonsensical, a contradiction. The famous command

Thou shalt love thy neighbour as thyself,

which the Old Testament Law promulgated (*Lev.* 19:18), and Jesus ratified (*Mk* 12:31; *Matt.* 19:19; *Lk.* 10:27; cf. *Rom.* 13:9; *Gal.* 5:14; *James* 2:8), is logically inescapable. The strained altruism which would prefer to say, 'Thou shalt love thy neighbour more than thyself,' is not more moral but less, not rational but silly.

Renunciation of the life beyond death, a readiness to leave it entirely to God without pretending to a view of our own on the subject, which seemed at first sight the goal to which the argument must plainly move, is thus not based on truth. If the lives of all men were in fact examples of fulfilment in goodness, then it might happen that a future life would occupy them less, because every part of their nature, even to its very highest ideals, would have been satisfied by this one. But this is not the case. Where men shrink from death – and not all do, since old age can bring gentle acceptance, fatigue or overwhelming problems evoke grateful welcome – where men do shrink from death, their reasons, it is true, are varied and often egotistical. They may hate the realisation that their personal identities and consciousness will cease; they may grieve at quitting family and friends, the beauty of the world and the light of the sun; they may be anxious about the fate of those dependent on them; they may regret the end of power and achievement, even of being feared and hated, knowing that their passing will bring the very happiness they have always bent their energies to destroy. But where there is brave and honest openness to truth, even a life devoted to the Good will not draw the sting of regret, since in one-self and in all the world around it is but too obvious that the good has not triumphed.

Nor is there even the consolation that it will certainly triumph one day. A death made easy by utopian dreams is simply anaesthetized by delusion. Progress can be of two kinds, by education or by evolution. Education has nothing to offer here. Nobility of character and conduct cannot be passed on, any more than any other acquired characteristic. All depends therefore on the perpetuation of ideals by training, mores, social institutions, and a propitious environment, aimed at enabling the ideals to be caught and appropriated as living realities by individuals. The business of living aright has to be begun over and over again in each person's life-story, in each hour of each community's corporate history, in each change of knowledge and circumstances. But, as we saw earlier,[1] the inherent conflicts in the human psyche and its fragility make a high degree of failure inevitable; and each failure, by destroying the conditions of success, breeds more failure in oneself and in others. The myth of Sisyphus is the arch-parable of Man's moral existence; and there is no ground so securely gained that it cannot ever be lost. As for evolution, it is at bottom irrelevant to our problem. A successful evolutionary development is one which is better able to cope with the problems of living in a particular environment; and such a mutation becomes established because those organisms which embody it tend to thrive and multiply. But the crux of the matter is that the organisms in question have changed. Willy-nilly they are a new being, and func-tion in a new way. If, then, Nature in due time moves beyond us, our inner predicament is not changed, only our circumstances. If we become the pets or helots of a super-race, our own struggle to be loyal to the Good in love, which is our special dignity, will remain our vocation,

[1] Cf. chap. 4 above.

ending only if we are forcibly exterminated or modified by our masters.[1] If, as is possible, and as some hope, Man 'takes charge of his own evolution' by controlling and changing his own genetic codes, beyond all the technical problems there must remain the moral issue – of what values do we wish the mutants to be capable? We are thus driven back to ask what is our essential definition of Man. Is it a being with a particular physiology and conformation, or is it one with a personality that finds fulfilment in living by a certain hierarchy of values? No doubt it is both; but just as the second without the first will not necessarily be human, neither will the first without the second.

Jesus, being a man like ourselves, is relevant to our actual situation. He offers not an escape from the human condition into a new transhuman order but a fulfilment of the original order, not a way to be more than Man but the way to be properly Man. And it is precisely this which is not accomplished here, and which the innate structure of Man forbids us to expect in a distant this-worldly future.

The more sincerely loyal, therefore, we are to the Good, the more eagerly we shall desire that this life should not be the end. For love's sake there must be an opportunity for created beings to attain their true fulfilment. In this perspective the Easter knowledge that God can give us a life beyond death takes on a new significance. Such a life is the only chance, even if an outside chance, of giving permanent embodiment to the particular good for which men were made. Will God, as the Father of love and forgiveness which we know him to be, refuse this chance?

'It is appointed for men to die once, and after that comes judgement' (*Heb.* 9:27). Traditional Christianity has, during most of its course, taught that there is indeed an existence after death for all men, but that the nature of that existence will depend on the use they have made of this one. It would be tedious and unhelpful to describe here the various ways in which Christians have envisaged the working out of this principle in detail. Suffice it to say that, within the confines of orthodoxy, all have had one feature in common: life after death brings the

---

[1] There is, of course, no reason to take it for granted that a more highly evolved species would behave in this way. There might well be amiable and beneficial co-existence, rather like that portrayed on an imaginary Mars in C. S. Lewis, *Out of the Silent Planet*. But the point is that the problem of incarnating goodness in Man remains.

person to a confrontation with God which is conceived in terms of an offender before a tribunal. The purpose of the court is to decide the fate of the person before it in the light of his life on earth. Strict justice will be done, for no evidence is lacking. Every nuance of every motive is known; all mitigating as well as aggravating circumstances will be fully and fairly weighed. Since, however, it is realised that such a standard would condemn everyone, there are ways of avoiding the seemingly inevitable outcome of the trial. These vary in different theologies, but each falls into one or other of two categories. Either the sentence is cancelled or the verdict is altered. In the former case, the sufferings of Christ are held to have paid already the debt of punishment due, so that those who belong to him are allowed to go free; in the latter, the righteousness of Christ is imputed to those who are his brethren, and they are therefore acquitted. The benefit that Jesus brings to mankind is thus seen as the opportunity, for those who will take it, of escaping at the last the just penalty of their wickedness, and of entering into eternal joy. Those who by their own fault have not availed themselves of this benefit receive the punishment which all have deserved, but which only they have been foolish, negligent, or proud enough to incur – eternal loss and torment.

It can safely be said that no doctrine general in Christianity has been so widely (and justifiably) denounced as this. Why beings not wholly evil should be wholly condemned; why a supposedly just judge should acquit the guilty because someone else is innocent; why he should adopt the view that so long as someone has been punished for a crime it does not matter whether or not it was the criminal; these are just the most obvious questions provoked by this distorted rigmarole, and questions which have been raised not only in modern times. In earlier centuries too there were those who sought anxiously for a way round a belief so dubious morally and so repugnant to decent human feeling. For example, Origen, the greatest speculative theologian of the early Church and, arguably, of any age, thought that by allegorical exegesis he could prove from the Bible that in the end good would triumph universally, and that all creatures, including the Devil himself, would be saved. This provided one major count on which after his death he was adjudged heretical. Or again, at the other end of the scale of theological eminence, a fourteenth century English priest, Uthred of Boldon, in the anguish of a kindly heart, attempted to argue that the vision of God in the moment of death might be the means of bringing

†

**Mother Amata
of the Mother of God**

Mary Isabel Long

**Born August 19, 1906
Professed May 5, 1936
Died October 17, 1989**

The Lord gave her wisdom and
understanding beyond measure,
and a heart as vast as the
sand on the seashore.

cf. 1 K 4:29

**Carmel of the Trinity
San Diego, California**

even an apparently obdurate sinner to the necessary repentance.[1] His opinions were formally anathematized by an ecclesiastical court. Many others, more, or less well-known, tried their hands at a solution, and met the same fate. To this day there are many devout Christians for whom belief in Hell is the acid test of sound religion, precisely because, being intolerable to 'natural' reason and moral feeling, it calls for the maximum degree of submission to the 'supernatural' revelation of God's will in Scripture and specifically in the alleged teaching of Jesus.[2] By the same token, no doctrine has done more to undermine the traditional faith, because its repulsive cruelty has forced even well-disposed people to reject official teaching and to formulate a theology of their own.

Nevertheless, this doctrine is, as we shall see, attempting to safeguard something of extreme importance. The absurdities and horrors of its classic formulation are basically the result of a failure to carry the message of the Gospel through to its logical conclusion. On the one hand, the doctrine respects human freedom; men must be allowed the liberty to decide for or against God. Yet on the other, it shies away from the direct personal encounter between God and Man without which there can be no chance of a free decision based on truth. When the human person for the first time meets God as he is, it is already too late. On the one hand, it accepts the reality of divine forgiveness; on the other, it limits that forgiveness to certain people. On the one hand, it asserts rightly that God is good as well as merciful; his generosity is not just a morally indifferent permissiveness. On the other, it forgets the essential nature of God's kind of goodness, the readiness to suffer for the benefit of others. At every point the truth about God is qualified by inferior human notions.

This has been more than enough space to devote to the well-known shortcomings of conventional teaching on this subject, teaching which in a large proportion of Christian congregations today is never mentioned from one year's end to another. If it is felt necessary to refer to it, almost all the offensive elements are left out. The stress is placed quite differently, by saying, for example, that the torments are those which we inflict on ourselves be refusing to accept God's love; or the suggestion may be made that in an existence which depends on God's

---

[1] A view which has affinities with the present-day speculations of Ladislaus Boros, *The Moment of Truth*.

[2] On the question whether this is a true reading of Jesus cf. pp. 294f. below.

re-creating us after death, rejection of God must lead to the annihilation of the self. Others have revived a modified form of Origen's teaching, and argue that continued exposure to God as he really is must in the end lead the most recalcitrant person to be reconciled to love, so that finally all will be saved.

A version censored, however, to conform with the requirements of current thought is not likely to have very much more theological validity than one elaborated to conform with the thinking of an earlier age. It will be best to return to our own line of argument, and to see where if anywhere it leads. We had maintained that for the sake of love there must be a chance for created beings to attain their intended fulfilment; and that therefore those who care most for the Good, and who know that God cares infinitely more, will confidently expect it. But how are we to think of that life? And what will be its impact upon us?

Two preliminary points must be dealt with. First, can anything useful be said about the mode of existence of the human person after death? Psychical research, though the phenomena with which it deals are extremely interesting and worthy of investigation, is irrelevant here, because there is as yet no reason to think that the vast majority of human lives leave any traces of this sort behind them; and we are thinking of a presumedly universal condition. Traditionally, there are two kinds of language used about this subject. One is in terms of an imperishable entity, the soul; the other stresses the physical nature of Man, and therefore leads either to the conclusion that there is no life after death or to a belief in resurrection, the new creation of a medium in some way appropriate to human nature. The latter type of language is favoured by a number of Christian thinkers today, both because it seems to take better account of the observable facts about human beings, and because it is the dominant Judaistic view found in the Old Testament. It is not, however, entirely adequate to the facts. The formative principle which makes a person what he is cannot be described in exclusively physical terms. We remarked earlier[1] that the human person is a 'feat of organization'. This organization establishes an identity with a continuous history maintained through perpetual changes in the physical organism. This identity is very like what the scholastic philosophers had in mind when they spoke of the soul as 'the form of the body'. It is natural, when someone dies, to speak of the soul having 'left' the body, because we are trying to express the fact that the

[1] Cf. pp. 66f. above.

vital organizing principle which made the material complex a recognizable person is no longer in operation. That pattern or principle is
unique; and if a human being were to be resurrected, the resurrection
'body' would have to be matched to and controlled by this pattern, if
the person were still to be the same person. If God is to give us a life
after death, therefore, we must assume that this pattern is preserved by
him to serve as the formative principle of the re-created being. In that
sense the 'soul' never dies. Something of this kind may have been part
of Paul's conception when he wrote to the Corinthians:

> For we know that if the earthly tent we live in is destroyed, we have a
> building from God, a house not made with hands, eternal in the heavens.
> Here indeed we groan, and long to put on our heavenly dwelling, so that
> by putting it on we may not be found naked. For while we are still in
> this tent, we sigh with anxiety; not that we would be unclothed, but
> that we would be further clothed, so that what is mortal may be swal-
> lowed up by life (*II Cor.* 5:1-4).

Secondly, there is the problem of Time. Is each individual inducted
into eternal life at the moment of his death, or does everyone wait until
a 'Last Day'? Theologies have varied on this point; but the argument
is seen to be unreal, as soon as we start to think of a future life as what
in essence it must be, namely the entry into a direct personal relationship with the God who gives us our new mode of existence.

We start from the assumption that any full encounter with God must
imply an encounter with total truth. This means a great deal more than
we might at first sight suppose. There is a tag which has been used
many times of the creature face to face with God at last – *solus cum solo*,
'alone with the Alone'. In the sense that this meeting will be concerned
with one thing and one thing only, the mutual relationship between
God and the individual, and that everything else which is relevant will
be so only in its bearing on that one focal point, the phrase is true. But
in the more obvious meaning of the words it is highly misleading. It is
based on an atomistic concept of personality which we now know to be
untenable, the idea of the soul as an entity which can be examined and
assessed in isolation. When, however, we remember that the human
self exists at all only in relationship with its 'world',[1] it will be realized
that any genuine meeting between God and the self must involve this
'world' as well.

The result, therefore, is a direct comparison of two very different

[1] Cf. pp. 70f. above.

pictures of a complex reality. Here am I with my patchy, censored, and egocentric version of that web of relationships – my family, friends, colleagues, enemies, casual acquaintances, nameless strangers, animals, plants, things, my own psycho-physical being, and my God, in short every item within the horizon of my existence – on which I depend to keep my 'self' in being. This version is the resultant of many factors; but in the end they reduce to two – the truth and my own apprehension of the truth. I am influenced, consciously or unconsciously, by other beings; but I also try to dictate what their influence is to be, and my very dictation is in turn shaped by their influence. Equally, I seek to affect others; but what I can effectively achieve is controlled in part by them themselves, and by other long-forgotten things. I take responsibility for my actions; but I neither understand fully what those actions are nor do I realize how much of my posture is an attempt to limit the area of my responsibility, and so to disown a part of every event. This buried or rejected truth of the self in interaction with its world is the favourite theme of many intelligent and sensitive modern novelists; and their work is often an excellent way-in to an understanding both of the nature of personal reality, and of how stylized and fragmentary is the awareness of it which constitutes our conscious self.

Into direct contact with this self now comes God's own self, with his total and precise awareness of me and my world in relation to all other systems of personal being, and of the relation of all of them to himself. Now, in my immediate involvement with him, I see with his eyes all that my own eyes could never see. Events take on their true personal value – kindnesses are revealed as egotism, failures as constructive charity, decisions as response to hidden pressures, hesitations as moral courage. I know all the evil done to me; but alongside it I know all the evil I have done. More shattering still, I learn for the first time all the love and concern, help and forgiveness bestowed on me, to which I was blind, or which in self-hatred or self-pity I misinterpreted as hostility or indifference. Above all, because every pattern of personhood is known to God with equal clarity and justice, there is a disclosure of that utter mutual dependence of all created beings which I have spent so much time and energy trying to ignore.

This is overwhelming enough; but it is not the whole truth now revealed. This covers only the static, the 'historical' aspect of what is past. This past, however, is in living, dynamic involvement with the present, with this moment of vision through the eyes of God, because every other being is in the same position. If they are part of my world, I also am enmeshed in theirs; and because both they and I are alive, feeling and understanding as never before, they now look at me and I at them with this divine perception. If, in Paul's words, 'I know even as I am known' (*I Cor.* 13:12), so do they know. We each of us know all these others, and are known by them. But because we are human, knowing can never be merely knowing, it is feeling as well. What will not such knowledge do to our feeling? What a cataclysmic release — and yet what realisation of utter poverty and impotence! We shall desire to respond as we 'ought' — yes, 'ought', because then for the first time we shall experience 'ought' for what it is, the free inner imperative of love in mutual belonging.[1] But where are we to find the inner resources to make such a response? They are not there. We are helpless, empty, borne hither and thither on the raging waters of reality.

But even this is not all; for 'the spirit of God moves on the face of the waters'. Every minutest aspect of this reality is not only known to him but is the object of his love. On all that is good his joy and approval shines; to all that is evil he brings forgiveness achieved through his own suffering. This too becomes known to us in the moment of vision. The response to goodness which we could not, and still cannot make, he has always made. The evil which we either did not recognize as such or, recognizing it, could not forgive, he has taken all upon himself. Jesus on the cross proves to be the only accurate picture of God the world has ever seen; and the hands that hold us in existence are pierced with unimaginable nails. God has used every evil done under the sun as the given framework of a new good, by enduring in unchanging love the infinite pain it has caused him.

It is at this point, as a very little imagination will help us to see, that the sword of judgement divides. To be forgiven is also to be condemned; hence pardon is the perilous moment. There are two possible reasons why the awareness of reality might destroy us. The one is self-love, the other self-hatred.

To take self-love first, we might be unable to accept the humiliation of facing how evil we have been, and how much suffering has been needed to forgive us. To be that indebted, to be so worthless in ourselves, could prove an intolerable demand. After all, it can happen all too easily even in the limited awareness of our present existence. Not

[1] Cf. pp. 103–106 above.

T

only is the knowledge of the pain we have caused lacerating to our self-esteem, the generosity of the victim's pardon makes it doubly so by contrast. The only escape is to insist that this assessment is false. We are not to blame, perhaps, or not so much to blame as they seem to think, or they are partly in the wrong themselves, or they are making a great fuss about very little, or they ignore what we have done to put matters right. In extreme cases the thought of someone whom we have greatly wronged, and by whom we have been forgiven, may be so excruciating that we cannot bear even to hear their name mentioned by others in a casual conversation. We want only to stay for ever as far away from them as possible, to forget that they ever existed. If we are forced by circumstances to have contact with them, this desire to pretend that the evidence of our own evil does not really exist is frustrated, and may then easily turn into an unconscious desire actually to do away with the evidence. If normal civilized restraints keep us from putting this desire into practice, it may still show itself in vicious enmity and prejudice. But if human forgiveness of evil in ourselves which we only imperfectly appreciate can have this effect, what may not be provoked in us by the divine forgiveness, which by its infinite suffering compels us to open our eyes to all the evil we have done in all its ramifications as it really is? 'Go, go, go, said the bird. Human kind cannot bear very much reality.' And if reality such as this is the only way to freedom, understanding, and love, what then? The risk has to be taken; and if the person concerned finds the reality too much for him, is it inconceivable that with a cry of rejection he should turn in on himself, close the doors of his soul and bar them tight against God and his fellow-creatures with their insufferable demands and even more insufferable goodness, and take final refuge in illusion?

On the other hand, there is equal danger from the seemingly opposite position of self-hatred, the inability to forgive ourselves. This too is a human commonplace. Certainly, others are very kind, very noble; but for that very reason we are unfit for their society. Nothing can persuade us out of our self-contempt. Why? Because in this way, deep, deep inside where no one can ever pry, we can be assured of our own essential goodness. We 'know' we are no good, and we shall behave towards ourselves accordingly, rejecting the comfortable superficiality of forgiveness. And this it is which proves that our 'real' self is immaculate in its integrity. We are so good that we know better than anyone else just how bad we are, and how irrevocably debarred from the

fellowship of those we have injured. From this position there can be no
evacuation because – because if we moved from it, we might have to
face the fact that we really are evil, even in that innermost sanctuary of
the soul. And that would be unbearable. But what is left for such a
person, when the full reality of their own defects makes this ultimate
lie indispensable to them, and yet relationship with God and with
other beings now means that this lie too is shown up for what it is?

Both types of person we have described are in fact prisoners of pride,
which the theologian rightly classes as the greatest and most radical of
sins. Pride is fatal, because where it has obtained a stranglehold there
can be no openness to truth, no genuine constructive sorrow for evil,
no acceptance of forgiveness. The proud soul is so eaten up with self
that the simplest and most obvious truth about other people never
enters its head – not even the thought that the forgiving person
presumably wants to forgive, and that therefore the kindest, indeed the
only kind thing the offender can do for them is to accept the pardon
they offer. In the last encounter, the moment of vision through God's
eyes, pride, naked or disguised, is the only vice that can bring the
creature to reject God. The people for whose eternal salvation one
fears most are those who seem utterly ignorant of their own character,
and oblivious of the motives and moral quality of their own conduct,
even though this is driving everyone around them to despair. At the
same time, because pride means that we make our very existence dependent on the rightness of our own evaluation of ourself, to surrender
it is the most complete annihilation of the self. In this schematic form
we have presented the case as though there were two separate types of
person – one addicted to all the sins except pride, the other enslaved by
pride as well. But clearly this is not so. Pride is present in all of us, and
could destroy all of us, if it is not itself destroyed by truth. What we
need to remember is that truth is hard to bear not just, as we might
imagine, when it comes in cold and clinical form – then it is almost
easier – but most of all when it comes with the warmth and humility of
forgiveness and suffering love, for this is a more piercing condemnation. Hence no preparation we can make in this life for the ultimate
meeting with God is more fundamental than to cultivate a passion for
truth.[1]

[1] It may be worth the reader's while to reflect what this implies for the convinced
atheist or agnostic. Someone who has arrived at atheism or at the suspended
judgement of genuine agnosticism by careful and honest investigation, can at the

How a person in the grip of pride, conscious or unconscious, will respond to the presentation of reality is unpredictable. The facts about the self may be accepted, either by admitting God's evaluation or by abandoning the last disguise. There may be submission to the dismantling of the whole structure elaborately built up and reinforced over the years, a plunge into annihilation. If so, then beyond that point of extremest pain, the self, we may be sure, will find itself miraculously reborn, purified, in communion with the truth. This in essence is the meaning of Purgatory. Or again, there may be rejection, in which case there is no reason why the pain should ever end, unless such a refusal of the good may dissolve existence. In either event the good is finally frustrated. The question, which of these two, acceptance or rejection of truth, *will* happen, no speculation can ever answer. It has been said[1] that while existentially we are faced here with a final and decisive Either-Or, theologically it is unthinkable that God should be defeated. Each part of this statement can be justified on its own by highly persuasive arguments. But this must not be allowed to obscure the fact that to insist that both are true simultaneously is to abrogate reason, and to descend to delusive doubletalk. The true lesson to be derived from the fact that logic forces us to such a contradictory position is that here logic has run out of steam. Its incompatible results indicate that we are at a dead end – and for a very good reason. Here at last we come to the moment of pure freedom. Here everything depends on the inner capacity of the unique individual self to engage reality, and this is essentially unpredictable. Precise and painstaking reflection on the direct encounter with God simply provides the final confirmation that God has destined us to share his own tremendous privilege, that the Good can be had only in freedom. With us, therefore, it rests whether his purpose of good in creation is to be at least a partial failure. He has put himself in our hands.

It follows then that even in Jesus God has not ensured our eternal fulfilment and happiness. Anything that could be ensured would not be

most be astonished to discover the true state of affairs. He may have much to learn, in which his concern for truth will help him; he will not, at least in this matter, have much to repent. He is in fact in less danger than the believer who has been worshipping not God as he is but an idol shaped by the twists and defects of his own character. The danger of the person who has, for whatever reason, done violence to his own integrity in choosing atheism is, however, another matter.

[1] Among British theologians notably by John Hick.

our fulfilment, since it would not be appropriate to our particular nature. But if our first feeling is that this is a rather depressing conclusion, we need to look again. If we do, the chances are that it will begin to appear in its proper and rather different light. For what is indeed inconceivable is that anyone who has grasped that this is the situation should at the last be beyond redemption by the power of the truth. Once we realise what lies ahead, our whole attitude both to this life and to the next is changed. We know for certain that if we keep ourselves open to truth, open to forgiveness, open to love, then, however imperfect our achievement, entry into the fullness of all these things in a living relationship with God will do for us what we could not do for ourselves. We no longer fear what is to come, we are eager for it beyond all else. The pain through which we are to pass to fulfilment becomes the thing we most desire. It is not a threat but a promise; and the light of that promise falls over the whole of our present existence, assuring us that not one of our tentative gropings and painful efforts will be wasted. Readers of Dante will recall the overwhelming sense of relief and exhilaration with which, at the opening of Book Two, one quits Hell for ever and prepares for the ascent of Purgatory:

> For better waters heading with the wind
>   My ship of genius now shakes out her sail
>   And leaves that ocean of despair behind. . . .
>
> Colour unclouded, orient-sapphirine,
>   Softly suffusing from meridian height
>   Down the still sky to the horizon-line,
>
> Brought to mine eyes renewal of delight
>   So soon as I came forth from that dead air
>   Which had oppressed my bosom and my sight.[1]

But we need also to remember that the *Divine Comedy* is not a literal description of Hell, Purgatory, and Heaven as the poet supposes them actually to be. The realms of eternity are used to give symbolic expression to the pilgrimage of the soul in this life. By presenting our acts and attitudes in terms of their eternal significance we learn to live differently, to acquire new values, to embrace a true purpose. The poet himself is throughout alive in flesh and blood, both when at the opening of the

[1] Dante, *Purgatorio*, Canto I, stanzas 1, 5, and 6, in the translation by Dorothy Sayers.

poem he is wandering lost and aimless in the wild wood, drifting to the very gate of Hell, and at the end when he attains to the Beatific Vision of 'the Love that moves the sun and the other stars'. The experience he has himself undergone he strives to make available to his readers also; and this is in all ages the only proper purpose of contemplating our final destiny. The revelation of God in Jesus enables us to know enough of the essential quality of that journey's end to avoid mistaking our journey itself, nay, to tread that journey with a joy and an anticipation which transform our whole self, so that with Paul we confidently affirm that

> the sufferings of this present time are not worth comparing with the glory that is to be revealed to us (*Rom.* 8:18).

It is significant that of the sayings on this subject attributed to Jesus in the Gospels those historically least suspect are those which concentrate on a person's attitude to life now rather than on a judicial verdict to be passed when it is too late to repent or on the horrific details of torment. We saw reason earlier[1] to think that Matthew's parable of the Great Assize (*Matt.* 25:31–46) had at least undergone considerable church recasting; and that the Tale of Dives and Lazarus (*Lk.* 16:19–31), with its mention of the agonizing thirst endured by the damned souls, was in fact a Christian adaptation of a Jewish original.[2] By contrast, a passage in *Mark* (9:43–48), which Matthew has also incorporated (twice! – *Matt.* 5:29–30; 18:8–9), though it too refers to 'hell, where their worm does not die, and the fire is not quenched',[3] is first and foremost an urgent exhortation to men to deal here and now with those traits in themselves that lead to evil. Jesus did not, it would seem, in any case concentrate on the active images of torment, such as fire. He is more frequently recorded as using those of exclusion from joy, such as that of the 'outer darkness, where men weep and grind their teeth' in regret. But it is striking that even this is found only in *Matthew* (*Matt.* 8:12; 22:13; 25:30) who devotes far more attention to this kind of teaching than any of the other evangelists (cf. *Matt.* 13:23–30, 36–43, 47–50); and it is hard not to conclude that here the preoccupations of Judaism are distorting the presentation of Jesus once again.

[1] Cf. p. 156 above.
[2] Cf. pp. 252f. above.
[3] A quotation from *Isa.* 66:24, commonly used by the rabbis as an image of hell. Matthew does not use this quotation.

The evidence taken as a whole suggests that Jesus devoted very little attention to this question, and when he did touch upon it, used it to stress the eternal importance of a right attitude to human life here and now. Moreover, what little there is has to be seen against the background of his teaching on forgiveness, which meant that anyone open to the truth about good and evil in himself and others had nothing to fear. Even Matthew has made this fundamental principle clear in the Sermon on the Mount (*Matt.* 7:1–2), drawing on the source which he shares with *Luke*, whose version of this saying makes clear why the teaching of Jesus did not impose on men the fear of hell, but rather liberated them from it:

> Judge not, and you will not be judged; condemn not, and you will not be condemned; forgive, and you will be forgiven; give, and it will be given to you; good measure, pressed down, shaken together, running over, will be put into your lap. For the measure you give will be the measure you get back (*Lk.* 6:37–38).

It must be said with emphasis (and even today it needs to be said) that *the fear of hell is present in the Christian faith only as a fear from which we have been delivered.* Hell is a possibility for humans simply because they have the capacity to become sub-human; it is by allowing themselves to be degraded into less than Man that they make this possibility a reality. For those who have found and loved the true spirit of Man in Jesus, hell is something that could have happened to them but now never can. As Paul puts it:

> There is therefore now no condemnation for those who are in Christ Jesus. For the law of the spirit of life in Christ Jesus has set me free from the law of sin and death (*Rom.* 8:1–2).

Indeed, we can go farther. We can say that no man truly knows what hell is until he is safe from it. Those who are afraid of hell do not know what the word means. They have an infantile picture of a place of punishment to which they may be sent if they fail to hold the right faith or do the right thing – make an act of contrition for their sins, believe in the atoning blood of Jesus, or whatever it may be. But those who have begun to grow up into the maturity which God intended for the human person, who have learned that openness to truth, openness to forgiveness, openness to love are the elements of the only atmosphere a man can breathe and live, they realize what they might have become, what they might have lost. The other hell is a phantasm, a nonsense, which has no basis in reality because it has no basis in God. Hence we say: no one can preach hell as a means to the gospel. If he does so, he tells us nothing about God or Jesus, only about himself and his neurotic, sub-human fears. But give men the spirit of Jesus which strives for the good that love would choose, and there is no need to tell them about hell. They will know without being told what it is that they have escaped.

> The dove descending breaks the air
> With flame of incandescent terror
> Of which the tongues declare
> The one discharge from sin and error.
> The only hope, or else despair
>   Lies in the choice of pyre or pyre –
>   To be redeemed from fire by fire.
>
> Who then devised the torment? Love.
> Love is the unfamiliar Name
> Behind the hands that wove
> The intolerable shirt of flame
> Which human power cannot remove.
> We only live, only suspire
> Consumed by either fire or fire.[1]

We see then that the transformation which Jesus effects in human existence is not, after all, something which has to wait for a heavenly future. Everything which will be in perfection and fullness is already present in part and in anticipation. We are forgiven here and now; we are united with all our fellow-beings here and now in the simultaneous and universal love of God. But there is more to it even than this.

Forgiveness, we noted, implies condemnation, and to accept it is also to accept one's own worthlessness. So much of oneself is bent and defective that really the whole person, despite the intermingled and partial good, has little intrinsic value. To be of value to someone who loves one in spite of oneself is undoubtedly better than to be unloved, unvalued. But in Jesus God has done something more; he has done the apparently impossible, and given us value in ourselves. Anyone who reads the resurrection aright as God's vindication of Jesus – which presupposes, as we saw, that he has faced the moral challenge, and found in Jesus the supreme good of human existence – can now hold up

---

[1] T. S. Eliot, *Little Gidding*, ll. 200–213.

his own head in pride. For he can say, 'I know that I am a failure, and
so, more or less, are all my fellow-men. But I am a man; and that means
that Jesus is my brother. And because of that fact, I am not ashamed
to exist.'

In Jesus something has been given back to the human race as a
corporate whole, a sense of dignity and worth. A species which could
produce such a member has no longer any need to write itself off as
worthless. We know the feeling well enough. To hear someone
admired, and to be able to say. 'Oh yes, he is a friend of mine', or, 'She
is my cousin', or, 'He comes from my town' or 'my country', or, 'I was
at school with him' – we do it all the time. And this kind of pride can
have very good effects; it puts us on our mettle. In the case of Jesus the
bond is far closer and more fundamental, and far more revolutionary
for our attitude. For we can say this about Jesus only by virtue of
belonging to mankind. It gives us value not as Christians, not as white
or black, not as Englishmen or Americans or Japanese, not as men or
women, but as human beings.[1] The intuition by which artists of all
races and cultures have represented Jesus as one of themselves is therefore a just one, and has often been commended as a sign of the universality of the Christian belief. But in a deeper sense it misses the creative,
transforming factor altogether, namely that this man whose life
enables the human race to hold up its head for the first time, was a
Palestinian Jew under the Roman Empire. There are no Boddhisatvas
in this faith, no new incarnations to meet the needs of different ages and
societies. Men are challenged to find their hero in a strange, even alien
figure; and by reason of the one thing they share with him, their
humanity, to recognize their unity with all the other strange and alien
beings who share that same condition.

We begin to see here an unexpected fulfilment of those expectations
in the New Testament which seemed at first to have been disappointed.
Jesus expected a coming judgement by one whom he knew as 'Son of
Man'; the Church continued to look for this in the immediate future,
only identifying Jesus as this Son of Man. What they overlooked was
that the judgement had already taken place, or rather had been instituted

[1] Cf. Paul's words in the New Testament: to the Galatians, 'There is neither
Jew nor Greek, there is neither slave nor free, there is neither male nor female;
for you are all one in Christ Jesus' (*Gal.* 3:28); and again to the Colossians, 'Here
there cannot be Greek and Jew, circumcised and uncircumcised, barbarian,
Scythian, slave, free man, but Christ is all, and in all' (*Col.* 3:11).

as a permanent fact of the human situation. Jesus is the judgement, and he judges precisely in his existence as 'Son of Man'. In him the question is put to each human being, 'Do you acknowledge this life as the true life of Man?' Is our ultimate criterion for choosing between the various possibilities of good to be that of sacrificial love? Do we stake our own lives on truth, understanding, forgiveness, freedom, with their total lack of guarantees for the triumph of goodness? Do we opt for the self-denial that reason can never commend or reject, since it is out of its depth in such matters? Or do we go for the seemingly more practical methods, and try to ignore that in this way goodness eventually eludes us? In short, are our values those of God or not?

In the New Testament itself, one writer has already made this explicit:

> Jesus said, 'For judgement I came into this world, that those who do not see may see, and that those who see may become blind.' Some of the Pharisees near him heard this, and they said to him, 'Are we also blind?' Jesus said to them, 'If you were blind, you would have no guilt; but now that you say, "We see," your guilt remains' (*John* 9:39–41).

Here, once again is reflection on the fact of Jesus, not Jesus' own teaching; but it is a true reflection. Not that the division effected by this judgement is a simple affair of 'sheep' and 'goats'. It cuts this way and that, and any individual may find himself in different categories at different times, or even simultaneously in respect of different aspects of his life. A man may acknowledge this hierarchy of values as the one for true human life, but not acknowledge God, or the values as God's values. A man may acknowledge both in theory but not in practice, or in practice only in certain contexts – in private life, let us say, but not in his public role. The Church which has the task of keeping men ever in touch with the challenge of Jesus may herself be governed so little by these values that millions of human beings never become aware of them at all, or at any rate not in connection with Jesus and so with God. The judgement is thus a permanent presence confronting every thought and activity of Man, both corporate and individual. At the same time, however, it is quite obviously not a judgement in the form of arraignment, condemnation, and sentence. The very essence of it is that it is embodied in a man who forgives and who by means of suffering takes the results of evil and uses them as the framework within which to create a new good. And in so doing he discloses God as this sort of person. In this way Jesus gives men yet another source of pride and confidence, by opening up to them the means of becoming genuinely partners of their Creator. Man is no longer the puppet of the gods, or a cipher whose life effects nothing eternal. He knows now that what he does in the spirit of Jesus is a real contribution to the triumph of good, because it works with God and not against him, and so hastens the achievement of the glory for which the world was made.

This has the further effect on human life of creating a new form of human society, one that runs across the boundaries of all existing groups, and yet is expressed in and through their life and culture. Yet again, we see how Jesus' apparently frustrated expectations turn out to be fulfilled. The Messianic kingdom is not unpeopled; it has its citizens everywhere, their ethos the one Jesus described and by which he himself lived. This kingdom is not to be equated with the Church. The perpetual argument among Christians whether the 'Church' is 'visible' or 'invisible' can never end because the two sides are talking, though they do not realize it, about two different things. There must be a visible Church, that is to say, a permanent and defined organization with an unavoidable presence. It must always be possible, so to speak, for the human race to bark its shins on the Church, because otherwise the truth will not be brought into judging and transforming contact with the world. A concrete body, dedicated to this task, is essential if the battle for human life is not to be lost by default. But the citizen roll of those who live by the truth can never be compiled. A human being may, as we said, be in this community at one time and not at another, he may be at once partly within it and partly outside it. He may be a conscious Christian believer or he may not. The Messianic kingdom is, as Jesus foresaw, salt in the food, leaven in the dough, the seed growing secretly. Its impact is not that of an institution with an image, but that of the sovereignty of God whose methods have been embraced by human individuals; and it is by their free co-operation that his purpose of freedom, understanding, and love is living and powerful. These individuals may at any moment come together in organizations for the service of the sovereignty – in a religious order, a secular humanitarian body, a small local *ad hoc* group that lasts a few months and passes unnoticed. Such pieces of practical machinery come and go; they are custom-built for the needs of the time. They may overlap the Church,

be within it, or independent of it; but they are never independent of the
Gospel or of Jesus, hidden or acknowledged.

But Jesus has brought yet another joy into the world's life. For
mankind now knows that the human society at large is not confined
within the borders of mortality. It runs through into eternity, and men
are at one with those who came before and come after them. The same
truth which alone can create the life of the race here holds good for
ever; and death is but the process by which men are laid open to direct
encounter with the Person in whom that truth is fully embodied, and
who by personal relationship can enable them at last fully and freely to
receive its perfecting power within themselves. The world does not end
here. Man can step out of the universe, and yet not cease to be or to be
Man. The human brotherhood endures and grows. Those who were
our friends are still our friends, and when we join them we shall know
ourselves at home; and those who were our enemies are now and ever
will be our friends, reconciled with us by the Man Jesus.

The present, then, and the future have been illuminated with joy.
But what of the past? Can even God change the past? This is the aspect
of the matter which Christians chiefly have in mind, when they speak of
'atonement'. In the deepest sense of the word, of course, the whole
work of Jesus is an atonement, as many modern writers have pointed
out, because it is a work of reconciling God and Man, bringing them
into a partnership of shared values, and as such involves the present and
the future as well as the past. But there is a narrower consideration in
which religion, like common parlance, is concerned with 'atoning for'
evil done in the past – making up for it, expiating it, enabling it to be
cancelled from the account. To clarify the issues a very brief historical
digression will be necessary.

In the Old Testament there are various ways of making atonement
for sins. The offender could go to the Temple, and offer a 'guilt
offering', for example. He would confess his offence (and in some cases
be expected to make reparation), and lay his hand on an animal victim,
which the Levites would then slay, and the priest offer to God as a
whole burnt offering on the altar. Such sacrifices would not cover every
kind of sin. Serious and wanton crimes, such as murder and adultery,
were outside their scope. Only once in the year was atonement made
for all the sins of the whole nation, in the great Day of Atonement. On
this day the High Priest confessed all the sins of the people over the
scapegoat, which was then driven out into the wilderness to be de-

voured by demons.[1] (At Jerusalem the animal was in fact killed by hurling it over a cliff.) In the period between the latest Old Testament writings and the time of Jesus, various good works, such as almsgiving, were held to atone for one's misdeeds. In the New Testament, there is a Christian continuation of this idea in *James* 5:19–20, where it is said that anyone who 'brings back a sinner from the error of his way' will also atone for ('cover') his own many sins.

There are here a number of different approaches to the problem of dealing with the evil past. The Day of Atonement is in essence a fairly primitive conception, in which sin is thought of as a quasi-material defilement, which is transferred to the scapegoat and thus removed from the human to the demonic realm. The guilt offering, however, is more subtle, and various misunderstandings of it are prevalent.

Clearly the fact that the sinner lays his hands on the victim while confessing his offence cannot have the same meaning here as it does in the Day of Atonement ritual. If it did, the animal would then become a polluted thing, and could not possibly be offered to God on the altar. Some have therefore seen the victim as a substitute for the sinner himself; but this too is unlikely for two main reasons. First, the sins for which this kind of atonement was valid were not ones requiring the death penalty. For such sins, as we have said, there was normally no method of sacrificial expiation. The idea of a life being taken in place of the offender's own life is therefore inappropriate. Moreover, if it were thought of in this way, the animal victim would hardly be offered to God as a gift; and this is the undoubted significance of the whole burnt offering, from which nothing was kept back to be eaten by the priest or the worshipper as happened in the case of other types of sacrifice. Secondly, the idea is anachronistic. The ancient world did not regard the life of an animal as having this sort of value. It is very much a modern attitude to concentrate on the thought of the lamb or goat or bird being deprived of its own 'right to live'. The correct interpretation is almost certainly that this is the imposition of a fine or penance. The

---

[1] The ritual is described in *Lev.* 16. It has sometimes been said that the Day of Atonement, like the ordinary guilt offerings, did not cover all sins; but the text seems to be perfectly clear on this point. Moreover, if it did not, there would seem to be no occasion for the warning shrewdly given by the Rabbis: 'If a man says, "I will sin, and the Day of Atonement will atone for my sin," the Day of Atonement will not atone for his sin.' Christians who use the Sacrament of Penance, please note!

stipulation that the animal shall be a perfect specimen arises partly from respect to God, partly to ensure that the sinner does not meet his obligations fraudulently by using stock that would be of no value to him anyway.[1] But when this has been said, we also have to bear in mind the striking fact that the value of the 'fine' was not proportioned to the seriousness of the offence but to the wealth of the worshipper. Atonement must be within the reach of all, and so the poorest of the poor need offer no more than 'a turtledove or two young pigeons'. This had two effects, both good. It made it impossible to suppose that the sacrifice itself expunged guilt by some inherent magical power; and it emphasized that the human act was simply a token, a penalty paid to show the seriousness of repentance, and that the real work of dealing with the past was done by God and his forgiveness. The same could not be said of the method of atonement by good works, which tended more and more to the credit-and-debit attitude of mind. The offender had to 'pay', certainly, but his payment was not sheer penalty, but instead something for which he was given merit, and which thus helped to outweigh his sins. Finally, mention should be made of one more ritual which played its part in the expiation of sin, the sprinkling of the worshipper with the blood of the sacrificial victim. Here the blood as the seat of life is thought of as reviving the life-force of the sinner which his guilt has seriously weakened. This too in later times is given a God-context. The danger to life comes from divine judgement; and God himself 'gives' men the blood on the altar to repair the peril. This is not, however, strictly a means of atonement.

All this is perfectly straightforward. In the ritual and symbolism of an ancient culture, indeed, it yet embodies the three basic human ways of dealing with the evil past: reparation, punishment, forgiveness. The complicating factor enters with the Christian Gospel. The early Christians were quite certain that the death and resurrection of Christ had dealt with all human problems, and in particular that the death on the cross had settled with the problem of sin. This was a connection so obvious that it would indeed have required considerable perversity not to make it. Not only had Jesus himself at the Last Supper characterized his coming death as a sacrifice to gain forgiveness of sins for all

[1] In practice the arrangement came to be that the worshipper had to buy his victim from the Temple authorities, who kept a supply of animals for the purpose. This ensured that the sinner could not defraud God, but created new temptations for the officials.

who believed in him, there was the Old Testament prophecy of the
righteous servant of God whose life God himself was to 'make an
offering for sin' (*Isa.* 53:10); and indeed, the basic datum of the killing
of a truly good man, designated, as they believed, by God to be his
appointed agent on earth, demanded interpretation, and that of blood-
shedding in sacrifice was clamant as the appropriate category for the
task. Thus it comes about that the formula, 'Christ died for us' or 'for
our sins' or 'for us sinners', enters Christian history as the map-
reference of an immense and mysterious depth in the ocean of the
spirit.

But what exactly had been done? and how had it been done? The
old sacrificial concepts could develop in two ways in order to handle
this new situation. Sacrifice thought of as a gift to God could be
stretched to cover this life of Jesus, perfect in every point, offered to
God in total obedience unto death. The utter loyalty to the good that
God wills made this the only worthy oblation that mankind had ever
made; and in response to this gift God could be thought of as granting
Jesus the right to bring into the eternal joy of God with himself all his
human brethren. Here we have the idea of Christ the High Priest,
exercising the priestly function of intercession on behalf of sinful
humanity with complete efficacy. This is one of the grand themes of the
New Testament *Epistle to the Hebrews*, and it continues through all
succeeding Christian theology. But while it provides a basis on which
God may, so to speak, properly let men off, it is not an expiatory view;
it does not cancel the sins of the world. To cover this aspect of the
matter, the concept of sacrifice grew out in a different direction, that of
punishment. Man had undoubtedly deserved death for his wickedness;
and a truly righteous God would therefore require that this penalty be
imposed. In the past, a token penance followed by pardon might have
been permitted; but this could not go on for ever. Sooner or later, the
account must be settled. But when the sacrificial victim is a human life,
how is this line of thought to be followed out?

Clearly the pain and death of another man is not a punishment of
me. The old animal sacrifice had at any rate taken something of mine
away. But this man was not my property. Death in striking him left me
untouched. The only way of using the punishment category was to say
that he had been punished on my behalf or in my place. And if this man
was also in very truth the Son of God from heaven, then God himself
in human form had borne this punishment for me. To many Christians

this statement is the heart of the Gospel. God satisfies the demands of justice by being executed in my place.

This view is today widely criticized and rejected, but more often than not for the wrong reasons. It inspires revulsion of feeling, when in fact its chief defect is not moral but logical. It is denounced for portraying a God who achieves inferior ends by evil means; but the truth of the matter is that the means described could never achieve their supposed ends at all.

Suppose that I have committed a crime. A friend of mine is arrested, charged, and wrongfully convicted and sentenced for my offence. As ill-luck would have it, he has no witnesses, no alibi, no evidence of any kind which might clear him. It would be quite permissible in ordinary speech to say that he was enduring 'my' punishment, or that he had gone to prison 'in my place'. After he has been in gaol some time, however, facts come to light which prove conclusively that I was the guilty one. The result is that my friend is released, given a free Royal Pardon, and paid compensation; and I am tried and sentenced. No one in his right mind would suppose for a moment that Justice could be satisfied with anything else. I do not receive a shorter sentence because my friend has already served two years of 'my' time. If I did, that would be grotesquely unjust. Punishment, to be punishment, must correlate with guilt. Justice can never be served by punishing the innocent.

But let us change the illustration slightly. Suppose that my friend could have taken steps which would have proved his innocence, but did not do so, because I am a family man with four children and he is a bachelor with no dependants. Again, after a time, the facts come to light. What happens now? He will be released, and may be given a pardon for this offence; and I will be tried and sentenced. But he will certainly not be compensated, and may lay himself open to a charge of perverting the course of justice. From a totally different standpoint his conduct may be regarded as admirable and heroic; but Justice will not think so.

What then of God? God knows all the facts. If God then deliberately takes on himself the suffering which is my due for the evil I have done, he is not satisfying Justice; he is perverting it. His conduct may be considered admirable from a different point of view, but not from that of Justice. In fact, we may say that Justice is being categorically rejected as a basis of action. But if Justice is to be rejected as the supreme principle, what is the point of talking in terms of punishment

at all? Whatever God is doing by suffering it cannot be this. The only
reason for speaking of the sufferings as 'my' sufferings was this
principle of Justice. It would seem, therefore, that it is nonsensical to
talk of God suffering in my place. Any sufferings he endures are his
own, and arise not from guilt but from some other cause.

There is a further difficulty in using Justice as the interpretative
category. Is Justice to be thought of as something independent of God
to which he is obliged to conform? If so, what becomes of God's
position as Creator, by virtue of which he determines the total nature
of existence including its moral basis? We must surely say that the
moral principles of the created order must have their root in the nature
of God himself. If Justice is the supreme end to be served, then it must
be the ultimate value for God himself, in his own personal being. In
acting in this way, therefore, he is being untrue to himself, he is denying
his own moral nature.

Justice, however, is not the only end which God fails to serve by
acting like this. He also fails to provide for expiation. The desire to
atone for one's misdeeds is not an ignoble yearning in Man. It acknowledges guilt, it aims at reparation, at adding to the good in the world to
counterbalance as far as possible the evil we have caused. It seeks by
penance to deprive ourselves of good in proportion to or even in excess
of the benefit we may have gained from wickedness. But it is something
we must do for ourselves, if it is to have any liberating or cleansing
effect on our own persons. We can, indeed, speak of atoning for someone else's sin in the sense of making reparation for it. But the subjective effect of dealing with the guilt can be achieved only by the guilty
person. If, therefore, God is supposed to have undergone suffering to
expiate our sins, he is in fact depriving us of any possibility of expiation. We are not even to have the dignity of being penalized for our
own wrongdoing. We conclude, therefore, that if justice and expiation
were God's intention, he could not have devised any method which
would more effectually frustrate them both.

Are we really desirous of believing in a God who is simply stupid?
Is not the moral of all this that Justice, expiation, punishment are
entirely wrong and inappropriate categories for interpreting the
sufferings of Jesus? If they lead to such ridiculous and self-contradictory conclusions, this ought to suggest to us that we are mistaken in
our methods of tackling the question, as if, for example, we were to
attempt a problem concerning spheres with the wrong kind of

U

geometry. It is not that there is anything intrinsically bad about the concepts of justice, expiation, or punishment as such; but rather that this is not a context in which they apply, or perhaps that they operate at a lower level of the hierarchy of values.

This inevitably prompts us to ask in what sense expiation can be said to deal with the past anyway? We have already noted ways in which it may, so to speak, set the record straight; but it does so not by erasing certain facts but by adding other, morally positive facts to counterbalance the existing negative ones. Nothing can rewrite history; all we can hope to do is to modify its future course. If I have committed murder, then a murderer I remain to the end of my days. It is a truth about that continuum which is my personal existence that I have killed a fellow-being without any of the commonly accepted justifications, such as war or self-defence. The constructive question now becomes, how is my life to go on from this given situation? Am I to become hardened, allowing it to make me a man so brutalized that I no longer consider the taking of life as a serious matter? Am I to go to pieces in self-pity or self-hatred? Am I to make this event a stimulus to radical change and reformation, and to spend what may remain of my life, so far as I am permitted to do so, in loyalty to the good, and to such goodness as my past crime makes specially fitting? I may do any of these things. But first of all I have to face and accept that none of them will alter the past or make it other than evil. To fail to grasp this is to fail to see the seriousness of decision attaching to any moral and personal act. Because I as a person am a child and partner of God, that relationship gives my personhood an eternal dimension, and gives what I do eternal significance. To demand that anyone, even God, should change this is to demand that I should cease to be a person, that I should be unmade, that the nature of reality should be destroyed – and not even for my benefit, since if this were done neither I nor anyone else would exist to be benefited. Whatever, therefore, has been done about the past in Jesus and his sufferings, it is not this.

If, therefore, we think that God may have done something about the past, we must look in a different direction to discover what this is. And here our earlier considerations about the true nature of forgiveness[1] come into play. It will be remembered that we defined one of the major works of forgiveness as the transmutation of evil by taking the new conditions created by the evil as the setting and material for a new good.

[1] Cf. pp. 120–125 above.

What has been done cannot be undone. It now constitutes the given situation, just as truly as the circumstances into which a person is born. Out of this and this alone the future has to be made; and it is the whole-hearted, unrepining acceptance of this which is the greatest of all the gifts which the one who forgives can bestow on the offender. Where the evil is serious, this creative, forward-looking acceptance can be achieved only through suffering, often protracted and intense; but this suffering is now the only path open to the completely good life, and it is this path therefore which love, in its loyalty to the Good, will take.

If we now apply these considerations to God, we see first that every evil is a blow to his purpose, which is to bring all his creatures to their proper fulfilment. In the case of Man this means the person's own free loyalty to the Good in understanding and love. By forming his grand design as Creator God committed himself to this purpose from the beginning, and thus exposed himself to the possibility of having to suffer. This is not, as it might appear, a contradiction of the old theological principle that God is 'impassible'. This term, usually construed as meaning 'incapable of suffering', certainly produces insuperable difficulties if it is taken in this narrow sense. But philosophically all that it necessarily implies is that God cannot be acted upon against his will. There is no other being, existing independently of God, who might so act. But if by his own decision and initial action God creates beings who can act upon him, then their power to do so comes from him, and his essential impassibility is unaffected. There is no need here to recapitulate all the arguments of the first part of the present work, where it was urged that the only credible God, in view of the nature of the universe, was one for whom sacrificial love was the supreme value. But if there is any force in these contentions, then it must be clear that it is open to God to meet evil by that forgiving acceptance of the circumstances created by the evil which uses them as the base from which to move forward to a new good, and through this new good to bring about in the end the fulfilment of his great underlying purpose. And this he can do only through his own suffering.

It thus becomes highly significant that Jesus should have stressed over and over again that forgiveness is God's fundamental attitude to human evil. It is also significant that he never, whatever his followers may have said afterwards, spoke of his own death as having expiatory meaning. At the Last Supper he is presented as defining the effect of his blood-shedding as the 'remission' or 'forgiveness of sins'. The saying of *Mk* 10:45 about the life given as a 'ransom for many', even if it has historical basis, does not contradict this. The ransom metaphor cannot in any case be pressed too literally, since, as has often been pointed out, there is no one to whom the ransom can be paid. Christian writers have sometimes explored the possibility that it might be paid to the Devil; but this leads nowhere, or rather it leads to totally immoral conclusions. Nor are men God's 'prisoners', so the ransom cannot be paid to him. The imagery connotes no more than the idea of a price paid in order to give men their freedom, and this, forgiveness most certainly does. Jesus, both in his dying and in his understanding of his death, exactly follows the path which, we believe, God laid down for himself in the act of creation: loyalty to the Good, even where this narrows down to the one line of ultimate suffering, because this is the only good which can be made out of the forces of human evil, and thus is the only form in which forgiveness can be made real.

The life, teaching, and death of Jesus are therefore the perfect revelation of what God is like. If we recall what was said earlier about faith, part of the significance of this will become apparent. Jesus provides the key which identifies one possible answer to the ultimate question as the right one; and his vindication in the resurrection gives final and eternal authority to this key. This means, however, that the key could never be provided simply in the form of teaching, a revelation in words. It had to be an event, a personal event, because this alone could be vindicated and so verified.

This brings us to the greatest of all the questions about Jesus himself, and drives us inexorably towards one particular answer. For it is simply inconceivable that a God such as we have described could ever have said: 'If men are to be free to find their true fulfilment, they must know the truth about their eternal situation. This truth can only be given to them in a personal existence, a human being who will be morally comprehensible to them. But this life will involve the most terrible suffering. *I will therefore send someone else to do the job.*'

Such a decision would not only be utterly unworthy, and incompatible with everything we know about love; it would also be pointless. If God suffers, then he has suffered whenever his personal relationship with free beings enslaved by moral evil has made him suffer, whenever the pains of his children have struck home to his compassion. The Talmud makes the point:

In the Midrash it is said: In the hour in which the Egyptians sank in the waters, the highest angels, those who were gathered round the throne of God, wished to sing a hymn of joy. But God said to them: 'My children are drowning in the sea, and will you rejoice?'[1]

What then, to put it crudely, had he to gain by not coming himself? Neither inability nor reluctance to suffer stood in his way. The tremendous moment of self-sacrifice, when God voluntarily surrendered perfect joy, was not the moment when an infant was conceived in the womb of a Jewish girl, but when the adventure of creation began. The purpose of becoming Man was not to enable God to suffer, but to bring that suffering into such a relationship with Man that Man could know it, respond to it, and co-operate with it, and so find his own fulfilment in freedom.

This is the great affirmation by which Christianity is marked off from all other answers to the riddle of life: the once for all, historical embodiment of the personal God in a particular human individual. Not the perfect obedience of a human being to an abstract principle, not the exaltation of such a being to eternal fellowship with God as his ideal Son: but the Incarnation of the Creator in a truly human life, decisive for the whole future and past of the human race.

The debate how this could be so has gone on ever since. To describe and assess all the complicated metaphysical arguments which have attempted to define the mechanics of the mystery cannot be done here, and would serve little purpose if it could. For the point which our whole line of argument has sought to make is simply this: that given the historic facts about Jesus, and given the only conception on which God is credible, it is here that the lines of thought inexorably meet. Check, turn, and twist as we may, this is the unavoidable conclusion – though why anyone should wish to avoid it, it is hard to fathom.

Nevertheless, it would be cowardly simply to say, It must be so, and therefore the difficulties can go hang. Let us therefore briefly examine the essence of the problem. As developed in the reflection of Christian theology it is this: how can a single personal being exist at the same time both as God and as true Man? Surely the same person cannot, as we argued in an earlier chapter,[2] be simultaneously a genuine human being and aware of himself as the eternal God? But if he is not aware of

---

[1] Quoted by Bovet, *That they may have Life*, p. 135.
[2] Cf. pp. 143–151 above.

himself as God, then his identity has been destroyed; he is no longer truly himself. Hence orthodoxy has tried to formulate the structure of Jesus Christ in various ways. It has conceived that two natures, the divine and the human, each complete in itself, were, so to speak, screwed together to make a single being. Since this implies only one centre of conscious identity, one person, and since, if God is to become Man, the person must be that of God himself, the human component comes to be thought of as 'impersonal'. The deity takes on not a human being, for that would be impossible, but 'human nature', complete with mind, feelings, will, and body, but not organized as the vehicle of an independent human personality. Such a conception leaves unresolved, however, the problem how a being conscious of himself as divine could live a normal human life. Hence the necessity is felt, sooner or later, of some kind of theory of *kenosis*, or emptying.[1] The divine person lays aside all his divine attributes. His power and knowledge and inviolable holiness are, as it were suspended, to enable him to conform himself to the narrow limits of human existence. In the end, therefore, we are left with the strange combination of a human nature without any personal centre, and a divine person existing in temporary unconsciousness of or detachment from his divine nature.

Such a diagram is the more unsatisfactory to us today, because of our very concept of 'person', which the ancient world did not possess. The idea of a person without his nature, or of human nature existing except in a human person, is to us a contradiction in terms. It would seem, therefore, that if faith in the Incarnation is to be made comprehensible to the present age – and, whatever some may say, a belief must be comprehensible, at least in the sense of using words in a way that is not self-contradictory – then it must be done by starting from the concept of person.[2] That this concept is as yet far from clear even in the human sciences no candid observer will deny. Too often it is used by writers today in a merely emotive sense: 'The dignity of the person', 'the great thing is to be a *person*' – where emphasis takes the place of analysis, and the hope seems to be that if only the word is repeated frequently and

[1] The use of the Greek word *kenosis* is inspired by the hymn in Paul's *Epistle to the Philippians*, where Jesus is said to have 'emptied himself, taking the form of a servant' (*Phil.* 2:7).

[2] For a preliminary essay along these lines cf. D. E. Jenkins, *The Glory of Man*.

intensely enough, light will eventually dawn. But this only implies what has been said throughout the present work, that we have to understand God's world before we can hope to understand God, even to the best of our no doubt very limited capacity.

To approach the question from both ends at once, however, is not necessarily a hopeless task; and it may be that something can be said from the angle of God's entry into human life as well. It makes some difference, in fact, if we put the proposition that God becomes Man the other way round, and say, that *when God chooses to exist within the terms of our environment a man is what he becomes*. Manhood, in short, is the only mode of being in which God can do justice under such conditions to what he is.

If we think of the matter in this way, then certain traditionally worrying problems turn out not to be real problems at all. Manhood, for example, implies limited knowledge and limited powers. Perhaps most significant of all, it makes it impossible to believe in one's own perfection. However good a man was, if he were truly sensitive to the facts of the human condition, he could never assert that he was sinless. He might *be* sinless; he would not be sure that he was. If God became truly Man, therefore we would not expect him to be infallible on all questions, we would not expect him to claim to be morally immaculate. And if we had good reason to think that God might have become Man, then we would also conclude that these characteristics were not indispensable to his expressing the essence of his nature. What would be indispensable is that sacrificial love in loyalty to the good which the nature of things declares to be God's supreme value, and without which indeed he cannot even be believed to exist. To put the matter in New Testament terms, belief in the Incarnation demands not the Christ of the Fourth Gospel (and to a lesser extent of the other three) but the Jesus of history.

The real metaphysical difficulty, in the view of the present writer, is not one of dissecting the structure of the incarnate God. He cannot be dissected; he is himself. But we find ourselves bewildered by the notion of a single person existing at once within the terms of the created order, and also being continuously present to that order as its Creator. It may well be, however, when we think how relative and fluid is the whole system of Space and Time, and how elusive of our grasp, that this in fact presents no obstacle at all. One thing, from the theological angle, is clear: we cannot invoke some conception such as

the doctrine of the Trinity to answer this question. God is not a committee, one of whose members can be detached to serve for a time on a
foreign posting. Even if we wish, as well we may, to think that something analogous to society and relationship exists within God, yet God
himself must remain indivisible, and be wholly committed to all his
acts.

Two misgivings which may arise, and which are more relevant to our
situation, are these. First, if we think in this way of God becoming
Man, is it not inconceivable that the Man whom he becomes could ever
be subject as we are to temptation? But why should this be so? As
we saw in an earlier chapter,[1] conflict and ambiguity are of the
essence of the human condition. Moral purity is attained not by an
enormous aggregate of 'correct' decisions in independent cases; for
many cases there is no single 'right solution', though there may be a
number which we can definitely say are wrong. What is vital is that
within the area of possible good solutions a man should choose in
accordance with the demands of sacrificial love; and the pressures upon
him not to do this are part of the condition of being human. The sinless
man is therefore no more free from temptation than any other. His
obedience to the true law of human existence is not a static and inde-
fectible quality but a fulfilment which has to be achieved through
suffering over and over again.

Secondly, it will be remembered that we argued earlier[2] that the
Jesus of history was mistaken about the programme which God
planned to follow. To many this would seem to rule out at once any
chance that he might be God in Man. But why? It is not merely natural
in human beings to be in error about the details of the future, it is
inevitable. This feature of the human condition could be overcome
only by investing Jesus with superhuman powers[3] which might
indeed have satisfied the tired old dreams of paganism but would
utterly exclude any true incarnation of God. What has an inspired
knowledge of the future to do with the point on which all really depends – perfect loyalty to the Good in love? In so far as such loyalty has
in the normal condition of Man to be exercised in ignorance of the

---

[1] Chapter 4 above.

[2] Cf. pp. 238–242 above.

[3] Whether it is right to think even of God as having a fixed detailed plan which
is bound to come to pass in a given form is itself questionable. But there is no need
to rest the present case on so abstruse a speculation.

future it would seem to be positively incompatible with it. The true vocation of Man is to be loyal to the Good here and now in fulfilling an immediate task, and to leave the ultimate outcome to God and to the free response of other men. Such a task may indeed include laying plans for the future, setting up groups to continue the work, handing on traditions and ideals; but determining what is to become of these creations after our part has ended it does not include. Our legacy may and usually does alter almost out of recognition in a very short time; but it may fulfil our purposes more deeply, and those purposes may have been an indispensable factor in bringing the greater good to birth. We must have some vision how things will go, or we cannot act morally and responsibly; and our vision will normally be shaped by the concepts of our time. But provided that this vision has led us to act in loyalty to the Good, the fact that it proves mistaken in detail is of total unimportance. To the extent that our intentions were in harmony with God's aims, they will be realized in essentials if not in outward forms. So with Jesus. If he did indeed expect the Messianic kingdom on earth, he may have been wrong in form and detail; but the goals and methods he pursued in preparing for it were God's goals and methods, and were fulfilled in God's way. The whole tenor of his life proves that what mattered to him was that this should be so. In short, the record at this point shows a closer conformity to what a true incarnation of God in Man ought to be than any unnatural knowledge would have done.

Is there then any joy, any good news, that could ever surpass the truth of which we have been given such assurance in Jesus? That Man should be, in his humble sphere, the partner of God is wonderful enough; that God should take us as his sons and daughters in a personal relationship transcending even death is surely sufficient for anyone. That all our errors and evils have been taken up by the divine love and made the source of perfect good, drawing the sting of the past; that we can hold up our heads in justifiable pride, even in our imperfect present; that we need have no fears for an eternal future – will this not transform any life? But when above all we learn that God himself has become our partner and our brother, sharing our own condition, this gives imperishable glory to every created thing. Never again can we despise or hate the earth trodden by the feet of God, the food and drink by which he lived, the family bonds which he shared, the human form which was found sufficient to express even his innermost being. Man is not merely Man but, in the old phrase, *capax Dei*, someone in whom

God can be himself. Because the heart of God is self-sacrificing love, it is by this capacity that we are 'in his image', and it is in Jesus alone that this has been proved. That is why, in the words of the Good Friday Liturgy:

> We venerate thy Cross, O Lord, and praise and glorify thy holy Resurrection; for by virtue of the Cross, joy has come to the whole world.

PART THREE

What Then Must We Do?

12

The Church and the World

BY FAR the most important thing to be said about Christians in the light of the long argument just concluded is that they are those human beings who have grasped the truth about the human situation. 'Grasped', not just in an intellectual way – because any complete presentation of this truth has at its heart, as we have seen, a moral demand. We have to choose love, we have to commit ourselves to a far from obvious or prudent attitude to life, before we are even logically entitled to believe. Hence to describe what Christians think is the truth is to confront oneself with this challenge, and with the stern condition that no one can claim to have made his own even the truth he has just so impeccably described unless he has decided for love, has acceded to this demand. The *Epistle of James* in the New Testament has some scathing words on this subject:

> You believe that God is one; you do well. Even the demons believe – and shudder (*James* 2:19).

For it must be admitted that to accept this picture of life as the true one, and yet not to be able to make the personal commitment to love, is the most terrible despair. It brings nothing but a deathly conviction that I am permanently alienated from the truth, a feeling that between myself and reality stands an impenetrable glass wall through which I can observe everything and enter into living involvement with nothing. Openness to joy, openness to suffering, a passionate interest and participation in the needs of others, and all this as a spontaneous attitude – this is what I must have, for this alone is the family likeness which marks God's children and partners. No wonder that, from the first, Christians have felt themselves compelled to use the word 'spirit' to describe this. It *is* a spirit, not a code; it is an attitude which issues in behaviour not a pattern of behaviour to be imitated or imposed. Yet this spirit is far more urgent and imperative than any code or system of conduct, for it is continually creating new obligations, new involvements. Everyone I meet calls on me for some particular response, some special contribution which, so long as I have strength and opportunity, I cannot refuse. A code might as often limit as enlarge what was asked of me. The spirit, the spirit of love and of Jesus, the spirit of God acknowledges no limits.

It might seem none the less that we are condemned to despair after all, for this spirit certainly does not come naturally. As we saw, there are natural growth-points, in the form of our common human affections, which give us an idea of what we require, of what is required of us. But these affections are neither absolute nor universal. Love as the criterion for choosing between the good alternatives offered to us by wisdom is not accepted by us as ultimate in our dealings with all persons or on every occasion. To accept it as such is to do violence to our natural disposition. In the ordinary way, when we say that something we want does not 'come naturally' to us, the remedy is to discipline ourselves, to practise, to make it habitual. But in this instance such an imposed behaviour will not suffice. For what we want is something free and spontaneous, otherwise it will not see the responses which the situation calls for, will not be alive and open to the possibilities. In short, we need a change in our fundamental attitude, and we cannot induce this in ourselves. It has, therefore, to be induced in us. We have to make this leap, this radical moral and personal decision, drawn, so to speak, by the compelling attraction of the decision itself. We have to fall in love with love – and we need that love itself should sweep us off our feet.

This can hardly be done in the abstract. Love has to be seen embodied in others as the creative source of living. Precisely because it is 'different', we need to experience its 'differentness' in those who live by it, before the adventure and excitement – and danger – of it become real to us, before we can intuit what it might feel like to be open and involved in this way. Because love in action cannot be adequately described by any formula or set of rules but always adapts itself to the uniqueness of the individual, we need to watch its style, and wonder at its strange presuppositions at work in our own group, on our own ground. It is by comparing the spontaneous reactions of real people who have this spirit with our own equally spontaneous reactions to the same situation that we begin to release the spirit in ourselves. If our response chimes with theirs, well and good; we become less hesitant. If it clashes against theirs, we become more aware of the dark, timid, prudential, impersonal side of our own nature, and, with luck, desire more intensely that it should be changed. In such a community the atmosphere is one of freedom. To give one example: because the good faith of others is taken for granted, malice is not suspected and offence therefore less often taken – with the paradoxical result that it is also less often given. There are homes and families like this, where the very children put one to shame because they accept spontaneously obligations impossible to one's own heart. But these are homes one enjoys visiting and regrets leaving. The gaiety and sincerity, the sanity and reliability, of the people who live in them, their readiness to attend or to help, and to think the best of others, mean that they are always the ones turned to in a crisis, and that their lives are constantly loaded with new burdens never shown by them to be so. There are other groups where in their own special circumstances recognizably the same air is abroad: shops, offices, small businesses, common rooms, schools, committees. Membership of any such group can induce in an individual the change which he needs but cannot impose on himself. It can change him so radically that long after he has moved on, and has lost all contact with anyone in whom this spirit is present, he still feels it challenging by contrast the dark, formal, insensitive wisdom of his new environment. 'We never had this trouble at X – we didn't do things this way.'

It might be thought that the Christian community above all others would be characterized by this atmosphere. For here, in theory, we have people who are committed first and foremost to this spirit, who cannot reasonably be Christians unless they have opted for it. But more than that, they are people who, having made this commitment, have had their eyes opened to the real meaning of the Cross and Resurrection of Jesus, namely that this is also the free personal commitment of the Heart at the heart of things. Knowing this, how bold, how irrepressibly happy, how serene, one would expect them to be! How infinitely patient, how unconcerned about their 'image', the 'success' of their group as such or their own individual position within it! Furthermore, should not such a vast and far-flung community (950,000,000 of them, we are told) inevitably impregnate the life of the whole world with their own spirit? One in three of the inhabitants of the world –

surely that should be enough to induce the same change in all but a small minority of people?

Sometimes, here and there, this atmosphere and its liberating effects are to be found, but not often. Why and how has this come about?

In the first place, from a very early stage in the history of the Christian Church the crucial logical and psychological sequence was reversed. Instead of making conviction of truth dependent on commitment to the moral demand, the moral demand was presented as deriving from a prior conviction of the truth. This was in a way natural enough. For Jesus, the temptation to make this mistake did not arise. The only doctrinal or metaphysical beliefs which he wanted to maintain were already common ground between him and his audience. Because they believed in God and his sovereignty, Jesus' task was to show them in what that sovereignty was to consist; and this inevitably gave primacy to the moral demand with its revolutionary scale of values. But after the resurrection the Church had to present not only the new moral demand but also certain claims about the identity of Jesus himself. The first disciples shared Jesus' basic religious presuppositions; hence they were free to be baffled, shamed, shown up, and changed by the moral character and assumptions of the man they followed.[1] Such claims as Jesus may have made for himself only reinforced this primacy of the moral element, since the stumbling-block was precisely, 'How could a man who lived and died like that be the agent of God's sovereignty?' But neither the Jews nor the Greeks to whom the Church went after the first Easter shared the disciples' conviction about Jesus, who and what he was. Hence this had to be formulated and put across. Moreover, because it was this conviction about Jesus which marked out the Christian community from Jews and pagans, because this was the

---

[1] *Mk* 8:33 = *Matt.* 16:23, Jesus' words to Peter: 'Get behind me, Satan! For you are not on the side of God, but of men', when Peter tried to dissuade him from running into crucifixion; *Mk* 10:42–45 = *Matt.* 20:25–28, Jesus' disciples are to turn human ideas of greatness completely upside down; *Lk.* 9:51–56, the disciples want fire from heaven to burn up those who reject Jesus, and he rebukes them; the words, 'You do not know what manner of spirit you are of; for the Son of man came not to destroy men's lives but to save them,' are missing from certain important MSS, and are therefore generally omitted in modern translations. What they say is implicit in the story anyway; but even if a Christian reflection rather than Jesus' own words, they superbly express his meaning, and show that somewhere the church had grasped the point.

distinctive platform by which they could be easily identified, it was inevitably this which new converts had first and foremost to accept before they could be admitted into the Church:

> If you confess with your lips that Jesus is Lord and believe in your heart that God raised him from the dead, you will be saved (*Rom.* 10:9).[1]

From this state of affairs comes the twofold division of the Christian message into 'faith' and 'morals', or, in the terms used by the early Church, *kerygma* (= preaching, or proclamation) and *didache* (= teaching, i.e., conduct and morals).[2] This has remained the controlling pattern for Christian theology ever since, and it is hard to see how this could have been avoided.

Nor is such a division necessarily harmful. In some ways it does not matter at all which part a man comes to first. Indeed, as was remarked earlier,[3] for most of those brought up in a Christian home the 'faith', expressed clearly and simply, for example, in hymns, carols, and prayers, is accepted before there can be any chance of properly understanding or responding to the moral challenge. This is of no consequence, provided that the true mutual relationship of the two is grasped later. What too often happens, however, is that the moral demand of Christianity is taught as a set of rules, outlined by Jesus and elaborated by his Church, which we ought to observe because Jesus was who he was and did what he did. Hence, when the maturing person stumbles at the 'faith' which he had accepted as a child, the key which alone can open the door to faith, namely the moral demand, is missing. It is either neglected because it is thought of as the 'authoritative' pronouncement of someone whose authority now seems to be bogus; or it is unknown. For the chances of any individual's being taught this demand in all its

---

[1] Or cf. *Acts* 8:37. When the Ethiopian eunuch asks Philip, 'What is to prevent my being baptized?', Philip's answer, according to many MSS, runs, 'If you believe with all your heart, you may.' To this the eunuch replies, 'I believe that Jesus Christ is the Son of God.' Here we probably have a profession of faith required of candidates for baptism in the early Church.

[2] This in its turn reflects an even older Jewish classification of the same general kind (*haggada* and *halakha*). It is not the division as such which is peculiar to Christianity, but the importance which circumstances inevitably attached to the 'faith', and the distortion which this tended to introduce into the total vision of the Church as inherited from Jesus himself.

[3] Cf. p. 68 above.

x

intensity as part of his conventional Christian upbringing are slim indeed.[1]

In this way everything is lost. We end up with neither 'faith' nor 'morals'. We may contrast this faulty presentation, so familiar to us from our own experience, with examples of the right method from the New Testament, beginning with Paul who, if anyone, understands the right relationship of the two. He writes to the Corinthians:

> You know the grace of our Lord Jesus Christ, that though he was rich, yet for your sake he became poor, so that by his poverty you might become rich (*II Cor.* 8:9).

The context in which he is speaking is the taking up of a collection at Corinth for the relief of poor Christians in the mother church of Jerusalem. His picture, albeit poetic, is essentially 'theological'; but he does not use it to say, '. . . *therefore* you ought to give your money to help your poorer brethren'. He is well aware that the connection is far more indirect. The verses immediately preceding the one just quoted run:

> . . . see that you excel in this gracious work also. I say this not as a command, but to prove . . . that your love is genuine (*II Cor.* 8:7–8).

The love already exists; he is confident of that, and does not instruct them to love in this instance, but to act in a way that will be in keeping with the love that underlies their whole life – just as Christ himself did. The same pattern – the explication of love first, then its exemplification in Christ – is found in the famous passage, *Phil.* 2:1–11; the second half of which is thought to be a Christian hymn quoted by Paul with perhaps one or two embellishments of his own. Love, affection, sympathy, are characteristics of those who are Christ's brothers, who share in his spirit (2:1), and this works itself out in humility and concern for others (2:3–4). It is the Christian's vocation to foster the working out of this mind which he already has in Christ Jesus (2:5), just as Christ himself was emptied and became a slave, obedient even to death, and death on a cross at that (2:6–8).

---

[1] It is interesting that while there are many who say that they cannot accept Christian dogma but claim to respect the Christian ethic, on examination their notion of that ethic turns out to be a heavily diluted or censored version. Those who assert that they want the Sermon on the Mount but not the Creeds have often (not always, but often) just not read the Sermon on the Mount, or not with any attention. On the whole the Creeds are a good deal more comfortable.

Elsewhere in the New Testament we find the same style of presentation, for example in *I Peter* (3:15b–18a):

> Always be prepared to make a defence to anyone who calls you to account for the hope that is in you, yet do it with gentleness and reverence; and keep your conscience clear, so that when you are abused, those who revile your good behaviour in Christ may be put to shame. For it is better to suffer for doing right, if that should be God's will, than for doing wrong. For Christ also died for sins once for all, the righteous for the unrighteous. . . .

Here again the reader's assent is claimed for the requirement of love, which is then showed to have been displayed in Christ himself. In this way the rigidities (and absurdities) of a legalism of imitation ('Christ behaved in this way, therefore you must do so too') are avoided, and a free acknowledgement is elicited that in Christ the good as chosen by love is both found and confirmed. It is important to be precise at this point. It is not being suggested that men and women already understood perfectly well what love entailed before Christ ever appeared on the scene, and that their ideas are simply verified by him. Christ does show for the first time what love on God's scale and with God's consistency implies, and he does so because the spirit, God's spirit, is in him as a spontaneous creative attitude which sees and seizes upon the works of God, the works of love, in each situation. But the work of love, as we have seen over and over again, is not to invent new kinds of goodness but to choose with absolute priority and universality one category of goodness, the self-forgetting, self-sacrificing kind, wherever there is a conflict, irreducible and unavoidable, between this and the goodness that would look after the interest of the self. Hence what Christ chooses is something already recognized as good, if only in a quixotic way, by the moral judgement of men. What they catch from him is the spirit that will tolerate no compromise on the point of this quixotic and imprudent good. This is 'the mind which you have in Christ Jesus'. The values of this mind are not necessarily something new, though their practical application may be new and surprising at times, simply because this has never before been carried through with such thoroughness. This means that Christians' behaviour can be convincingly argued to be good at the bar of men's general moral thinking, 'so that . . . those who revile' it 'may be put to shame'. But this is only in theory, so far as the world is concerned. The world's own verdict, as regards its own conduct, is that some other goodness may well be more appropriate in the given situation. The world does not live by love absolutely and universally. Nevertheless, it can do so to a marked extent and surprisingly often. Hence it is no surprise to find Christ's type of love in people who have never known Christ.[1] When Justin Martyr in the second century A.D. maintained that Socrates was a foreshadowing of Christ, a Christian before his time, he was absolutely right; and the same kind of comment ought to be made about any man or woman anywhere who chooses from the possible good courses open to them in accordance with the priority of love. The only change one might wish to make in Justin's phrasing would be to say that Socrates was a foreshadowing of Man, of what Man can become and should become – and did become once the spirit of God was enmanned. For we are not concerned with claiming adherents for the Church, as if the Church were a separate organization in competition with the world for membership, but with identifying those human beings who are bound together by that spirit, pre-eminently present in those who are brothers and sisters of the 'proper Man', the one who was truly the son of God.

When, therefore, Paul writes to the Corinthians

Be imitators of me, as I am of Christ (*I Cor.* 11:1).

– Christ whom he himself could have imitated only through what he had learned from the companions of Jesus' brief career – what he has in view is not an imitation consisting in the slavish reproduction of gestures, ways of living, ways of talking. His own life-story proves that. It is the imitation practised by someone who has caught the authentic spirit of his model, and who lives by it in his own circumstances.

A slightly different way of stating this relationship between love and faith is found in the N.T. letter known as *I John*. The author is quite clear about the importance of true belief on the subject of Jesus:

Whoever confesses that Jesus is the Son of God, God abides in him, and he in God (4:15).[2]

---

[1] By the same token there is nothing odd in the fact that much of the ethical teaching in the N.T. is material shared with Jews (since Christ as well as before his time) or with pagan teachers of the ancient world or with secular moralists since. If the 'faith' could not command men's free moral homage it would necessarily be either degrading or unbelievable.

[2] Cf. 1:7; 2:1, 22; 3:8, 23; 4:2–3, 10, 14; 5:1, 5, 10–11, 20.

But equally it is he 'who abides in love' who 'abides in God'; and abiding in love entails above all loving our brother whom we have seen, for if we do not love him we certainly do not love God (4:16–20). Faith and love are inextricably intertwined (5:1–5). Those modern expositors who give the impression that loving our neighbour is the whole content of 'loving God', or of believing in Jesus, so that the 'faith' element is absorbed in the moral and ethical, have missed the distinctively New Testament viewpoint, for which the Gospel is the joyful and liberating fact, now put beyond a peradventure, that the supremacy of love has been established for all time by the confirmation that there is a God and that love is his spirit.

Nevertheless, the New Testament can describe love as obedience to Jesus' commandments,[1] and the same applies on occasion even to Paul.[2] This is not serious so long as the sense that love commends itself as a value and an ideal, and that this value and ideal are displayed in Jesus and vindicated as God's own value and ideal by the resurrection, is genuinely alive. Moreover, there is inevitably an extended sense in which we can apply the word 'commandment' to this situation, since this conviction about God's scale of values implies quite inexorably that any other scale is mistaken and futile. The use of commandment language cannot hurt provided that the sequence of thought is right. The paradox expressed in the famous words, 'whose service is perfect freedom', presents no problems so long as we remember that assent to the moral challenge of love comes first, and is the one thing which makes it possible for us to have our eyes opened to the fact that God is in Jesus, and that therefore love *is* the 'law of life'. For such an assent, albeit induced in us by our encounter with love in Jesus or in other people, is essentially the freest of free acts, as anyone who has ever loved knows perfectly well. When, however, this is forgotten, everything alters. The resurrection then becomes simply proof of certain facts about the divine order, evidence of Jesus' eternal status; and this status is seen as giving him authority to lay down laws for mankind. 'Loving one's neighbour' then turns into a duty which we must try to

---

[1] Cf. esp., *John* 13:34; 14:15; 15:12; *I John* 3:23–24; 4:21.

[2] Paul's ruling about divorce, for example, is based simply on the use of Jesus' words as a straight moral directive (*I Cor.* 7:10–11). He does not quote Jesus' argument from the creation on which the directive is based, though we ought perhaps to assume that this would be known to the Corinthians from the stereotyped form of the missionary preaching (*Matt.* 19:3–9 = *Mk* 10:2–9).

undertake because Jesus says so. The results of this can be seen in those strained and forced exercises of 'charity' so painfully characteristic of many Christian people. The same attitude produces the continual parroting of clichés to the effect that love is not a matter of 'feeling' but is an 'act of the will'. This is disastrous, because it allows us to think that grimly doing our duty is 'real love', and so destroys all the life and joy in human relationships which alone make the mutual doing of duty worthwhile or tolerable. It is also based on woolly thinking. It is quite true that our 'feelings' are not a reliable guide to the good that love would choose; but this is no possible logical basis for saying that love has nothing to do with 'feeling'.[1] No wonder the listener often concludes that Christian love has nothing in common with love as he knows it.

There are similar dangers in a different approach, which at first sight seems more sensitive and satisfactory. Here the believer begins by accepting the 'faith-story', that God sent his only Son to die on the cross, that the Son willingly gave himself for that mission, and that therefore he ought to do as God wills in gratitude for such generosity:

> Love so amazing, so divine,
> Demands my life, my soul, my all.

Words such as these mean a great deal to a great many people, the present writer included. But they do still miss the point. It is not just God's extreme sacrifice which faces me with the challenge to give my life, my whole being; it is love itself. God's cross can do no more than blackmail me, unless I have made my prior free decision for sacrificial love. And when I do, then the thought that even God has accepted its most extreme sacrifices in his own person does not put me under an obligation, so that I then have to buckle to and start loving. It transforms me, and gives me courage to entrust myself to the spirit of love which I already approve.

The divergence may seem too small to matter, certainly too small to labour. But when the diverging lines are extended through twenty centuries of history the gap between them can become astronomical.

---

[1] Even Fletcher, *Situation Ethics*, p. 79, makes this mistake – though it is hard to be sure, since he seems to regard 'will' as also 'disposition' or 'an attitude'. Cf. the critique by A. von Hildebrand in D. and A. von Hildebrand, *Morality and Situation Ethics*, 1966, p. 189. It is one of the great services of the von Hildebrands to have attacked this strange Christian notion about love.

For if it is assumed that life in the spirit of Christ starts as my response to a 'faith' which I have first to accept as an independent set of propositions, then certain practical consequences follow. To begin with it becomes indispensable to embrace the faith in a fairly elaborate form – as summed up, for example, in the creed used at the baptism of converts, with all the prior instruction necessary to explain it – before one can hope to make any progress at all; for nothing less will have enough ingredients to effect the necessary change in the new member. This at once sets a high hurdle at the entrance to the Church, with ludicrous results for theology. For one thing it rules out any rationale of natural human goodness, driving some theologians to conclude that what people do before they believe in Christ, and so come into contact with his transforming spirit, must all be in some sense sinful.[1] It also makes for highly artificial answers to common-sense questions, such as, 'Why are the people who don't go to church often so much better and nicer than the ones who do?' Given the assumptions we are examining, there can be only two answers to this one: either, 'Those who do go would be much worse if they didn't, and those who don't would be much better still if they did' – which has the great advantage of being quite impossible to prove, and equally to disprove; or, 'There is nothing wrong with Christianity – it's simply that Christians don't live up to their beliefs.' This last is a strange defence from a faith which claims to 'change' people. It also (and this is its immediate relevance) shows clearly how those who use it see the structure of their religion: you accept certain statements, and then try to generate appropriate attitudes and actions in the light of those statements. Obviously, if this analysis is correct, the reasons for failure are to be sought in inadequate belief, lack of insight into what belief entails, or lack of determination to act accordingly. But the analysis is, as we have seen, incorrect. We need the moral attitude before belief can become living and real. Since, however, this attitude develops in us as the result of genuine and open personal involvement with those who already have it, and who by way of this relationship are able to provide a climate in which the natural potentials for love within us can have a chance to grow, it should be utterly clear that any fences which keep those who have the attitude from community with those who have it

---

[1] Cf. Article XIII of the Thirty-nine Articles of the Church of England. Under proposals at present before the Convocations assent to every item of these Articles will no longer be required of Church of England clergy.

only partially or not at all defeat the whole purpose of Christianity. So far from belief in the Christian creed being a pre-condition of membership it is one of the results of membership, one indeed which may take a whole lifetime to achieve. It is the end of a process, not the beginning. The process begins with the natural growth-points of love present in every human being who has not been fatally distorted or mutilated by external forces. The dogmatic hurdles at the entrance to the Church therefore succeed in doing only two things: they let in people who for the most part have made a purely mental and superficial assent to the formularies, and who then spend their lives putting on an act, an external and artificial mimicking of a way of life that is spontaneous or nothing; and they keep out a great many people in whom the root of love is growing and flowering but who for one reason or another cannot commit themselves sincerely to the full dogmatic faith of the Church. In this way those inside are cut off from the very fellowship which would help them to mature in love,[1] and those outside are denied the opportunity to move towards a real understanding of the faith. Everyone gets the worst of all possible worlds; and only an open church offers any hope of putting this right.

No wonder then that, as things are, the Church falls back on authority and a kind of remote 'example' as her only means of influencing the world. It has ruled out the chance of changing people by involving them, where they are, in a group of those who live by the spirit of Jesus, by co-operating with them in the life which all genuinely share – the common ground of the family and the street, the factory and the farm, the nation and the world. Even the Church's example may be of little use, if it exhibits love operating in artificial circumstances. A religious order, for instance, can be a magnificent thing; but by the very fact of being a like-minded *corps d'élite* under a stringent rule, impracticable in ordinary life, it may get its results not by overcoming the problems of human life but by avoiding them.

Yet in the eyes of most churchmen the consequences just described, so far from being disastrous, seem highly desirable, authentic signs that the Church is doing her work. The elect will always of necessity be few; the truth will always scandalize men, and stick in their gullet if it is uncompromisingly proclaimed; and to be the voice of divine

---

[1] How many congregations there are, for example, which cannot carry out even the childishly simple project of a Christmas bazaar without enough envy, hatred, and malice to power a dozen major crimes.

authority and to display a supernatural quality of life is her central
vocation. Is this so gross a parody of Christian attitudes? And is there
not something suspicious in the fact that all of them are also watertight
excuses for what the ordinary person would call failure? Does no one
see anything odd in declaring in one breath that 'God wills all men to
be saved', and in the next that most men will never manage to accept
the means God is supposed to have provided for their salvation; or
that Jesus is the truth that will make men free, and yet that most men
are incapable of responding to this truth? Both the premises and the
evidence shout aloud that somewhere the Church has gone off the
rails; but rather than listen to an argument so chilling to her ego, she
withdraws behind a screen of protective rationalizations, and pulls
more closely around her the tattered coat of self-righteousness, the
smug illusions of the perpetually 'misunderstood'.

The history of the Church in the west during the last twenty
centuries confirms this diagnosis by one striking fact: the way in which
she quickly became and remained a new version of the Judaism which
Jesus so drastically criticized. The only comprehensive synthesis, the
only all-embracing system of thought produced by this branch of
Christianity was that of mediaeval Catholicism. All subsequent systems
have taken their colour from that one, because they were either re-
forming it or reacting against it. This mediaeval system, however, was
essentially Later Judaism with a Greek philosophical substructure.
That these two ingredients could be successfully combined had been
discovered long before. Between the beginning of the second century
B.C. and the end of the second century A.D. there was considerable
mutual influence, Judaism interesting Greek thinkers in her concept of
a personal, Creator God, and borrowing from the Greeks a great deal of
metaphysical language which her own tradition was unable to supply –
notably the terms of the so-called 'negative theology', which defines
God in terms of what he is not.[1] The general thinking and piety of this
kind of Judaism was markedly different from that of the Old Testament,
in which some of its most important ideas appear sketchily or not at all.
But it does bear a strong resemblance to mediaeval catholic Christianity, especially in the feel of the religion, the ways in which it
impinged upon ordinary men and women, and made itself effective in
their lives. The catholic ideas of merit, especially the 'treasury of

[1] As, for example, 'impassible', i.e., unable to suffer, 'infinite', 'illimitable',
'ineffable', and so on.

merits' accumulated by the saints, which made them powerful intercessors before God for sinners, the consequent cult of saints, the important role of angels and demons, the ideal of heroic asceticism, the detailed visions of heaven and hell and judgement to come at the Last Day, these and many other details are characteristic of Judaism at the turn of the eras. The discoveries at Qumran have familiarized many people with the existence of monasticism in Jewry at this period. Above all, the whole 'church-centredness' of Christian thinking was supremely Judaistic. It is fascinating too to see how in the course of the centuries catholic Christianity and Judaism develop similar cultic features. The lay-out of the synagogue is in some ways very like that of the Catholic church building, with a tabernacle at the far end in which the divine presence is sacramentally mediated – in Christianity by the consecrated eucharistic host, in Judaism by the scrolls of the Law.

How far did Protestantism break away from this pattern of religion? Obviously some of the features we have mentioned were the particular targets of the Protestant reformation. Yet looked at as it turned out in practice rather than in terms of its theory there never was a society where skirts were so ostentatiously pulled in from the harlots and tax-collectors, where the outward appearance of correct moral behaviour was the only passport to the congregation, as European and American Protestantism. Never were so many people condemned to deep-seated anxiety neuroses about their guilt or innocence – an affliction from which Catholics were largely delivered by the institution of the confessional. Even the great watchword of 'justification by faith not works' lost its point, because faith became the one work needful for salvation. If you could not 'believe', you were lost. Such a religion is of use only for those whose psychological development has endowed them with immense faculties of will-power and self-control. It works for the 'strong' who need no sanctification; the weak either fail to stand the strain or take refuge in intense and morbid forms of emotionalism and religiosity.

It is in keeping with the markedly Judaistic character of both Catholic and Protestant piety that they should be so book-minded. The great theological systems, whether of Aquinas and his successors on the one side, or of Calvin, the later Lutherans, and Karl Barth on the other, are from one point of view exactly like the Jewish Talmud, elaborate attempts to make a coherent intellectual structure out of the conflicting data of the Scriptures. Likewise the astounding edifice of Christian moral and ascetic casuistry (not by any means the contemptible thing it is fashionable to consider it) works by weighing and reconciling authoritative dicta from the ancient tradition. (The parallels in details between Catholic and Rabbinic casuistry are, it must be added, highly thought-provoking.) But has not Protestantism followed basically the same method? The corpus of authoritative material may be smaller, being confined in effect to the Scriptures, but the approach is the same. Just as the Rabbis strove to find guidance for their own day by comparing passages from the archaic texts, and squeezing them dry of every possible implication, so Protestant exegetes struggled to direct life in the modern world by the Bible. The only result, however, was that the conclusions arrived at were either dubiously relevant to real life or palpably not what the plain words of the Bible meant. It is hardly surprising then that all this labour achieved only the discrediting of the Scriptures. We reap the fruits today in the standard objections: 'Life's different now; that was a long time ago'; or, 'You can't take the Bible literally; it doesn't mean what it says, does it?' Of the inhuman atrocities justified from the sacred text, from the burning of heretics to modern doctrines of the inferiority of certain races, there is no need to speak in detail. Ways to a better use of the Scriptures will be discussed in the next chapter.

Perhaps the best news our day has to offer is the collapse of this Judaistic Christianity under the pressures of history; for this affords Christians the best chance they have ever had to regain the perspective of the original Gospel. Because men are ceasing to believe in a Providence of simple retributive justice, or in a magician-god who will wave his wand to give them whatever they ask; because they are beginning to value freedom and the responsibility which has to learn by making mistakes; because they are more acutely aware than ever before of being one small single family of Man in a universe too vast for their imagination to take in; because of all these things, what Jesus said and how he lived has more meaning, more relevance, not less. The world has not left Jesus behind; it is getting to the point where it can just see him, far ahead, blazing the trail. In the so-called 'ages of faith' it made endless false Christs in its own image. Now these images are for the most part broken and abandoned; only in the churches do men and women in any numbers still fall down and worship them. What Jesus said to the chief priests and elders of his own people could come true again in this generation:

> Truly, I say to you, the tax-collectors and the harlots go into the kingdom of God before you (*Matt.* 21:31).

Nevertheless, despite all the pungent criticisms that can justifiably be made, despite all the upside-down notions and the lapses into conventional 'religion', the Church remains, so far as anyone can see, necessary if men are to come to the truth about their human condition. This is so not simply because, alongside the others, there are men and women within her who do see things the right way round, and in whom the spirit is very much alive. It is so because the Church is the only human society within which the data about Jesus are preserved (even if they are often misunderstood), and for which Jesus is acknowledged as the key to the riddle of human existence (even if people persist in putting that key into the lock upside down). The frightening urgency is that if Christians continue to misrepresent the information they have, and go on fiddling ineptly with the key, in time everyone will have given up and gone home.

The earliest Church began with a handful and conquered an empire. What God did once he could do again – if necessary. But why should it be necessary? Perhaps it will not be. There are on all sides encouraging signs. But if the gathering light is not to prove a false dawn, there must be a far more thoroughgoing reconstruction than any yet envisaged, both in the Church's structure and in her presentation of her teaching. The latter involves nothing less than a fundamental change of perspective. What that change is we have already seen; how it can be brought about is one of the subjects for consideration in the next chapter. In what remains of the present one let us examine the problem of structure.

Any group of people which exists for a common purpose needs organization planned to make it as easy as possible to achieve that purpose. No structure is sacrosanct. This is not to say that an organization which is failing in its aims is necessarily defective in structure. The structure may be excellent in principle, and the fault lie with the indolence, incompetence, or corruption of those who man it. But it cannot be assumed that this will always be so. Structures may cease to be effective as circumstances change, and may then break the hearts of good men and women who have to work within them. Christians are not exempt from these possibilities, or from the accompanying responsibility to scrutinize their organization, and change it when necessary.

The first and perhaps the most important element in the current problem is that of creating an 'open' Church. Cells can move freely in a body only where there is continuous living tissue, and the Church needs to be in this sense an organic part of mankind. This at once raises the question of entrance qualifications, and of Christian 'initiation'.

At present the almost universal form of admission to the Church is the rite of baptism. Leaving aside many of its symbolic and theological aspects, its significance in our present context is twofold. First, no one can baptize himself. In this action he is entirely a passive recipient. This expresses the fact that the relationship into which he is now inducted is genuinely two-way. One cannot simply announce oneself a partner, friend, and adopted son or daughter of God. As with any human partnership, friendship, or adoption it is necessary not merely to desire it oneself but to be freely accepted by the other party. It is true that God has already accepted us long before we ever ask him, since, as we saw, the coming of Jesus has effected an objective change in the situation of every human being. By virtue of the Incarnation we are all of us brothers and sisters of God's Son. But the need to submit to a formal adoption ceremony emphasizes that this is a free, personal decision by God with regard to each individual human being. His acceptance is as much a true commitment as is our own desire. Secondly, no one is baptized to himself. He joins a community, the community of those who have found the true vocation of Man in the brotherhood of Jesus, the family of God. In this community above all others the potential of true community is to be found. For entry into this community is achieved only by entering upon the supreme fulfilment of individuality, in that each one lives by his unique relationship with God, which gives him an infinite personal value. Yet that very relationship can be lived out only in community with our fellow creatures.

This moment of baptism is, in a sense, not a point in earthly Time, but an entry into God's infinitely adaptable Time, a beginning of something which exists on more than one level, and so cannot be ended by death, an event which takes effect on only one of these levels. Hence the community into which the individual enters passes uninterruptedly across the boundaries of mortality; it is simultaneously both here and elsewhere. Nor is its membership confined (if what we have discussed earlier concerning our ultimate meeting with our Creator is true) to those who are admitted through the ceremony of baptism here. In God's presence the Church is finally and completely an open Church. But that ultimate openness is brought about by the presentation of total truth.

In this life the relation of truth to entry into the community is more complex. In infant baptism obviously there is no awareness or acceptance of truth by the person baptized. Since, however, to grasp the truth about human life is the all-important goal, important both for the individual and for the community into which he has been received, it is right that there should be a point later on at which he can commit himself freely and formally to that truth, should he wish to do so. The opportunity for this in some branches of the Church is provided by the ceremony of confirmation or an equivalent. The individual's life between these two points is ideally a movement towards this moment of free commitment, and it is to fostering that commitment that the sponsors of the infant, the godparents, dedicate themselves at the baptism. Some Christian groups, however, find this an artificial procedure, and postpone baptism until the individual can understand what is involved and declare his allegiance for himself. They do not thereby imply that the child of Christian parents is not a member of the Church – simply that his relationship with God is not yet that of full human maturity, but one adapted to his natural limitations. So long as there is agreement about the actual state of affairs, it is hard to see that it matters very greatly which programme is followed. Whenever we try to mark the course of growth and process by fixed ceremonial points, there are bound to be elements of anomaly and transition.

Nevertheless, recognition that there is process in the individual even after he is formally 'inside' the community (and this process, of course, continues all through one's life, and is not confined to the years before confirmation or believer's baptism) surely carries important implications for the idea of an open Church. If one can count as a member a small child whose grasp of the truth is inevitably limited, why not an adult who likewise can accept only part of that truth? The famous Swiss doctor and writer on pastoral theology, Theodor Bovet, has some pertinent remarks on this subject:

> ... faith is not something we can construct for ourselves, but ... is given bit by bit. If someone can believe no more than that Jesus was an especially good man, then he should quietly begin by following this good

man to the best of his ability, by living as he imagines Jesus would have wanted him to live. Nothing could be more perverse than to turn such a person away, and to tell him that a faith of that kind was worthless. Faith is constantly on the move; change is of its very essence.[1]

That there will in the nature of things be a minimum, below which any assertion of membership would be unreal, is obvious; indeed any reasonably conscientious person who could not sincerely profess such a minimum would not wish to enter the community anyway. But if, as was argued earlier, the life of every Christian is a pilgrimage towards the fullness of truth, if the Creeds of the Church set out not a minimum entrance requirement but a formula which is virtually a series of chapter headings to an account of a mature faith, why make at initiation a demand which assumes that those who wish to begin in the community will already have attained a stage not yet reached by many members of long standing? Is this not an invitation to hypocrisy and formalism? Does it not actively encourage people to lapse when they reflect that the profession which they made, either on their own behalf or that of their godchild, does not tally with their genuine convictions?

It is still an all too common assumption in church circles that whether the world understands the faith or not, whether Christians understand it or not, at any rate Christians believe it and the world does not. This is a very questionable assumption. If the majority of clergy knew what their people actually believed, they could never preach as they do. They would not produce arguments to defend or attack notions that have never entered the heads of the men and women in front of them. They would not exhort people to behaviour in accordance with tenets which their congregation simply ignore. The average English churchgoer believes just as much as he or she can swallow as not improbable, namely, that there is Someone or Something behind it all, that Jesus was a good man, and that the betting on survival after death is evens. These are not the vestiges of Christianity lingering in the dwellers on the housing estate, who have never been near a church since they were sent once or twice to Sunday School. This, at bottom, is what a large proportion of regular worshippers would sincerely uphold if pressed. This may also explain why most of the rank and file reacted in the way they did to the 'Honest to God' debate. Some, of course, fulminated; others exulted. But the solid

[1] Theodor Bovet, *That they may have Life*, 1964, p. 194.

squadrons merely sighed and said, Oh dear, theologians do make things so difficult. It was neither a liberation nor an offence, because there were no firm convictions to be either offended or broken open. The new theology was just as sophisticated and intellectual and useless as the old.

It would introduce a note of reality into Christian initiation if the parents and godparents or, when dealing with adults, the persons to be admitted to membership, were allowed to make, after discussion with the minister, a profession of what they truly did believe and of the obligations which in their eyes went with this. Such a procedure would, of course, compel the Church to acknowledge in general the wide range of belief actually found among existing members. This would be in no way incompatible with corporate affirmation of the fuller truth about the world and Man as summed up in the teaching of the Church. It would simply be a recognition that to make this truth one's own is a lifelong vocation, and that no one ought to be excluded by impossible demands at the outset from the milieu in which he can most easily discover that truth. It would also enable the correct test for admission to be applied, in that the Church could begin by confronting the intending member with the moral demand on which everything else turns.

This kind of change is one way in which Christianity could move towards the open Church; but only one, and in some respects the most superficial one. Valuable, indeed essential as it may be, it is still the product of thinking in terms of the separation between the Church and the world. To do this is right enough since facts compel it. Between those who hold one thing for truth and those who do not there cannot but be a line drawn; and to cross that line is to move out of one community into another. Nothing should ever be allowed to blur the decisiveness both of the difference and of the move across it. But to think only in terms of the difference, the separateness, is wrong. So wrong that it makes a wrong even of the right awareness of separation:

> If today Jesus lives in devout men and women, then he will be just as little desirous of cutting himself off from the world; on the contrary, he will still want to come incognito as close as possible to ordinary heathen people who are far from God, and to win them in the same way as his first disciples won those around them. Christ is the Door, through which all men can enter into the Kingdom, not a hedge of thorns to block the way of anyone who is not a 'true believer'. Nay more: Christ is already

here and now the friend and ally of all men, even of those who do not know him, or who deny him and fight against him. He is here and now the friend and ally not only of the Catholic Spaniard and the Calvinist Dutchman, but of the Soviet Russian and the Communist Chinese; for it is his will that all should be one.[1]

It is by the separateness that the Church preserves – no, not her own identity! that is insignificant – but the identity of Jesus and his Gospel. If she does not do that, there is no humanly discernible hope for the world:

> You are the salt of the earth; but if even salt has lost its taste, what will you use for seasoning? (*Matt.* 5:13.)

But just as there is no point in having salt unless you put it into the cooking, so there is no point in the Church's separateness unless she is also united with the world, integrally involved in it. Her separateness and her involvement are totally different in kind. The separateness is separateness as to the truth, and this cannot be preserved by refusing involvement, for it is a truth that means anything only in involvement. Similarly her involvement is involvement in the human condition, and it is falsified if the truth about that condition is perverted or abandoned. Something much more radical is required, therefore, than the stock recipe of piety, that in their church life Christians come apart to be with God, and then go out, strengthened and illuminated, to witness to Christ in the world. The mental pictures behind this view – of the world as an alien land, of God as fully encountered only within the community, and of grace as mediated not through life but through specialized religious activities – make any sense of genuine brotherhood with mankind very difficult, to say the least. If the truth is to reach men through the spirit of the Christian community, then the organization and structure of that community must be adapted to establish a living continuity with them.

For a great part of her history the Church used as her basic structure a simple pyramidal system of organization. Local congregations, each under the jurisdiction of a single minister, were organized into a diocese, ruled over by a bishop who had his own church in a major population centre.[2] Dioceses in turn were grouped in provinces or patriarchates,

---

[1] Bovet, *ibid.*, p. 152.
[2] In the East it not infrequently happened that the city and its immediate environs formed the full extent of the diocese.

Y

their bishops being presided over by the bishop of the regional metro-
polis. In the West the provinces came more and more under the direction of the central bishopric of Rome; in the East the patriarchates
retained a much larger measure of autonomy. This fundamental system
was diversified and complicated in innumerable details: by the growth
of religious orders as independent power structures within the community; by the development of a central bureaucracy staffed with
lawyers, diplomats, and prelates with titular sees; by the superimposing
of missionary clergy on to the local priests in certain areas; by cathedrals
and their chapters, and many other *ad hoc* arrangements. In the West,
which more particularly concerns us, the diagram of organization seen
from above is a series of webs, more, or less densely strung, placed one
on top of the other and all radiating from Rome. Viewed in elevation,
the shape is still that of a pyramid.[1]

This system was manned by the priesthood, taking that term in its
widest sense. Feared, venerated, and loved as the agent of God's own
power and mercy; despised, denounced, and satirized for its human
failings; nevertheless, as the only supra-national organization since the
fall of the Roman Empire (whose mantle it consciously put on) it
disposed of unequalled authority over the minds and hearts of men, and
used it to do much good as well as evil. Furthermore, the clerical
calling was the only opportunity for the man from the lower orders of
society to rise in the world. Supplying, as it did, the universities with
their teachers, and rulers with their principal officers of state and their
only approach to a civil service, it created some degree of much needed
social mobility, and put to work talent that would otherwise have run
to waste. Its patronage also provided the challenging commissions that
evoked some of the world's finest art and architecture. But, for all this
interaction, Christians both clerical and lay thought always in terms of
the sacred versus the secular. The world had its own order, and its
salvation was to be brought about by obedience to the supernatural
direction of the Church, not by a sacralization of its own structures.

The Reformation did something to change this, the Renaissance and
the rise of modern Europe much more. But these changes rather
hindered than helped a solution of the problem we are considering.
The division of Europe into Catholic and Protestant states meant that the

[1] The alleged attempt of the Byzantine Empire to integrate Church and
State – a system to which the name 'Caesaro-papalism' has been given – cannot
unfortunately be discussed here.

various churches looked to their particular secular power to be the champion of the 'true faith' against its Christian 'enemies'; and this inevitably deprived them of the will or the capacity to criticize effectively the 'godly princes' on whom they depended for victory and even for survival. (It is ironic but instructive that only once did the leaders of the established Church of England abandon the doctrine of passive obedience even to the worst of kings; and that was when one of those kings, James II, admittedly for reasons of self-interest, attempted by decree to enforce toleration for Roman Catholics.) The result was that the heads of each national church, from being predominantly spokesmen of God to the world, became the representatives of the world's interest to God. Furthermore, Protestantism itself divided into an ever-increasing number of denominations, most of which lacked all standing in the state, and were often actively persecuted. This turned them inwards, tending to make their ethics individualistic,[1] their primary concern the religious activities of prayer, preaching, and theological argument, and their attitude to the outsider exclusive. A third solution, differing both from establishment and sectarianism, was sought by Calvinism, which first in Switzerland, then in Scotland, and later in America, attempted to set up theocratic states, dominated and directed in all their activities by the ministers of God's word and the elders of the local community. This ideal will call for attention again shortly.

The effect of these developments, however, was simply to reduce the area of life common to the Church and the world still farther. The divisions of Christendom made any united Christian social attitudes impossible, and ensured that those ecclesiastics whose voice was still heeded in the secular sphere did not in fact speak for more than a minority of Christians. 'Establishment', far from giving the churches solid moral control over the state, merely made them dependent on the state, if not for money, at any rate for a public platform and an impressive image. Moreover, church leaders, who as late as the seventeenth century still provided heads of civil government, now ceased to hold administrative office. English bishops continued to figure in the House of Lords, but the 'inferior' Anglican clergy could not be elected to the Commons, and the feeling was growing that the Church should not meddle with politics – a feeling reinforced by the naïveté and ineptitude of much ecclesiastical comment on secular issues. How the clergy were to comment intelligently when they were virtually

---

[1] A noble exception here, of course, is the Society of Friends.

excluded from a share in the practical life of the nation no one bothered to enquire.

The widespread and intense anti-clericalism to be found in parts of Europe never took firm root in Britain, though impatience with the clergy and mockery of their mannerisms and ineffectiveness was (and still is) a national habit. The English in particular gradually ceased to be a churchgoing people. The nineteenth century, regarded in folk-lore as a time 'when everyone went to church', was nothing of the kind. All the denominations put together touched less than a quarter of the population now crowded into the industrial cities. Apart from the Salvation Army, and some devoted individuals and voluntary groups in the older bodies, congregations and clergy became too busy keeping the institution of the church afloat and solvent to have much energy to spare for the world around them. In the United States this latter problem was not so severe; but inter-denominational hatreds, and a tendency to act as Public Relations Officers for the American way of life, minimized Christian influence for creative change. In Africa and Asia the fact that Christianity was a white man's religion, linked inseparably with foreign domination, ensured the impermanence of much seeming success by missionaries. Finally, the ebb of the Christian tide was hastened by the three great revolutions – Darwin, Marx, and Freud – which for many educated people in all classes of society made the then current presentation of the faith unbelievable.

Yet throughout these centuries of recession the churches persisted in fighting the battle with only a tiny proportion of their manpower – the ordained ministries. Whenever a new challenge arose, it was the clergy who were expected to meet it; and the intellectual, personal, and physical demands were too great. Where the laity was employed, it was in a quasi-clerical role as teachers and parish visitors. There was no chance of deploying the Christian people as a whole; the basic pattern of organization did not permit it. Today on all sides Christians are realising their mistake, and we hear continually of the vital role of the laity. What that role should be our argument has already suggested: the restoring of organic continuity between the Church and the world as members of the one human race. Before considering, however, in what ways this can be done in practice, we obviously need to ask a more fundamental question: is there any value in retaining the distinction between lay and clerical anyway? Does the concept of an ordained ministry have any permanent and essential significance?

At first glance it might seem that it does not. In New Testament times certain local churches, namely those founded and guided by Paul, seem to have managed with a minimum of fixed organization. They undoubtedly did allocate special duties and responsibilities to individual members; and there are clear signs in Paul's Epistles that there was a natural movement towards stereotyping this system. But while his inspiration was there to influence them this process was held in check; the master vision was that of a community of varied gifts to be used as and when available for the benefit of the whole. Pre-eminent among these gifts were those of prophecy, the ability to act as a mouthpiece for the direct guidance of the spirit of God, and teaching, the ability to expound scripture and tradition. But there is no evidence that these ever constituted 'orders of clergy' into which men could be officially admitted. Certainly, when permanent clerical office does emerge, prophets and teachers are not sections within it.

To work out the various schemes of church order, embryonic or fully developed, implied by the New Testament accounts is an impossible task. But two points are fairly clear. First, Paul's ideal was not attempted elsewhere. Secondly, the eventual Catholic system of bishops, priests, and deacons did not exist anywhere in the first generation church, and possibly not until the end of the first century A.D. The most likely solution, pending further evidence, is that this system was the result of fusing two other patterns. One was an imitation of the Jewish synagogue structure, where the congregation was ruled by a board of 'elders' (Greek: *presbyteros* = presbyter). The origins of the other are more obscure, though it may owe something to Jewish sectarianism like that of the Dead Sea community. In the Christian version we find a group of 'guardians' or 'superintendents' (Greek: *episkopoi*, the word from which 'bishop' derives) with 'assistants' or 'servants' (Greek: *diakonos* = deacon), particularly for charitable work.[1]

The most important point to note about both these systems is that the titles of the various offices are either neutral, organizational terms

[1] Paul, in the opening address of the letter to the *Philippians*, refers (1:1) to 'all the saints in Christ Jesus who are at Philippi, with the bishops and deacons'. If, as many think, this letter dates from the end of Paul's life, when he had already been some time in prison at Rome, then this may indicate the assimilation of a Pauline church to the more general structure. But it should be remembered that Corinth, the church about which we know most from Paul's writings, may have received a special share of his personal attention, and may therefore not be typical even of congregations founded by Paul himself.

('superintendent', 'assistant') or derive from the ordinary structures of society ('elders', who were originally no doubt in fact the senior members, these being the natural officeholders in a strongly patriarchal tradition). In time, however, religious meanings of a very specific kind attached to at least two of these terms, presenting them as roles or descriptions of Christ himself. Thus, *I Peter* speaks of Christ as the 'shepherd and guardian (*episkopos*) of your souls' (2:25); and in *Mark* Jesus is presented as saying that 'the Son of Man came not to be served but to serve' (10:45), where 'serve' is a verbal form from the word *diakonos*, 'deacon'.

This process was not, it would seem, applied to the term 'elder'. For this there may be two reasons. The first is quite simply that 'elder' does not commend itself as an appropriate title for Jesus, who held no position of seniority or status in any community, and who died a young man. Secondly, the boards of elders in one type of congregation must have been virtually indistinguishable from the boards of guardians in another, with the result that the two words became interchangeable as contact between local churches increased. Thus, the writer of *I Peter* urges the elders to 'tend the flock of God' under the 'Chief Shepherd', Jesus (5:2–4), whom he has previously called 'shepherd and guardian'. Similar language is used in connection with the elders of the Ephesian church in *Acts* (20:28–30).

The decisive transition came with the emergence of what is called the 'monarchical episcopate', that is to say, the selection of one man in each congregation to preside over the board of elders and to hold ultimate authority over all church members. To him as the superintendent and guardian *par excellence* the term *episkopos*, bishop, came to be reserved. This system is already reflected in the New Testament letters known as *I* and *II Timothy* and *Titus*, documents written under the name of the apostle Paul but certainly much later than his day. It is attested too in the *Epistles* of Ignatius, bishop of Antioch in Syria, which date from the year 107 A.D., and which give us a glimpse of church life in Asia Minor at that time. There are now three grades of clergy: bishops (guardians), presbyters (elders), and deacons (assistants). There is still a certain parity of status between bishops and elders, since bishops sometimes use the form of address 'co-presbyters' when referring to them.[1] This usage persists to a late date, even

---

[1] The fact that the writer of *I Peter* uses this form may therefore suggest that he himself was one of the new monarchical bishops.

after the actual degrees of authority of the two grades had become very different.

We now have the framework of developed Catholic order, but one important element is still missing – the characterization of the second grade as 'priests'. This element comes in by a rather different route. The New Testament *Epistle to the Hebrews* is largely an extended essay on the subject of Jesus as the true High Priest, whose sacrificial dedication of himself to God even to the point of death, is seen as at once fulfilling and superseding the old offerings of animal sacrifices to God under the Jewish Law. Here a wholly new religious concept is introduced, the paradox of the Priest-Victim. A priest who offers other lives as his sacrifice is only a shadow of the true; the true priest offers his own life (*Heb.* 9:26; 10:1–10), and institutes a new priesthood (7:15–22; 8:4; 9:24), the essence of which is that its sacrifices are spiritual, the offering of the self in obedience to the purposes of God. Christians are called to enter this newly created priesthood by self-dedication carried, if need be, like that of Jesus even to the blood of martyrdom (12:4).

Under one aspect, therefore, the Christian calling is to a new kind of priesthood which is essentially the same as that of Jesus himself. It is true that Jesus' priesthood is unique, in that he alone can perform the supreme rite of the Day of Atonement (*Heb.* 9:7), and sanctify those who are called (2:11). Once sanctified, however, Christians are his brethren, and holy (3:1), with the right to eat of the true altar (13:10), to offer spiritual sacrifices (13:15f.), to intercede (13:18), and to join their sufferings with his (13:13). This is a paradoxical condition, often and easily distorted; but it reflects Christian experience as recognized elsewhere in the New Testament, notably in *Colossians* (1:24).

But if this priesthood is a mark of all Christians, how did the term 'priest' come to be confined to certain individuals? The answer is probably to be found in the central observance of Christian worship, the Eucharist. Here we have an act which by Jesus' own words is connected with the breaking of his body and the shedding of his blood on the Cross, the supreme act of his own priestly vocation. It was almost inevitable therefore that those who were privileged to preside at this act of worship, to pray the eucharistic prayer, and to offer the symbolic form of Christ's sacrifice, should be thought of as the Christian equivalent of 'priests'. Thus it is that bishops and presbyters together come to constitute the Christian 'priesthood',[1] even though

[1] This is correct Catholic doctrine to this day.

the whole body of Christians is also a 'kingdom of priests, a holy nation' (*I Pet.* 2:9).

One more connotation remained to be added, that of apostle. Originally this term designated someone sent as a plenipotentiary representative or agent, and therefore the men sent out by Christ to preach the Gospel to the world and, above all, to be witnesses of his resurrection.[1] It acquired heightened significance from the thought that Christ himself had been 'sent' to mankind by God; and the parallel is explicitly drawn in the Gospels (*Mk* 9:37; *John* 17:18; 20:21). The writer to the *Hebrews* can use the word 'apostle' even as a title of Christ (3:1). Having already to hand, therefore, the first two links in a chain of sending and being sent, it is not surprising that before long attempts were made to carry this down to the contemporary heads of the Christian community, first to the collective episcopate of the boards of guardians or elders,[2] then to the monarchical bishops – or, perhaps we should say, attempts to carry their succession back to the apostles, and so to link it on to the great primary sequence of God's sending his Son and the Son's sending out his first and closest disciples. Backed by this kind of association, the apostle-bishop eventually became the man supremely responsible for maintaining purity both of faith and morals in the Church.

The structure of Catholic ministry as it finally emerges, therefore, is a powerful symbol of the threefold Christian calling: to proclaim the faith revealed in Jesus and to bring it into saving relationship with the realities of human life (the work of the apostle, shepherd, and guardian); to sacrifice oneself in wholehearted devotion to God's cause of love and forgiveness (the priest); and to serve the practical needs of all mankind (the deacon); and in each of these to be ready to commit oneself even to death.[3] But – and it must be repeated with emphasis – this is not just the vocation of a select cadre within the community but of the community as a whole and of every individual member. These

[1] Cf., e.g., *II Cor.* 5:20: 'We are ambassadors for Christ, God making his appeal through us.'

[2] A letter of Clement, bishop of Rome, to the church at Corinth at the end of the first century A.D. presents an early reconstruction of Christian history along these lines.

[3] This aspect of the priesthood and the diaconate has already been illustrated. For the shepherd-bishop cf. Christ's words in *John* 10:7–18, a passage which undoubtedly has the life of the Church in mind; esp. the famous verse 11: 'I am the good shepherd. The good shepherd lays down his life for the sheep.'

are not roles which can be delegated, which some group can live out on behalf of the rest; they are the features of Christ which must be found in anyone who claims the spirit of Jesus and of God. In short, there is not just a 'priesthood of all believers', but an apostolate, a pastorate, a diaconate as well.

If this is so, then it may well be asked what is the role of the special cadre, of the ministry as such? The answer is given in principle by Paul in his letter to the Galatians:

> My little children, with whom I am again in travail until Christ be formed in you! (*Gal.* 4:19).

Not many Christian ministers have ever earned or will ever earn the right to address their lay brethren as 'my little children', but that is not the immediate point. The task of the ministry is the fostering of the spirit of Christ, the formation of the mind and heart of Christ in the whole community, themselves included. It is for this purpose that certain special functions are entrusted to them: the expounding of the faith, the celebration of the Eucharist, the proclamation of forgiveness, the assurance of God's love and partnership in blessing, the acceptance of the free commitment of believers to Christ in confirmation or its equivalent, and so on. All these things are means, not ends. They serve to bring certain realities into being; they are not those realities themselves. For the bishop and priest as much as for any layman all that matters – or should matter – is the growth and power of the spirit of God in himself and others. The actions which he is called upon to perform are of no special value in themselves but only by their usefulness for achieving that goal which is the goal of all Christians equally. The true purpose of setting aside Christians especially commissioned to continue these actions is to ensure that the task of making men God's sons, daughters, and partners by the most appropriate means shall never lapse by default. This is the supreme purpose of the community's existence, and in her ministry she makes provision for fulfilling it.

But this makes no sense at all unless the Church is an open Church. All three aspects of the Christian vocation here symbolized are outward-looking. To understand them as concerned to form an in-group of really good people, whose own salvation is thereby assured, is to pervert them. The aim of making every member of the community into an apostle, a pastor, a priest, and a servant in the moral and personal, not the official sense is to enable them to carry out that vocation to the world at large. It is in a way like a series of concentric shapes, each of which is a larger version of the one immediately inside it: Christ, the ministry, the church, the world. Such a diagram is, of course, inadequate, since the ministry, like Christ himself, can never be content with simply training Christians. Unless the clergy are in apostolic, pastoral, priestly, and serving contact with human life in general, they will neither be true ministers themselves nor will they be able to help their fellow-Christians to become such. Hence they must always work alongside their fellows as equals in a team. But within that team their special responsibility is to make sure that the spirit of the community is the true spirit of God, that the creative factor shaping all their lives is the truth as found in Jesus and not some diluted or adulterated substitute.

The education of her ministers is therefore a prime factor in the vitality of the church; and the heart of that education must always be theological. But this is very far from implying merely a thorough grounding in 'sound theology' before ordination, however important that may be. For no one can hope to make the faith his own, so that it determines the way in which he spontaneously looks at life, by a few years' concentrated intellectual study in a training college. It ought to be taken for granted that every ordained minister is released from his church duties for several weeks in every year to live with other clergy and laity in a time of study, thought, discussion, and quiet, recovering the perspectives which he is losing, discovering others which he has never had, giving and receiving the lessons of Christian experience, and so reviving and strengthening the spirit of God in all.[1] Even for those who have retired from active work this ought to be a primary obligation, if only for the sake of all that they have to contribute. Such a system would also provide an opportunity of keeping Christians in living awareness of the problems of mankind at large. Nothing could be sillier than to suppose that a few pre-digested courses of 'psychology' or 'social studies' at seminary will meet this need. All that this achieves is to supply the clergy with superficial and over-simplified notions which thereafter they trot out at, for the most part, inappropriate moments.

In the life of the congregation there is the further problem of making

[1] Provision for this, as yet rather rudimentary, is now being made in some churches.

use of this essential theological understanding. Here Christians badly need to recover the *ad hoc* flexibility of the Pauline approach. The Christian community must learn to organize itself in any given area in response to the particular needs of its environment. This includes the traditional activities of counselling the individual and of helping the suffering and the unfortunate. But such work must be done with the openness of the Church constantly in mind. Help of this sort is not, and never has been, exclusively Christian; and today more than ever it will, if it is to be effective, involve co-operating with those who may not be Christians – doctors, psychologists, trade unions, the state welfare services, and so on. Similarly, if sensitivity leads Christians to notice some evil which others have so far overlooked, there ought to be no question of making a corner in remedying it. If others can be brought to see it in the same light, and are willing to join in the work, so much the better. There will inevitably be features in human life which the Church sees to be evil but which society blindly accepts; and in such cases the Church has no option but to go it alone. But 'meeting human need' in joint ventures is one of the prime ways in which the Church can become truly an open Church, and mankind be drawn more deeply into God's kingdom.

This drawing, however, is brought about in the fact of the works of love that are done, and in any insight that the world may acquire in the process concerning the attitudes that prompt Christians to do them. They are not an opportunity to buttonhole one's fellow-workers with a view to converting them – much less those who are being helped. Far too often in the past help from a church member has been cause for apprehension, for expecting the suggestion of a *quid pro quo* in the form of church attendance or interest in religion. Good can be done only in good faith. There must be no strings attached.[1] Finally, tackling projects in this way may well involve Christians in political action – standing for Parliament or local government, lobbying representatives, attending meetings and asking questions, engaging in freelance journalism. This is not something to be feared. What should be feared is that Christians should ever give automatic support to any particular political group or party, or that they should descend to slanting statements, bending facts, misrepresenting arguments, or smearing motives in the process of trying to secure political action. It is

[1] The work of many Christian relief organizations is a welcome sign that this lesson is at last being learned.

not undesirable that individual Christians should enter politics for Christian reasons,[1] to pursue ends which they see, because of their Christian insights, to be good for men in general; and in such a course they ought to have the support of their own Christian community.

An aside may be in order here on the subject of a current platitude to the effect that of course there cannot be a specifically Christian view on technical matters, but only on the moral and personal dimensions of any programme. If this means that the Christian has no special light to shed on the theory of road-building or the making of a systems analysis, then it is no doubt true. It is also hardly worth saying. The danger is that Christians may weakly accept that certain questions are purely technical when they are nothing of the sort, and so fail to look for the damage to human life hidden behind such technical-sounding phrases as 'maximum cost-effectiveness', or succumb to the current blasphemy that the needs of the collective automatically take precedence over the individual's efforts to make something personal and distinctive of his own small allowance of life. The Christian will often be against the godlings of Efficiency and Economy, when these are secured not by skill but by lazy or arrogant indifference to human dignity and freedom.

This train of thought, however, opens up further possibilities. Human need is not to be defined solely in terms of such conditions as sickness, destitution, loneliness. It covers the normal lives of normal people at their work, at leisure, at home. It ought to be possible for Christians to find help and advice in their community for improving the quality of life in any sphere where they are themselves engaged. The necessary knowledge may not always be available within any one congregation. If so, it should be sought from others – and not only from other Christian groups or individuals. The open Church will learn quite as much as she teaches. In this context the question of specialist ministries (not necessarily ordained) is relevant. The Church needs men and women who have been enabled to combine a special professional qualification with a theological training which will make them expert counsellors on particular subjects, and who can be made available, within the limits of their professional commitments, to congregations which can use their guidance. It is, moreover, out of the personal vision of such men, especially when there is a number of them in any given

---

[1] Gladstone is one well-known historical example among many who have done this.

field – the physical sciences, education, medicine, the law, industry – to make mutual conference possible, that the Church at large is aroused to the specifically Christian attitudes to these areas of human concern. Specialists too on prayer and worship, theology and ethics (perhaps the holders of teaching posts) ought to be accessible to the local church, if necessary living among them for a time while problems are clarified and plans laid. The benefits in such contacts would certainly not be all on one side. It is obvious, however, that to make this kind of cross-fertilization possible there must be planning of work and resources on at least a provincial scale. It is no good relying on the spare time and personal generosity of individuals who try to crowd such activities into an already overfull working life.

Co-operation of this sort does not, however, call only on those with 'intellectual' gifts. Christians must learn to think in teams where any skill or craft may be of essential importance for an effective piece of work. Surely in the Christian community above all the person who drives the car or keeps the files and accounts or makes the equipment is recognized as of equal standing with the specialist in labour relations or housing or biblical studies whose skill he helps to make available? Lastly may be mentioned the possibility of training and seconding certain individuals (and ordaining them if desirable) for an extended but definite period to serve on particular projects at home or abroad, after which they would be enabled to return to their former career without detriment to their families or loss of such things as pension rights.

Once thinking has moved on to these lines, the practical possibilities are almost endless. But this at once raises the question of cost. Many Christians today are querying whether it is true to the Gospel to have so many economic resources tied up in the maintenance of plant working at ten per cent capacity – church buildings of scant artistic or historical value being the prime targets for criticism. It is worth remembering that all that is strictly needed to equip a congregation for its religious life is water, bread, wine, a copy of the Bible, and possibly a basic manual of worship. Everything else is dispensable; and every congregation would find it illuminating to discuss how it would organize its life if it were in fact reduced to this level. Would it, for example, in fact be disastrous if the community had to manage without any full-time, salaried clergy at all? If every minister were required to support himself and his family by an ordinary job? Where would

Christians worship if they had no special place set apart? And would this strip the practice of religion of all meaning for them? Some of these questions will occupy us when we come to consider worship in a later chapter. For the moment it must be sufficient to ask them, and particularly to raise the fundamental question of priority, namely: ought not many things which at present are customarily a first charge on the available resources to be provided out of surplus, and vice versa? There are no easy answers or universal solutions to this one; but one thing is quite certain. Until priorities are reversed, the Church will never become an open Church, for it will never be able to afford the activities which alone will make it open.

All that we have so far considered arose out of the meaning of the Catholic concept of ministry – the Church's duty to be apostle, pastor, priest, and servant of the world, and thereby (let us repeat it) to make all men the apostles, pastors, priests, and servants of each other, and it may be of the Nature that surrounds them. But in addition to thus developing Christian approaches to the business of human living, with the resultant involvement alongside men and women who are not Christians, there is another way towards the open Church. It will be recalled that in the earliest days some Christian communities were organized on a different system under a board of elders. After being for many centuries submerged in the Catholic order, this pattern reappeared after the Reformation in Presbyterianism; and to this day Christianity is divided between these two structures. The division goes deep, and is one of the most intractable issues in discussions of Christian reunion. This is, indeed, only to be expected. The reason (often overlooked) is that the two systems represent two quite different intuitions about the nature of the Church. The Catholic order is the result of creating a specifically Christian symbolic structure, which then seeks to change human life by co-existing and interacting with it. It expresses – when it is true to its Lord – the aspect of revelation and redemption from evil through the cross. The presbyteral system, by contrast, is a 'baptizing', an incorporation into the kingdom of God, of that which is already good in human existence, of the natural structures of human life. It conforms the church to the family, the village, the clan, and the city, placing at the head of the community those who would be men's natural leaders. The function which we have been examining in connection with the Catholic ministry is still catered for, and by precisely the same method of a trained and consecrated clergy.

But these clergy are summoned by the community to serve them, and can be dismissed by them; nor are there any higher clerics to bear down upon the autonomous local elders. In Catholicism redemption invades the natural order; in Presbyterianism the natural order takes redemption into its system.

For this reason Presbyterianism is at its best where the Christian community and the natural community coincide. The old Calvinist ideal of making the world into a theocracy here finds its fullest opportunity. It was the cardinal error of the Catholic clergy, that in a world where everyone was nominally Christian they came to look upon their own lay fellows, in their corporate if not their individual identity, as the 'world' and upon themselves as the 'church' — an idea which is only now dying and even now dying hard. Hence 'secular' became the opposite not of 'sacred' but of 'clerical'. Everyone, from the Holy Roman Emperor downwards, was organized into secular structures, and these could serve the purposes of God only by submitting to direction from the separate clerical order. Human individuals had been baptized; human society was not.

If the human race were suddenly to be converted to Christianity, we might all look at this question quite differently. It might then seem right that the structures of the world should become the structures of the 'Church', for the two bodies would be one and the same. The natural heads of the human community would be the obvious candidates for heads of the race in its awareness of itself as the family of God, and the Church, like the Marxist State, would wither away. This would indeed be the fulfilment of the seer's vision:

The kingdom of the world has become the kingdom of our Lord and of his Christ (*Rev.* 11:15).

Until the world can sincerely think of itself as simultaneously the world and the Church, that is to say in effect as neither but as the human race living life as it should be lived, in the all-sanctifying context of God, the world's joy can never be fulfilled. Here the problem how to achieve the open Church finally vanishes:

You shall know that I am in the midst of Israel, and that I, the LORD, am your God and there is none else. And my people shall never again be put to shame. And it shall come to pass afterward, that I will pour out my spirit on all flesh; your sons and your daughters shall prophesy, your old men shall dream dreams, and your young men shall see visions (*Joel* 2:27–28).

Meanwhile a tension exists; but it is easy to mistake that tension and to express it wrongly. It is not simply a tension between the Church and the world as separate entities, but between mankind on the way to the spirit of God and mankind living by that spirit, or, in biblical language, between the present age and the age to come. The Church therefore must embody both ages. She must approach the world as God approaches it in Christ; and she must also baptize the world, drawing it constantly as far as she can into the already existing kingdom. It is to this second condition that the presbyterian ideal relates; and this is the ultimate reason why it must never be allowed to perish.

Easier said than done, no doubt. But one obvious step in the right direction is for the Christian community to draw part of its leadership now from the heads of the local 'secular' community, and to operate not only in the gathered congregation but also in the social groupings of the world.[1] That heads of families and rulers of nations, for example,

[1] It may be pointed out that it is a sense of this aspect of the Church's vocation which lies, sometimes inarticulately, behind the misgivings of serious people about the ordination of women. It is the 'enlightened' attitude at the moment to say that there is no 'theological' objection to women's ordination; and fair-minded people (including women) therefore quite commonly remark, 'I can't see any real argument against it, but I don't like the idea all the same,' The assumption here is, of course, that attitudes arising from centuries of human cultural tradition do not constitute a 'real argument'. In fact they are of great theological importance. The tension between the revolutionary Church, turning the world upside down by the spirit of God, and the Church baptizing the natural orders of human life is just as real in this issue as in any other. Society itself does not know very clearly what it wants the human vocation of women to be; and the Church at large is only now starting a new quest for the mind of Christ on the subject. The present writer is of the opinion that the following would be the right steps by which to work into the matter: (1) in accordance with the ideal of the open Church, to stimulate and participate in much more widespread and serious consideration in society at large of the human vocation of women, and what changes are needed to realize this; (2) in view of the inevitably over-emotional reaction of the clergy to this subject, some of them being attached to the old order, others perhaps too intellectually 'progressive' as a result of guilt feelings about that order, to encourage informed discussion by the laity, and to give them an equal voice; (3) possibly, since data can never be complete without actual trial and, if necessary, error, to build up the role of women in the specialist ministries mentioned earlier, and to ordain some of them in this context, where the job would normally demand it. It must also be appreciated that the traditions of any given society are bound to be decisive in this matter. What might be feasible in western society could well be mere fantasy for the Church in other parts of the world. This does not necessarily imply that all churches ought to keep in step – after all, they do

should have special status in the worship of God is a feature of human history almost everywhere except in the Christian Church; and the barriers to full integration of the natural order into God's kingdom can hardly be lowered, much less done away, until the representatives of the former are admitted into the heart of Man's relationship with God. And this means not simply a seat on church councils but the right to perform certain offices, such as presiding at the Eucharist, and teaching, which are at present confined to 'professional' ministers.

Looming over the whole discussion has been the problem of authority. Here at last that overworked word 'problem' is entirely in place. Neither is there, nor will there ever be any means of getting rid of it, for the simple reason that to talk about authority at all in a Christian context is to create a problem. The authority of Jesus one can talk about, since it is the root of the matter. But we should remember what a strange kind of authority that is. We accept Jesus' authority not because he holds any official position, nor even because he has been consecrated and appointed by God. His authority does not rest ultimately even on the resurrection, since – and here we come once again to our reversal of the conventional Christian sequence – the resurrection confirms Jesus' divine authority only to those who have already responded to his message and his life. Jesus' authority rests on the unique fact of himself. The Church in turn fulfils her calling only as she lives by his spirit, which is God's own spirit; and in so far as she does so, she confronts men with the same challenge: Is this the key to our human living or not? The spirit of love has to be accepted on its own merits or not at all; hence the Christian community has authority only by virtue of what it is. The false notion of authority is that the truth can be enshrined in forms of words,[1] and that some individual or group, regardless whether they live by the spirit of that truth, has the power to decide on such words or to guarantee that given forms of words are true. From this it is but a short step, and often taken, to saying that because the individual or group has this power, it is wicked

---

not do that now. It does suggest that the right attitude may be to stop thinking about the ordination of 'women' as such, as though they were simply an aggregate of uniform objects, but to consider, as is done with men, whether on a realistic assessment of the position and needs of the Church at the time, any individual woman is the best person to do a particular job, in competition not just with other women but with men as well.

[1] On this whole subject cf. chapter 13 below.

z

or dangerous not to accept what they say, *even if it does not seem to one-self to be true.* This is nonsense, and evil nonsense. A person may quite properly say: 'I would like to believe so-and-so, and I hope that one day I may; but at the moment it does not seem to me to be true. Meanwhile I will go on thinking about it.' That is as far as one can go. For there are three things which lie at the heart of Christianity: belief, love, and worship – and not one of them can be achieved in obedience to authority. They are all free personal commitments or nothing. Hence even if God were to find some way of investing the Church or the Church's spokesmen with this kind of authority, it would do no good. Moreover, while statements can be promulgated in this manner, a living spirit cannot thus be communicated. Unless it is present in some-one or some community, it remains inaccessible. It can neither be approved nor caught.

If this applies to the relations between the Church and the world, it also holds good in the internal life of the Christian community, though with one qualification. Very few of us are clear in our minds all the time what is right or good or true.[1] When in doubt, therefore, we may wish to be guided by others; and for a Christian the most obvious place to seek this guidance will be the mind of Christ in his fellow-Christians. But to put such trust in others is possible only where we are already confident that the truth and the spirit are present in the com-munity. Acceptance of 'authority' in this sense presupposes that on fundamental issues all concerned share a common free commitment; and it always looks ahead to the day when personal conviction will supersede even this dependence on authority.

Authority in the Church, however, has other aspects; and one more must be considered here. This is the question where power to deploy resources and to lay down policy is to reside. The present systems vary considerably from one denomination to another, but they have a number of vices in common. Since they are concerned primarily with moving ordained men around the board,[2] the lonely 'spiritual tech-nician' is posted from one place to another, and very probably has no

[1] Cf. the discussion on pp. 94ff. above.
[2] In the Church of England a bishop or a diocesan patronage committee may have to play an elaborate game of solitaire, shifting six or seven marbles in order to get one particular marble into the hole desired for it. This marble may be ideal for that hole; whether the other six are equally well placed in the process we perhaps ought not to ask.

personal roots in any of them. On arrival he finds no living structures of ministry, no local ordained men already operating, with whom he can work himself in as one of a team. He has few sources of information about his new position that are not either partisan or malicious. Small wonder that he falls back on a set of standard techniques that have served reasonably well in other settings. Unless he is exceptionally resourceful or lucky, his style becomes stereotyped; he ceases to respond, and simply functions. A weariness settles over his days. His character becomes a set of mannerisms. What is more, he has little prospect of changing even temporarily to a different type of job, or, when he has gained experience, of rising to a management-type post with wider responsibilities. In the non-hierarchical churches this is at least the lot of all his colleagues too. In the hierarchical ones there is something analogous to promotion and a career for a few; and this in some ways makes things harder, since it adds the temptation to disappointment to his other frustrations. It is not uncommon, therefore, to find those in authority exhorting the rank and file to lay aside such ambitions as unworthy of a Christian. This may be true; but they ought to reflect that they are the last people entitled to say so. The simple fact is that if you deny men the chance of any deep fulfilment in their work, if you condemn them to isolation and a life of scratching the surface of the real task while keeping up an appearance of profitable activity, then those with any honesty at all will be sickened by the perpetual falsity, and will hanker after some sort of escape; and this, unless they abandon their calling altogether, only promotion can provide.

The answer, however, is not to be found in supplying a more elaborate career structure. The work of the Church does not call for the vertical expansion needed. The answer is to offer the chance of such fulfilment in the job, that promotion becomes of secondary importance; and this the kind of community life in an open Church which we have been considering would do in abundance. A good deal has been heard in recent years of 'group ministries'; but these have too often turned out to mean half a dozen identically trained personnel sharing out identical chores spread over half a dozen identical congregations. This may provide company for lonely evenings. It hardly offers fulfilment. But a local church such as we have envisaged, with lay groups actively engaged on the real needs of the world, and co-operating with people outside the church; with leaders of the community also ordained and exercising a ministry; with worker-priests in industry or agriculture attached to the church; with visiting specialists from outside helping to guide the congregation's own efforts; and with regular periods of conference and contact to deepen and increase one's own resources; this could offer anyone with a genuine vocation a satisfying life, which would make preferment a far less significant issue. This is not the justification for it, but it is interesting that it would very likely have this effect. And not only this. It would also ease the invidious burdens of authority, which compel those who themselves have achieved a fulfilling and rewarding field of work to move their 'subordinates' from one hopeless and distasteful job to another. It would reduce the number of personal problems and breakdowns, which they are now required to handle without having the one remedy needful (square holes for square pegs) at their disposal. It would increase the control of the local congregation over its own staffing and destiny, because the people's awareness of their needs, and their resultant application for suitable help, would play the larger part in deployment, instead, as at present, of the top administration's guess about those needs. In so far as it created the chance to do a real job it would also increase the number of vocations, and so of the men available to deploy. Last but not least, such a vision of the Church, open on all sides to the world, alive with complex and responsive activity, giving and receiving the spirit of Jesus, makes a little more sense of the New Testament metaphor of the Church as a living 'body'. Too often now the congregation, even the wider Church, seems not so much a highly articulated organism with a thousand different capabilities as a collection of left ears and big toes – a macabre anatomical exhibit rather than a living personal being.

Nothing has been said in this chapter about one of the greatest questions in the life of the Church: her unity, and the current efforts to recover old unities and create new ones. Of two major aspects of this question, however, there is hardly need to say more. If the Church is to be an open Church, ready to co-operate with the world in the business of human living, then all the more should Christians be ready to work with each other in this field. This is already happening to an encouraging extent. In many countries all over the world local congregations of different allegiances are joining together to study and take concerted action on social affairs. The second aspect is more difficult. This concerns the reconciling of different concepts of church structure and order. Here progress can be hoped for only by a return to first principles. To amalgamate systems that have been built up by centuries of divergent development is an impossible task. Any apparent solution could be no more than a diplomatic compromise. But a discussion of first principles will certainly bring us to the third and hardest aspect of the problem. Different churches have evolved distinctive understandings of Christian faith and life as a whole, and these control not only their official formularies but their atmosphere, their piety, their way of doing things. It is in this third area that the real barriers to unity are to be found; and any attempt to lower these must wrestle with the problem of expressing and communicating truth, which is the subject of our next chapter.

One final but important function of the Church must be mentioned. That Christians should be alive to and informed about contemporary problems is indeed essential; but they need also to be thinking in the present, as any serious human being does, about the future. There is absolutely no reason why the Church should always be taken by surprise by every new development. We know, for example, that ahead lies an immense extension of automation with its concomitant of more and more 'free time', when the business of earning one's living, which today gives meaning to so many lives, will become the least of our concerns. We can see already how technological advance, and the global economic and financial structures on which this has to be based, may lead to increasing tyranny over individual lives. It will become increasingly imperative that people do the work assigned to them, go where the system demands, live in officially provided dwellings. At present such mobility can often be achieved by carefully calculated incentives, which have the advantage of eliciting a better level of work than can be secured from directed labour. But will economically feasible incentives always produce enough labour quickly enough? Or contrariwise, if ordinary employment becomes too dull and controlled, will the problem not be to keep people at the humdrum? What is this going to mean for the rights of the free individual? We can guess that an industrialized world where economic inequalities between societies have been ironed out may also entail tremendous consequences. Are nations to eke out a precarious existence taking in each other's economic washing? It looks very much as though the whole current concept of relative national wealth will become meaningless, and that the international monetary structure, already crumbling before our eyes, will one day disappear except as the central accounting system of a single world 'firm'. In such a global unit what becomes of private property? It is a nuisance; the individual changes into a tenant or lessee of an all-embracing authority, which supplies him with his approved 'needs', and lays down permitted levels of procreation, thus obliterating in large measure the situation to which ethics as we know them are relevant. In such a world there might be no outlet for human creative energies except in the dangerously narrow intensities of feeling and contemplation, or in art and leisure – but how much of their present value do the latter derive from their contrast with the indispensable hard graft of survival? How do we give our actions real importance when there is less and less that anyone can 'do' for anyone else? Have Christians nothing to say about all this? Have they no views how in the context of God and of the nature of Man as God has created him we should take charge of our own becoming, to decide where we really want to go, and how we ought to act now in order to get there? The whole Church throughout the world will need to pool all its resources to answer these questions, and to work together to influence events.[1] There can be no truly moral attitude to the present which does not consider the possible future.

[1] The department of Humanum studies in the World Council of Churches is a promising move in this direction.

13

The Word and the Words

COMMUNICATION IS a mysterious process – how mysterious perhaps only those generations can appreciate which, like our own, are faced with the acute problems that arise when it breaks down. Of course, incompetence in the use of language, failure on the part of the communicator to be clear even in his own mind and terms what it is he wishes to say, may be expected to block understanding. A person may be so fixated on a particular point that even a closely related question, to which he could give a perfectly satisfactory answer, defeats him. But these are superficial difficulties.

A rather more serious frustration, which most people will have experienced, occurs when a perfectly straightforward statement apparently conveys a meaning quite different from the one intended. We are thinking here not of those occasions when emotional factors cause the other person to 'take it the wrong way' (which is sometimes, alas, the right way in terms of our own hidden feelings!) but rather of those dispiriting moments when someone says, 'Ah, I see what you mean . . .', and then proceeds to expound an idea which has never entered our head. (Those who have to give talks and lectures often encounter this kind of reaction in conversation afterwards.) Probing a little more deeply, however, we may then come across the reason. What we have said has not communicated our meaning, but it has triggered off a reflection dormant in the listener, who has been brought by our words to a moment of vision of his own. A train of thought has been set up so new, interesting, and convincing that he is quite sure this is what we must have meant; and this insight will normally spring from his own position. It has not involved a radical change of that position. It is an organic development of his existing outlook.

Moreover, even where words heard or read do induce a seemingly fundamental change – as in experiences of moral, political or religious conversion, or in psychological release – the results that unfold prove still to be plainly in keeping with the basic make-up of the person concerned. Again and again, biographies of men and women whose lives have contained some momentous turning-point from which they move in a drastically new direction bring to light the essential continuity between the two parts of the drama. In the end, if our lives are to be personally genuine and not a pose destructive of personality, we can only be what we are. Any perfection or fulfilment we may attain must be *our* perfection. If we come to see things in the 'right' way, yet it will still be our particular way, even though it may be recognizably right in principle. The purpose of communicating truth to others, therefore, can only be that they should see truth for themselves, with their own eyes.

If truth were simply a matter of words, of composing reasonably viable formulas for describing experience, then this fact would imply total relativism. Whatever formula suited me would be the 'truth', and one could get no farther than that. But if there are ultimate facts, existing independent of any description that may be made of them, then at least certain statements will come nearer to conveying that truth than others. Certainly, we may have a range of statements, all of which are personal approximations to the truth; and we may not be entitled to treat one as normative and reject the rest. We may have statements that are true 'as far as they go', and which must be respected as such. But we can also have statements which are false, or so predominantly false that any truth which is in them is better expressed another way or in a different setting. Thus, the Christian is bound to say that some of the teachings of Buddhism are simply untrue, and that others present partial truth in so wrong a context or perspective that it is advisable to scrap them and start again. A Christian is bound to say that the western atheist who asserts flatly, 'There is no God', is incorrect. If the atheist adds, 'Your God is a product of your own imagination', however, then the Christian, if he is honest, will agree that there is some truth in this, just as he might half admit that 'There is no God as you imagine him'. But he may still feel that the truth-content of either is much better expressed by saying, 'There is a God, but our ideas of him are in many ways distorted or fictitious'.

In this question of ultimate truth God plays a unique and vital role. If the sum total of cosmic facts is the sum total of all facts, then no one

interpretation can effectively compete with another. However susceptible of coherent scientific description things may be, even if the
microcosmic and the macrocosmic can in the end be arranged in a
single consistent scientific pattern, yet when we come to descriptions in
terms of value the contradictions and conflicts within reality make every
world-view a matter of emphasis, selection, and mood. But if behind
the cosmic aggregate there is a unified, morally consistent personal
being, who is responsible for this mass of contradictions and is bringing
a purpose to fruition out of it and by means of it, then it makes sense to
talk of 'ultimate truth'. With the universe as it is, ultimate truth can
exist only if the universe is not everything.

This state of affairs invests the believer in God with an unpopular
but necessary intransigence. Unfortunately, he is apt to carry this
hard-edged attitude not merely into the area of essential affirmations
but far below that, into the precise phrasing of his own systematic
presentation of details. Not content with his creed, he takes his stand on
speculations interpreting that creed; and when others disagree with him
on the latter, he accuses them of dissolving the former as well. Alternatively, he may credit certain hallowed interpretations, such as the
Bible, with verbal inerrancy throughout, disregarding the fact that so
large and diverse a collection of writings contains almost as many conflicting elements as the universe itself, and appears in as many different
guises when attempts are made to describe it in a comprehensive and
unified view.

The Scriptures indeed present the thorniest of all problems in this
matter of communicating religious truth. The product of at least
twelve hundred years of history, containing laws, narratives, romances,
lyric poetry, proverbial wisdom, metaphysical speculation, moral
instruction, prayers, liturgies, cosmogonies, family trees, sermons,
predictions, and heaven knows what else, and written in three different
languages, they display not even one feature common to every part.
We cannot even say with certainty that all the writers were Jews or
directly connected at some time in their lives with Judaism; and if they
were, they undoubtedly borrowed from other faiths, cultures, and
philosophies. One book, indeed, has only the faintest link with the idea
of God.[1] And the whole of this literature stands, at its nearest, almost

---

[1] The *Song of Solomon*, where the divine name occurs once, but only in its
purely linguistic use as a means of giving intensive or superlative force to the
word to which it is attached. The book of *Esther* is notorious as not mentioning

two thousand years away from us, and on the far side of several radical revolutions in human thought.

Nevertheless, it is possible to find without falsification one theme running through this collection, even if not instanced in every part. What this theme is as regards the Old Testament was analysed in some detail in the first chapter of the present work,[1] and there summarized as the attempt to see all existence in terms of the sovereignty of God, and to define Man's place in that overall scheme. The unifying key to the Old Testament, therefore, is its great fundamental question, not its answers, explicit or implied. It might be considered frivolous, but it would not be far from the truth to say that the question is in fact the only thing which the Old Testament does get right, and that the answers, at least in their Old Testament form, are all wrong. But in the end it is the question which matters, for it is this question which is answered correctly in Jesus; and it was because Israel was the only nation that did ask this question that God incarnate had to be a Jew. In no other setting would his life have made any sense. The New Testament writers in their turn, therefore, are able to communicate and interpret God's own answer because, through the medium of Judaism, they shared the question. But had the cross and resurrection of Jesus not made that answer so clear and definite, they would never have realized that Israel's own ancient answers were inadequate. As it was, however, they were able, as Paul for example so often did, to bring out the new truth by contrasting it with the old mistakes – though some of them, as we have seen, at times found the gravitational field of those mistaken systems too strong for them.

If this were all, however, why was it that the Christian Church for so long found parts of the Old Testament, such as the Psalms, the best available expression for her own thoughts and feelings? There are several reasons. The first and most obvious is that these were the sacred writings of Judaism, which Jesus himself had quoted and treated as the oracles of God (though, as we shall shortly recall, he did so in an unusual way). They contained the promise of the Messiah,

---

God at all, but in fact he is a much more real presence behind the narrative and the attitudes of the characters than he is in the *Song*. It is a tribute to the vigour of religious re-interpretation that both Judaism and Christianity have at various periods turned every line of the *Song* into an allegory of the relationship of the soul with God.

[1] Cf. pp. 27–33 above.

which Jesus believed to be his own vocation, a belief in which he had been vindicated by his resurrection. It was natural therefore that Christians should approach these documents with reverence and expectancy, and find in them numerous other predictions and promises which Jesus had fulfilled. The second reason, let us admit it, is that the Church had not yet been emancipated from the wrong answers; her view of God's operations was still in many ways less than that of Jesus himself.[1] The third reason, however, is more subtle and of enduring importance. Much of what the Old Testament has to say about God and Man is basic imagery; that is to say, it deals in the fundamental concepts of life and death, health and sickness, victory and defeat, truth and the lie, light and darkness, the cruel sea and the firm rock, food and hunger, drink and thirst, offspring and sterility, loyalty and treachery, love and hate, friends and enemies – the list is immense. These are the images which the writers used to express their particular historical feelings and situations in relation to God. But because they are so primitive and permanent, because they tap the deepest springs of feeling in the human psyche, the same phrases that served so well to voice, let us say, the enthusiasm of a tenth-century B.C. Israelite for the glory of the Davidic kingdom proved equally effective to express the exultation of a Christian at the kingdom which was not of this world. The result was that the Church used the old words, almost without realizing it, in a completely transformed, though not extravagant sense. One very early example may be cited. In *Psa.* 96:10 we find the words: 'Say among the nations, "The Lord reigns!"' The early Christians changed this. What they said was, 'Say among the nations that the Lord reigns *from the Tree.*' It is clear from the citation of this passage in the second-century writer Justin Martyr that Christians of his day were quite satisfied that their version was the original text, and that the Jews had maliciously excised the last three words to conceal the fact that the Psalm referred to Christ. The fact that Justin is unaware that his version is a falsified one shows that he has inherited it from a respectably old tradition, and that the change must therefore have been made at an early stage in Christian history. Now the reason why it was made is almost certainly this – not because men wanted to invent a prophecy which would support their case, but because to them it seemed obvious that the words of the Psalm could refer only to the Cross. They knew that this was where God had truly reigned, and that this was the Gospel to be

[1] And still is: cf. pp. 329ff. above.

preached to all nations. This therefore was what the words meant, and their addition only made this explicit.

As time went by, an elaborate system was developed for working out this approach in comprehensive detail, expounding Scripture by what are called the 'allegorical' and 'typological' methods. Much criticism and indeed ridicule has been expended on this kind of exegesis, and on the fantastic ingenuity by which the most unpromising texts were given a Christian meaning. No doubt it will not do, and there is no intention of defending or commending it here. But fairness demands that we recognize that in one vital respect they understood the essence of using Scripture, and we do not. They knew that the words of Scripture come alive and blaze with meaning only when in some respect they chime in with what we ourselves want to say.

There is a simple fact which is often forgotten, namely that thoughts (other than mathematical ones) are not *expressed* in words – they *exist* in words and only in words. When we read the words of an ancient culture, therefore, we are reading their thoughts, their concept of truth. Certainly, the greater and perhaps the most significant part of that truth, the myriad feelings and associations that clustered round it, the 'feel' of it, is beyond our reach. But something comes through, otherwise we could neither accept nor reject it; even when we cannot believe or share it, we can form some notion of what it was. What we cannot do, however, is to apply some principle of re-interpretation to the words which will discern behind them a quite different truth which we can believe and share. There is nothing to find; their words are their thoughts, and that is as far as you can go.

It is impossible, therefore, to join in the almost universal admiration voiced today for the celebrated methodological question in which Leonard Hodgson sought to describe what our attitude ought to be to the religious teaching of the past: 'What must the truth have been and be if that is how it looked to men who thought and wrote like that?'[1] The hidden assumption behind this question is that truth is, as it were, clothed in thoughts and words, and that by understanding the idiomatic structure of the imagery of a particular world we can formulate our own expression of the same truth which they were stating in their own terms. But truth does not come to men clothed in words, it comes to them as words; and when as far as possible we know what the words meant to them, then as far as possible we know what the truth was to

[1] L. Hodgson, *For Faith and Freedom*[2], 1968, p. x.

them. We can go on to agree or disagree in whole or in part, but we cannot, so to speak, allow for the index of refraction in their minds, and say, 'The truth must therefore be so-and-so.' This is the fallacy behind the so-called 'demythologizing' approach. You cannot, for example, say, 'Because these were people who believed in supernatural beings behaving in such and such ways, *therefore* the truth which they were expressing when they thought and wrote about them was a moral and existential one.'

If we shared the world-view and presuppositions of the biblical writers, then their words would present no difficulty. We could dispute them or echo them, moving naturally in the same mental environment. Now we cannot and do not. Nevertheless, if we find in Jesus of Nazareth a fact of crucial importance for human life, we have to enter into some sort of living relationship with Scripture, because Scripture is the primary point of contact with him and with the context in which he originally made sense. Clearly we cannot adopt a reproduction of the biblical world-view for religious purposes only. If men's faith is to have anything to do with their life, they have to come to it with their own honest picture of existence. When they do, we observe the operation of a kind of sliding scale of response. A contemporary Western atheist may be able to take certain passages of Scripture, and say, 'Yes, in the plain sense of their own terms these seem to me to be saying things which I myself would wish to say – for example, "All who take the sword will perish by the sword," or, "Whatever you wish that men would do to you, do so to them," and so on. The majority of the material, however, I cannot make my own in any sincere way.' An idealist in his turn might have a somewhat more complex attitude. He could use some material in a literal way, other as a legitimate poetic or metaphorical expression of his own thoughts. He would know that this was not what the writers meant, and he could define the change in use that he wished to make; that, for example, the value which the writers attached to God, and the feelings which the thought of God aroused in them, he himself would relate to the principle of Love or the concept of the Good. A modern theist, that is to say, someone who has worked out an interpretation of the world in terms of a good God, and who holds to this as the most probable hypothesis of existence, will find himself very much more at home with the material. Again, there will be the passages taken as they stand in agreement with the original writers; again the metaphorical and poetic applications of the idealist type. But there will now also be numerous instances in which the words of Scripture are used in much the fashion of the early Church, treating statements about God, for example, as truths about an existent personal being, but referring them to God's nature, influence, or activity conceived in a new way.

This, however, is not the only new development, nor by any means the most important. For, once the reader's underlying world-view has approached this close to the view of the biblical writers themselves, it now becomes possible for his own understanding of existence to grow in ways stimulated by the beliefs of Scripture. The classic example of this process is the central doctrine of Christianity, the Incarnation. This is not the kind of thing which someone would envisage for himself, simply because on general grounds he believed in a personal God; but it is very much the kind of thing which, once suggested, might seem to grow naturally out of his belief, and to fulfil it in a way beyond his wildest hopes. If this does happen, then a good deal more of what Scripture has to say becomes meaningful to him, not metaphorically but directly; and deriving from this new advance comes a new insight into the possible relevance of a great range of other passages. Thus, he may not wish to follow Paul to the letter in his interpretation of the death of Jesus in terms of the demise of the Old Testament Law. But he may be led to conclusions of his own which he recognizes as corresponding in his own day to the point that Paul was making in his.

This may suggest ways in which the difficulties found today in preaching on a text of Scripture can be overcome. Ordinarily, if we start from the chosen passage, it is first necessary to initiate the hearers into the background of the original writer. Once they are in his shoes, then they can be led along the path of his argument to his conclusion. But at this point we are only a third of the way to making the words come alive. The next stage is to look around for points of contact in our own situation, and to draw an analogy with the biblical one; and this is often extremely difficult to do convincingly. The effect is artificial, and rather intensifies than reduces the listener's initial prejudice that the Bible is likely to be irrelevant. Finally, more often than not, he is then asked to accept that the modern application is what the biblical text is 'really saying'; and this outrages his common sense. A more straightforward method would be better. To start from human life in the context of God and to see where, for us, the argument leads; and then to say, 'Look! in his own situation this was the kind of insight which Paul or John or Jesus was expressing' – this is of infinitely more value, because it brings home to the reader that the great perspective in which the Scriptures view human life is one that he can usefully adopt for himself. It gives him not a series of piecemeal dogmatic statements but a way of looking at existence, and a growing confidence that he can use it and get reliable results. As he does so, he then discovers for himself more and more in the Scriptures with which he has a feeling of kinship. Sometimes he will exclaim, as we all do in our ordinary reading, 'That is just what I wanted to say, but could never have put so well.' Then the scriptural language will become definitive for him. Sometimes he will prefer to put it his own way, but will nevertheless develop a deepening respect for the Scriptures. Sometimes he will be led on to expand his own outlook by seeing that the biblical writers themselves move on from the point which he shares with them; but he will do so by pondering for himself on life as he knows it, and only then discovering that they have been there before him. In this way he grows into the mind of the Bible, but he remains his own man and lives in his own day. Finally, and this is equally important, there will be times when he concludes that certain pronouncements of Scripture are mistaken or inadequate. Even in the present work we have already seen enough examples of this, comparing one passage against another, to know that this is so. What is vitally necessary, however, is that people should not be encouraged to feel that in reaching such a decision on any particular point they are 'sinning' or inevitably mistaken; for this is the surest possible way to kill in them anything that can be called a living faith.

If individuals are to be encouraged to develop along these lines, then it goes without saying that the Church as a teaching body must have tried, through her thinkers and writers, to work out fundamental positions, valid and possible for the thought of her time, which men can use as their starting-points. In other words, the present contempt for natural theology must be exorcised. It is in any case fatal, since it implies that with the most important of all questions for us, the truth about human existence, reason has nothing to do. Small wonder, then, that Christians today seem to divide with increasing sharpness into two embattled camps: those on the one hand who have nothing but a natural theology, decked out here and there with scraps from the Christian heritage; and these on the other who hold to the static perfection of the faith once delivered to the saints, whether in the Bible or in church formularies, and who reject with contumely (and perhaps a modicum of fear) any attempt to question or to hold only what intellectual integrity will allow. But an appeal for a return to the study of natural theology must also make clear that that theology has in its past forms made a disastrous mistake. It has been assumed that by reason certain basic truths could be established; and that on this solid foundation other truths, unattainable to unaided reason, could be added by revelation. As we have already argued, however,[1] this is to mistake the situation. Reason cannot lay such a foundation. It can only construct a hypothesis. It can say, 'If you try to answer the ultimate question in terms of God, then an adequate answer will have these characteristics and will exclude those.' What revelation does in Jesus of Nazareth is to confirm the general outline thus put as a possibility, and to carry it farther, showing which potentials within it have in fact been realized, and revealing new potentials which we had never noticed. The supposed conflict between reason and revelation is a phantasm. What is revealed is seen to be perfectly rational; what is rational is confirmed by what is revealed. Revelation is necessary, but the explanation, as we have argued all along, is a moral, not an intellectual one. Reason could never say that God would be governed by the law of sacrificial love, because reason herself is powerless to prove that this must be obeyed. She can recognize it as a possibility; she cannot advise it. The choice which God has in fact made in harmony with his eternal nature is a free choice on this account; and being truly free it was unpredictable. He might have been different – we had no means of being sure. Hence he had to disclose the fact, and so confound the prudential wisdom of men by his own 'foolishness'.

It is at this central point, the point of Jesus, that Scripture is seen in her true sovereignty. It might be thought, from what was said above, that we could arrive in time at a formal, logical normativeness of Scripture. If different types of contemporary answer to the ultimate question make differing proportions of Scripture meaningful, then surely it would be possible eventually to work out a vision of reality which would make every part of the Bible a medium of revelation? But the contradictions within Scripture put any such systematic achievement for ever out of the question. No, the control which Scripture exercises over men is a moral one, not that of a moral law indeed, but that of a moral challenge. To anyone who will not follow

[1] Cf. pp. 277f. above.

her into the foolishness of God she speedily becomes meaningless. She gives light only where divine loyalty to the Good in love is the supreme value. Because of this her dominion, like that of God and of Jesus, does not impose authority but creates freedom. Because of this she is not only the words of men, but also the Word of God.

It is, perhaps, worth noting also that she is this only in her range and variety, warts and all. It would be hard to argue that the exact canon of Scripture which we now have is ideal, or that any serious loss would be sustained if some books had been excluded.[1] But by representing the widest possible scope of human thought and experience, and offering problems as well as answers, errors and half-truths as well as truths, she places the key figure of Jesus in its right setting and enables us to see more clearly the real and distinctive significance of his life and person. She gives us practice in relating him to alternatives, and so encourages us to place him correctly with reference to the immensely wider alternatives which open up with the growing experience of mankind. The method of Scripture herself is to come to the truth of God on the basis of our own openness to all possibilities.

Significantly enough, both the points we have made are supported by Jesus himself. That which he taught in parables comes alive to men only as they see it in a certain perspective, and challenges them precisely by its obscurity when they do not.[2] Again, the parables take as a starting-point men's direct experience of life and the world. Similarly, in Jesus' approach to Scripture he taught his followers to find God first in the terms of their existence, and then to pass by way of Scripture more deeply into God's mind.[3] For us the task is that much easier, because in Jesus himself we have the decisive fact of our situation. But the principle remains the same.

What we have said of the Bible applies also to all later reflection on the truth. Scripture is in a class by itself not because she has an authority

---

[1] Those churches which regard the Apocrypha as of inferior value have, of course, the chance to consider the further question whether, say, *Ecclesiasticus* or *Wisdom* or *Tobit* might not well replace *Esther* or *Nahum* or *Obadiah*. But why exclude any? The distinction between the two sets of books is based on a wrong approach to Scripture anyway, namely the idea that certain doctrines can be proved by selected texts. Since the Apocrypha encourages 'pernicious' ideas such as praying for the dead, it is in some Christian circles considered safer outside the pale!

[2] Cf. pp. 200ff. above.

[3] Cf. pp. 215ff. above.

AA

which makes her words inherently more correct than any others, nor because we are to approach her in a different attitude of mind, but because she is the direct witness to the unique event of Jesus. Without her we can never check our course by him; and where the Church has abandoned constant attention to the Bible, her own theory of human life strays more and more away from the mind of Christ. But this does not imply that all insight is to be found in Scripture. In many ways the Church today understands the purposes of God and her own vocation better than it was understood by some of the writers of the New Testament. This is not because we are better men, but because we are standing on their shoulders, and on the shoulders of all the intervening generations. We have more material, for there has been two thousand years of history in between. We have more knowledge, because we have penetrated far more deeply than they ever had opportunity to do into the nature of Man and of the Universe. We have more chance to correct even their mistakes, because we see them against the background of their own times, and can discern some of the pressures to which they were subject. We may even, though this is perhaps a fond illusion, have learned better to detect the pressures that play upon ourselves, and to realize that we are merely drifting with the tide of the age, when we thought we were striking out towards the shore of truth. And it may confidently be hoped that as history moves on, and understanding increases, so we shall unlock more doors in the house of God, and becoming better acquainted with his design, co-operate with it more effectively. But we shall unlock them only with the key of Jesus. As the setting in which Jesus stands is revealed more and more in all its vastness and wonder, his figure does not recede nor shrink. He grows in proportion, becoming more significant not less, more necessary not more dispensable.

The effect of Scripture then on other writings is not to belittle them but to enhance. We learn to approach all of them in the way we approach the Bible. They all become sacred texts, just as through Jesus life is not divided any longer into sacred and secular but becomes in every part sacred. This applies not merely to writings on religious subjects, or words that consciously look towards God or Jesus. It applies to every serious consideration of the human condition, and even to those flashes of insight that occur from time to time in the not so serious, because we have learned to see everything in the context of God as he really is. The only thing that cannot serve to advance us in the understanding of God's purpose is the lie; and even this we can relate to him, since his light shows it up for what it is.[1]

If only Christians would begin to see this, instead of taking refuge in the past, half the problems of Christian unity – the theological problems anyway – would become insignificant. Those who have given up extracting truth from past words, and have begun to stand first on their own honest vision of truth, moving on from there to learn what all words mean, can never regard inherited formularies as justifying separation.

But it is naïve to talk like this. Division is the very purpose for which Christians unconsciously use these formularies. So long as they can say, 'This is the truth, this document here – if you cannot accept that, there can be no real fellowship between us,' they are safe from the anguish of having to consider that they might be mistaken. The adequacy of their vision need never be rigorously scrutinized in the only circumstances in which such scrutiny is possible, namely close community with others who believe differently.

It is becoming common form nowadays in oecumenical circles to say that the common beliefs that unite us are far greater and relate to far more profound questions than those that divide. If this were true, it would condemn all Christians out of hand, because there could be no possible justification for not uniting immediately. But in fact it is not true. It is a psychological trick to protect one from reality. If we agree that we are agreed, then this makes it only proper to behave to one another with civil courtesy, to take a benevolent interest in the activities of other Christians, to co-operate in good deeds. Fine! We have made great progress. Perhaps now we need not hurry quite so precipitately towards actual community. For if we joined together we might find that we were not agreed after all, and cherished beliefs would come under fire.

The real divisions within Christendom do not correspond to the boundary-lines between churches. These are drawn indeed, or very often, between different opinions on church government, the right sort of ordination of clergy, the exact nature of the sacrament of the Eucharist, and so on. The real divisions plunge deep as the abyss between those who disagree passionately on fundamentals: on the Incarnation

---

[1] A corollary here is that Christians should be far more ready than they are to censor or jettison inadequate past attempts at the truth – the positively corrupting ideas, for example, in their hymns and liturgies.

and the nature of Jesus; on the nature of human life and morality, and what God has done to redeem it; on the scope and manner of his revelation of himself to men; on the meaning of the very affirmation of his existence. There are beliefs on these subjects held by fellow-Christians which seem to the present writer to be so profoundly and so immorally wrong, so destructive of true human life and of God's love, that he has no difficulty whatever in understanding how men felt in the old days when they persecuted heresy; and he has no illusions about the similar effect which the present work will have on any one of them who may happen to read it. But what hope is there for either party if we retreat into fortifications garrisoned by companies of totally like-minded and defensive believers?

What is the answer? There has never been but one. Like it or like it not, warring factions must be put into one boat and set adrift on the sea of God to find the better answer together or perish. But this cannot be done simply by institutional means. The Church of England proves this. It is a single organization, containing the most diverse points of view on Christian truth. The result is simply – polarization. Those with shared interpretations flock together, community is destroyed and replaced by aggregations. The will must be there to inquire together into the things that matter. This will is unlikely to be created by political mergers, it must be fostered wherever it happens to be, wherever the spirit of God lists to blow. Small cells of the unlike-minded, however unimportant they are by worldly standards, who want to explore into God together, and come to a new and shared understanding, must have the arrogance to decide to do so, whether others will hear or whether they will forbear. If the lions are too cowardly, the mice must be brave. Then the Word will unite where words have only divided.

14

Man in the Presence of God

IT IS very difficult to generalize with accuracy about Man. If we so much as say that every man must die, someone will object to us Enoch or Elijah. Especially precarious are the statements, of which some writers are so fond, to the effect that Man is 'by nature' this or that sort of animal. At one time it would have seemed perfectly safe to say that Man was a religious animal. Now it is apparent that what had seemed to be a trait of nature was in fact a response to circumstances. Human beings can manage to live easily enough without any religion, in the strict sense of that word, given favourable conditions; and therefore any return to religion induced by a worsening of those conditions can no longer impose such a view upon us.

Even if, however, religion is no more 'natural' to Man than city-dwelling or any particular form of society or culture, yet he has within himself the needs from which all these phenomena take their rise. He has the need to become free, the need to understand, and the need to love and be loved. What is more, all these three are interdependent. If we do not understand our world and ourselves, we can never become free nor ever love, for we operate with a set of illusions. If we are not loved, we never acquire the courage to be free, we never catch the spirit of love, we never understand enough about other people to love them in our turn. If we are not free, we can never take the decision to love or to forgive or to suffer independently of reason, which is to say, that we do not understand the nature of our world.

All of these three purposes of our human condition are concerned, in their different ways, with the same object. That object is Truth. Loyalty to truth is not so much a necessary virtue for human beings as a necessary pre-condition of all virtues. The 'pilgrimage to seek Saint Truth' on which that archetypal man, Piers Plowman, set out, is not an activity additional to the quest for freedom, understanding, and love;

it is those same journeys under another guise, or, let us say, it is the
common character which makes them all in the end the same journey.
Thus it comes about that likewise all the cultural and social forms
which are the by-products of the triple quest for freedom, understanding, and love also depend on loyalty to truth for any strength or value
they may have. Without this they all corrupt into various modes of
tyranny, bigotry, and hate. And the same applies to religion. Religious
faith is worth having only if it is an expression of and a relationship
with truth. Christianity is of no value at all unless it speaks and lives by
truth. The only justifiable pattern for her theology, the only respectable method of proceeding which it can use, is, as the last chapter tried
to argue, one which is oriented not towards faith but towards truth, one
which could in theory lead as easily to refutation as to confirmation of
belief, one which is concerned not with exploring the insights into
existence available from a particular standpoint but with finding the
right standpoint from which that existence can be truly and completely
known.

It is this loyalty to truth which alone can give reality to the aspect of
Christianity which the modern world finds least sympathetic: worship.
The whole history of the word 'worship' is bound up with the notion
of truth. To 'worship' someone is to give them their worth, the
honour which is their due. When, in Malory or some other old writer, a
man goes out to 'win himself worship', the object is not to acquire
simply reputation but justified reputation, to perform deeds which men
will acknowledge as truly of high worth. The husband who in the old
form of the Anglican marriage service declared to his bride, 'with my
body I thee worship', was concerned not merely with his own subjective desire to pay honour to his wife through the devotion of his body
but with her right to be so honoured. It was not just a promise but a
praise. And when we talk about the 'worship of God', we can rightly do
so only if two things are true: that there is a God, and that he is worth
worshipping.

It is because both these propositions are doubted today, that men
find worship empty and meaningless. When a young clergyman,
newly ordained, said to a reporter, 'I'm not sure about God, and my
views about prayer are unprintable,' he was certainly speaking as a
child of his time. One may well wonder what led him to be ordained,
but his worries were assuredly addressed to the right points. The outward forms of worship, the ceremonies and the words, may or may not

have some psychological value, helping men towards a spirit of brother-hood and mutual concern, and creating inner tranquillity. If they do, then that is a good thing; but it should not be called worship.[1] To worship is to acknowledge God for what he is, to render him the honour which is his due, to base one's relationship with him on the truth about him and about ourselves.

Sincere worship, therefore, is exactly proportionate to the strength and content of the worshipper's beliefs. It is an inward reality, and cannot be faked. Surprising though it may seem, most men do in fact worship sincerely. The vacancy of mind, the lack of attention, the concern with petty external trivialities, the surges of superstitious awe or emotional enthusiasm ungeared to the business of living, the critical appraisal of other worshippers and of those 'taking the service', which characterize so many churchgoers at their devotions are not to be ascribed primarily to human weakness. They correspond with terrifying honesty to the vagueness and remoteness of the concept of God, to a failure to face the profound moral challenge on which belief must rest, to an immense indifference to the implications of belief.

The same lack of reality in the idea of God is the root cause of some other vices typical of much Christian worship. One is the bland inertia of the worshipper in face of much that he is expected to say or sing, or to endure while it is said or sung to him. There are, of course, those who, as we considered in the last chapter, have a framework of belief, and a living, constructive approach to it, which enables them to make their own much scriptural and other material that at first sight seems unpromising or even hopeless. Such people are content to accept what they cannot appropriate, partly from a general respect for its source and context, partly because they have every reason to expect that it may come to have personal value or usefulness for them some day. But this is far from being the situation of most. They will listen to or join in nonsense or worse, and then, if challenged, calmly remark, 'Oh, but the words don't really matter, do they?' There is an irreducible

[1] It is a theologian's views on worship which indicate most accurately whether God is for him an objective personal reality or not. The chapter on worship in Bishop Robinson's *Honest to God* is a striking illustration of this. There is no sign in his treatment of the subject that either corporate worship or individual prayer are anything other than means to self-improvement by conforming the personality to the principle of love.

minimum (which even the adepts just mentioned ought to recognize) that has no place in any lectionary, hymnbook, or order of service pretending to be Christian. That it is allowed to slide past without involvement is no doubt a sign of some grace. Matters would be worse if it were relished. But where the truth about God is a living reality to the individual such casual *laisser-faire* is impossible; the words can be tolerated neither by the congregation nor by those appointed to select the material for use. Worse still, their continued employment merely deadens what sensibilities there are, and encourages that lack of clear and concerned thinking which we have seen to be such a dangerous and disgraceful defect.

The other vice is of a different sort, and peculiarly clerical. Public prayers, as well as private, are in theory and in form addressed to God. In practice this is all too often forgotten. The prime concern of the leaders of worship is 'taking the service', which means giving an aesthetically pleasing or emotionally satisfying performance. It is said that many clergy are actors *manqués*; and it would seem to be true. Such might try to justify their preoccupation with a 'beautiful' or 'expressive' rendering by arguing that, where one has to speak for all, this is the best way of helping the congregation to direct to God words that they themselves do not actually say. But how, unless the leader of the prayers is addressing them to a God who is a vivid reality to him, can he know whether the particular beauty or expressiveness he supplies is the appropriate one? Yet even this is not so bad as the fake sincerity which, perhaps only half-consciously, is saying, 'I will put across by my manner the fact that I am speaking to God.' How could such attitudes survive for a moment, if God were a reality? But indeed, if he were, half the prayers – set or extempore – would never be finished. They would falter and die in the throat of the one speaking them.

A third and related vice is especially prevalent in those Christian traditions whose worship is predominantly sacramental. A sacrament, theologically considered, is a divinely appointed means by which God wills to come into saving and sanctifying contact with the worshipper. It is the supreme and effectual symbol of God's real and personal involvement with Man. This is not all that there is to be said about sacraments, especially the sacrament of the Eucharist, but it is certainly a part of it, and an important part. At the moment we are not concerned with its adequacy as an account of the truth but with the undoubted fact that this is believed. That being so, one would expect that anyone with a vital sense of the reality of God would approach the sacrament with an almost intolerable tension of passionate desire and extreme diffidence. It could assuredly never be a light or commonplace matter. Sincerity and truth would urge both a reluctance and a sense of need such as could be reconciled only by a total honesty in the worshipper, acknowledging his failure as a human being to live his whole life in an awareness of the reality of God as intense as that produced by the sacrament itself. That this is recognized as an ideal can be seen from the fact that it is a constant element in the advice given by the great writers on the spiritual life. The widespread neglect of the ideal, and its replacement by a kind of routine of frequent communion accompanied by stereotyped pious exercises, is possible only because of the vague, remote, and unreal nature of God in the communicant's own consciousness. Ironically, this is reinforced by the sacramental act. Instead of mediating the awe-inspiring reality of God it has reduced that reality to the level of its own mundane and unexciting form. What was meant to sacralize ordinary human life, to place it dramatically in its true divine context, has been given quite the reverse effect. Those Christians who complain about the secularization of Christianity should reflect that nowhere has this been so successfully achieved as at the average communion rail.[1]

A deep conviction of the truth, with all its moral and personal corollaries for every aspect of human life, issuing in a constant awareness of the reality of God – that is the source of worship in spirit and in integrity (cf. *John* 4:24). We have already had occasion to note the conventional Christian approach which sees corporate acts of worship (and indeed, private prayer) as a time of recollection, spent in the presence of God, from which the worshipper derives renewed strength and wisdom for the business of everyday living.[2] At the other end of the scale there are those who argue that because God is just as real anywhere, there is no need for special religious observances. In T. S. Eliot's phrase, 'Neither are these justified nor the others.' The right

---

[1] It is just another of the many, many paradoxes of Christian history that a true sense of the implications of the sacrament is more obviously alive in such eighteenth-century Protestants as John Wesley or Dr Samuel Johnson (the latter of whom frequently took weeks or months to prepare for his annual communion, and even then might abstain from a sense of unworthiness) than in many Catholics who hold a far higher sacramental doctrine.

[2] Cf. p. 337 above.

perspective is different from either, though each has hold on part of the truth.

It is undoubtedly better that people should remember God for one or two hours a week than not at all; and in this respect participation in formal, corporate worship for those who forget God the rest of the time is something to the good. But inevitably it means that they remember him only when they find themselves in a particular, specially designed setting, going through actions which bear no obvious resemblance to anything else in their lives. Psychologically this is likely to have an effect the very opposite of what is desired. Memory, as we know, is closely bound up with a mechanism of association: recall is triggered off by one or more stimuli associated with the object to be remembered. An exclusive association of the object with stimuli not encountered except at special times and in special environments then tends to have an actively repressive effect. The memory is unlocked and released only when a specific key is available. Hence too restricted a link between 'God' and 'church', far from helping, positively hinders a continuing awareness of his reality. The same applies in the case of private prayer, if this is performed only at set times and in the same or similar places. Furthermore, the 'God-church' association is bound to have a dulling effect on awareness even when the person concerned finds himself in the 'right' setting. If God is to be real to him, then he must be a God who is intimately associated with the rest, that is, the very much greater part of the person's life. But when, in church, he tries to think of God in this way, his mind has nothing to work on, for he cannot recall any ordinary life situation in which he was aware of the present reality of God. Hence he is never able to apply the excellent admonitions which may be given him, since he cannot picture their relevance in terms of remembered experience.

There is, therefore, a serious practical flaw in the 'preparation for ordinary life' view of worship. There is little or no chance of its working. This defect can be overcome only if awareness of God becomes frequent or habitual for the individual. In that case, however, what is left for formal worship to do? We must return to this point shortly. First, there is more to be said about the cultivation of awareness.

When people start to cultivate awareness of the reality of God, they almost always run at once into the same difficulty. Their picture of God is so lacking in precision and detail that the attempt is wearisome and frustrating, and they quickly lose interest. There is no cure for this except a living picture which they can use; but this must be a picture of a certain kind. It is no use having a picture that is static or historical – for example, one based on a knowledge of the Gospel stories of Jesus as actual finished incidents. What we need is a sense of the attitudes and values, the behaviour patterns, underlying such stories; or, in the case of God as such, the attitudes behind his role as Creator and Saviour. When we are with another person or with other people, we have to be aware of God as the one who knows us all, as we are, in this very moment. When we seek each other's good with the readiness, if need be, for sacrificial love, we know that he rejoices. He is happy at the good, however struggling and rudimentary, in what has just been said; are we then to react with cynicism, cavilling, or envy? Where there is any kind of evil, he suffers and forgives; are we to be merciless and self-righteous, where he is neither? His pardon, however, is always linked with two other elements. First, he tries to bring home to the offender the truth of the whole situation in such a way that the fault may be fully and freely recognized, the pardon accepted, and the relationship restored. At once, therefore, we are faced with a series of questions: are we clear and fair as to the whole truth? is there any way of bringing this to the attention of those who are at fault, without driving them on to the defensive and so hardening them in their attitudes? can we perhaps hope to make them more aware what those attitudes, and their accompanying presuppositions, really are? can we do all this while keeping them in relationship with ourselves? Secondly, there is the transmuting of the results of wrongdoing by making them the given framework of a new good. Instead of limiting ourselves to censure or admonition, however wisely and fairly put, can we also find ways to do something positive with the new situation, if necessary at some cost to ourselves? But if none of these lines is open, if we are baulked by intransigence and cannot communicate the truth, may we not have to make a stand, break, again perhaps at cost? Finally, it is clear that if decisions taken are going to affect people who have no say in making them, then an awareness of God, to whom all those involved are the completely known objects of his love, will challenge us to be as informed and imaginative about their real needs as we possibly can.

And when we are alone, what then? Not that we are ever alone, since (barring very exceptional situations) what we do with our selves, our time and resources, will have some effect, however indirect, on the lives of others. Here too the presence of God in joy, sorrow, forgiveness, and judgement constantly stirs us to a greater candour about ourselves, to a sense of responsibility for the hours and days in which he holds us in existence, for the care of body and mind, for the lighter as well as the more serious side of life. This kind of awareness was very much alive in the piety of a century ago. Unfortunately it was governed by a picture of God which, in the case of many at least, was a distorted one. They thought of God as critic and judge, as a presence which inevitably induced anxiety and fear, instead of as a friend and partner who was inviting us to share his loving and creative concern for our common situation, and who allowed us as his partners a real freedom of decision concerning what was best to be done.

They tended perhaps to think of him also as a God without joy. There is no need to subscribe to the exaggerated notion that our great-grandparents and their own immediate forebears were a universally grim lot who frowned on the most innocent high spirits. There is ample evidence that many of them did no such thing. But some undoubtedly (and these as the 'unco' guid' may have tended to set the tone of 'correct' piety) forgot that God could be happy. They knew that Jesus had pointed to the wild flowers of the Galilean countryside and re-marked that even Solomon in all his glory could not stand comparison with beauty like that; but they tended to forget that God felt the same. They knew that Jesus was attacked for enjoying a good meal and a drink, and that he made a joke of the criticism. But the idea that God might approve the enjoyment of food, drink, and even (save the mark!) of jokes seems to have passed them by. As for a universal openness to joy and beauty, such as the Creator might be supposed to have had in making the universe at all, this perhaps has never been a characteristic of many men and women in any generation. As human beings, it is true, we do need something to be happy about; but there is no reason why the list of things that can make us glad should be so limited. Convention, prejudice, weariness, preoccupation with our own troubles, desire for the security of the familiar, narrow down and down, as the years go by, the scope of our joys and admirations. To walk down a street with God then would be an unnerving experience – 'You don't mean to say that you find *that* "very good"?'

But if an awareness of the reality of God lets us in for an alarming increase of pleasures, it also exposes us to a more clamorous necessity of sacrifice. There are many things which men refuse to admit are evil, precisely because they could do something about them. Once God becomes real to us as our companion and partner here and now, and we begin to realize that he values and cares about every man's life as much as our own, then we are no longer able to ignore that such-and-such is an evil, and – what is worse – that it is within our power to help to overcome it. On the instant a host of reasons, some genuine and sensible, some excuses and rationalizations, some just plain lies, rush to our rescue. If we keep our awareness of the reality of God with us, then we shall be capable of sorting the valid from the invalid, and of facing whatever demands love's standards of goodness and justice may make upon us. As for the sacrifice itself, whatever it may be, here above all we know that God is with us:

> Christ leads me through no darker rooms
> Than he went through before;
> He that into God's kingdom comes
> Must enter by this door.

And if Christ, then God. That is the heart of the good news. To be alive to the reality of God is to be aware of his glorious foolishness, and of the infinite sufferings which make him the Father and friend of all the fools of love.

With this realisation comes a further transforming of our vision of life. For to be constantly with God is to be with all those others who keep the same company:

> He wants not friends that hath thy love,
> And may converse and walk with thee,
> And with thy saints here and above,
> With whom for ever I must be.

> In the communion of saints
> Is wisdom, safety and delight;
> And when my heart declines and faints
> It's raisèd by their heat and light.[1]

Indeed, a familiarity with the lives and thoughts of those for whom every hour was spent in an awareness of the true nature of God and of his presence can sometimes be of more help to us than our necessarily

---

[1] Both these verses and the one quoted in the previous paragraph are by Richard Baxter (1615–91), the brightest ornament of the English Puritan tradition.

more general understanding of God himself. But here a word of warning is needed. Merely to read and admire what others have been and done may lead to no solid achievement; in fact, by engaging our sympathy it may simply induce self-deception. Because we feel stirred by their goodness and courage, we fancy that at bottom we are already like them. If they are to help us, it will not be as figures in some other drama of which we are simply the spectators. It will be only in the same way as God himself changes us, namely as real and present men and women who also see our situation with the eyes and spirit of God. The question we need to ask about anyone whose qualities have won our admiration is: how do they see this? what is their response? This at once confronts us with the proper moral challenge; and it does so the more effectively because as the friends of God they are at all times in living relation with our condition. The question is not the one we might ask about a hero of fiction, 'What *would* he have done?' It is the one we can ask about any colleague or acquaintance; it is in the present tense, and is actual, not theoretical.

God does not love his saints more than he loves anyone else. The difference is that, living constantly in the awareness of him, they become people in whom he finds more joy and in whom his spirit is more clearly shown. Moreover, he is not more truly present to them than to others; it is just that they are aware of a presence which is the same for all. We are all continually in the immediate company of God whether we know it, whether indeed we like it or not. It is this fact which takes us straight into the heart of the matter of prayer.

If our lives are lived in the way just described, then there will be no need for anyone to argue us into the practice of private prayer. We shall need it and want it. To reflect on the day that has been spent with him, to sort out where we failed to keep pace, to see with his eyes, to act with his love, even though this means pain and regret; to ask his forgiveness for what has gone wrong, and to think what can be done about it; to thank him for the joy of what has been good, beautiful, and right, and most of all for the joy of himself with us at every moment; all this will be a help and a blessing not to be foregone for any consideration. But it should be quite obvious that where the remembrance of God as the third person in every encounter has never come to mind, where nothing has been seen at the time in this context, to try to create this awareness after all is past and done with, is bound to be heavy and artificial. No wonder at all, therefore, if the practice is more often than not neglected as producing no benefit proportionate to the effort required. Prayer, spontaneous, devoted prayer, is possible only to those who know the truth about human life and do their utmost never to forget it – the truth of the immediate and constant reality of God.

It must, however, be equally obvious that reflection based on the sense of such a relationship can never be concerned only, or even chiefly with oneself. The prime motive for attention to oneself is preoccupation, whether in joy, gratitude, sorrow, or concern, with the world around us and the people and other creatures in it. As we come increasingly to focus our love and understanding on them, directing our gaze to the objects on which God himself is concentrated, many remarkable changes take place in us unbeknown to ourselves. We become humble, because we cease to be egotistically modest; we become brave, because what has to be done overrides the daunting prospect of doing it; our habitual weaknesses begin to wither because they are crowded out; and what we could never hope to achieve by an introverted programme of self-improvement, however energetic, starts to happen behind our backs. Paradoxically, we find it easier to receive, because we are delighted with the kindness of the giver; we become more circumspect in giving, because we are less interested in our own merit, and more concerned with the real needs of the other person.

When, therefore, we turn in conscious partnership with God to quiet contemplation of all that has happened during the past day, more and more it is these others who occupy our thoughts. And because it is our keeping company with God which has made us aware of them in a new way, we feel more and more intensely the fact that he is perpetually present with them too, and that his eyes are always upon them for their good. Wherever they are, then, they are intimately close to us and we to them, because we are all in the same 'spiritual place'. This place is more truly a single place than any spot in physical space-time, nor is any distance, of however many hundreds of thousands of miles, as 'real' as this proximity. For this nearness is nearness to the eternal and indestructible God.

It is the sense of this nearness which lies at the root of prayer for other people. They, like ourselves, are under the eyes of the everlasting mercy, and by virtue of this fact they are under the eyes of our own love also; for it is in tune with this love, of which we are ever more conscious, and following its own gaze, that we ourselves love to any effect. When, therefore, we think of them in love at this place of nearness, it is through the presence of God with them that our love, in complete co-operation with the love of God, is brought to bear upon them. We remarked in an earlier chapter[1] that Christians had no right to expect any considerable number of miraculous 'interventions' in the regular functioning of the universe, because these regularities themselves are the necessary environment in which we grow towards freedom, understanding, and love; and any extensive interference with it would inhibit rather than encourage these divinely intended fulfilments of human existence. But this does not mean that effects of the most wonderful kind cannot be produced through the 'natural' endowments of the spirit when these are opened to the transforming love of God. If natural telepathy for example, can communicate ideas and feelings across half a world, as well attested cases suggest, then there is something, as yet imperfectly understood by us, some capacity of Man to be open to non-physical reality. Prayer is not telepathy; but at the natural level it may use this openness. For if our weak human affections can link up through seemingly impassable obstacles and separations, why should not the power of God's love, which at all times is immediately present to each one of us, penetrate the self, bringing strength, joy, healing, and fortitude, prompting to this or that action? When we and those for whom we pray are bound in the deepest possible personal union by the common reality of God, when our love for them and theirs for us are consciously in tune and harmony with his for us all, is it in any way incredible that the work of love should be done? That prayer, in short, should be 'answered'?

Certainly this is speculation. Certainly these are vague and simpleminded phrases, a groping in words after something half glimpsed, half guessed at. Nevertheless, they are in accord with the observed phenomena of the natural order, albeit on the outer frontier of the small province of that order as yet known to us, and they are most decidedly in accord with the fundamental truths which we know about God. In the view of the present writer, we shall not go far wrong if we think in general terms of the efficacy of intercessory and petitionary prayer along some such lines as these. It is to the openness of the human self to the power of divine love mediated through the activity of prayer that we may most reasonably attribute those cases of healing,

[1] Cf. p. 62 above.

guidance and inspiration, for many of which the evidence is so strong.

All that we can even conjecture about is, of course, the human side; of the way in which God 'functions' in his part of the relationship we can know nothing – and indeed, we do not need to know, once we have grasped that the essential thing, his goodwill, is a fact. The nub of the matter is that our love for the person prayed for is united with God's love for that same person, and communicated to them by God for their good. Once we have understood this, then certain troublesome points in the theory and practice of prayer are easier to resolve.

To take the practice first, it should be clear that many customary ways of interceding make no sense at all. The long effusions which mar too many 'prayer meetings' are quite irrelevant. If they serve any purpose at all, it is to clarify the mind of the petitioner on what he really is praying for (which should have been done before he spoke), or to edify the other people present. Frequent references to 'claiming the promises', sermonettes in parenthesis designed to stimulate faith or feeling – of course, there is nothing obnoxious in these things in themselves; but it does sometimes seem that they are treated as a necessary part of praying 'well'. In more formal settings or traditions the use of the 'collect' type of prayer, beginning with mention of some appropriate characteristic of God or of Christ before going on to the actual petition, serves the same purpose, and is equally superfluous. Both methods carry with them the insidious temptation to regard the speaking of suitable words as the essence of the act of prayer. And sadder still, many people follow the same procedure when praying on their own, in effect haranguing themselves, or wasting their attention on verbalizing that which most often does not need to be put into words at all. Similarly undesirable is the habit of working oneself up into a great emotional lather when praying, or inducing a sense of tremendous concentration in order to project, as it were, by sheer mental energy one's thoughts either up to God or over to the object of our prayer. There is a phrase, 'wrestling in prayer', which has an honourable history, but which is based on a misapprehension. Sometimes, it must be said with regret, such wrestling or 'praying with power' is pure self-indulgence, and a sign that the attention is directed not to God or the person prayed for but to one's own magnificent spiritual performance. Once we have grasped clearly what we are doing when we pray for others, we shall see that the most important requirement by far is inner calmness and tranquillity. We are not engaged in creating or producing anything, but in becoming aware of what is already the fact, namely that God is immediately and intimately present both to ourselves and to the ones for whom we are praying. Our task is to hold the awareness of this fact in the still centre of our being, to unite our love for them with God's love, in the quiet but total confidence that he will use our love to help bring about the good in them which we both desire. In technical terms, therefore, intercession is a form of that kind of prayer known as 'contemplation', with the special feature that here we contemplate not God in himself but God in his relationship of love towards those whom we also love; and on the basis of our partnership with him we entrust our love into his hands to be used in harness with his own for their benefit.

If we bear this character of prayer in mind, some of the theoretical problems that surround it may become easier to resolve. Jesus' own teaching on prayer cannot be used to support the simplistic view that any request made in faith will be granted. Gethsemane shows that. So far as praying for others is concerned, if we stop to think for half a minute, we shall realize that we would not want this to be true anyway. It assumes that what we ask will always be the best thing for the person concerned; and it totally ignores any wishes they may have in the matter. In other words, it exaggerates our own understanding and right to freedom and minimizes theirs, to say nothing of God's. In any petitionary prayer for people, three personal beings are involved, and what happens as a result will emerge from the interplay of all of them; it is not to be conceived in terms of mechanism or physical action. This is the old primitive desire for magic raising again its sub-human, and even on occasion demonic head. God is not going to emit some sort of ray, and hey presto! the patient jumps up cured or converted.

This, of course, prompts us to rush at once to the opposite conclusion. We will not interpose our own wishes at all; we will leave it all to God, who must know best what is needed, and will simply pray, 'Thy will be done.' But this will not do either. In the first place, love does not function like that. It does not content itself with wishing 'the best' in the abstract for those it loves. Its very intimacy means that it thinks in terms of actual needs and hopes. Even where it is perplexed, the perplexity relates to specific possibilities. When, therefore, we pray in love for someone, these particular wishes or doubts are the form which our prayer is bound to take. Secondly, a mere blank cheque to God fails to do justice to God's own relationship with the person prayed for. Because they are what they are, that relationship can grow in some directions but not in others. If our interest is serious, therefore, we shall be praying not just for some abstract good to be done to them or for them, but for the constructive personal developments which are appropriate to them and which they alone can make.

Serious intercession always seeks to express itself in personal and specific terms. Are these ideas there just to be overruled or ignored, if they do not coincide with God's wiser knowledge of what is 'best'? This is how many people think of the matter, but to do so is to relapse once more into an external and impersonal conception. These particular requests of ours spring from the common life we share with those for whom we pray; they are the concrete articulation at the conscious level of the unseen but real bond that unites us. Because that bond is a living one of mutual influence, they do not merely state the possibilities to which we suppose the other person might be open. They help to create an openness for these things. When, therefore, through this natural medium of our psychical communion the love of God is brought to bear on the other person, its power works within the existing potentials, and thus issues in those very changes (or ones akin to them) for which we have asked. In this way human freedom is respected, human co-operation with God is made real, and yet prayer is genuinely answered. Because the relationship is truly personal throughout, there are no automatic fulfilments. There may be obstacles which even the love of God cannot, or cannot yet overcome. But equally there is no reason to doubt that if, as happens especially often when the human relationship is close and deep and alive with the genuine spirit of Christ, what is prayed for comes to pass, then the prayer has indeed helped to bring about what men by themselves could never have done – and what even God could not have done without our aid. It may seem incredible, even blasphemous to some, to suggest such a thing. But if we reflect on the great human destinies of freedom, understanding, and love, which God designed, and which he will always respect, then it not only ceases to be incredible, it becomes probable. Moreover, that living communion at the unconscious level which all mankind undoubtedly enjoys, even though contemporary individualistic western Man has forgotten it, is now seen to have not merely a natural but a supernatural purpose. Like so many other aspects of the created order it proves to have a special relevance not only to this age but to the age to come. It has its part to play in the kingdom.[1]

Fundamental to true prayer, therefore, are a genuine concern for others, a respect for and knowledge of what they are, and as great a degree as possible of contact with them. This means that prayer for others, like every other kind, has its roots in and draws its strength from the quality of our whole life. Writers on prayer have always stressed the importance of what they call 'remote preparation', by which is meant the creating in our everyday living of a situation and state of mind in which prayer can be living and effective. The cultivation of an awareness of the reality of God at all times, which was described earlier, is an example of this. The same principle applies forcibly to intercessory prayer. If we want to be able to help others in this way, then we have to take trouble to be 'in touch' with them; and, what is more, in touch at a level of sincerity and concern which will help to open the other person to love and truth. And this is yet another of the factors which make all prayer a creative judgement on our own life.

Does this mean, then, that there is no point in praying for victims of distant wars, or world statesmen, and suchlike? Not necessarily, though it may suggest that our priorities in prayer are likely to be those people and causes with which we are in touch, or with which we might be in touch, if we were not so unimaginative and idle. But there are two quite simple reasons why we should not arbitrarily restrict the objects of our prayer to the family circle or the parish pump. The first is, that if we have any ordinary human feelings at all it will be impossible to do so. If we care about those injured or homeless as the result of an earthquake in Iran or a bush fire in Australia, we shall want to pray about them; and no theories of the how of prayer can have sufficient substance to justify our saying that such matters do not fall within our assignment. If we care, genuinely, then no one can stop us from loving and suffering with God over this cause. The real danger is that caring about distant and colossal disasters is too easy. We feel harrowed,

[1] If what has been argued in this section has any substance, then there is no need to play complicated games with Time and Predestination, as so many defenders of intercessory prayer have felt it necessary to do. The idea of God foreseeing all the prayers ever made, and programming history to take account of them, is not only remote in its sophisticated intellectualism from the Gospel, it also relies in the last analysis on a falsely deterministic view of the method of God's operation.

especially when the misery but not the whole difficult fact of the situation is dramatized for us by television or journalism, and a pity springs up within us which is hardly ever awakened by the small agonies down our own street. In praying for needs that have no point of contact with our own experience all that we have to do is to *feel*. To have no feeling would be an even worse state; but merely to feel is still very far from the self-forgetting and sacrifice that mark the response of love – indeed, precisely because our own feeling is the staple ingredient of the prayer in such a case, that prayer tends to self-absorption and self-indulgence. Prayer for the distant and unknown, therefore, has to be conducted with great humility, with eyes open and will ready to act in any way at all that may be helpful, and with the expectation that our being thus drawn into the fringe of one great need may prompt us to new ideas of what we can do in our own circle of work and contact. The second reason is this. It may seem to me, with my modern limitations of individualism and rationalism, that I have no natural unity with the victims of flood or famine in Bengal or Bihar. But this may not be true. The very fact of common humanity may be a link at the deepest level of the psyche which not only can be put at the disposal of the love of God but which fulfils its greatest potential only in so doing. Moreover, when the mesh of human relations is spread so far as it is today, we can often find one point of personal contact at least through which, however distantly, our love and practical concern can be linked to the network of which the central object of prayer – be it a national leader, soldiers in a war, mentally retarded children, a nation invaded – is part. The fact that our contact may be at a hundred removes from the apparently 'important' person or situation is of no significance. All concerned are in the immediate presence of God, and the simultaneous objects of his love; and so what might seem to be help so remote as to be useless is, when harnessed to God, as directly in touch as the prayer of a wife or mother or lifelong friend.

Finally on this topic, a word about prayer for the dead. If this were, as it is sometimes conceived to be, simply a request to God to alter or remit a judicial sentence, it would indeed be a misguided and pointless proceeding. If, however, we bear in mind what was said about judgement, purgatory, hell, and heaven in an earlier chapter,[1] it becomes what so many find it, a compellingly natural thing to do. That which we are, God has made and sustains; and this includes the continuum of

[1] Cf. pp. 287–294 above.

our human relationships. Why should we suppose that he who upholds us through and beyond death will denature us by stripping out this essential part of our being? In the fourth century Paulinus of Nola, writing to his friend and tutor Ausonius, rejects such an idea in a poem of classic but heartrending simplicity:

> I, through all chances that are given to mortals,
>   And through all fates that be,
> So long as this close prison shall contain me,
>   Yea, though a world shall sunder me and thee,
>
> Thee shall I hold, in every fibre woven,
>   Not with dumb lips, nor with averted face
> Shall I behold thee, in my mind embrace thee,
>   Instant and present, thou, in every place.
>
> Yea, when the prison of this flesh is broken,
>   And from the earth I shall have gone my way,
> Where'er the pole our common Father stay me,
>   There shall I bear thee, as I do today.
>
> Think not the end, that from my body frees me,
>   Breaks and unshackles from my love to thee;
> Triumphs the soul above its house in ruin,
>   Deathless, begot of immortality,
>
> Still must she keep her senses and affections,
>   Hold them as dear as life itself to be.
> Could she choose death, then might she choose forgetting:
>   Living, remembering, to eternity.[1]

And if this continuum is there, why should we imagine that God's love and truth will not still make use of it, as they did before, to find their way into the heart of those for whom we pray, judging, purifying, transforming by joining forces with our love for them, coming in its company, being welcomed on its surety? So long as the personal identity exists, and stands in the presence of God, prayer makes sense; and death sets the person praying and the one prayed for no farther

---

[1] Helen Waddell, *Mediaeval Latin Lyrics*, p. 47, where the Latin text will also be found. Miss Waddell's translation is here printed with one change. In v. 3 l. 3 she wrote: 'Wheresoe'er in the wide universe I stay me'; the present writer's literal version, though crude by comparison, has been substituted simply because it renders the theological point which Paulinus explicitly made, and which, as we have seen, is the crucial one. It is our 'common Father' (*communis Pater*) whose love makes our continuance in communion possible.

apart than they were in this life. While it is true, therefore, that Time in the everyday meaning of the word has no relevance in the encounter of the person beyond death with God, and that the old pious stories of souls whose stay in purgatory was shortened by the intercession of their holy friends on earth cannot be taken literally, they can be taken seriously. Indeed, they must; for in their pictorial idiom they express a very dear truth, namely that by love's continuing prayer those who have gone before us can be assisted in their inner growth from glory to glory to find their fulfilment in God.[1]

That help should come in the reverse direction also, and that those who have died should in their turn help us by their prayers is as little surprising. The more their capacity for love is purified and deepened by God's own love and truth, the more effective indeed we would expect their co-operation with God on our behalf to be. But the notion of asking them to obtain specific requests from God for us has little to commend it. God's care is already so great, and shown to be so, that there can be no reason for not making our request to him direct; nor can any human holiness add weight to a prayer, when God is much more ready to respond to the petition of the worst man who ever lived than even the best man can ever be to make one. In this crude form, therefore, the custom of asking the prayers of the saints will not stand up. But it is one of the joys of the Gospel that their prayer for us and their joint-prayer with us are always active to make us more alive and open to the reality of God, and more at home where we should be most at home – with them and him.

Having said thus much, it will be necessary to touch only briefly on the question of prayer for and by ourselves. Not that there is ever such a thing as prayer concerned only with ourselves. If we 'pray' with any such exclusive concentration, then what we are doing is not 'prayer'. Prayer is conscious attention to our involvement with God; and since he sees us and is related to us in the truth of our situation or not at all, prayer which does not attend to that truth is not prayer. The fundamental truth of being a human person is, as we saw early on, that our self exists only in relationship with other persons, experienced or re-membered; and therefore proper attention to our own condition must mean awareness of our relationships, with a great sense of indebtedness

[1] By the same token, however, there is obviously no justification whatever for ideas of shortening time spent in purgatory by the mechanical recitation of devotions, the purchase of indulgences, or any other sub-personal means.

and humility for the gift of existence which under God they have bestowed upon us. It is not altruistic idealism but plain objective fact that we owe our genuinely personal existence as much to our enemies as to our friends, to the critical and difficult and unfeeling as much as to the sympathetic and encouraging and helpful. Perhaps indeed we owe them more, since, unless we have the misfortune to be seriously psychologically deprived, antagonism stimulates the growth of inner resources and keeps us alive, where comfortable people allow us to drift and atrophy. To consider our self in relationship with God, therefore, is to consider that self in its whole human setting, with its loves, hopes, fears and responsibilities. What we seek in such prayer is a true understanding of our role in that setting as God's partner, child, brother, and friend.

Hence this kind of prayer sends us to the task of deepening our general insight into the character and values of God and the truth of the human condition. For this every kind of serious and honest material will be apposite. In literature it will include poetry, fiction, history, biography, books about the world and its cultures, every kind of science, as well as specifically religious writing. If we are not inclined to much reading, then television, radio, journalism, and sensible conversation; art, music, drama, keeping pets, voluntary social work, leisure occupations that make demands upon us and bring us into touch with a wider variety of people – all these things and many more help to open ourselves to the world. And if, but only if, we remember that it is God's world then the world becomes the Word. Presentations of reality which are already religiously oriented are helpful only to start us thinking, to help us to see existence from a new angle, to stir in us new responses of the heart. If we rely on them too much, we absorb our conclusions pre-digested, we cease to be ourselves, and adopt a pose, even if a congenial one. What we need is the opportunity to grow into our own conclusions, and to test them as we go against the reality of life in a world which we know to be God's world.

It is this openness to reality in the context of God which equips us for one of the permanent and vital elements of prayer, the Bible. We shall find truth in Scripture in proportion to the experience and understanding of existence that we bring to it. This is the application, at the individual level, of the principle set out in the previous chapter, and of the general basis of prayer and worship with which the present one began. But what would this involve in practice? Without going into wearisome detail, the following suggestions may be useful.

On the conventional method of using the Bible in prayer we take a short section, study it, perhaps with notes, think about it, and try to extract from it a relevant lesson. This tends to be a rather inefficient method, in the sense that the proportion of passages which come alive to us is often rather low. Instructions on prayer normally ascribe this to failures on our part, or to natural difficulties such as tiredness and preoccupation, or occasionally and for some to periods of dryness which occur from time to time in the slow maturing of the spiritual self. Certainly, these are all operative factors; but the list leaves out the commonest of all reasons for a blank lack of response to Scripture, namely that the passage in question means nothing to us, because there is nothing in our own experience to give it meaning. Whether we take our series of sections for consideration from a course or anthology, prepared for the purpose, or simply start at the beginning of a biblical book and work straight through makes little difference. The chances of a meeting of minds between the scriptural writer and ourselves are equally random.

The practice already recommended of increasing our scope either by direct or by vicarious experience is one step towards dealing with this. An intense interest in life in all its forms, and a constant endeavour to see it in the context of God, must multiply the number of points of contact. A further obvious practical step is to familiarize ourselves with the contents of the Bible in a less concentrated way. Many of our fore-fathers simply read the Bible as a book, two or three chapters a day; and one noticeable result of this was that after a time more and more situations in life began to call to mind scriptural echoes and analogies. Before we can hope to sip the Bible like wine, we need to drink it like beer. Anyone who wishes to be able to pray effectively with short passages would therefore be well advised to spend a year or two simply reading it. At various points, undoubtedly, he will be brought up short by some sentence or story which speaks to him as true, which brings ideas into focus, and which thereby places his own experience clearly and firmly in the light of God. When he does, that is the time to stop, ponder, and make the insight his own, with any decisions for action that may occur to him. But if such times are rare, this does not matter. It is no use being in a hurry, or straining for results. God's seed

grows secretly. If we try to change ourselves at once by tearing messages from our reading by brute force, we shall achieve nothing. Any
morals we draw are likely to be purely superficial, clever notions from
the top of our head, and quite unrepresentative of any fundamental
attitude. When, however, we have become broadly familiar with the
whole, we shall be able to move on to a new stage. Then our current
situation will begin to prompt us to turn to particular areas of Scripture
where, as we recall, the material may be helpful. We go back, let us
say, to one of the Epistles; we find that it makes sense, and, what is
more, from the point at which we see eye to eye with the writer we are
now led on by his argument. From our common ground he has
developed a train of thought which we too can follow along a parallel
track of our own. He may, of course, lose us quite quickly; but it will
be surprising if, before he does, we have not enlarged our own vision of
life under God. This stage is likely to last most of our lives. Only great
experience, and great spiritual wisdom, will equip us to open the Bible
at any point and find some relevant enlightenment. But we shall come
nearer and nearer to this condition.

The reason why the Bible will not disappoint us, if we approach it
gently in this way, is quite simply that it is the product of such a
variety of people all striving to see life as the kingdom of God, and, in
the case of the New Testament, working out this vision in terms of
Jesus Christ and of the traditions about him deriving from those who
knew him at first hand. We, in our generation, will see implications
which they could never have known. That is one of the things which
we mean when we say that life in Christ is a matter of the 'spirit' and
not of the 'letter'. The Bible prompts us to see things for ourselves in
the new way, with God's eyes. Because the world is God's world, the
word of Scripture is God's Word to us.

This Word is also the safest way to a knowledge of ourselves. Just as
contact with people who have the mind of Christ challenges our values
and visions, so does contact with the people whose adventure of faith
the Bible records. We grow into a free and spontaneous dissatisfaction
with this or that aspect of our own lives. This is a much better and more
effective form of penitence than the anxious scrutiny of our conduct
carried out with a check-list of sins. There are, of course, enough
thoughts and words and acts in our lives already of which there is no
need for the Bible to tell us to be ashamed. But the Scripture helps us to
deal with these in a more radical way, by fostering a positive vision of

life in which they become steadily more intolerable to us, and therefore more spontaneously avoided.

A private regimen of this kind bears fruit in another way. It makes more and more of the Scripture used in the worship of the Church meaningful. The lessons, the Epistle and Gospel at the Eucharist, begin to come home to us. Even sermons may start to make sense, especially if they are preached on the lines suggested in the previous chapter. It is, incidentally, much to be wished that preachers would be more content with planting ideas which their hearers could take away and develop for themselves, rather than elaborating finished arguments which set out only what the Scripture has said to the preacher himself. By the time the congregation has struggled to follow him along his personal pilgrimage – and failed, more often than not, because his private experience is not theirs – the starting-point, from which they might have taken their own step forward, has been forgotten.

We thus come back by a natural progression to the corporate worship of the community. Here two factors are at work: what is said, and what is done. The Word of God is present not merely in words but in actions, and in one pre-eminent action, that of Jesus himself. It was once remarked to the writer that when a certain priest, in the course of celebrating the Eucharist, came to the words of institution, he seemed not to be reciting a set form of prayer but 'telling a friend with wonder of an event at which he had been present'. Ever since the second century A.D. at the latest, what Jesus said over the bread and wine at the Last Supper, what he did with them, has figured at the heart of the eucharistic rite.

Sometimes, however, the ideas behind this centrality have been tragically mistaken – a complete misunderstanding, indeed, of Jesus's own wish. As we remarked earlier,[1] the command, 'Do this in remembrance of me', cannot originally have meant, 'Repeat the words, "This is my body" – "This is my blood".' These were once-for-all words intended to establish the symbolism of the action, to define it as a representation of Jesus' death for mankind. What he asked his friends to do was to distribute the bread and wine among themselves with prayer of blessing and thanksgiving to God – blessing and thanksgiving for the reality which the action represented. This reality, the saving death, had completely and fundamentally altered the situation of all

[1] Cf. p. 237 above.

men everywhere. It had, in ways which we have been investigating throughout this book, liberated them for a life of freedom, under-standing, and love, in accord with the truth of their existence. On this side of Good Friday and Easter nothing could ever be the same again.

Hence the Eucharist is not, never can be, a re-enactment of the Last Supper. The Supper was before things were changed, and it looked ahead to the event which was to change them. We celebrate that event; we celebrate it in God's presence, praying that what the event has done for us and for all mankind may bear its proper fruit in the transforma-tion of human lives and the setting up of God's sovereignty. And we celebrate it in the only possible way, namely, by using that symbolic representation of the event which Jesus himself created. Consequently, the status of the story of the Last Supper in the eucharistic rite is first of all a narrative and directive one. It explains why we do this, and the meaning of what we do. The words of institution do not have a magical force, changing the bread and wine into some new mystical reality.

But this is not all there is to be said. For the command to 'do this' was not just to pray, to break, to bless, but also to take, eat and drink. This second part of the action has two meanings, both of which stem from the fact of intimate fellowship with Jesus himself. First, because the eating and drinking together which in all ages and cultures has been a natural sign of unity and brotherhood is an eating and drinking of the symbols of the Cross, we affirm by this that our brotherhood with Jesus and with each other is possible only on the terms of the Cross, and thus we pledge ourselves to those terms of sacrificial loyalty to the good in love. Secondly, because eating and drinking is the indispensable natural means of receiving and preserving life, the eating and drinking of the symbols of the Cross declares that it is through the Cross alone that we receive the necessities of our true life – forgive-ness for our past, the spirit of love for our present, confidence for our future, both now and in eternity. But these two meanings also belong, as does the narrative and directive aspect of the story, to this side of the Resurrection. We are not engaged in a mere exercise of imagination, reconstructing Golgotha with its crowds of long-dead Jews and Romans, its vanished Jerusalem, as though we were transported back to A.D. 30. We are faced with the fact that the liberating power of the Cross is a reality bringing heaven to the earth of 1970, as it will to that of 19070, if the world lasts that long. The Jesus who has inspired in us this pledge, has given us this new life, has welcomed us as his brothers and sisters, is not the dead hero of an old saga, but the living companion of our present existence. (We saw in our examination of the Resurrection narratives[1] how the Gospels express this in the stories of Jesus' presiding at the fellowship meal after his rising from the dead.) Moreover, he is thus present with the family of God not on a purely individualistic basis, but as the head of a community; and it is by making the Eucharist at Jesus' direction a corporate act that we acknowledge our inescapable need of each other, our dependence on each other, our devotion to each other.

It is clear that in such a rite the mechanistic, the magical, the sub-personal has no place. To try to safeguard the centrality of the Cross by elaborating some theory – transubstantiation, consubstantiation, real presence – which will identify the bread and wine as 'actually' the body and blood broken and shed only tends to defeat the whole purpose of the action by making reception of the sacrament the vital necessity for Man, not openness to the spirit of Jesus in his sacrifice. Moreover, such theories blur the fact that 'things are different now', that the Cross really has changed the whole human situation. Likewise, if we speak of the celebrant as *alter Christus*, a 'second Christ', we do away with the ever-new sufficiency of the primal event, and sub-stitute for it a piece of magic; for since the celebrant unquestionably does not have that identification with God's sacrificial love which alone made Jesus the wellspring of life for men, what he does has on this interpretation no organic personal relationship with what he is, and can be only a feat which he is enabled to perform by some external power. Certainly, a priest who is sensible of the infinite privilege delegated to him on behalf of the people of God will be moulded by it, as every man is by his calling and circumstances. He will become for ever something which he could never have been if this were not his vocation. But what he becomes is not Jesus, but the servant of Jesus, and himself needs and receives healing and transformation through what he does. Participation in this act is essentially a matter of the mind and heart.

It is the sense of this which above all creates true worship. For worship, as we saw, is to pay the due honour, to acknowledge the truth about the object of worship. Because the Sacrament operates

[1] Cf. p. 264f. above.

in the realm of the personal, in the understanding mind and heart alive to what God is doing, we find that *in the Eucharist to receive what God has to offer is to give him what is his due.* To know what we receive is to know that this is God's offering of himself freely through human death to bring us joy; therefore to value this is to value not some extrinsic gift but God himself as he is. Rightly then is this Sacrament called 'Eucharist', 'thanksgiving'. Rightly too the Christian Church has insisted that no other form of religious act is worship in so complete and essential a sense. For all other rituals and forms of devotion are our attempts to express our response to God's gifts. This alone is gift and response in one.

This celebration of the crucified and living God is at home any-where in Man's Here and Now, for it is that Here and Now with which God is concerned. Hence the Eucharist is at home in the factory canteen, on the kitchen table, in the napalm-scorched bunker, by the hospital bed, in the centre of the sports arena, as it will be in the space-craft or on any distant planet to which men may come. This is not the secularization of God but the sacralization of Man. That is why the Eucharist can never be converted into just another meal. It is not the universal sign of human brotherhood, eating together, given ultimate value; for Man's symbols of fellowship, like his fellowship itself, are imperfect. They can never command our total loyalty and veneration, for they are ours, and we know that we are not worthy of worship. This symbol is the medium not of our marred and inade-quate existence, but of God's perfect dedication to the Good in love. As such it must preserve its distinctive reality by clothing this in distinctive form; and the right and obvious form is that which the In-carnate God bestowed upon it. By preserving the slightly unfamiliar, the deliberately hieratic and traditional rite of the sacred words and the unleavened bread and the wine we confess the truth without which there is no hope: that we cannot save ourselves, because we are en-slaved to lovelessness. God saves us by the act in which he makes us free to love.

Let us then keep this simple action for what it is, the world's heart that beats to eternal life. Let us honour it with all the wealth the world affords. Let the cathedrals soar, let art and music wait upon it and feel themselves privileged. If we are truly honouring it for what it is, we shall never in order to honour it deprive the poor and the hungry, the sick and the despairing, we shall never lift gun or bayonet against our brother. These crimes are compatible indeed with the distorted self-regard that finds religious satisfaction in gorgeous externals. They will never be compatible with worship in spirit and in truth. If only truth be there, if the kingdom comes, then with an undoubting and untroubled heart we can give due honour to this eternal moment of Man.

Postscript
The Simple Truth

THE TRUTH is not hard to put into words. It is not necessary to have a degree in philosophy or science, or to have taken a course in the history and culture of the ancient world in order to understand it. To a large extent the gigantic labours of theologians down the Christian centuries have been spent on resolving problems not in the Gospel but in the complications which men have made of the Gospel. The present work, like every other, suffers from this predicament. It is far too long for all that really needs to be said; but it is not long enough to justify the saying of it, in view of that very human amalgam of good, evil, and plain mistake which constitutes the Christian past.

This disproportion means that the thing which most needs to be said, and which can be said to any kind of people in any language, is buried under the justifications and explanations. It is as if one were to sink a huge mine to excavate some valuable mineral – and then, as it was brought to the surface, pile the waste from the excavation on top of it. At the end of a book like this it is important to stop and to ask: What does it all amount to? This chapter tries to say just that in the most straightforward possible way. The author would therefore ask his reader to allow him to abandon the impersonal conventions of literature, and to set out in the first person the faith which this book has been, as much as anything, an attempt to clarify.

I believe that there is indeed a God. He is eternal; no one created him, but to him everything there is owes its existence. He alone is responsible for the way things are, and he gave them their nature and being out of sheer love. This was no unfulfilled longing, so that he needed to make something on which to lavish his affection. All the giving and receiving of life and joy which we find in our many kinds of

love for each other he has always known in himself, to a degree and
with a perfection beyond our imagining. How we are to describe this
does not really matter. We can be certain that it must be so, because he
made some of his creatures at least to find their joy in just this kind of
existence. For these, life has three special goals: understanding, freedom, and love. It has meaning only to the extent that they move and
strive to achieve these conditions, all of which depend on one another.
To become aware of them, and to attain them, in however small a
degree, is to be in the image of God; for they are the heart of his own
nature.

The world God has made can be understood by us, and we have both
a duty and a need to understand it. Thus he puts his blessing on all the
sciences and arts of Man. In proportion to our understanding of things,
both outside and within ourselves, we have the chance to become free
and the means to do good. But the very regularities of the world
which make it possible for us to understand it also mean that no one in
his lifetime can avoid either enduring or causing pain. I believe that
God intended this, because without the possibility of pain there could
be no courage or adventure, no doing good for its own sake, no loyalty,
no concern or responsibility for others, no sacrifice, no self-forgetting –
and without self-forgetting there could not even be happiness. Happiness and love spring from the same root, the surrender of the self. This
surrender is not something which can be enjoined on us by reason,
wisdom, common sense. No argument can prove to me that I ought to
put someone else's need before my own. I am left to make a naked
choice, the choice for or against love as the law of life.

The qualities in the world which make love possible also open the
door to evil; and it is this which makes freedom a necessity for us. We
see easily that the man who is ignorant or afraid is enslaved, and will do
harm. It is imperative both for himself and for others that he should
become free. But slavery is also the lot of the man who lives by wisdom,
for in the end he has no means of making the most important decision of
all, the decision in principle for or against love. Like a man in a night-
mare he wants to wake up, but all his efforts are of no avail; he cannot
decide his own fate, but sinks back into the grip of something which
sweeps him along to its own dénouement. 'Prudence dictates . . .', we
say, and we are right. It is because the one who loves is a fool that he is
free. Who would make himself vulnerable, open to be cheated, mocked,
betrayed, slandered, robbed, hurt, killed, if he had any sense? No one.

cc

And so long as we accept this as an overriding argument, we are enslaved. God has made a world in which he who loves absolutely and he who loves so far as good sense permits must both suffer; but to the fool who loves absolutely the general possibility of suffering has a point, to the man of sense it has none. God, it would seem, is on the side of the fools of love.

But there is something else which this foolishness can do which all the ingenuity of wisdom cannot. It can turn evil into good. There is evil that stalks abroad and sickens every man's stomach. There is also evil so in tune with the spirit of an age that only the truly good suffer when they see it. Particular forms of Man's cruelty, greed, and arrogance may pass in and out of fashion, be checked or allowed by law. But the capacity of the human being for evil in general does not change. There is no 'progress', because progress here depends on the individual and his growth towards understanding, freedom, love. Each generation, each single life has to begin again, and to decide for itself what is good in its inheritance, what it will keep, what it will change. Therefore the battle to eradicate evil ebbs and flows, it can never be decisively and finally won, while the world lasts. But if we cannot win this kind of victory, there is another kind which we can win, for it rests entirely with the individual and his willingness for sacrifice. This is the victory of forgiveness, which takes the results of evil, and without a backward glance of self-pity or resentment, makes them the raw material of a new good. It is as if one were born to this condition, and yet it is greater than that. For someone who is born blind or deformed may be sorry for himself or resent his fate, but the forgiving person will not. In this way evil in the heart is rooted out, evils of circumstance become the means to a good life, and the evil of despair in the guilty is taken away. But this can be done only by those who, however much they respect the just rights of others, refuse to let mere justice dictate their own feelings or conduct. They obey only the absolute and universal law of love, whose fools they are.

And if God is on their side, then he himself must be one of them. For love cannot be explained; you cannot give lessons in it. You either 'see' what it is about or you do not; you either catch its spirit or you go through life without it. You cannot imitate it, or do its works as a duty. It has to be spontaneous, a free commitment. If therefore God has made the world an arena for love, then he himself is a lover. This means that he is vulnerable – not by nature, as we are to help us discover love, but by deliberate choice, that is, by love itself which must be the heart of his own being. It means that he is one who forgives utterly, and who uses all the results of evil as the means to a new good.

There was a man, a Jew named Jesus, born in the Roman province of Syria during the reign of Augustus. Something over thirty years later, when Tiberius was on the throne, the Romans executed him by crucifixion on the orders of the procurator of Judaea, Pontius Pilate, probably at the instigation of the Jews themselves. This man had grasped the essential truth about human life in a way that no other man in history has ever done, completely and exactly. He saw the world as the kingdom of a God who loves, a Father whom each human being can address as such, intimately and affectionately. For him, therefore, the men and women who had the stamp of God upon them, who were recognizably members of God's family, were those whose lives were dominated by the two requirements of the law of love: to try to meet the needs of one's fellow-men by doing what was truly best for them, and to forgive all the evil done to oneself, whatever the cost might be. This meant sacrifice and suffering, and nothing else would meet the demands of human life. Hence he taught that anyone who sincerely wished to follow him in living by the truth must carry on his back at all times the stake of his own execution. This challenge confronted all men, and it was urgent. The time was short. For his own nation, eaten up with self-righteousness and self-pity, and set on a suicidal policy of hate, it had almost run out; for each individual, with no notion of the hour when his life would be required of him, it was at its end here and now. In the demand of the truth which Jesus proclaimed, the sovereignty of God was already standing across the path of each individual, compelling him to give his answer. On the right answer ultimate fulfilment and happiness depended; but that right answer was an acceptance now of tears, poverty, hunger, rejection.

From this answer Jesus himself never shrank. He declared the truth entrusted to him, plainly and without qualification; but he wept for those who rejected it. He gave up the security of his home and trade; he forwent the joy and fulfilment of marriage and children. He used every gift he possessed in order to meet men's needs, to rescue them from sickness of mind and body. He forgave his enemies to the uttermost, using their cruelty as the given means of loyalty to the Good. And he refused to compromise the Good to save himself from a horrible death, even when that death seemed to mean the total defeat of the cause of God to which his life had been dedicated. And in all this he was an ordinary man, with an ordinary man's fatigue and desolation of spirit, an ordinary man's natural shrinking from torture and execution.

But though he died a failure, in his own eyes and in the eyes not only of the world but even of his friends and family, he was vindicated, and his message declared to be the truth. For on the third day God raised him from the dead. I believe this not just because of the experiences of those who had known him and lost him, and who now found him again in a new and transfigured life, experiences which it clearly strained all the resources of their words to convey; but chiefly because his teaching, which they had never been able to accept, and which his death had seemed finally to refute, also lived again in power, and laid hold on them never to let go. This is the inexplicable thing. Hallucinations might have solaced grief for their friend and master. Something more was needed to turn upside down their whole scale of values, to re-lay the moral foundations of their lives, and to transform them into the fools of love, the apostles of the Cross.

Nevertheless, if they were the heralds of a creed of suffering, they were remarkably happy about it. The reason is not far to seek. The vindication of Jesus was not just a vindication of him as an individual. It confirmed the yearnings, the conjectures, the hopes so apparently ridiculous that men were half-ashamed to acknowledge them. More than we dared believe is in fact true. For this was not the resuscitation of a corpse; it was the gift, to a man who had died, of a life of new and unimagined glory. This only God could have done; and if he thought it right to do it for this man alone out of all the men who have ever lived, then what this man said, what he was, is the truth. There is a God. More than that, there is a Father, and it is

Love which moves the sun and the other stars

– forgiving, suffering, sacrificial love.

This is not something mooted for the first time. It is not that, while reason could prove that there is a Mind behind the Universe, now we know that there is a Heart as well. That is a false notion of the matter. All our thoughts about God are conjectures, and those conjectures, before the time of Jesus, had already envisaged a God of love as a possibility. Now we can be sure that this possibility is the right one. Yet the change brought about by the first Easter is still not a proof in the ordinary sense, namely that if we can understand the words used, and can think clearly, we are forced to admit the conclusion. It is a proof on one condition. It carries conviction only to those who are willing to be the fools of love, who feel in their heart of hearts that, however far their own performance may fall short, sacrificial love is the highest of all values, the only thing which has a just claim to be the absolute and universal law of life. If I cannot accept this, then the whole affair remains an irrelevant enigma.

When, however, I do accept it, what God has done and the manner of his doing it increase my wonder and gratitude. For this means that God leaves me my freedom. He does not wish to overwhelm me, to batter me into submission. Somewhere within me, however choked and starved, there is this natural endowment of sacrificial love that comes from my blessed solidarity with all living things, and with the myriad ages of creatures who have gone before me and brought me to birth. If this perilously feeble flame can breathe and blaze up, it will enlighten me from within to see clearly, and to know where God is to be found – in Jesus.

Jesus, then, was not only right; he was the agent of God's truth, as he claimed to be. No hero, king, or sage can pretend to one smallest fraction of the honour due to this man. And why? Because through him all the immemorial fears – the fear that life might be built on nothingness or be the plaything of demonic forces – are destroyed for ever:

We venerate thy Cross, O Lord, and praise and glorify thy holy Resurrection; for by virtue of the Cross joy has come to the whole world.

His achievement transforms all the most fundamental aspects of human life. It unites the human race; for it is now by virtue of being Man that we acquire our only solid value. It enables us to hold up our heads for the first time. Every man, if he is honest about his life, knows that in face of the abstract ideal of goodness he stands condemned. Now, however shameful his own story, he has something to be proud of. Mankind has produced one man who did not merely *know* or *teach* (though that would have been a great thing) but *lived* the good. I am proud to be human not because of my own history or that of the race – I know too well what these have been – but because of Jesus; and I claim the right to exist not for what I am in myself but as his brother. Nay more, I know that that right now belongs to all men on the same grounds, however evil they may be; and in the transfiguring joy and liberation given to me without any effort of my own I find myself committed to love and forgiveness as the true law of human relations. Believing what I do, not to forgive would be the lie in the soul, the ultimate treachery which would put me, as nothing else could, beyond the pale of humanity, and would finally extinguish within me the free fire of genuine personal existence. For a man can rightly give away only what belongs to him. If I am willing to give away everything, even life itself, in order to forgive and to love – then that life is indeed my own. By drawing me into the kingdom of love Jesus gives me myself, trusts me with my own life, wholly and for the first time.

But at what a cost! – and a cost made necessary by my own pride in my wisdom and my fear of love. If I can now forgive, it is only because I have been forgiven, I and all the other men and women who have ever lived. Certainly one can forgive only what has been done to oneself. But all the evil ever done has been done to God, because it is a misuse of his good gifts, a rejection of the purposes he set in motion from the beginning. The crucified Jesus is the only accurate picture of God the world has ever seen, and the hands that hold us in existence are pierced with unimaginable nails. But on this Cross God fulfils the nature of forgiveness by using the evil done to him as the means to a new good; for it is the Cross of Jesus which creates within me a free, unhesitating acceptance of the law of love.

If the fear of love has gone, so has the fear of death. I do not need to believe in some imperishable spirit within myself, for which there is no evidence. I rest on God, who will assuredly not allow me to find the meaning of life in his love and forgiveness, to be wholly dependent upon him for the gift of myself, and then destroy that meaning, revoke that gift. He who holds me in existence now, can and will hold me in it still, through and beyond the dissolution of my mortal frame. For this is the essence of love, to affirm the right of the beloved to exist. And what God affirms, nothing and no one can contradict.

Does a shadow here fall across the sunlight? My confidence in God rests not only on him but also on my readiness to acknowledge my own evil. If I forget that, I deny his forgiveness. It ceases to be real. I deny his crucifixion; to suffer over what is not there is mere neurosis. If I reject the truth about myself, I lose the self which God has given me, and fall back into the grip of nothingness, of the demonic.

My freedom then is no comforting fiction, but a reality; and because that is real, hell is a reality too. Hell is not something with which God threatens me to bring me into line. His attitude to me is always and unchangingly one of forgiveness and welcome for me as I am. Hell is a truth about myself, that goes everywhere with me like my own shadow. Indeed, it is my shadow, the dark side of myself, my private province in the kingdom of the lie. This is the shadow that falls across the sunlight, but it can do so only when I turn my back on the sun. Hence even the shadow of hell holds no terrors for me. In the light of the everlasting mercy I am safe from being swallowed up by my own darkness; and by turning my face to that light I at last declare with my whole being that it is by love alone that men live.

It is for this reason that I fear so horribly for those who say that God is dead and that Love is God. All their words have the sickly scent of decay, of rottenness under a bright surface of optimism. They will not face the truth about Man. Our most important need is not to love and to forgive but to be loved and to be forgiven. To reverse this priority is to walk straight into the realm of the lie, where my broken and inadequate love either becomes the sum of all possible righteousness or the measure of my condemnation. A superficial collectivism may blind men to this. They may think that we can do for each other what God, in the old belief, did for all. My love and mercy are to give fullness of life to my neighbour, and his to me. If so, we are both lost, even if the collective view is an adequate account of the human situation. But, of course, it is not. In the last analysis we are alone. We are alone in those deep levels of our being which even we do not know, much less our neighbour; we are alone in our deaths. And if there is no one to love us in our solitariness, then our own demonic evil, our own central nothingness will inexorably devour us. But there is Someone, whose love has laid hold on us in Jesus; and even my own darkness is no darkness with him.

'Whose love has laid hold on us in Jesus.' Jesus is the image and likeness of God in human terms; he has done God's work in human space and time. Faced with this truth, I cannot stop there. I have to go beyond it to an even greater affirmation, because of the very nature of love. It is inconceivable to me that love could ever say: 'I must save these children of mine, and that will mean the most terrible suffering. *I will find someone else to do the job.*' Love does not send others to suffer in its place. Love comes itself. And at this point I am struck dumb. I dare not frame the thought that faces me, and yet there is no other thought to which I can turn and escape. This is no clever theory, no remote possibility, no wild imagination. It is something that I *know*. It is absurd, it cannot possibly be true, but deep inside there is no question about it. The Cross is not a picture of God. This was God himself.

Because I am sure of this, I learn something else – not about God but about Man. When God enters our space and time, a man is what he becomes. There must therefore be something appropriate about manhood which makes it a possible way of life for God. This seems ludicrous, when we think of Man's ignorance, frailty, and wickedness; but there is one thing – our capacity for sacrificial love. In us it may be only a capacity, an unrealized potential; but that is no reason why it should not be developed to the full. When God, who is just such love through and through, enters a particular world, he can do so only in a form which will allow that love full play; and in our case that means the form of Man. This then is the family likeness between God and ourselves; not our brains, not our self-awareness, not our conscience – just our love.

To belong to this family of God is the true life for which all human beings are made; and they can in the end find their way to that life only through Jesus and the truth that is in him. The Church is that part of the human race which has the guardianship of this truth, the key to the gate of life, that is, the record of Jesus, his life, death, and resurrection, and the true understanding of that record. One would think then that her members would be the first to use it, and would welcome all who by any roads were closing in on that gate. In her surely the spirit of Jesus and of God, the spirit of free commitment to the absolute and universal law of love and forgiveness, would be alive and infectious. It is, alas, not so. We hang the key up and let it rust. We argue whether it is the key or not. Some of us try their hand at making new keys; others occasionally take it down and try it in the gate, but upside down. And any new arrivals are encouraged not to use the key for themselves, but to take sides in the argument about the key. And yet the only justification for our separate identity is that we are the keepers of that key, with the solemn trust of giving it to all who come to the gate. I am tempted to say, God forgive us! But that is too easy. O brother men, will you forgive us too?

And you, the other members of our community, where she crosses the borders of mortality, and enters the light of the everlasting mercy, will you forgive us? You who are no longer just Christians, but men

and women united with all in whom the small flame, catching at the
fire of God, has wrought transfiguration, pray to the Father for us.
Pray that the Spirit may kindle our hearts too with the fire of his love,
to make us all men, all one, and to renew the face of the earth.

> My song is love unknown,
>   my Saviour's love to me;
> love to the loveless shown,
>   that they might lovely be.
>   O, who am I,
>   that for my sake
>   my Lord should take
>   frail flesh and die? . . .
>
> Here might I stay and sing,
>   no story so divine;
> never was love, dear King,
>   never was grief like thine!
>   This is my Friend,
>   in whose sweet praise
>   I all my days
>   could gladly spend.

Christmas 1968